£ 15

BIBLIOTECA DI «LETTERE ITALIANE»
STUDI E TESTI
XLIII

VICTORIA KIRKHAM

THE SIGN OF REASON
IN
BOCCACCIO'S FICTION

FIRENZE
LEO S. OLSCHKI EDITORE
MCMXCIII

ISBN 88 222 4111 8

ACKNOWLEDGMENTS

I thank the friends who persuaded me to undertake this project, above all Vittore Branca, without whose encouragement and backing it would never have materialized. Family and colleagues helped me put the manuscript in final form: my mother, Mary E. Kirkham, edited the entire English text; my sister, M. B. Kirkham, read large portions of it; Janet Levarie Smarr commented on the complete manuscript, and Pier Massimo Forni reviewed the new chapter on the *Amorosa visione*. Initial research on Boccaccio's numerology was made possible by my year as a Fellow at Villa I Tatti, the Harvard Center for Italian Renaissance Studies in Florence, 1977-1978, on funding from the National Endowment for the Humanities. Additional support that allowed me to begin thinking about allegory in the *Amorosa visione* came from the University of Pennsylvania in the form of a Junior Faculty Summer Grant and a sabbatical semester in 1980. A reduced teaching load in 1991 expedited the process of revising and updating previous publications for the present anthology. Monica Oberthaler assisted with the typescript, and Helen McFie Simone lent an expert eye to final editing. Generous subvention for this volume has been provided by the University of Pennsylvania School of Arts and Sciences through the willingness of two colleagues, whom I warmly thank. Richard R. Beeman, Associated Dean for Humanities, made available funding from his office to match an amount contributed by Stuart A. Curran, Director of the Center for Italian Studies, from the Center's Henry Salvatori Research Fund.

* * *

My thanks to the publishers for permission to reprint in revised and updated form essays that originally appeared as follows: '*Chiuso parlare*' *in Boccaccio's 'Teseida'*, in *Dante, Petrarch, Boccaccio. Studies in the Italian*

Trecento in Honor of Charles S. Singleton, ed. A. S. Bernardo and A. L. Pellegrini, Medieval and Renaissance Texts, Binghamton, 1983, pp. 305-351; *Boccaccio's Dedication to Women in Love*, in *Renaissance Studies in Honor of Craig Hugh Smyth*, I, ed. A. Morrogh, F. Superbi Gioffredi, P. Morselli and E. Borsook, Florence, Giunti-Barbèra, 1985, pp. 333-343; *An Allegorically Tempered 'Decameron'*, «Italica», XLII, 1985, pp. 1-23; *The Word, the Flesh, and the 'Decameron'*, «Romance Philology», XLI, 1987, pp. 127-149; *Love's Labors Rewarded and Paradise Lost ('Decameron' III 10)*, «The Romanic Review», LXXII, 1981, pp. 79-93; *Painters at Play on the Judgment Day ('Decameron' VIII 9)*, «Studi sul Boccaccio», XIV, 1983-1984, pp. 256-277; *The Classic Bond of Friendship in Boccaccio's Tito and Gisippo ('Decameron' X 8)*, in *The Classics in the Middle Ages. Papers of the Twentieth Annual Conference of the Center for Medieval and Early Renaissance Studies*, ed. A. S. Bernardo and S. Levin, Binghamton, Medieval and Renaissance Texts, 1990, pp. 223-235; *The Last Tale in the 'Decameron'*, «Mediaevalia», XII, 1989 for 1986, pp. 205-223 («A Special Volume in Honor of Aldo S. Bernardo»).

V.E.K.

Philadelphia, January, 1993

INTRODUCTION

No trespassing the sign of reason

In the voice of a woman, Boccaccio recorded a cautionary dictum that could well stand as his philosophical credo: Nothing without reason. It was prudently spoken by Pampinea, whom he imagined in the sanctuary of Santa Maria Novella, late March of 1348, as she enjoined the ladies in her circle to flee plague-stricken Florence, dishonesty, and death:

> io giudicherei ottimamente fatto che noi [...] di questa terra uscissimo, e fuggendo come la morte i disonesti essempli degli altri onestamente a' nostri luoghi in contado, de' quali a ciascuna di noi è gran copia, ce ne andassimo a stare, e quivi quella festa, quella allegrezza, quello piacere che noi potessimo, senza trapassare in alcuno atto il segno della ragione, prendessimo.[1]

Clinging to the city they are at risk both physically and morally, but country retreat promises preservation of life and renewal of values — provided the women not «trespass in any act the sign of reason».

Boccaccio's phrase «trapassare il segno» resonates, through his spokesperson Pampinea, of Dante's *Paradiso*. It catches a fragment of conversation with Adam during a poetic moment that imparts some of the most critical information in the history of humanity, the facts about the Fall. Privileged to hear them from Adam in person, Dante learns that gluttonous fruit tasting was not the cause. Rather, the first parents lost Eden because in their presumption they 'went beyond' the limit of what God

---

[1] G. BOCCACCIO, *Decameron*, ed. V. Branca, Milan, Mondadori, 1976 («*Tutte le opere*», IV), I, Intro. 65.

allowed and did what he had forbidden. Adam and Eve «trespassed the sign», that is, they overstepped a moral limit:

> Or, figliuol mio, non il gustar del legno
> fu per sé la cagion di tanto essilio,
> ma solamente il trapassar del segno.[2]

Adam, that master of language who gave things their names, picks his words carefully as he dialogues with Dante. The verb 'trapassare', cognate with 'trespass' in the sense of 'sin', derives from the late Latin form *transpassare*, which is synonymous with 'transgress', from *transgredire*. Both mean, literally, 'to go beyond', 'to overstep'. They gravitate toward the lexicon that medieval etymologists summoned to expose the origin of 'pride' (*superbia*), responsible for the Fall. Isidore of Seville, the most authoritative, derived *superbia* from *supergredire* ('to overgo', 'overpass'), and that definition anchors the discussion on pride by Thomas Aquinas in his treatise on the virtues and vices:

Isidore says (*Etymologiae* X): "A man is said to be proud [*superbus*], because he wishes to appear above [*super*] what he really is; for he who wishes to overstep beyond what he is, is proud". Now right reason requires that every man's will should tend to that which is proportionate to him. Therefore it is evident that pride denotes something opposed to right reason, and this shows it to have the character of sin.

Pride, as Thomas continues, can be understood doubly:

First, as overpassing [*supergreditur*] the rule of reason, and in this sense we say that it is a sin. Secondly, it may simply denominate overreach [*superexcessus*]. And in that sense, whatever overreaches can be named pride.[3]

---

[2] *Paradiso* XXVI 115-117. I cite throughout DANTE ALIGHIERI, *La Commedia secondo l'antica vulgata*, ed. G. Petrocchi, Milan, Mondadori, 1966-1967 («Società Dantesca Italiana, Edizione Nazionale»).

[3] *The Summa Theologica of St. Thomas Aquinas*, trans. Fathers of the English Dominican Province, London, Burnes Oates and Washbourne Ltd., 1921, II-II, Qu. 162, Art. 1; cf. *Summa theologiae*, ed. Instituti Studiorum Medievalium Ottaviensis, Ottawa, Studii Generalis O. Pr., 1941-1945: «Dicendum quod superbia nominatur ex hoc quod aliquis per voluntatem tendit supra id quod est; unde dicit Isidorus in libro *Etymol.*: "Superbus dictus est quia super vult videri quam est; qui enim vult supergredi quod est, superbus est". Habet autem hoc ratio recta ut voluntas uniuscuiusque feratur in id quod est proportionatum sibi. Et ideo manifestum est quod superbia importat aliquid quod adversatur rationi rectae. Hoc autem facit rationem peccati, quia secundum Dionysium, IV cap. *De Div. Nom.*, "malum animae est praeter rationem esse" [...]. Dicendum quod superbia dupliciter accipi potest. Uno modo, ex eo quod supergreditur regulam rationis. Et sic dicimus eam esse peccatum. Alio modo potest superbia

Original Sin resulted from pride of both kinds, 'overpassing' the rule of reason and 'superexcessive'. It deprived man of original justice, the guiding inner disposition that prevented him from ever wanting anything wrong, and when that happened, the parts of his soul fell out of harmony. Desire, seated in the concupiscible faculty, could now contradict reason. Human beings began to have inordinate wishes for things not good and right:

Since, in man, the concupiscible power is naturally governed by reason, the act of concupiscence is so far natural to man as it is in accord with the order of reason; while in so far as it trespasses beyond the bounds of reason, it is, for a man, contrary to reason. Such is the concupiscence of original sin.[4]

Backed by Adam alone, Pampinea's turn of phrase could sound like nothing more than a casual echo of Dante's «trespass the sign», one of those tiny vernacular sound bites that Boccaccio repeats by the hundreds and thousands in his own new literary contexts.[5] Nevertheless, the Adamic phrase, so poetically fraught for the *Divine Comedy*, filters into the *Decameron* not just as another nugget panned from an earlier poet's wordflow, but as a cameo mounted to display renewed and serious meaning. Boccaccio cites 'Adam' knowing full well, as Alighieri had known, the underlying etymological and theological ramifications. Trained in canon law, he too had absorbed a solid medieval ration of Thomas Aquinas. The *summae* whose substance he memorized in youth retained their authority in his later years and buttress a powerful profes-

---

nominari simpliciter a superexcessu. Et secundum hoc omne superexcedens potest nominari superbia».

Pride in the sense of trespassing is built into the canto structure and topography of Dante's poem, as demonstrated by V. KIRKHAM, *Eleven is for Evil: Measured Trespass in Dante's 'Commedia'*, «Allegorica», X, 1989, pp. 27-50. K. BROWNLEE, *Language and Desire in 'Paradiso' XXVI*, «Lectura Dantis», VI, 1990, pp. 46-59, connects Adam's «trapassar del segno» with St. Thomas' «supra suam mensuram» (*Summa theologica* II-II, Qu. 163, Art. 1 ff.). Both formulas, which evoke the «transgressive voyage» of Ulysses in *Inferno* XXVI, in contrast to Dante's own journey, have important poetic implications for the *Comedy* as a whole.

[4] *Summa theologica* I-II, Qu. 82, Art. 3: «Dicendum quod quia in homine concupiscibilis naturaliter regitur ratione, intantum concupiscere est homini naturale, inquantum est secundum rationis ordinem; concupiscentia autem quae transcendit limites rationis, inest homini contra naturam. Et talis est concupiscentia originalis peccati».

[5] They have been compiled and characterized by, e.g., C. DELCORNO, *Note sui dantismi nell'Elegia di madonna Fiammetta'*, «Studi sul Boccaccio», XI, 1979, pp. 251-294; A. BETTINZOLI, *Per una definizione delle presenze dantesche nel 'Decameron' II. Ironizzazione e espressivismo antifrastico-deformatorio*, «Studi sul Boccaccio», XIV, 1983-1984, pp. 209-240; R. HOLLANDER, *Boccaccio's Last Fiction. 'Il Corbaccio'*, Philadelphia, University of Pennsylvania Press, 1988, pp. 59-75.

sion of faith in the autobiographical passages of his *Genealogia deorum gentilium*, where he recites a credo shared with Aquinas.[6]

If Dante is the 'missing character' in the *Decameron*,[7] Aquinas is its absent philosopher. The Angelic Doctor dwells by metonymy in the seat of Florentine Dominicanism, that great Gothic church Boccaccio privileges in the spatial plan of his book as the spiritual *domus* of his storytellers. The author could have placed them within the Franciscans' equally grand Santa Croce (which does enter the *Decameron*, but most unflatteringly in I 6) or, say, in the Baptistry so venerated by the city whose patron was San Giovanni, yet that octagon is present only as a backdrop to Cavalcanti's acerb wit (VI 9) and Calandrino's artlessness (VIII 3). The *brigata* meets instead after Mass in Santa Maria Novella, thence to depart on the circular excursion that will close with their return to its holy walls.

During the same decade that Boccaccio was composing the *Decameron*, Andrea Orcagna, Nardo di Cione, and Giovanni del Biondo decorated the Strozzi family chapel in Santa Maria Novella with a program dominated by Thomas Aquinas. The haloed saint presides overhead from Giovanni del Biondo's four ceiling medalions, flanked in each portrait by two personified figures. His eight companions are the seven canonical Virtues plus Chastity, a quality close to Temperance with symbolic attributes of Purity. The lily and ermine designate Chastity, whose partner is Charity, identified by the flaming heart which Thomas holds in his right hand (fig. 2). All together the overhead virtues paired as personified women are: Charity-Chastity, Faith-Prudence, Justice-Temperance, and Hope-Fortitude. These icons canonize Thomas as the philosopher whose *Summa theologica* was the definitive authority on the virtues and vices. The Strozzi Chapel, best known for Nardo's frescoes of the Last Judgment and Hell, inspired by Dante's *Divine Comedy*, still

---

[6] When his recitation comes to Christ's Crucifixion, Boccaccio defers to Thomas, «Cuius cum iam humanitate victa suppliciis in finem suum ivisset (seu, et melius reor, ut Thome de Aquino placet, cum voluntarie, collectis viribus, spiritum emisisset), tremuit orbis omnis» [When His human strength was overcome by His punishment, His end came; or rather, I believe with Thomas Aquinas, that He gathered up His strength, and of His own will gave up the ghost. And the whole earth shook]. See G. Boccaccio, *Genealogia deorum gentilium*, ed. V. Romano, Bari, Laterza, 1951, XV 9 (p. 771), trans. C. Osgood, *Boccaccio on Poetry*, Indianapolis, Bobbs-Merril («The Library of Liberal Arts»), 1956, p. 126; and cf. *Summa theologica* III, Qu. 47, Art. 1.

[7] The happy turn of phrase is from F. Fido, *Dante, personaggio mancato del 'Decameron'*, in *Boccaccio: Secoli di vita. Atti del Congresso Internazionale: Boccaccio 1975. Università di California, Los Angeles. 17-19 Ottobre, 1975*, ed. M. Cottino-Jones and E. F. Tuttle, Ravenna, Longo, 1977, pp. 177-189; rev. as *Dante personaggio mancato del libro galeotto*, in F. Fido, *Il regime delle simmetrie imperfette*, Milan, Franco Angeli, 1988, pp. 111-123.

holds its magnificent altarpiece, commissioned of Orcagna in 1354 and completed in 1357 (fig. 3). Christ in a mandorla consigns the keys to St. Peter with his left hand, while with his right he reaches down to receive the *Summa theologica*, offered by a kneeling St. Thomas, whom the Virgin presents. Symbolically, the Redeemer's act affirms and advocates Thomistic doctrine. Powerful in both Naples and Florence from the late Duecento, preached in charismatic sermons and diffused on the wings of Dante's poetry, the Dominican influence finds a visual *summa* in fresco by Andrea di Bonaiuto da Firenze at the Spanish Chapel of Santa Maria Novella, *The Triumph of St. Thomas* (1366-1368)[8] (fig. 1).

Restoring Aquinas to Boccaccio's intellectual picture, we recover the significant connection Pampinea makes between «trapassare il segno» and «ragione». That is, Dante alone cannot account immediately for both terms, only the words «trespass the sign». To link them with the idea of 'reason', we must look beneath the letter of the *Comedy* and think back to its Scholastic matrix. More open in ways than Dante and always more expansive — or more 'prosaic', one might say — Boccaccio restores to the surface of his masterbook the Thomistic concept of *ratio*, suppressed through artistic ellipsis and tensions in his predecessor's *terzine*. The *Summa theologica*, founded on Aristotle, spells it out logically: prideful 'trespassing' opposes 'reason'; whatever opposes reason is sin. The rational, by contrast, shuns excess or extreme. It respects limits; it seeks the happy medium; it presumes and requires the proportionate. Reason is measure, that tempered mean synonymous with virtue in the *Nicomachean Ethics*, so important for St. Thomas.

Such language as Pampinea speaks, absorbed from Dante's poetry and Scholastic philosophy, was already forming in Boccaccio's mind fifteen to twenty years earlier. We find it in his first romance, *Filocolo*, which he composed during times off from law classes at Naples, city of a

---

[8] S. BATTAGLIA RICCI, *Ragionare nel giardino. Boccaccio e i cicli pittorici del 'Trionfo della Morte'*, Rome, Salerno Editrice, 1987, provides good background on Tuscan Dominicanism in the first half of the Trecento, but argues that Boccaccio programmatically rejected it in his *Decameron*. On dating the decoration of the Strozzi Chapel and on Giovanni del Biondo's contribution, see R. OFFNER and K. STEINWEG, *A Critical and Historical Corpus of Florentine Painting*, IV 4, New York, New York University Institute of Fine Arts, 1967, pp. 21ff. Offner calls the virtue whom I identify as Chastity 'Moderation'. On Orcagna's altarpiece see R. FREMANTLE, *Florentine Gothic Painters from Giotto to Masaccio. A Guide to Painting in and near Florence 1300-1450*, London, Martin Secker and Warburg, 1975, pp. 135-137 and fig. 274. A curious monument of Dominican influence from the same era as the *Decameron* is the panel by the Master of Terenzano, also known as the Master of the Dominican Effigies, after 1340, in the sacristy of Santa Maria Novella, *Christ and the Virgin Enthroned with seventeen Dominican Saints* (*ivi*, fig. 206).

flourishing Dominican *studium* whose history Aquinas had personally distinguished as a chaired professor in 1272. A formula that now rings familiar served the young author for the scene where King Felice falsely charges Biancifiore with attempted murder by serving at his table a poisoned peacock. Then, concerned about the danger of public censure, the monarch masks his treachery by staging a mock trial, «acciò che alcuno non potesse dire che io i termini della ragione in ciò trapassassi».[9] Needless to say, Felice's determination to eliminate the lady his son loves is nothing if not unreasonable. Boccaccio's irony will have us see how the storybook king, he who most of all should rule most rightly, does instead «trespass the limits of reason». In fact, as Steven Grossvogel has demonstrated, «Felice fits Aquinas' definition of the tyrannical sovereign to the letter».[10]

When a later figure in Boccaccio's fiction refuses to accept 'Reason', Boccaccio again tailors his Scholastic language to fit the fictional setting, this time a humorous philosophical allegory. The character in question is a Dreamer who strolls self-indulgently through the *Amorosa visione*. He is strongly inclined to follow his appetites on the leftward 'sinister' way, contrary to tireless efforts of his heaven-sent guide, a woman symbolic of Reason. Only when he awakens at dawn and discovers her still standing beside his bed in broad daylight does his stubborn resistance end. Now that his eyes have each been opened, literally and morally, he humbles himself and will obey her so as to please the woman he loves, Maria d'Aquino: «Humile e pian, quanto io posso, m'assegno / a te: fa sì ch'al piacer di colei, / di cui son tutto, i' non trapassi 'l segno».[11] Allegorically, he asks Reason to prevent him from «trespassing her bound» so that he may keep in the good graces of his lady, an 'Aquinas' whom we deduce personifies Prudence. In other words, Reason has led him to the love of Wisdom. Now that his rational faculty has made him 'philosophical', he will stay within reasonable bounds and sustain in his behavior virtuous measure.

---

[9] G. BOCCACCIO, *Filocolo*, ed. A. E. Quaglio, Milan, Mondadori, 1967 («*Tutte le opere*», I), II 39, 3.

[10] S. GROSSVOGEL, *Ambiguity and Allusion in Boccaccio's 'Filocolo'*, Florence, Olschki, 1992, pp. 135-136. This thoughtful study analyzes the *Filocolo* in a philosophical framework, emphasizing Thomas Aquinas and his shaping influence on Boccaccio. For an overview of Boccaccio's Neapolitan cultural milieu, see G. BOCCACCIO, *'Diana's Hunt'. 'Caccia di Diana'. Boccaccio's First Fiction*, ed. and trans. A. K. CASSELL and V. KIRKHAM, Philadelphia, University of Pennsylvania Press, 1991, pp. 4-6.

[11] G. BOCCACCIO, *Amorosa visione*, ed. V. BRANCA, Milan, Mondadori, 1974 («*Tutte le opere*», III), B Text, L 34-36.

* * *

My title for this collection of essays, *The Sign of Reason in Boccaccio's Fiction*, cites Pampinea, the storyteller in the *Decameron* who personifies Prudence. She asserts her identity as an antitype to Eve when she alludes to the Fall while arguing for restraint.[12] Her formula «senza trapassare [...] il segno della ragione» is a semantic magnet. Into its field of force flow prior usages by Boccaccio, Dante, and St. Thomas. On their authority, I take the phrase to have several meanings. Literally 'reason's marker', it denotes the limit beyond which reason forbids us to go, something that says 'no trespassing beyond this sign'. Reason, Pampinea asserts, should rule our actions and arbitrate our decisions. Poetically, her view of reasonableness comes filtered through Dante and thus comports moral categories of good and evil, virtue and vice. Philosophically, Boccaccio's 'no trespassing reason' calls forth an Aristotelian-Thomistic system of ethics, which forges a great chain of being: as the soul rules the body, so must the appetites of concupiscence and irascibility obey reason, so must woman obey man, so must citizens obey their ruler, so must good Christians obey God. Such an ideal world, mirrored in the pastoral utopia of the Florentine *brigata*, requires rational order in the individual and rational order in the state.

For all its wit and spice, the jokesters and philanderers among its population, the *Decameron* is a microcosm founded on the principle of reason. Boccaccio, who would continue arguing the case for rational conduct in his Latin compilations, had already long been committed to that enterprise, as far back as his earliest fiction. My article *Numerology and Allegory in Boccaccio's 'Caccia di Diana'*, interprets the hunt at a moral level as a *psychomachia* between human reason and bestial passion, virtue and vice. That study became the nucleus for the Introduction to *'Diana's Hunt'. 'Caccia di Diana'. Boccaccio's First Fiction*, in which A. K. Cassell and I collaborated. From it the present volume follows, with respect both to the chronology of Boccaccio's works and interpretive orientation.

The Sign of Reason in Boccaccio's Fiction is an updated gathering of already published English language pieces along with a new monograph, *Amorous Vision, Scholastic Vistas*. From *Teseida* (1340-1341 with glosses written later) to *Amorosa visione* (1342-1343/1355-1365) to *Decameron*

---

[12] D. WALLACE makes the point in his delightful manual *Giovanni Boccaccio. 'Decameron'*, Cambridge, Cambridge University Press, 1991 («Landmarks of World Literature»), p. 13.

(after 1348), these papers bridge Naples and Florence, Boccaccio 'minore' and 'maggiore'. To argue ideological continuities in the poet's art, I privilege his order of composition over mine. Hence, even though *Amorous Vision, Scholastic Vistas* (Ch. 2) was the last essay to be written and synthesizes thinking of twenty years, I place it second after *'Chiuso parlare' in Boccaccio's 'Teseida'*, which I wrote in 1978 (Ch. 1). The *Teseida* makes a logical starting point for this anthology because there Boccaccio first spoke directly in a Thomistic vocabulary.[13] Scholastic psychology dominates the long glosses he attached to the structural center of the epic, where he unveils his allegorical intent. Like *Caccia di Diana*, the *Teseida* describes a soul-battle. Redesigned to suit the content of an epic, it pits the rational faculty (Teseo, Duke of Athens) against irascible and concupiscible passions (the Theban knights Arcita and Palemone). Identical contending forces return to the oneiric landscape of the *Amorosa visione* as personifications that vie for control over Dreamer, who must be taught that he should prefer rational discipline over sensual pleasure.

The *Decameron* frame will restage these allegories, transmitted via the *Comedia delle ninfe fiorentine*, but it downplays and distances them into allusive registers. Irascibility and concupiscence, characterized by Filostrato and Dioneo, are countered by Panfilo as Reason. His allies are the Seven Virtues, corresponding to the female narrators. Their leader is Pampinea-Prudence, the virtue that according to St. Thomas 'commands'. As they rule by turn, the stories move programmatically toward culmination on Day X, which dramatizes the 'perfecting' Aristotelian virtue, magnanimity. The final Day rises to cloture with two men, Tito and Gisippo, who are models of friendship, a supreme Ciceronian virtue. It climaxes in the woman Griselda, 'the last who will be first' for her Biblical quality of humility, antidote to pride for Augustine and foundation of the entire Christian edifice for Thomas Aquinas. My seven essays on the *Decameron* start with the Proem, *Boccaccio's Dedication to Women in Love* (Ch. 3), and the *cornice*, *An Allegorically Tempered 'Decameron'* (Ch. 4). Next *The Word, the Flesh, and the 'Decameron'* encompasses all the *cento novelle* to chart the ethics of discourse and show how Boccaccio correlates human locution with reason in traditions that the Middle Ages inherited from Aristotle, Cicero, Quintilian, and Augustine (Ch. 5). Then come two essays related both by theme and placement of the tales

---

[13] There is Scholastic language in the earlier *Filocolo*, as Grossvogel amply demonstrates, but in strands woven into the texture of the fiction. In the glosses to the *Teseida*, by contrast, Boccaccio speaks not as poet but as commentator, hence in a more 'direct' expository mode.

they treat, respectively on the first and second Sundays of storytelling: *Love's Labors Rewarded and Paradise Lost ('Decameron' III 10)* (Ch. 6) and *Painters at Play on the Judgment Day ('Decameron' VIII 9)* (Ch. 7). The last two essays also pair logically because they pertain to the peroration of the *Decameron*, those extreme examples of virtue that give Boccaccio his grand finale: *The Classic Bond of Friendship in Boccaccio's Tito and Gisippo ('Decameron' X 8)* (Ch. 8) and *The Last Tale in the 'Decameron'* (Ch. 9).

The Sign of Reason in Boccaccio's Fiction does not reprint everything I have written on Boccaccio, articles as well as reviews. But more is here than not. Exclusions, like inclusions, have been my choice. For instance, I omit *Numerology and Allegory in Boccaccio's 'Caccia di Diana'* because that was reworked as an introduction to the translation with commentary that Cassell and I co-authored. Another absent piece, *Reckoning with Boccaccio's 'Questioni d'amore'*, will appear in *Boccaccio's Tuscan Muse*, a book I am currently preparing that explores the Certaldan's vernacular poetics and focusses on the *Filocolo*. My work on Boccaccio's portraits and authorial iconography, *A Preliminary List of Boccaccio Portraits from the 14th to the mid-16th Centuries*, in V. Branca, P. F. Watson, V. Kirkham, *Boccaccio visualizzato I*, «Studi sul Boccaccio», XV, 1985-1986; and *Renaissance Portraits of Boccaccio: A Look into the Kaleidoscope, Boccaccio visualizzato II*, «Studi sul Boccaccio», XVI, 1987, will reappear in *Boccaccio visualizzato*, ed. V. Branca, Turin, Einaudi, 1994, and my book in progress, *Under the Laurel. Poets in their Renaissance Portraits*.

Here I pull together for convenient reference between two covers essays that have appeared during two decades in scattered sources — scholarly journals, Festschrifts, and conference proceedings. So bound, they can be consulted one at a time, as they were composed, or they can be read as a more comprehensive statement. When I configured *The Sign of Reason in Boccaccio's Fiction* it was my wish to shape a volume, what medievals would have called a *compilatio*, to assemble and order pieces into a whole unified not just by my scholarly signature, but by Boccaccio's philosophical poetics.

1.

«CHIUSO PARLARE» IN BOCCACCIO'S *TESEIDA*

In his dedicatory Proem to Fiammetta, the Author of the *Teseida* announces that he will tell a long forgotten love story. Hopeful of regaining Fiammetta's lost favors by appealing to her fondness for fictional romance, he reports having rendered into vernacular verse «una antichissima istoria e alle più delle genti non manifesta, bella sì per la materia della quale parla, che è d'amore, e sì per coloro de' quali dice, che nobili giovani furono e di real sangue discesi».[1] Love, however, is not this Author's only avowed concern, for at the close of the twelfth and last book of his epic, he proudly proclaims its true subject to be Mars. Bidding the work farewell, he writes that ever since the Muses began appearing «naked» among men, some poets employed the Italian language «con bello stilo in onesto parlare, / e altri in amoroso l'operaro; / ma tu, o libro, primo a lor cantare / di Marte fai gli affanni sostenuti, / nel volgar lazio più mai non veduti» (XII 84).[2] Finally, a pair of postscripted sonnets reveal that at the Author's request, the Muses have delivered his completed book to Fiammetta, who is to have the honor of giving it a name. She sighed after reading the tale of such valiant heroes, «Ahi, quante d'amor forze in costor foro!» and has decided to call it «Teseida di nozze d'Emilia».[3]

---

[1] G. BOCCACCIO, *Teseida delle nozze d'Emilia*, ed. A. LIMENTANI, Milan, Mondadori, 1964 («*Tutte le opere*», II), *A Fiammetta*, p. 247. Boccaccio's term 'istoria' here implies not just 'story', but 'history', following his definition of epic as a form «more like history than fiction». See below, n. 4.

[2] The 'naked' Muses are those who have doffed their traditional Latin garb. Boccaccio here recalls, of course, the passage in *De vulgari eloquentia*, ed. A. MARIGO, rev. P.G. RICCI, Florence, Le Monnier, 1968, II 2, where Dante states that Italian, which has so far produced poetry of love and moral rectitude, still awaits an epic voice to sing «armorum probitas» [righteous feats of arms].

[3] It sounds as if Fiammetta has read Francesca da Rimini's story in *Inferno* V. Fiammetta's title has been Englished as *The Book of Theseus* by B. McCOY, New York, Medieval Text Association, 1974. Her translation so often disregards the original that it has rightly dwelt in

Fiammetta's choice is surprising. While the Author tells of love in a song inspired by Mars, «nuptials» form the conceptual nucleus in her title. She therefore takes the poem's theme to be marriage. His protagonists are two enamored knights descended from Theban Cadmus, Arcita and Palemone. Omitting any nominal reference to them, she calls our attention instead to Teseo, Duke of Athens, and Emilia, the Amazon maiden whose affections the Thebans vied to win. The terms in her title, which provide an alternative perspective on the epic, must have been selected for good reason. As we learn from the Author's Proem, she differs from the unintelligent mob of women generally by virtue of her intellect and knowledge. He has consequently not hesitated to put in his work «né storia né favola né chiuso parlare in altra guisa». This challenge, alerting Fiammetta to the necessity of looking creatively beyond the letter of the text, invites us to do the same. «Storia», «favola» and «chiuso parlare» all imply an allegorical intent,[4] but the last phrase may refer more specifically to another occult system of literary discourse, namely numerology. The *Teseida* is, in fact, a numerical composition,[5] and one that is particularly rich because it has so many quantifiable elements − books, the 'chapters' into which they are separated by rubrics, stanzaic octaves, verses, glosses, and sonnets − all ordered and

---

obscurity. Like scribes of some early *Teseida* manuscripts and book inventories, who referred to the epic as *Libro di Teseo*, McCoy evidently thought that a name as odd as «Thesead of Emilia's Nuptials» needed to be altered. But Boccaccio intended it to be a strange, ear-catching composite. It announces his poetic strategy to merge a martial hero with marriage, arms and the man with love and the woman.

[4] Boccaccio defines 'fabula' (literally 'fable', but more broadly 'fiction'), of which he distinguishes four types in his defense of poetry. See *Genealogia* XIV 9: «Fabula est exemplaris seu demonstrativa sub figmento locutio, cuius amoto cortice, patet intentio fabulantis» [Fiction is a form of exemplary or demonstrative discourse set beneath a fantasy, from which, when the cortex is removed, there appears the fictionalist's intent]. The first kind of 'fable' is that form in its strict definition (e.g., Aesop's). Myths ending in metamorphoses exemplify the second, which has been used from earliest times by the most ancient poets, «quibus cure fuit divina et humana pariter palliare figmentis» [whose object it has been to clothe in fiction divine and human matters alike]. The third, «potius hystorie quam fabule similis» [more like history than fiction], is represented by the epic writings of Virgil and Homer, «longe tamen aliud sub velamine sentiunt quam monstretur» [yet their hidden meaning is far other than appears on the surface]. The last are old wives' tales («delirantium vetularum inventio»). Applying this scheme to the *Teseida*, 'storia' corresponds with the Author's epic narration proper, an allegorical form with 'historical' ties to Statius's *Thebaid*; 'favola' describes many of the myths, also open to allegoresis, related in the commentary as short stories by his Glossator. Both 'storia' and 'favola' qualify, then, as «chiuso parlare», or «closed discourse». The adjective must call to mind the *trobar clus* of Provençal poets like Arnaut Daniel who cultivated a difficult, hermetic diction.

[5] For an introductory excursus on *Numerical Composition*, see E. R. CURTIUS, *European Literature and the Latin Middle Ages*, trans. W. R. TRASK, Princeton, Princeton University Press, 1953, pp. 501-509.

transcribed by Boccaccio himself on the pages of the Laurentian holograph.[6] Each contributes to the numerological plan of the epic, in which, under the moral guidance of Teseo and Emilia, an arithmetic union signifying 'marriage' silently joins 'love' and 'Mars' at the poem's center.

We may begin our search for symbolic numbers hidden in the *Teseida* by recalling the Author's divisions of its content as outlined for Fiammetta in his Proem. He informs her that before relating the tale of Arcita and Palemone's love for Emilia, he will first tell two other stories:

Dico adunque che dovendo narrare di due giovani nobilissimi tebani, Arcita e Palemone, come, innamorati d'Emilia amazona, per lei combattessero, primamente posta la invocazione poetica, mi parve da dimostrare e donde la donna fosse e come ad Attene venisse, e chi fossero essi e come quivi venissero similemente; laonde sì come premessioni alla loro istoria due se ne pongono.

The poem then opens with a five-stanza invocation to Mars, Venus, and Cupid. As the actual narration of events begins, the epic's Glossator (none other than Boccaccio himself, feigning yet a different literary persona) reiterates why it was necessary for the Author to include these two preliminary stories, which occupy respectively Books I and II:

Con ciò sia cosa che la principale intenzione dell'autore di questo libretto sia di trattare dell'amore e delle cose avvenute per quello, da due giovani tebani, cioè Arcita e Palemone, ad Emilia amazona, sì come nel suo proemio appare, potrebbe alcuno, e giustamente, adimandare che avesse qui a fare la guerra di Teseo con le donne amazone, della quale solamente parla il primo libro di questa opera. Dico, e brievemente, che l'autore a niuno altro fine queste cose scrisse, se non per mostrare onde Emilia fosse venuta ad Attene; [...] e il simigliante fa della sconfitta data da Teseo a Creonte, re di Tebe, per dichiarare donde e come alle mani di Teseo pervenissero Arcita e Palemone. (I 6, gl.)

As if these apologetic explanations were not sufficiently clear, he again alludes to the prefatory nature of Books I and II in his gloss on II 10. «Poscia che l'autore ha dimostrato di sopra, nel primo libro, donde e come Emilia venisse ad Attene, in questo secondo intende di dimostrare come Arcita e Palemone vi pervenissero». Boccaccio could hardly be more emphatic. Two accounts precede the third and main story in the *Teseida*,

---

[6] Florence, Biblioteca Medicea-Laurenziana, Ms. Doni e Acquisti 325. The manuscript was described by G. VANDELLI, *Un autografo della 'Teseida'*, «Studi di Filologia Italiana», II, 1929, pp. 1-76. For subsequent editions, see A. LIMENTANI, *Nota al testo*, in his edition of the *Teseida, cit.*, p. 873.

which begins with Book III. The Author has already announced its subject, «a most ancient story [...] beautiful for the matter of which it speaks, which is love». So too has the Glossator, «the principal intention of this little book's author is to treat of love».

Now love, the poet's acknowledged main theme, is also given as the matter most specific to Book III, where his story proper commences. To document fully the case for an identification between this Third Book and love, we must here recall the guiding role played by the sonnets that frame Boccaccio's epic: a general proemial sonnet summarizing its complete contents, plus a «sonetto particulare» preceding and paraphrasing each single book, plus the two postscripted sonnets mentioned above in connection with the book's name. The general proemial sonnet, line 3, announces love's conquest of the Theban knights, «nel terzo [libro] amore Arcita e Palemone / occupa». From the «particular sonnet» heading Book III we hear that Mars, who had motivated Teseo's battle triumphs in Books I and II, will here be allowed to rest:

> Nel terzo a Marte dona alcuna posa
> l'autore, e discrive come Amore
> d'Emilia, bella più che fresca rosa,
> a' duo prigion con li suoi dardi il core
> ferendo, elli accendesse in amorosa
> fiamma [...].

Appropriately, the stanzaic octaves of Book III open with an invocation to Cupid: «con più pio sermone / sarà da me di Cupido cantato / e delle sue battaglie, il quale io priego / che sia presente a ciò che di lui spiego». Lest we should have any doubts about what «di Cupido» means, help is not far away in the commentary: «cioè d'Amore».

Arcita and Palemone, who have so far been suffering supreme sadness in their Athenian prison tower for nearly a year, will soon have reason for more bitter woe: «per Vener, nel suo ciel lucente, / d'altri sospir dar lor fu proveduto» (III 4). Before entering upon the description of their enamorment, which constitutes the longest chapter in the *Teseida* (forty-two stanzas), Boccaccio reports the season, as his rubric promises, «Il tempo prima, e poi come Arcita e Palemone s'innamorarono d'Emilia». He does so with a complex astrological circumlocution condensed into a single stanza that will require the longest astrological gloss in the poem. The stanza in question is III 5, and as we shall see, these numerical signs (3 and 5) are significant. Phoebus is rising in Taurus, Venus accompanies him, and Jupiter is in Pisces. The Glossator by no means tells us everything he knew about the auspicious and amorous implications of this horoscope, but he does correctly assess its general meaning. The Author's purpose here is to «dimostrare il cielo essere ottimamente disposto a fare altrui innamorare» (III 5, gl.).[7]

Beneath the stars so favorably configured all terrestrial life reawakens to love. Their joyful celestial influence is felt by plants, flowers, trees, birds, animals, «e' giovinetti lieti, che ad amare / eran disposti, sentivan nel core / fervente più che mai crescere amore» (III 7). The spring brings Emilia into a garden below the prisoners' tower, where one day she sits down to make a garland, «sempre cantando be' versi d'amore». Arcita espies her and calls Palemone to the window, «vieni a vedere: / Vener è qui discesa veramente!» (III 13). Palemone looks down exclaiming, «Per certo questa è Citerea». Almost immediately and in quick succession the archer Cupid wounds each knight with a golden arrow shot from the goddess-like lady's eyes. The knights begin to burn; Emilia's image is fixed in their hearts and minds because «Amore, / ladro sottil di ciascun gentil core» and a crueller lord than Teseo, now holds them in his sway. Captives twice over, as with the passing days Cupid's chains bind them ever more tightly, they are given to copious sighing and can scarcely sleep or eat. Their only comfort is to watch Emilia for a short while each morning in the garden and praise her high worth by composing sonnets and *canzoni*. While this fiery desire increases, so does their suffering, to the point that all recollection of Thebes, their noble heritage, and present humiliating circumstances vanishes. Sighs yield to tears of grievous lament, leading them to wish for solace in death, and finally, after Arcita's release from prison, nagging jealousy enters the heart of his once so loyal companion Palemone. Eventually, Palemone will escape from the tower to find Arcita and resolve their rivalry, challenging him to a nearly fatal duel. For that encounter, however, we must wait until Book V.

Meanwhile, some explanations are in order concerning the abundant and largely canonical love matter of Book III. Why does Boccaccio postpone the beginning of his love story until this moment in the poem? He has already defensively justified the delay, affirming that Books I and II are not irrelevant, as they might seem, because they give needed

---

[7] A more complete anaylsis is given by A. E. QUAGLIO, *Scienza e mito nel Boccaccio*, Padua, Liviana Editrice, 1967, pp. 101-106; 177-82. The programmatic literary function of the planetary allusions in the epic is lucidly unveiled by J. L. SMARR, *Boccaccio and the Stars: Astrology in the 'Teseida'*, «Traditio», XXXV, 1979, pp. 303-332. Discussing the horoscope at III 5, Smarr points out that Venus, powerful to begin with since she is ascendent, gains influence by being in Taurus, her day house, and becomes stronger still through proximity with the sun.

background information. But textual clues planted early in the Third Book hint at another, unstated, reason for reserving it as the narrative locus of the Theban knights' enamorment. The onset of their passion is attributed to the operation of «Venus, shining in her heaven». The elaborate astrological periphrasis following casts a horoscope with Venus ascendent close to the sun in her lunar house, Taurus, which means that her influence is maximal. Both passages direct our attention to the goddess of love in her planetary aspect. Dante's «bel pianeto che d'amar conforta», she shines from the third heaven of the Aristotelian-Ptolemaic universe.[8]

Boccaccio chose the number 3 for his 'book of love' in the *Teseida* because it is the number of Venus in her cosmic sphere of influence. Dante was, no doubt, the authority who sanctioned the association for him, but many others before, of course, had also reckoned Venus as the third planet.[9] References to the goddess and her heaven elsewhere in Boccaccio's early works echo both the opening of Dante's *canzone*, «Voi che 'ntendendo il *terzo* ciel movete», and the context in which this verse is repeated in *Paradiso* VIII by Charles Martel, first of the light-bathed souls to address the pilgrim after he and Beatrice have risen to Venus, star of the third heaven. Thus as Boccaccio begins to recount his *Amorosa visione*, the poet-dreamer invokes Cytharea, «O somma e graziosa intelli-

---

[8] Cf. *Purgatorio, cit.*, I 19; VIII 1-12. 'Love' literally penetrates *Teseida* III through its opening stanzas. The word 'amore' itself recurs often, and so, too, do its variations in the *figura etimologica*, or the rhetorical device of paronomasia (e.g., 'amore' and 'amare' both used as rhyme words in the same stanza). Here also Boccaccio alludes to Guido Guinizelli's famous *canzone*, a *locus classicus* for the Italian lyric love vocabulary, «Al cor gentil rempaira sempre l'Amore».

[9] See Dante's catalogue of the spheres in *Convivio* II 3, 7 and its precedents, e.g., ALFRAGANUS, *Il 'Libro dell'Aggregazione delle stelle'*, ed. R. CAMPANI, Città di Castello, Casa Tipografico-Editrice S. Lapi, 1910, p. 109: «Minor vero earum est illa quae est propinquior terrae et est spaera Lunae, et secunda est Mercurii et tertia Veneris est et quarta est Solis et quinta est Martis et sexta est Iovis et septima est Saturni et octava est stellarum fixarum» [The smallest of them is the one that is nearest to the earth, and it is the sphere of the Moon; and the second is Mercury's, the third is of Venus, and the fourth is of the Sun, and the fifth is of Mars, and the sixth is of Jove, and the seventh is of Saturn, and the eighth is the sphere of the fixed stars]. Typical also is the list in ISIDORE OF SEVILLE's *De natura rerum*, in *Patrologia Latina* 58:995-996: «In ambitu quippe septem coelestium orbium, primum in inferioris sphaerae circulo luna est constituta. Inde proxima terris posita, ut nocte nobis facilius lumen exhibeat. Dehinc secundo circulo Mercurii stella collocata, soli celeritate par, sed vi quidam, ut philosophi dicunt, contraria. Tertio circulo Luciferi circumvectio est, inde a gentilibus Venus ita dicta [...]» [In the revolution of the seven celestial circles, first in the ring of the lower sphere the moon was placed. It was set next to the earth so that at night it could display its light for us more easily. Next in the second circle the star of Mercury was located, equal to the sun in speed, but contrary to it, as the philosophers say, in influence. The revolution of Lucifer is in the third circle, thence called Venus by the gentiles].

genzia / che muovi il *terzo* cielo e ogni sua idea, / metti nel petto mio la tua potenzia: / non sofferir che fugga, o santa dea, / a me l'ingegno all'opera presente» (B, II 1-5). Troiolo, protagonist of the *Filostrato*, praises Venus ecstatically after consummating his love for Criseida, an event described in the third chapter of the Third Part of the romance, stanzas 30-39: «O luce etterna, il cui lieto splendore / fa bello il *terzo* ciel dal qual ne piove / piacer, vaghezza, pietate ed amore, / del sole amica [...] / sempre lodata sia la tua virtute» (III 74). In the *Filocolo*, the madrigal composed by Caleon for Fiammetta, queen of the debate on thirteen questions of love, is recited by an enamored spirit who sings, «Io son del *terzo* ciel cosa gentile, / sì vago de' begli occhi di costei, / che s'io fossi mortal me ne morrei» (IV 43, 10). When love's pilgrim, Filocolo, reveals his true identity later in the same tale, Dario will raise his eyes heavenward, expressing wondrous thanks, «O più che altro potente pianeto, per la cui luce il *terzo* cielo si mostra bello, quanta è la tua forza negli umani cuori efficace!» (IV 83, 1; italics mine).[10]

Although in the *Teseida* Boccaccio refrains from openly numbering the circle of Venus, he clearly understood it to be the third. Through this connection, the number 3 becomes the arithmetic attribute of the goddess herself and therefore a number signifying 'love'. Other triads would, of course, have reinforced the identification, above all the 3 of Trinitarian love that governs so visibly structure and verse in Dante's *Divine Comedy*. Boccaccio consistently accepts, too, the Scholastic distinction defining three categories of love. His last work, the *Esposizioni sopra la Comedia di Dante*, enumerates them and cites Aristotle as the source;[11] but as early as the *Filocolo*, Queen Fiammetta was already discoursing on that subject, her concern at the very center of the love debate.[12] «Honest

***

[10] *Amorosa visione, cit.*, B, II 1-5; G. BOCCACCIO, *Filostrato*, ed. V. BRANCA, Milan, Mondadori, 1964 («*Tutte le opere*», II), III 74; *Filocolo, cit.*, IV 43, 10; IV 83, 1. Boccaccio's lyrics also assume a bond between love and the third heaven. One sonnet, «Dietro al pastor d'Ameto alle materne», tells of an unidentified widow who appears to the poet «accesa con quello splendore / che è *terza* luce nelle rote eterne»; in another, «Dante, se tu nell'amorosa spera», Boccaccio asks Dante to intercede on his behalf with Fiammetta so that she may grant him the mercy of death, «Io so che, infra l'altre anime liete / del *terzo* ciel, la mia Fiammetta vede / l'affanno mio dopo la sua partita: / pregala [...] / a sé m'impetri tosto la salita» (italics mine). See G. BOCCACCIO, *Rime*, ed. V. BRANCA, Milan, Mondadori, 1992 («*Tutte le opere*» V, pt. I).

[11] G. BOCCACCIO, *Esposizioni sopra la Comedìa di Dante*, ed. G. PADOAN, Milan, Mondadori, 1965 («*Tutte le opere*», VI), V 1, 160: «Piace ad Aristotile esser tre spezie d'amore, cioè amore onesto, amore dilettevole e amore utile: e quell'amore, del quale qui si fa menzione è amor dilettevole».

[12] *Filocolo, cit.*, IV 44, 3-7 and n. 5, p. 872. Fiammetta's stern lecture on love recalls as well Dante's analysis in *De vulgari eloquentia, cit.*, II 2, 10 of man's threefold nature (vegetative, animal, and rational), a triplicity determining the great subjects on which worthy

love», «love for pleasure», and «useful love» are the three types that seem to appear symbolically as the three figures crowning the fountain in the garden of worldly vanity in the *Amorosa visione*. The number of Venus is metrically prominent in that cryptographic *tour de force* with three acrostic sonnets preceding a narrative in *terza rima*.[13]

Since Venus and her number preside over one book in the *Teseida*, we should not be surprised to discover that another is ruled by Mars, the god of whom the poet sings for the «naked» vernacular Muses. His numerical territory, like hers, depends on the sphere he occupies in the sevenfold planetary hierarchy. With Venus shining in the third position, he has the fifth. Consequently, just as Arcita (alias Penteo, or 'Fively') and Palemone begin loving Emilia because of Venus in Book III, so in Book V, «Marte, secondo gli antichi pagani iddio delle battaglie» (I 3, gl.) will compel them to fratricidal combat. The general proemial sonnet announces masculine battle as the theme of the Fifth Book: «il *quinto* [mostra] la battaglia virilmente / da *Penteo* fatta col suo compagnone». The Fifth Book's «particular sonnet» then informs us that Mars, «who had rested too long» — presumably since assisting Teseo with the military campaigns of Books I and II — will now return. His name, twice mentioned here, launches the rhymed résumé:

> Marte, che troppo s'era riposato,
> entrato in Palemon novo sospetto
> il suo compagno udendo ritornato,
> dimostra il quinto a lui entrar nel petto;
> [...].
>   Poscia le lor carezze, e' l quistionare
> d'ognun volere Emilia, e 'l fiero Marte
> può chiaro assai chi più legge trovare.

Palemone has learned that Arcita, whom Teseo had released from prison but banished from Athens, is back in the city incognito as Penteo, a servant in Duke Teseo's household. The knowledge causes Palemone to fear that Arcita has furtively conquered Emilia's love. Fuming with the same poison of discord that Tisiphone had instilled in the hearts of Eteocles and Polynices (V 13), he determines to escape from the tower

---

poets should write: arms, love, and rectitude. Dante ends this chapter of his treatise with precisely the passage that inspired Boccaccio to compose the first Italian epic: «Arma vero nullum latium adhuc invenio poetasse» [I do not find, however, that any Italian has as yet written poetry on the subject of Arms].

[13] *Amorosa visione, cit.,* B, XXXVIII 79-88 and note, p. 710. See further below, ch. 2.

and conquer Emilia by force, «per arme» (V 14). At midnight he goes «armed» to the grove where Arcita, unsuspecting, lies sleeping. Dark, infernal forces continue to stir his passion as he pauses and prays to Luna-Proserpina, «Acciò che per battaglia io possa avere / l'amor di quella sol che m'è in calere» (V 31). Arcita tries to dissuade him from his «mad plan», but then in resignation agrees to fight. First, however, he recites nine tragic episodes from the history of divine wrath against Thebes: the battle of the men sprung from the dragon's teeth, Actaeon, Athamas, Niobe, Semele, Agave, Oedipus, Eteocles and Polynices, and Creon. Largely based on material drawn from Statius's *Thebaid*, Arcita's declamation, which begins in stanza 55, belongs to the central and longest chapter of Book V. The digression is appropriate in a book dominated by the impulse to strife emanating from Mars because «Martian Thebes» had been the warrior god's city, its inhabitants his children.[14] Arcita and Palemone, «nepoti» or grandsons of Cadmus (II 88), are furthermore Mars' descendants since Cadmus had married Harmonia, daughter of Mars and Venus.[15] Arcita sadly concludes, «or resta sopra noi, che ultimi siamo / del teban sangue, insieme n'uccidiamo. / E e' mi piace, poi che t'è in piacere, / che pure infra noi due battaglia sia». We hardly need the Glossator to realize, «Vuole qui mostrare Arcita che tutti li suoi predecessori, discesi di Cadmo, facitore e re primo di Tebe, abbiano fatta mala morte, e così convenire fare a loro due che rimasi n'erano, cioè a Palemone e a sé» (V 57, gl.). After they have been fighting some hours, Emilia arrives (V 77) in a hunting party with Teseo, who adjures the knights in the name of Mars to lay down their weapons. He decrees that each choose a hundred men to fight on his side in a tournament one year hence, and whoever routs the other «by force of arms» shall have Emilia's hand in marriage.

Book III belongs to Venus and Book V to Mars because 3 and 5 are their planetary numbers. Although for readers today the alternation between amorous and martial matter in the *Teseida* seems to cause awkward, abrupt narrative shifts, it follows a well-conceived plan in which number is a significant ordering factor. This plan also applies to a

---

[14] See STATIUS, *Thebaid*, trans. J. H. MOZLEY, 1928; Cambridge, Mass., Harvard University Press, 1967 («Loeb Classical Library»), I 680, where Polynices identifies himself, «Cadmus origo patrum, tellus Mavortia Thebe» [Cadmus was the ancestor of my sires; my land Mavortian Thebes]; and III 269-270, as Venus pleads with Mars for peace, «bella etiam in Thebas, socer o pulcherrime, bella / ipse paras ferroque tuos abolere nepotes?» [War even against Thebes, O noble father, war dost thou thyself prepare, and the sword's destruction for all thy race?].

[15] *Thebaid, cit.*, II 265 ff. and III 269 ff.

third major deity in the epic, Diana, patron of its chaste heroine, Emilia. On the eve of the tournament that is to decide which of the knights she will wed, the Amazon maiden goes to Diana's temple. Her propitiatory sacrifice, her prayer, and the portents through which Diana communicates an answer are set in three successive chapters of Book VII. The first is announced in the seventh rubric of Book VII, «Come Emilia sacrificò a Diana». This rubric heads a chapter of seven stanzas that begins at VII 70. The following rubric, «L'orazione d'Emilia a Diana», then precedes VII 77. In the next chapter, «Ciò che ad Emilia orante apparve e come ella si partì del tempio», Diana's chorus speaks, «e già nel ciel tra l'iddii è fermato / che tu sii sposa dell'un di costoro, / e Diana n'è lieta» (VII 89). If the first chapter in this three-part sequence has seven stanzas starting with VII 70, the next two, which start with Emilia's prayer at VII 77, contain a total of seventeen stanzas. The entire sequence is placed, moreover, at two structural centers in Book VII. Since Book VII has 145 stanzas in all, the seventy-third is their midpoint, and VII 73 marks precisely the central octave in the chapter that introduces Diana's temple at VII 70. Reckoning alternatively by rubrics, we find that the reply to Emilia's prayer is announced in the ninth chapter. Since Book VII has in all nineteen chapters, the ninth marks a numerological center. (In strict arithmetic terms, of course, ten would be the middle in a sequence of nineteen, and here at Chapter Ten of Book VII, which is VII 94, Boccaccio brings us to a new narrative departure, sunrise on the tournament day.) We can envision the chapter sequence centered on Emilia and Diana as follows.

VII, Rub. 7 = VII 70	«Come Emilia sacrificò a Diana»	seven
VII 73	= cent. stanza of Ch. 7 and Bk. VII	stanzas
VII, Rub. 8 = VII 77	«L'orazione d'Emilia a Diana»	seventeen
VII, Rub. 9 = VII 88	«Ciò che ad Emilia orante apparve»	stanzas

The above patterns, coinciding twice with 'centers' in the Seventh Book, indicate that the number 7 must be Diana's number in the *Teseida*. Her name is not mentioned in the poem proper until the Seventh Book. Excluded, for example, from Palemone's nocturnal prayer to Luna (V 30), which begins, «O di Latona prole inargentata», it appears in that context only as a part of the commentary: «Scrivono i poeti che Latona fu bellissima donna, della quale Giove innamorato e avuto a fare di lei ebbe due figliuoli, Appollo e Diana, cioè la luna» (V 30, gl.). Diana as a name makes its first appearance in the octaves, as distinct from the three rubrics just discussed, at the description of the palace of Venus (VII 61), where many broken bows from her faithless nymphs, including Callisto's, hang on a wall as trophies. The sum of the digits designating this stanza (61 = 6 + 1 = 7) probably alludes to the goddess of chastity. The last references to Diana in the epic form a short sequence starting with the seventh chapter of Book XII, when Emilia protests that she should not marry because the Scythian women had all taken vows of chastity to Diana. Fearing the goddess's vengeance, she prefers to continue obediently serving her. Teseo, however, quickly dispels her resistance, «se Diana ne fosse turbata, / sopra di te verria l'ira dolente, / [...] / la forma tua non è atta a Diana / servir ne' templi né 'n selva montana». With his speech (XII 43), again in a stanza that could conceal her number (43 = 4 + 3 = 7), Diana is dismissed from the poem.

Like the 3's and 5's accompanying Venus and Mars, Diana's number in the *Teseida* is also astrological. Silvery daughter of Latona and sister of the sun Apollo, she is the moon. When Emilia invokes the goddess in her «gran deitate / triforme» (VII 80), the Glossator remarks, «È questa dea in cielo chiamata luna e ha quella forma la quale noi veggiamo; e in terra è chiamata Diana, dea della castità, e allora si figura con l'arco e col turcasso a guisa di cacciatrice; in inferno si chiama Proserpina, e allora si figura come reina perciò che è moglie di Plutone, iddio e re d'inferno». In her lunar aspect Diana can be the seventh planet, providing, naturally, we reverse our perspective on the celestial spheres and count them downwards from Saturn.

This alternative system of reckoning the planets was practiced both before and after Boccaccio's time, and he was not the only author to combine the two. Dante, for example, admits that one can number them starting with either the lowest or the highest. In the *Convivio*, adding to the seven revolving heavens a starry eighth and a ninth (the Prime Mover), he correlates each with a branch of learning. To Mars he attributes Music, in part because that planet is at the center and so enjoys an especially harmonious relationship with the others: «E lo cielo di Marte si può comparare a la Musica per [...] la sua più bella relazione, chè, annumerando li cieli mobili, da qualunque si comincia o da l'infimo o dal sommo, esso cielo di Marte è lo quinto, esso è lo mezzo di tutti, cioè de li primi, de li secondi, de li terzi e de li quarti».[16]

Chaucer, who surely perceived numerical patterns in the *Teseida*, also counts the orbiting stars both ways. In *The Knight's Tale*, he is looking up

---

[16] *Il Convivio*, ed. G. Busnelli and G. Vandelli, rev. A. E. Quaglio, Florence, Felice Le Monnier, 1968, II 13, 20.

from earth at Venus, whom he links with the number 3 and her votary, Palamon. Palamon escapes from his seven-year imprisonment «in the seventhe yer, of May / The *thridde* nyght» (vv. 1462-63); before the tournament that Theseus ordains «this day fifty wykes» (v. 1850), it was «The *thridde* houre inequal that Palamon / Bigan to Venus temple for to gon» (vv. 2271-72). Similarly, in *Troilus and Criseyde* love's keen shots happen to strike Pandarus «on Mayes day the *thrydde*» (II 56-58), and amorous Venus opens the Prohemium of Book Three, «O blisful light, of which the bemes clere / Adorneth al the *thridde* heven faire! / O sonnes lief, o Joves doughter deere, / Plesance of love, O goodly debonaire, / In gentil hertes ay redy to repaire!». Conversely, however, it is her mythological and astrological lover who is the lord of this heaven in *The Complaint of Mars*. So the English poet has here shifted his perspective and views the planets from above:

> Whilom the *thridde* hevenes lord above,
> As wel by hevenysh revolucioun
> As by desert, hath wonne Venus his love,
> And she hath take him in subjeccioun,
> And as a maistresse taught him his lessoun,
> Commaundynge him that nevere, in her servise,
> He nere so bold no lover to dispise.
>
> (vv. 29-35; italics mine)[17]

Chaucer then freely interchanges the spheres of Mars and Venus, counting in either direction and accommodating their numbers to the poetic scheme dictated by his different works.

In spite of these alternations, the number 7 had been well-established from antiquity as Diana's defining number. Cicero's *De natura deorum* so counts her: «Diana is called All-Wandering not from "hunting", but because she is numbered seven just as the wandering stars».[18] As we know from the *Commentary on the Dream of Scipio* by Macrobius, the moon is also seen as last among the planets by the two Scipios, who gaze from a «lofty perch» in the Milky Way down through the ranks of the underlying

---

[17] G. CHAUCER, *The Knight's Tale*, *Troilus and Criseyde*, and *The Complaint of Mars*, in *The Works of Geoffrey Chaucer*, ed. F. N. ROBINSON, Boston, Houghton Mifflin Company, 1957². For a rich study on number symbolism in Chaucer, see R. A. PECK, *Numerology and Chaucer's 'Troilus and Criseyde'*, «Mosaic», V, 1972, pp. 1-29.

[18] CICERO, *De natura deorum*, trans. H. RACKHAM, Cambridge, Mass., Harvard University Press, 1951 («Loeb Classical Library»), II 27, 68: «Diana, *omnivaga* dicitur, non a venando, sed quod in septem numeratur tamquam vagantibus».

spheres in the cosmos, one by one from Saturn to the earth. Scipio the Elder makes a cryptic reference to the «seven times eight recurring circuits of the sun» his grandson will live. This requires Macrobius to expound at length on numbers generally. The digit that receives his fullest attention is 7, most venerable in the Pythagorean decad, and the one that motivates the moon: «the number 7 motivates the moon, which is in the seventh planetary sphere, and regulates its course».[19] Many proofs, he asserts, can be adduced to demonstrate the truth of this statement. To begin with, the moon completes its cycle in twenty-eight days, and 28 is the sum of the first seven digits ($1 + 2 + 3 + 4 + 5 + 6 + 7 = 28$): «seven is the source of this number of twenty-eight, for if

---

[19] MACROBIUS, *Commentary on the Dream of Scipio*, trans. W. H. STAHL, New York, Columbia University Press, 1952 («Records of Civilization, Sources and Studies», XLVIII); *Commentarii in somnivm Scipionis*, ed. J. WILLIS, Leipzig, B. G. Teubner Verlagsgesellschaft, 1970: I 5, 2: «nam cum aetas tua septenos octies solis anfractus reditusque converterit»; I 6, 48: «lunam quoque quasi ex illis [vagantibus sphaeris] septimam numerus septenarius movet cursumque eius ipse dispensat». The inventory of Boccaccio's books that passed into the «parva libraria» at Santo Spirito includes a «Macrobius de sopno Scipionis conpletus», the incipit of which coincides with the beginning of Cicero's *Somnium*. See A. MAZZA, *L'inventario della 'parva libraria' di Santo Spirito e la biblioteca del Boccaccio*, «Italia Medioevale e Umanistica», IX, 1966, pp. 1-71.

Recall PHILO's reverential encomium of the heptad, *De opificio mundi*, I, trans. F. H. COLSON and G. H. WHITAKER, Cambridge, Mass., Harvard University Press, 1929 («Loeb Classical Library»), p. 73: «I doubt whether anyone could adequately celebrate the properties of the number 7, for they are beyond all words. Yet the fact that it is more wondrous than all that is said about it is no reason for maintaining silence regarding it. Nay, we must make a brave attempt to bring out at least all that is within the compass of our understanding, even if it be impossible to bring out all or even the most essential points». Cf. MACROBIUS, *Comm. in somnium, cit.*, I 6, 45-47: «hic numerus ἑπτάς nunc vocatur, antiquato usu primae litterae, apud veteres enim σεπτάς vocitabatur, quod Graeco nomine testabatur venerationem debitam numero. nam primo omnium hoc numero anima mundana generata est, sicut Timaeus Platonis edocuit [...] non parva ergo hinc potentia numeri huius ostenditur quia mundanae animae origo septem finibus continetur, septem quoque vagantium sphaerarum ordinem illi stelliferae et omnes continenti subiecit artifex fabricatoris providentia, quae et superioris rapidis motibus obviarent et inferiora omnia gubernarent». [This number is now called [h]eptas, the first letter no longer being in use; but the ancients used to call it septas, the Greek word testifying to the veneration owing to the number. It was by this number first of all, indeed, that the World-Soul was begotten, as Plato's *Timaeus* has shown [...]. The fact that the origin of the World-Soul hinges upon seven steps is proof that this number has no mean ability, but in addition the Creator, in his constructive foresight, arranged seven errant spheres beneath the star-bearing celestial sphere, which embraces the universe, so that they might counteract the swift motions of the sphere above and govern everything beneath.] Note also what awe before the number bursts from the discourse on Arithmetic by MARTIANUS CAPELLA, *De nuptiis Philologiae et Mercurii libri VIIII*, ed. A. DICK, Leipzig, B. G. Teubner Verlagsgesellschaft, 1925; *The Marriage of Philology and Mercury*, trans. W. H. STAHL and R. JOHNSON with E. L. BURGE, in *Martianus Capella and the Seven Liberal Arts*, II, New York, Columbia University Press, 1977 («Records of Civilization, Sources and Studies», LXXXIV): «quid autem te, heptas, venerandam commemorem?» [What reasons should I recount for your veneration, O Heptad?]. For further references see V. F. HOPPER, *Medieval Number Symbolism*, New York, Cooper Square Publishers, 1969², pp. 43-44.

you add the numbers from one to seven, the total is twenty-eight». Then, too, its monthly course can be divided into four quarters of seven days each, «twenty-eight, evenly divided into four quarters, marks the number of days required by the moon to complete its course out and back across the zodiac». Finally, this mutable body regularly waxes and wanes through seven phases, «following the same arrangement of seven-day periods the moon also regulates the phase of its light under a fixed law».[20] Other notable authorities, among them Martianus Capella and later Isidore of Seville, reasoned along just these same lines, which compound Diana's number in the planetary hierarchy with the 7's characterizing the lunar cycle.[21] They, like Macrobius, were known to Boccaccio, who preserves a learned tradition by selecting 7 as the number for that goddess in the *Teseida*.

The numerological descent of Venus, Mars, and Diana from their celestial homes to the poetic terrain of the *Teseida* reaches beyond the primary structural areas of influence that I have thus far outlined for Books III, V, and VII. Venus and Mars, who will directly intervene in the tournament on behalf of Palemone and Arcita respectively, also quietly determine the hours of its duration. When the two knights march with one hundred combatants each into the arena, «già del cielo al *terzo* salito era / Febo» (VII 104). As Arcita is borne triumphant back to Athens, «Passata avea il sol già l'ora *ottava*, / quando finì lo stormo incominciato / in su la *terza*» (IX 29).[22] The chivalric contest, stemming from courtly enamorment, begins at a time of day carrying the number of

---

[20] MACROBIUS, *Comm. in somnium*, cit., I 6, 52-54: «Huius ergo viginti octo dierum numeri septenarius origo est. nam si ab uno usque ad septem quantum singuli numeri exprimunt tantum antecedentibus addendo procedas, invenies viginti octo nata de septem. hunc etiam numerum, qui in quater septenos aequa sorte digeritur, ad totam zodiaci latitudinem emetiendam remetiendamque consumit [...] similibus quoque dispensationibus hebdomadum luminis sui vices sempiterna lege variando disponit».

[21] MARTIANUS, *De nuptiis*, cit., pp. 373-374: «ex tribus et quattuor septem fiunt, qui numerus formas lunae complectitur [...]. hic numerus lunae cursum significat»; *The Marriage*, cit., p. 282: «seven consists of three and four. It is the number that marks the phases of the moon [...]. This number also marks the orbit of the moon». ISIDORE echoes the tradition in his *Liber numerorum*, *Patrologia Latina*, 58:188: «Idem quoque septenarius numerus formam lunae complectitur; tot enim habet luna figuras [...] hic etiam numerus et nomina lunae significat. Nam unum, duo, tria, quatuor, quinque, et sex, et septem viginti octo faciunt» [this number seven marks the phases of the moon, for the moon has seven phases [...] this number also defines the moon, for one, two, three, four, five, and six, and seven make twenty-eight].

[22] Boccaccio is guilty of an oversight in these calculations. He glosses 'terzo' in VII 104 as «Cioè era già sesta o presso, perciò che in quella stagione, cioè verso l'uscita di maggio, il dì è di xviii ore o presso, il terzo delle quali è presso a sei». But in IX 29 he clearly says that the battle, which ended with the «ora *ottava*», had begun in «[l'ora] terza». The inconsistency indicates confusion between solar and symbolic time.

Venus, and it brings an end to the knights' militant rivalry with the victory of Arcita in a period of exactly five hours. Moreover, after setting the rules for this 'love battle', Teseo had stated, «Questo sarà come un giuoco a Marte, / li sacrifici del qual celebriamo / il giorno dato» (VII 13). Referring to Boccaccio's discussion of the commonly acccepted astrological relationship between the planets and the days of the week in his *Genealogia*, Janet Smarr has rightly deduced that the «given day» in question must be 'martedì', the first hour of which is governed by Mars. According to the above scheme for matching successive diurnal hours with the planets, the third and eighth on this tournament Tuesday acquire greater symbolic resonance because Venus governs the former and Mars returns to rule the latter.[23]

Our Narrator may also be pointing numerically to Mars as he registers the size of the amphitheater, which has «più di *cinquecento* giri» rising up from the ring in circular steps (VII 110). This possibility is strengthened by the fact that his Commentator, too, has a predilection for the number 5 and its multiples by 10, an interest evident much earlier in the *Teseida*. It happens, for example, that the glosses on Book I cite the number 50 just five times. In I 7 the Author compares the Amazons' mad slaughter of their menfolk with the ferocity of the «granddaughters of Belus», and the Glossator then explains:

Belo fu re in una parte di Grecia, e ebbe due figliuoli; l'uno ebbe nome Danao, il quale fu re dopo la morte del padre e ebbe *cinquanta* figliuole; l'altro ebbe nome Egisto e ebbe *cinquanta* figliuoli maschi; e di pari concordia diedono le *cinquanta* figliuole di Danao per mogli alli *cinquanta* figliuoli d'Egisto.

---

[23] J. L. SMARR, *Boccaccio and the Stars*, cit., refers to *Genealogia* I 34: «Sed cum longe alius sit ordo planetarum quam in nominibus dierum habeatur, est sciendum secundum planetarum ordinem successive unicuique diei hore dari dominium, et ab eo cui contingit prime hore diei dominium habere, ab eo dies illa denominata est, ut puta si diei dominice Veneri secundam horam tribues, que Soli immediate subiacet, et Mercurio terciam, qui subiacet Veneri, et Lune quartam, que subiacet Mercurio, quintam autem Saturno, ad quem convertendus est ordo cum in Luna defecerit, sextam Iovi, et sic de singulis XXIIII[or] horis diei dominice, sub nomine vel dominio Mercurii invenietur hora XXIIII[a], et XXV[a] que prima est diei sequentis sub nomine vel dominio Lune» [But since the order of the planets is quite different from that of the names of the days, it must be understood that the planets, according to their order, are given dominion successively over the hours of each day, and the one that has dominion over the first hour of the day is the one from which that day takes its name. So, for example, if you attribute the second hour of the day Sunday to Venus, which lies immediately below the Sun, and the third to Mercury, which lies below Venus, and the fourth to the Moon, which lies below Mercury; and the fifth to Saturn (to whom the order must revert because it runs out at the Moon), the sixth to Jove, and so on for each of the 24 hours of the day; the 24th hour of Sunday will appear under the name or dominion of Mercury, and the 25th, which is the first of the following day, will be under the dominion of the Moon]. See also A. E. QUAGLIO, *Scienza e mito*, cit., pp. 200-201.

Seven stanzas later, he tells how a magnificent deed of valor accomplished by a man called Tydeus inspired Teseo to attack so courageously the Amazons. The heroism of Tydeus, which he knew, of course, from Statius,

fu in questa forma: Etiocle e Polinice figliuoli d'Edippo, re di Tebe, composero insieme di regnare ciascuno il suo anno, e mentre l'uno regnasse, l'altro stesse come sbandito fuori del regno [...]. E essendo finito l'anno che Etiocle dovea avere regnato, venne a Tebe Tideo, a richiedere il regno per Polinice; il quale non solamente non gli fu renduto, ma fu di notte in uno bosco assalito da *cinquanta* cavalieri, li quali Etiocle avea mandati a stare in guato, perché l'uccidessero; li quali Tideo, fieramente combattendo, tutti uccise, e poi consecrò a Marte, iddio delle battaglie, il suo scudo. (I 14, gl.; italics mine)[24]

If the marginalia of *Teseida* I yield a 50 five times, three further pentavalent referents appear in its preliminary companion piece, Book II. So the rubric introducing II 10 with the Author's «Transgressione dalla propria materia, per mostrare qual fosse la cagione per la quale Teseo andasse contra Creonte» prompts a longer annotated account of the war between Eteocles and Polynices, which again requires mention of the fifty slain by Tydeus. Lexicon calls our attention to the ensuing march of «five» against Thebes, as opposed to the more predictable seven:

fu, tornandosi egli [Tideo] ad Argo, assalito una notte da *cinquanta* cavalieri d'Etiocle, gli quali egli tutti uccise; e, tornato ad Argo, commosse ad andare a vendicare la ingiuria fatta a Pollinice, e quella che stata era fatta a lui, Capaneo re, Anfiorao re, Ippomedone re, Partenopeo re, e Adrasto suo suocero; e con grandissimo esercito di gente a piè e a cavallo, e egli e Pollinice co' predetti altri *cinque* re andarono ad assediare Tebe. (II 10, gl.)

Finally, at II 70, as Boccaccio's Teseo advances victorious into the fallen city, his Glossator proffers a last reminder — the third in the epic — of the fifty who had ambushed Tydeus, «que' *cinquanta* de' quali è detto di sopra» (italics mine). In other words, the Italian epic's commentary thrice alludes to these fifty in a broader pattern proceeding from the Danaids and containing 5 + 3 occurrences of 5 and 50 that extend from I 7 to II 70.

Our Glossator, privy to his Author's numerological plan, collaborates with him in another tripartite scheme matching Diana and her twin, Apollo, with the number 7 doubled. During Teseo's preparations for

---

[24] Cf. *Thebaid, cit.*, II 482 ff.

Arcita's splendid funeral, the author borrows a formula from Dante to report that the Athenians' grief was surely greater than that of the Thebans «quando li sette e sette d'Anfione / figli fur morti en la trista stagione» (XI 16).[25] Here the Glossator notes, «Detto è sopra come per la superbia di Niobè fossero uccisi i suoi xiiij figliuoli» (XI 16, gl.). «Above» turns out to be X 8, where we find that the number of those killed in the tournament equalled that of the funeral urns Niobe carried after Latona's vengeance. Again the commentary refers us to an earlier passage.

Mostrato è di sopra come i figliuoli e le figliuole di Niobè per la sua superbia fossero uccisi da Apollo e da Diana, figliuoli di Latona. Li quali furono xiiij, e ciascuno fu dalla madre, cioè da Niobè, messo per sé in una urna [...]. E così mostra [l'autore] che xiiij fossero coloro che in quella battaglia morirono.

For a full account of Niobe's pride and punishment, we must retrogress to Arcita's synopsis of his city's history, that is, the grim recital starting in V 55. Explaining the verses, «Latona uccise i figliuoi d'Anfione / intorno a Niobè, madre dolente», the Glossator writes that Amphion was a king of Thebes married to Niobe, «della quale aveva xiiii figliuoli, vii maschi e vii femine». He goes on to narrate the familiar Ovidian myth, concluding that, as Niobe was disporting in a meadow «con tutti questi suoi xiiii figliuoli, in poca d'ora, saettando, Apollo uccise li vii maschi, e Diana le vii femine».[26] Understood as 7 + 7, this trio of 14's in the marginalia on V 58; X 8; and XI 16 reiterates the numerical structure tying Diana to the heptad at the Seventh Book's center.

Another line of textual exploration reveals figurative patterns of kinship linking Mars, Venus, and Diana with their earthly fictional counterparts, Arcita, Palemone, and Emilia. Arcita, who will pray to Mars for victory the night before the tournament, decides to conceal his identity after embarking on the bitter path of exile, and he changes his name to Penteo. The pseudonym, which then accompanies him through the duel in Book V, is derived from the Greek word for 5, 'pente'. This poetic cipher, which we could English as 'Fively', would have been suggested to Boccaccio by Latin treatises on the Pythagorean decad, which often used the Hellenic forms to designate each number, *monas*, *dyas*, *trias*, and so forth.[27] Palemone is apprized that Arcita has returned

---

[25] Cf. *Purgatorio*, *cit.*, XII 37-39: «O Nïobè, con che occhi dolenti / vedea io te segnata in su la strada, / tra sette e sette tuoi figliuoli spenti!».

[26] Cf. OVID, *Metamorphoses* VI 165 ff.

[27] Characteristic is the section on Arithmetic in MARTIANUS, *De nuptiis, cit.*, pp. 369-370: «pentas, qui numerus mundo est attributus; nam si ex quattuor elementis ipse sub alia forma est

secretly to Athens «e ch'e' servia Teseo / e faceasi per nome dir *Penteo*» in V 5. The rubric entitled «La forma e l'esser d'Arcita» introduces the fifth chapter and fiftieth stanza of Book III (III 50, rub.). In Book IV Arcita will lament the destruction of Thebes for five stanzas (13-17) and raise a plea of five stanzas for help from Love (67-71). His rehearsal of Theban history beginning with V 55 also occupies five stanzas, as does the «Orazione d'Arcita a Marte» in Book VII (24-28).

We have already seen the cluster of 7's surrounding Diana in conjunction with her temple and vengeance on Niobe. So the arrival of her devotee Emilia on the scene of the duel in V 77 may have been calculated by Boccaccio to coincide with this number, especially since the princess comes as a huntress: «sopra d'un bel pallafreno / co' can dintorno, e un corno dallato / avea e [...] / dietro alle spalle, un arco avea legato / e un turcasso di saette pieno» (V 79). These verses recall Boccaccio's gloss on Emilia's prayer to the goddess of chastity at VII 80: «On earth she is called Diana, goddess of chastity, and then she is depicted with a bow and quiver in the guise of a huntress». The poet will withhold his description of «la forma e la bellezza di Emilia» until the twelfth chapter of Book XII. It begins, as does the epic itself, with an invocation to the Muses, this time in the name of Amphion, whom they had helped build the city walls for Thebes. The stanza's number (XII 52) suggests a 7 (52 = 5 + 2 = 7), a sum implicitly related to the three preceding cross-referenced allusions to Amphion's 7 + 7 children.

«La forma e l'esser di Palemone», who entrusts himself to Venus before the tournament, is the title of the central chapter in Book III. It consists of a single stanza, the forty-ninth. Again, the sum of these digits (49 = 4 + 9 = 13) could count symbolically since Boccaccio elsewhere had already used 13 as a number of love, most obviously for the thirteen «questioni d'amore» debated in the *Filocolo*. We are told how Palemone's confidant, appropriately called Panfilo ('all love'), engineers his escape from prison in a chapter of three stanzas, the third of Book V. Palemone,

---

quintus, pentade est rationalibiter insignitus»; *The Marriage, cit.*, p. 279: «The pentad comes next, the number assigned to the universe. This identification is reasonable, for after the four elements, the universe is a fifth body of a different nature». Boccaccio's choice of 'Penteo' as an alias for Arcita may also allude to the tragic story of the Theban king Pentheus whom the Bacchantes destroyed, a connection suggested by W. WETHERBEE, *History and Romance in Boccaccio's 'Teseida'*, in *Boccaccio 1990: The Poet and his Renaissance Reception*, «Studi sul Boccaccio», XXI, 1991-92, pp. 173-184. R. MARTINEZ, *Before the 'Teseida': Statius and Dante in Boccaccio's Epic, Ibid.*, pp. 205-219, characterizes Arcita-Penteo as «the moral microcosm of the poem» — a kind of summation of its major themes because of his reversals at the hands of Fortune, his lovesickness, his awareness of the nature and danger of Theban origins, his loss of Emilia, his painful violent death, and his *contemptus mundi* after dying.

who invokes «Latona's silvery offspring» for three octaves beginning with V 30, will then reach Arcita sleeping in the wood at V 33, that is, at the start of the fifth chapter of Book V.

Finally, the 3 of love fulfills Palemone's good fortune in marrying Emilia because she had twice before been a bride-to-be. Several times vague mention is made of Acate, a man to whom Teseo would have given her hand had cruel fortune not caused his untimely death (V 94). Next she is wed to Arcita, who had emerged victorious, but gravely injured, from the tournament. Arcita, of course, never recovers and dies but ten days later. Thus it must be thanks to the protection of Venus that Palemone, third in line, becomes her spouse in a true marriage, sealed by consummation and a formal nuptial celebration ('nozze').[28]

These numeric ties between mythological and mortal participants in the *Teseida* invite three working conclusions. First, the poem's governing numbers signal important thematic content, such as planetary dispositions (III 5), prayers to the gods (V 30; VII 70), and crucial shifts in narrative development hinging on character action or intersection: Palemone comes armed to Arcita at midnight (V 33) for a duel preordained by the curse on Thebes (V 55) that will be halted by the morntide arrival of Emilia (V 77) with Teseo. Second, what seemed at first a simple relationship between Venus and 3, Mars and 5, Diana and 7, now becomes an interlocking system involving these numbers collectively because they tend to keep occurring in conjunction with one another. Third, the glosses share in the numerical plan governing disposition of material into books, chapters, and stanzas. Scattered traces intimate that both what the Commentator says and where may be significant on this count. He thrice recalls the death of Amphion and Niobe's 7 + 7 children beginning with a gloss (V 58) in which the sums 7 and 14 are named seven times. All told, he finds occasion to use the number 50 seven times, first in I 7 (the Danaids) and last in II 70 (the Theban fifty who ambushed Tydeus). These curious coincidences bring us now to a closer consideration of Boccaccio's marginalia.

Almost all the glosses on the *Teseida* exemplify the first kind of commentary Boccaccio will later apply to his readings of Dante's *Comedy*, «literal exposition». Only a handful go deeper, disclosing some of the moral truth the Author means to convey «poeticamente fingendo». Early in the epic, as Mars returns from Tydeus's bloody triumph and musters

---

[28] H. A. KELLEY discusses the terms 'sponsalizie' (the act of marrying) and 'nozze' (the feast that follows it) as used by Boccaccio in *Love and Marriage in the Age of Chaucer*, Ithaca, Cornell University Press, 1975, pp. 180-185, 194-195.

«Teseo magnanimo» to sail with an army against the Amazons, the poet gives us a first glimpse of his work's allegorical possibilities by establishing a connection between the god of war and the emotion of anger (I 14-15, gl.). But he chooses not to exploit them more fully until the night preceding the tournament, when Arcita and Palemone pray for assistance in the Athenian temples of Mars and Venus. Their «Orisons», which fly personified to these deities' abodes and view them in virtually every detail, occasion the two longest, most rigorously constructed, moralistic glosses in the entire poem. They are attached through a striking numerical chiasmus to the thirtieth stanza (for Mars) and the fiftieth stanza (for Venus) of Book VII.

The resulting conjunction of the numbers 3, 5, and 7 should not at this point be surprising. After all, it is precisely in this pair of dense, didactic expositions at VII 30 and VII 50 that Boccaccio finally extends a key opening the way to the *Teseida*'s underlying allegory. In the former, which resumes the note on Mars' Thracian home accompanying I 15, he states that all men have two principal appetites, «de' quali l'uno si chiama appetito concupiscibile [...] l'altro si chiama appetito irascibile». Each in turn may be laudable or reprehensible depending on whether it is subject to the higher power of reason. The god Mars can therefore represent righteous anger as well as blind wrath:

due maniere d'ira sono, e ciascuna fa arrossare l'adirato: l'una si è l'adirarsi senza ragione, e questa è viziosa e è quella di che qui si parla; l'altra può essere ragionevole, sì come il turbarsi d'alcuna cosa non giustamente fatta, e questa riceve il consiglio della ragione in riprendere e in fare ammendare quella cotale cosa mal fatta. (VII 30, gl.)

Venus is similarly twofold, either a goddess of matrimony and generation or an incitement to wanton concupiscence:

La quale Venere è doppia, perciò che l'una si può e dee intendere per ciascuno onesto e licito disiderio, sì come è disiderare d'avere moglie per avere figliuoli, e simili a questo; e di questa Venere non si parla qui. La seconda Venere è quella per la quale ogni lascivia è disiderata, e che volgarmente è chiamata dea d'amore; e di questa disegna qui l'autore il tempio e l'altre cose circustanti ad esso. (VII 50, gl.)

Applying these distinctions to the narrative in the *Teseida*, we can say that the 'good' Mars and Venus assist 'good Teseo' in his just warfare against the Amazons' proudly truculent, unnatural, antimatrimonial society (Book I). Announcing imminent surrender, Ipolita informs her subjects, «Se di ciascuna qui fosse il marito, / fratel, figliuolo o padre che fu morto / da tutte noi, non saria stato ardito / Teseo mai d'appressarsi al nostro porto; / ma perché non ci son, ci ha assaltate, / come vedete, e ancora assediate. / Venere, giustamente a noi crucciata, / col suo amico Marte il favoreggia» (I 116-117).

The same Mars moves Teseo to end the tyranny of King Creon (Book II), whose hubris had also led him to violate social custom, more particularly another aspect of the marriage bond, by denying aggrieved widows the time-honored privilege of granting their husbands ritual burial. Scythia and Thebes stand in moral juxtaposition to Athens, recognized by the Commentator as the city of Minerva and wisdom: «Minerva tenevano gli antichi che fosse dea della sapienza, e questa oltre a ogni altro iddio era onorata in Attene, sì come i Fiorentini più che alcuno altro santo onorano San Giovanni Batista» (I 60, gl.). Having conquered Ipolita's kingdom, Teseo's first act on returning to Athens is to enter the temple of Pallas-Minerva: «diritto andò al tempio di Pallade / a reverir di lei la deitade. / Quivi con reverenza offerse molto, / e le sue armi e l'altre conquistate» (II 23-24). Minerva's is, moreover, the first of several religious sanctuaries visited in the poem by the wise Duke of Athens. An embodiment of moral enlightenment, he will end toward high noon the duel begun in a dark wood at midnight between Arcita and Palemone, whose rivalry had been caused by the irrational Mars and his adulterous, concupiscent consort, the 'wrong' Venus. To these gods the Thebans pray, again at night, before the civilized, rationally planned tournament, through which, as Apollo shines for five hours, reason personified by Teseo dominates the knights' destructive appetites. Its outcome will permit the poet to end the Twelfth Book of his matrimonial epic as he had the first, with a nuptial ceremony celebrated in the temple of the 'good' Venus, who fosters the legitimate desire to marry and bear children.

But there is more to be said about the marginalia surrounding Arcita and Palemone's prayers to Mars (VII 30) and Venus (VII 50). The stanzas to which these conceptually central glosses are attached stand exactly at the poem's structural centers. Again, as we saw for Book VII, there are two, one based on a verse count and the other on the sum of the chapters demarcated by rubrics. The *Teseida* has 1,238 octaves, making a total of 9,904 verses, which puts the central stanza (the 619th) at VII 30. The central verse (4,952) coincides with VII 30,1, where the solemn description of Mars' tenebrous castle begins, «ne' campi trazii, sotto i cieli iberni».[29] The rubrics distributed among the twelve books of the epic create 176 chapters. Their center is the eighty-eighth, which is the sixth chapter of the seventh book: «Come l'orazione [di Palemone] pervenne a Venere, e come fatto e dove sia il tempio suo» (VII 50, rub.). This chapter opens with VII 50, and recalls explicitly the corresponding description of Mars' dwelling that had begun in VII 30: «Come d'Arcita Marte l'orazione / cercò, così a Venere pietosa, / se n'andò sopra 'l monte Citerone / quella di Palemon» (VII 50). The Author's main theme, announced in the Proem, is love. It is therefore appropriate that the gloss on this stanza, running to nearly five thousand words, should be by far the longest in his poem. The second longest is its pendant on Mars, the god of whom Boccaccio first sang in the noble vernacular of Latium. These glosses, together with the conspicuous absence of any analogous

---

[29] R. HOLLANDER also discovered independently that VII 30, 1 is the central verse in the poem, noting that it is «precisely the numerical center of the work that Boccaccio chooses for the first of his two 'chiose singolarissime'». His detailed discussion of the glosses, which he suggests were written to make the epic «an instant classic», appears in *The Validity of Boccaccio's Self-Exegesis in his 'Teseida'*, «Medievalia et Humanistica», n.s., VIII, 1977, pp. 163-183. S. NOAKES dedicates to the *Teseida* a chapter of *Timely Reading. Between Exegesis and Interpretation*, Ithaca, Cornell University Press, 1988. She reaches conclusions that dovetail with Hollander's findings and my own: artistically conceived, the commentary goes far beyond simple explication to enhance poetically the text. Such devices as thematic repetition enrich our perspectives on the characters and foreshadow events in the plot. Although condescending in his attitude toward the *Teseida* (it suffers from invidious comparison with Chaucer), P. BOITANI does recognize what importance Boccaccio attached to the center of his poem, «a triumph of 14th-century iconography», in *Style, Iconography and Narrative: The Lesson of the 'Teseida'*, in *Chaucer and the Italian Trecento*, ed. P. BOITANI, Cambridge, Cambridge University Press, 1983, pp. 185-199. J. MCGREGOR studies the temples of Mars and Venus as parts of a programmatic series of ancient monuments in the poem, which he sees as «a repossession, to the fullest extent Boccaccio ever encompasses, of his classical and epic heritage». See his *The Shades of Aeneas. The Imitation of Vergil and the History of Paganism in Boccaccio's 'Filostrato', 'Filocolo', and 'Teseida'*, Athens, University of Georgia Press, 1991, esp. pp. 77-78.
My own line of argument on the central glosses owes much to R. HOLLANDER's interpretation of the *Teseida*, initially shared with me in collegial discussion and later published in *Boccaccio's Two Venuses*, New York, Columbia University Press, 1977, pp. 53-64. Hollander gives special and rightly deserved attention to the prayers and their glosses in Book VII, where «the crucial moral action of the *Teseida* occurs». I have also drawn informing suggestions from J. L. SMARR, *The 'Teseida', Boccaccio's Allegorical Epic*, «NEMLA Italian Studies», I, 1977, pp. 29-35. Her essay identifies Teseo as Reason, the power that combats the appetites, epitomized by Arcita and Palemone.
Boccaccio's information on man's «two principal appetites» suggests Aristotelian, Thomistic, and Augustinian antecedents. For example, the two kinds of anger, irrational and righteous, come from Aristotle. *De anima* (402a) describes how the first blinds the mind; the *Nicomachean Ethics* (1105b, 1125b) gives justifiable circumstances for the second. See the commentaries on these by Thomas Aquinas, also his *Summa theologica, cit.*, I, Qu. 59, Art. 4: «Philosophus dicit, in III *De An.*, quod irascibilis et concupiscibilis sunt in parte sensitiva» [The Philosopher says that the irascible and concupiscible are in the sensitive part]; I, Qu. 81, Art. 2: «appetitus sensitivus est una vis in genere, quae sensualitas dicitur; sed dividitur in duas potentias, quae sunt species appetitus sensitivi, scilicet irascibilem et concupiscibilem» [the

text following Emilia's prayer to Diana, allow us to see Venus and Mars, who rule for better or worse successive portions of the *Teseida*, as a couple presiding allegorically at its numerologically determined structural centers.

Now we must recall that if the Author declares love and battle as his «matters», Fiammetta's title marks marriage as the poem's theme. Could she have seen in the pairing of Mars and Venus a symbol of matrimonial union? Through survival of the Homeric account of their affair, medieval mythographers had condemned them as archetypical adulterers, and some found in Venus's seduction of Mars a pagan counterpart of Eve's temptation of Adam.[30] There was, however, a second way of interpreting the influence of the goddess on her heroic warrior lover, under a positive

---

sensitive appetite is one generic power, and is called sensuality; but it is divided into two powers, which are species of the sensitive appetite – the irascible and the concupiscible]; Qu. 82, Art. 5: «Philosophus dicit, in III *De An.*, quod voluntas in ratione est: in irrationali autem parte animae concupiscentia et ira» [the Philosopher says that will is in the reason, while in the irrational part of the soul are concupiscence and anger]. Thomas draws here on Aristotle's *De anima* III 9-11. If Boccaccio's glossarial nomenclature is Scholastic, he seems also to be recalling Augustine when affirming that the Venereal and Martial appetites may operate either for good or evil. So in AUGUSTINE's *City of God*, trans. G. E. McCRACKEN *et al.*, Cambridge, Mass., Harvard University Press, 1966-1972 («Loeb Classical Library»), XIV 19, we read that the rational mind commands as from a citadel the defective divisions of the inferior soul, anger and lust (*ira, amor*), so that justice may be preserved among all the soul's parts: «ut eas [iram et libidinem] ab his rebus ad quas iniuste moventur mens conpescendo et cohibendo refrenet ac revocet atque ad ea permittat quae sapientiae lege concessa sunt (sicut iram ad execrendam iustam cohercitionem, sicut libidinem ad propagandae prolis officium)» [It is for this reason that the mind by repression and restraint curbs and recalls anger and lust from things that they are wrongly moved to do but allows them to follow any course that the law of wisdom has sanctioned. Anger, for example, is permitted for the display of a just compulsion, and lust for the duty of propagating offspring]. See below, ch. 2 and ch. 4 for more on the appetites in the soul as Boccaccio knew them from Thomas Aquinas.

[30] FULGENTIUS, *Mythologies* II 7, in *Fulgentius the Mythographer*, trans. L. G. WHITBREAD Columbus, Ohio State University Press, 1971, interprets Mars caught with Venus in Vulcan's net as manly valor fettered by ardor. Similarly, the Third Vatican Mythographer, known to Boccaccio as Albericus, in *Scriptores rerum mythicarum latini tres Romae nuper reperti*, ed. G. H. BODE, Hildesheim, Georg Olms Verlagsbuchhandlung, 1968[2], pp. 231-232: «Mars igitur complexu Veneris pollutus, id est, virtus libidinis illecebris corrupta, sole teste apparet, id est, tandem veritatis iudicio rea esse cognoscitur. Quae quidem virtus prava consuetudine illecta vinclis constrictioribus, ostenditur catenata» [When Mars had thus been stained by the embrace of Venus, that is, virtue corrupted by illicit passion, the sun appeared as a witness; that is, in the judgment of truth his virtue was seen to be corrupted. This virtue, seduced through depraved habits with constricting bonds is shown enchained]. On these understandings, as well as how Arnulf of Orléans read the myth, see T. D. HILL, *La Vieille's Digression on Free Love: A Note on Rhetorical Structure in the 'Romance of the Rose'*, «Romance Notes», VII, 1966, pp. 113-115. R. P. MILLER discusses the Venus-Mars story as illustrating «the essential conflict of Christian life – the tempting allurements of the flesh against the rational "manliness" of the spirit», and «a mythological reenactment of man's fall to sin», in *The Myth of Mars' Hot Minion in 'Venus and Adonis'*, «Journal of English Literary History», XXVI, 1959, pp. 470-481.

aspect, or *in bono*. She could have the beneficent capacity of tempering his ferocity. Statius sees such a potentially tender relationship between them in the *Thebaid*, when Mars affectionately consoles her, «O thou who art my repose from battle, my sacred joy and all the peace my heart doth know: thou alone of gods and men canst face my arms unpunished, and check even in mid-slaughter my neighing steeds, and tear this sword from my right hand!».[31] This more favorable view was reinforced by a parallel astrological tradition in which, since Mars 'follows' Venus through their planetary revolutions, she becomes his gentle, subduing mistress. Boccaccio alludes to this pairing in the first *ternario* of his *Comedia delle ninfe fiorentine*, when he invokes the power of Venus «per lo tuo Marte, o graziosa stella». Chaucer fills out the picture of her effects on her warrior lover in his *Complaint of Mars*, vv. 36-42:

> For she forbad him jelosye at al,
> And cruelte, and bost, and tyrannye;
> She made him at her lust so humble and tal,
> That when her deyned to cast on hym her ye,
> He tok in pacience to lyve or dye.
> And thus she brydeleth him in her manere,
> With nothing but with scourging of her chere.

By the end of the next century in Italy, Mars and Venus will evolve to legitimate status as figures typifying man and wife. A subject for paintings on marriage chests by Botticelli and Piero de Cosimo,[32] they also appear in nuptial portraits, symbolic as well as real, by Mantegna, Titian, and Paris Bordone. The Renaissance artists were reviving ancient usage. Erwin Panofsky reports a Roman custom, dating from the Antonine period, of sculpting distinguished married couples in the guise of Mars and Venus.[33] The Lehmanns find literary precedent for the icono-

---

[31] *Thebaid, cit.*, III 295-299: «O mihi bellorum requies et sacra voluptas / unaque pax animo! soli cui tanta potestas / divorumque hominumque meis occurrere telis / impune et media quamvis in caede frementes / hos adsistere equos, hunc ensem avellere dextrae!».

[32] P. SCHUBRING, *Cassoni. Truhen und Truhenbilder der italienischen Frührenaissance*, Leipzig, Karl W. Hiersemann, 1923, plates 313, 410. See also P. F. WATSON, *The Garden of Love in Tuscan Art of the Early Renaissance*, Philadelphia, The Art Alliance Press, 1978, p. 115.

[33] E. PANOFSKY, *Studies in Iconology*, New York, Harper and Row, 1962², p. 164; IDEM, *Problems in Titian. Mostly Iconographic*, New York, New York University Press, 1969, p. 127. See also E. H. GOMBRICH, *Botticelli's Mythologies*, «Journal of the Warburg and Courtauld Institutes», VIII, 1945, pp. 7-60:46-49; E. VERHEYEN, *The Paintings in the 'Studiolo' of Isabella d'Este at Mantua*, New York, New York University Press, 1971, pp. 35-38. I thank Peter Porçal for bibliographical guidance and generously sharing information from his research on the Renaissance iconography of marriage.

graphy in Ovid's *Fasti*,[34] a work that Boccaccio already knew when he glossed the *Teseida*.[35] There, Mars and Venus, whom Romulus considered his «parents», are mated in the calendar as god and goddess of the first two months: «the month of Mars was the first, and that of Venus the second; she was the author of the race, and he its sire»; Venus can rightly claim April because all growing things, for whose creation and continuation she is responsible, then return to life: «And no season was more fitting for Venus than spring. In spring the landscape glistens; soft is the soil in spring; now the corn pushes its blades through the cleft ground; now the vineshoot protrudes its buds in the swelling bark. Lovely Venus deserves the lovely season and is attached, as usual, to her dear Mars».[36]

Did Boccaccio intend Mars and Venus as a marriage couple in the *Teseida*? He does report the myth of their adultery (VII 25, gl.).[37] At the center of this poem he asserts that *there* he is talking about the god of senseless wrath (VII 30, gl.) and the goddess of unbridled sensuality (VII 50, gl.). Conjunction of these two deities as planets portended adultery and fornication for many medieval astrologers, including those whom Boccaccio cites on Mars in his *Genealogia*.[38] This evidence combines to shape a strongly negative image of the couple. On the other hand, we have from antiquity the tradition of a matrimonial Mars and Venus that has firmly reasserted itself in the visual arts by the end of the Quattrocento and rests partly on literary texts familiar to Boccaccio. His Glossator distinctly says that Venus and Mars are not always bad; each can also be a morally and socially positive force. If this holds for the two separately, it must be true of their coupling as well. The title given the story by Fiammetta (but chosen by Boccaccio) clearly marks it as a marriage piece, *Teseida delle nozze d'Emilia*. Mars and Venus, who rule the poem by turn, are present at its center. Its protagonist, Teseo,

---

[34] P. W. LEHMANN and K. LEHMANN, *Samothracian Reflections. Aspects of the Revival of the Antique*, Princeton, Princeton University Press, 1973 («Bollingen Series», XCII), pp. 157-166.

[35] A. E. QUAGLIO, *Scienza e mito, cit.*, p. 178.

[36] OVID, *Fasti*, trans. Sir J. G. FRAZER, Cambridge, Mass., Harvard University Press, 1931 («Loeb Classical Library»), I 39-40: «Martis erat primus mensis, Venerisque secundus: / haec generis princeps, ipsius ille pater»; IV 125-130: «nec Veneri tempus quam ver erat aptius ullum: / vere nitent terrae, vere remissus ager, / nunc herbae rupta tellure cacumina tollunt, / nunc tumido gemmas cortice palmes agit. / et formosa Venus formoso tempore digna est, / utque solet, Marti continuata suo est».

[37] In *Genealogia* IX 3 he condemns it in much the same terms as the Third Vatican Mythographer.

[38] Albumasar, Andalò, and Aly; *Genealogia* IX 3-4. J. L. SMARR, *Boccaccio and the Stars, cit.*, also adduces Firmicus Maternus and strongly affirms the dire consequences of Mars in astrological combination with Venus.

vigorously combats the powers, both human (Ipolita, Creon) and abstract (ire, concupiscence), that threaten lawful union between husband and wife. He himself will marry at the close of Book I, and he arranges the marriage promised by the title that is realized in Book XII. Both marriages take place after Martian conflicts have been met and overcome. It is, as Robert Hollander has argued, the matrimonial Venus who then triumphs at the beginning and the end of the *Teseida*.[39] I am therefore inclined to think that Boccaccio's Mars and Venus are ambivalent. Their menacing presence at the poem's center stands in explicit, admonitory contrast to the implicitly constructive influence they are capable of exercising ideally. Baneful as appetites, they are amicably beneficent when serving the rational goals of order in the soul and the state. Their 'friendship', furthermore, seems to symbolize a prototypical union between male (σ) and female (φ) in the *Teseida*, because union of the sexes is signified in its numerological plan.

The number 5 that accompanies Mars and then crosses over to Venus at the center of the *Teseida* is a Pythagorean marriage number. According to the Pythagorean theory, numbers have gender. Odd ones, being superior to even, are masculine; the latter, feminine. The monad, origin of number, does not count in the sequence leading to 10, which therefore proceeds from 2:

Consequently, since two makes the first of the even numbers and three the first of the odd, and five is produced by the union of these numbers, very naturally five has come to be honoured as being the first number created out of the first numbers; and it has received the name of "marriage" because of the resemblance of the even numbers to the female and of the odd number to the male [...] let it suffice to say that the Pythagoreans called Five a "Marriage" on the ground that it was produced by the association of the first male number and the first female number.[40]

Here I cite Plutarch's explanation, a convenient synthesis of Greek reasoning on this marriage number. Although Plutarch himself was not known to Boccaccio, the tradition he describes was. Boccaccio could have learned it from the respected allegorical encyclopedia on the seven Liberal Arts by Martianus Capella, who refers to 5 as a coupling of male and female, «the pentad [...] represents natural union, for it is the sum of number of each sex, for three is considered a male number, and two a

---

[39] R. HOLLANDER, *Boccaccio's Two Venuses*, cit., pp. 64-65.
[40] PLUTARCH, *De E apud Delphos*, in *Moralia*, V, trans. F. C. BABBITT, Cambridge, Mass., Harvard University Press, 1936 («Loeb Classical Library»), pp. 217-219.

female number».[41] He had apparently read Martianus by the summer of 1339, and he also certainly understood by then the «virtues» of odd and even numbers. We find mention of them in his *Sacre famis*, one of four rhetorical epistles dating from that summer.[42] The accomplishments attributed to the letter's unnamed, and probably fictitious, recipient include mastery of the seven Liberal Arts, divided into Trivium and Quadrivium. First among the latter is arithmetic: «and because you had reached a fuller age, having seen through arithmetic the virtues of even and odd numbers, you took up delightful music [...]».[43]

From antiquity through the early modern period, many authorities knew 5 as the number of marriage. Jewish commentary and mysticism from Philo to the Cabbala,[44] as well as the most erudite Christian poets made the association — Edmund Spenser, Ben Jonson, Sir Thomas Browne.[45] Boccaccio himself exploits the connection elsewhere in his own works. The Fifth Day of the *Decameron* (excluding Dioneo's usual exception) is given to love stories that turn out happily, and their endings always coincide with a marriage. This is not true for any other Day in the

---

[41] MARTIANUS, *De nuptiis*, cit., p. 279: «pentas [...] qui quidem permixtione naturali copulatur; nam constat ex utriusque sexus numero; trias quippe virilis est, dyas femineus aestimatur».

[42] On these epistles and Martianus see G. BILLANOVICH, *Restauri boccacceschi*, Rome, Edizioni di Storia e Letteratura, 1945, pp. 68, 72; G. BOCCACCIO, *Opere in versi, Corbaccio, Trattatello in laude di Dante, Prose latine, Epistole*, ed. P. G. RICCI, Milan, Riccardo Ricciardi Editore, 1965, p. 1064, n. 2. The *Teseida*, which has important affinities with the letter *Sacre famis*, is tentatively assigned to 1339-1341 by A. LIMENTANI in his Introduction to the text, cit., p. 231, following V. BRANCA, *Giovanni Boccaccio. Profilo biografico*, Florence, G.C. Sansoni Editore, 1977, p. 49.

[43] G. BOCCACCIO, *Sacre famis*, in *Epistole*, ed. G. AUZZAS with A. CAMPANA, Milan, Mondadori, 1992 («*Tutte le opere*», V, pt. I), IV 7: «et quia in fortiorem etatem evaseras, viso iam per arismetricam parium dispariumque numerorum virtutes, voluptuosam musicam sequebaris [...]».

[44] PHILO, *De opificio mundi*, cit., I, pp. 83-85, remarks that the fifth of the seven stages in men's growth brings «ripeness for marriage». As evidence, he cites a sequence of couplets on the seven ages of man by Solon, who writes of the fifth, «Let him in his fifth week of years a bride bespeak, / Offspring to bear his name hereafter let him seek». J. MACQUEEN, *Numerology. Theory and Outline of a Literary Mode*, Edinburgh, Edinburgh University Press, 1985, p. 7, cites what Thomas Browne wrote in the Renaissance on 5 and the Cabbala: «The same number in the Hebrew mysteries and Cabalistical accounts was the character of Generation; declared by the letter *He*, the fifth in their alphabet».

[45] Spenser's understanding of 5 is confirmed in the now classic study by A. FOWLER, *Spenser and the Numbers of Time*, New York, Barnes and Noble, 1964, p. 35. To explain why we must wait until Book V in the *Faerie Queene* for the marriage of Marimell and Florimell, Fowler cites the later writer Thomas Browne as an exemplary authority: 5 is «the Conjugall Number, which ancient numerists made out by two and three, the first parity and imparity, the active and passive digits, the materiall and formall principles in generative Societies». I am indebted to Carol Kaske for calling to my attention the marriage number in B. JONSON's *Hymenaei*. Among the symbols in the masque are five waxen tapers whose meaning Reason

Decameron. Before the *Teseida*, too, Boccaccio had so applied the pentad in his *Filocolo*, another tale of two lovers who marry. It begins as *Quintus* Lelius Africanus and his wife, Giulia Topazia, after *five* years of marriage are blessed by conceiving a child under the sign of the Virgin. She is Biancifiore, born like Florio on *Pente*cost, the same feast day that brings a blissful end to Florio/Filocolo's quest. Florio and Biancifiore wed twice for good measure, once privately before consummating their love, and then in a public ceremony arranged by the Admiral. The felicitous outcome of this nuptial romance, written in *five* books, depends in good part on Mars and Venus, who generously help the protagonists master all the plotted obstacles to their well-deserved marriage.

In the *Teseida* Boccaccio construes both 5 and its numerological variant, 15, as marriage numbers. Teseo promises that one of the two knights shall take Emilia «as wife» at the end of Book V, stanza 96 (96 = 9 + 6 = 15). Emilia's marriage will be celebrated at the temple of Venus in a chapter of three stanzas, the thirteenth of Book XII. It culminates with the exchange of vows at XII 69 (69 = 6 + 9 = 15): «E poi in presenza di quella santa ara / il teban Palemon gioiosamente / prese e giurò per sua sposa cara / Emilia bella, a tutti i re presente; / e essa, come donna non già gnara, / simil promessa fece immantenente; / poi la basciò sì come si convenne / e ella vergognosa sel sostenne». The next chapter, «Come, tornati al palagio, si celebrarono le nozze» (XII 70) has five stanzas, and in the first we learn when the wedding banquet began: «e l'ora *quinta* già venia del giorno, / quando, venuti nel palagio, messe / trovar le mense, e assisersi ad esse». The fifteenth chapter playfully accounts for the wedding night, when «Venere, anzi che 'l dì fosse chiaro, / sette volte raccesa e tante spenta / [era] nel fonte amoroso» (XII 77). It reports as well how long the ensuing celebration went on: «Durò la festa degli alti baroni / più giorni [...] / ma dopo il dì *quindecimo* si pose / fine alle feste liete e graziose» (XII 80; italics mine).

This latter chapter recalls the marriage of Chrétien's Erec and Enide: «Ensi les noces et la corz / durerent plus de *quinze* jorz / a tel joie et a tel hautesce; / par seignorie et par leesce / et por Erec plus enorer, / fist li rois

---

reveals: «And lastly, these five waxen lights, / Imply perfection in the rites: / For five the special number is, / Whence hallow'd Union claims her bliss. / As being all the sum that grows / From the united strength of those / Which male and female number we / Do style, and are first two and three. / Which joined thus, you cannot sever / In equal parts but one will ever / Remain as common; so we see / The binding force of Unity; / For which alone the peaceful gods / In number always love the odds, / And even parts as much despise, / Since out of them all discords rise». *Hymenaei*, in *Works of Ben Jonson*, X, ed. C. H. HEREFORD *et al.*, Oxford, Clarendon Press, 1950, vv. 196-211.

Artus demorer / toz barons une *quinzaine*».[46] For the French poet «quin-zaine» may mean simply a two-week period, typical for plenary court gatherings in Old French romance, but Boccaccio's «fifteenth day» is more than a calendrical quantity. Before the wedding, «Disegna l'autore la forma e la bellezza di Emilia» (XII 52, rub.) This rubric introduces the twelfth chapter of Book XII, which is fifteen stanzas long. Here Boccaccio reveals the bride's age: «Né era ancor, dopo 'l suo nascimento, / *tre* volte *cinque* Apollo ritornato / nel loco donde allor fé partimento». Our conscientious Glossator kindly solves this problem in multiplication. Equating «three times five» with «*quindici*» and «Apollo» with «il sole», he pithily rephrases the Author's solar circumlocution, «aveva xv anni» (italics mine). Emilia had reached the proper age for a woman to enter wedlock.[47] The number 15, here explicitly divided into 3 and 5, is especially suited to Boccaccio's epic bride, for it is another product of union between Venus and Mars, the two gods secretly at work as nuptial forces in the tale.

Appropriately, this product also regulates the number of sonnets framing the *Teseida*'s twelve books. There are fifteen: a general proem; an individual sonnet preceding each book and summarizing its contents; and after the close of Book XII, another pair of sonnets in which the Author speaks to the Muses and they reply. Since these last two are missing in many manuscripts,[48] Boccaccio may have added them, as he apparently did the glosses, after writing the rest of the poem in order both to enhance and better articulate its internal numerological design.[49] Fifteen

---

[46] C. De Troyes, *Erec et Enide*, ed. M. Roques, Paris, Librairie Honoré Champion, Editeur, 1953 («*Les Romans de Chrétien de Troyes*», I), vv. 2065-2071: «Thus the nuptial feast and courtly gathering lasted more than fifteen days with such joy and such grandeur; in lordship and happiness, and to honor Erec the more, King Arthur had all the barons stay on for a fifteen-day period». We also find a fifteen-day marriage celebration in the thirteenth-century Provençal *Flamenca*, whose author had read Chrétien. See A. Limentani, *Dalle nozze di Erec et Enide alle nozze di Archimbaut e Flamenca, Miscellanea di studi offerti a Armando Balduino e Bianca Bianchi per le loro nozze*, Padua, Presso il Seminario di Filologia Moderna, 1962, pp. 9-14. Limentani also points to Chrétien's *Erec* as a model for Boccaccio in his Introduction to the *Teseida*, p. 244.

[47] It is often fifteen for Boccaccio, as V. Branca notes, *Decameron, cit.*, I, Intro., 49 and n. 13, p. 991; II 6, 35 and n. 8, p. 1088.

[48] S. Battaglia, ed. *Teseida*, Florence, Accademia della Crusca, 1938, describes twenty-eight manuscripts in his Intro., pp. XI-XXIII. Excluding two that are fragmentary and three others that are incomplete at the end, thirteen lack the last two sonnets. Of these thirteen, however, allowance being made for missing inital folios and occasional internal lacunae, all but one manuscript contain the general proemial sonnet and those preceding each book. A personal communication from W. Coleman in 1983 reported that of forty-seven complete manuscripts thus far known, only seventeen have sonnets at the beginning and end, while thirty lack the introductory or postscripted poems.

[49] There has been general agreement that the commentary postdates the text: G. Van-

sonnets so disposed would have had the further advantage of generating a center (the eighth sonnet) standing before the epic's central Seventh Book. A diagram better illustrates the relationship:

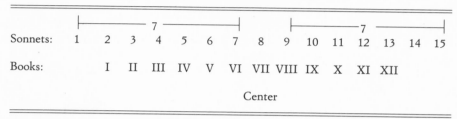

Sonnets:	1	2	3	4	5	6	7	8	9	10	11	12	13	14	15
Books:		I	II	III	IV	V	VI	VII	VIII	IX	X	XI	XII		

Center

Now, in an epic of twelve books, the symmetrical halfway point would be the end of the sixth. As we have discovered, however, each of the *Teseida*'s formal components marks the number 7 as the center: the central verse, the central chapter, the central glosses, and the central sonnet all gravitate within the Seventh Book. If 3 is for Venus and love, 5 for Mars, battle, and marriage, what might 7 stand for beyond Diana? Singularly honored as the arithmetic sign at the *Teseida* center, the number 7 has manifold potential meanings in medieval numerology, more than for any other integer. The problem of isolating solutions is therefore a difficult one. I shall present those that seem most plausible to me.

The numbers of Venus, Mars, and Diana derive immediately from their positions in the ranks of the seven wandering stars. For this reason it would be logical to take the 7 marking center in the *Teseida* as a sum embracing the planets collectively. Book VII might then have special astrological implications pertaining to the plan of the poem more generally. When casting horoscopes, the astrologers divide the zodiac according to a mobile scheme starting from the ascendent into twelve houses that describe twelve aspects of the life or event under examination. A traditional pair of mnemonic verses lists them, «Vita lucrum fratres genitor nati valetudo / Uxor mors pietas regnum benefactaque carcer». Based on slightly variant terminology, the houses and what each concerns can be given as follows: 1, Life; 2, Wealth; 3, Brothers; 4, Parents; 5, Sons; 6, Health; 7, Nuptials; 8, Death; 9, Duty; 10, Honors; 11, Friends; 12,

DELLI, *Un autografo*, cit., p. 70; *Teseida*, ed. S. BATTAGLIA, cit., Intro., p. CCCXV, n. 2; *Amorosa visione*, ed. V. BRANCA, Florence, Sansoni, 1944, pp. XXLVIII-CXLIX; G. BILLANOVICH, *Restauri boccacceschi*, cit., p. 85 and note; A. LIMENTANI, *Tendenze della prosa del Boccaccio ai margini del 'Teseida'*, «Giornale Storico della Letteratura Italiana», CXXV, 1958, pp. 524-555:529. The glosses were themselves written in stages, as ascertained by W. and E. Agostinelli Coleman, who have identified three successive authorial redactions. See E. AGOSTINELLI, *A Catalogue of Manuscripts of 'Il Teseida'*, «Studi sul Boccaccio», XV, 1986, 1-83.

Enemies.[50] In the seventh place we find the marriage house. There could thus be a correspondence between this astrological marriage house and Book VII in Boccaccio's nuptial epic, at the center of which we find Diana-Luna following a paired poetic conjunction of Mars and Venus. In the Seventh Book of the *Teseida* might the combination of these three pagan gods, who had survived from antiquity as planets, refer to a heavenly configuration auspicious for marriage in a fourteenth-century Italian horoscope? Perhaps, in other words, the epic celebrates a real marriage.

Turning from astrology to literature, we can see other possibilities for 7 at the center. Charles S. Singleton has found that at the center of the *Divine Comedy* Dante concealed the number 7 as a symbol of Christian conversion.[51] The number expresses a «turning» from this world, created in six days, to the next and God, represented by 7 because it was on the seventh day that He rested. Whether or not Boccaccio noticed the pattern in the *Comedy*, he would have understood Dante's iconographic intent. Explaining in the *Genealogia* how the seven-day week originated, he writes,

Moreover, since out of respect for the number seven, which for various reasons the ancients held to be perfect, human ingenuity disposed that all time proceed by weeks of days, and to those days of the week they gave various names; some people were wont to seek out the reasons for those names, which I retain to be as follows: Since in our times five are named after the planets, the sixth, which was called Sabbath by the Hebrews, was not changed afterwards by the Christians because they say it means "rest" in Latin as can be seen from the fact that God created all things in six days and on the seventh He rested from all his labor. The day Sunday, however, which for us Christians is the seventh, is so named because on that day Christ the son of God not only rested from all His labors but arose truly a victor from the dead, and thus the learned fathers named it after our Lord, "the day of our Lord".[52]

---

[50] F. BOLL, C. BEZOLD, W. GUNDEL, *Storia dell'astrologia*, Intro. E. GARIN, Bari, Laterza, 1977 («Biblioteca di Cultura Moderna», DCCCI), pp. 87-89: «Life wealth brothers parents children health / Wife death piety power benefactions prison».

[51] C. S. SINGLETON, *The Poet's Number at the Center*, «Modern Language Notes», LXXX, 1965, pp. 1-10.

[52] *Genealogia* I 34: «Insuper cum humana solertia respectu habito ad septenarium numerum, quem quibusdam ex causis veteres voluere perfectum, disposuerit omne tempus per septimanas dierum efflui, et dies illas septimane nominibus variis nuncupare, consuevere nonnulli nominum talium exquirere causas; quas ego has puto, cum a planetis apud nos quinque denominentur, sexta sabbatum ab Hebreis dicta, a christianis postea immutata non est, eo quod requiem dicant significare latine, ut appareat cum creavisset omnia Deus in sex diebus, eum septima ab omnibus operibus suis quievisse. Dominica autem dies, que nobis christianis est septima, sic eo dicta est, quia ea die Christus Dei filius, non solum ab omnibus laboribus suis

Conversion could underlie the «perfect» 7 at the center of the *Teseida* because its Book VII is preeminently a book of prayer. Each of the protagonists respectfully enters a place of worship and turns to a power above, gentile gods dwelling in the sevenfold planetary hierarchy. Mars receives Arcita's winged prayer (VII 30), Palemone's reaches Venus (VII 50), and Emilia sacrifices to Diana (VII 70). After these pious vigils and orisons, on the tournament morning Teseo himself escorts the two Thebans into the temple of Mars (VII 96). Their devotions last through nocturnal quiet and the peaceful dawn of a new day, marked contrasts to the violent battle clash that begins with Book VIII. The number of conversion might also apply to the *Teseida*'s overall allegorical thrust, which moves in a morally corrective direction toward triumph in the soul over sinful, irrational appetites. Two spiritual forces that counter the appetites, virtue and wisdom, may be signified as well by the number 7.

Denoting Diana-Luna, 7 implies both virginity and virtue. For the Pythagoreans it is «virgin» because it is the first prime that has no multiple within the first decad, «indeed, it is regarded as a virgin because, when doubled, it produces no number under ten, the latter being truly the first limit of numbers».[53] This Pythagorean virgin may well serve in the *Teseida* as an emblem of chastity, a maidenly quality and wifely attribute appropriate to the symbolism of a marriage piece. When transferred to a Christian frame of reference, the virgin heptad evolves to define more broadly the Seven Virtues, women in their personified forms. They are Diana's numerological consorts as early as Boccaccio's *Caccia di Diana*,[54] and they return to accompany her for a time in the *Comedia delle ninfe fiorentine* as ladies who had been her chaste nymphs before becoming followers of Venus. After each Florentine lady has told her tale, seven swans and seven storks fly across the sky. The birds begin to fight each other fiercely, «in sette e sette divisi» and the swans drive away the storks. Trinitarian Venus descends, to whom Ameto prays, thanking her for the «seven flames» now entwining his soul.[55] Seven

---

quievit, verum victor surrexit a mortuis et sic illam a domino nostro patres incliti vocavere dominicam». See also V. Kɪʀᴋʜᴀᴍ, *Reckoning with Boccaccio's 'Questioni d'amore'*, «Modern Language Notes», LXXXIX, 1974, pp. 47-59.

[53] Mᴀᴄʀᴏʙɪᴜs, *Comm. in Somnium, cit.*, I 6, 11: «nam virgo creditur, quia nullum ex se parit numerum duplicatus qui intra denarium coartetur, quem primum limitem constat esse numerorum».

[54] V. Kɪʀᴋʜᴀᴍ, *Numerology and Allegory in Boccaccio's 'Caccia di Diana'*, «Traditio», XXXIV, 1978, pp. 303-329; A. K. Cᴀssᴇʟʟ and V. Kɪʀᴋʜᴀᴍ, *Diana's Hunt, cit.*, Intro. pp. 25-27; 30-32.

[55] G. Bᴏᴄᴄᴀᴄᴄɪᴏ, *Comedia delle ninfe fiorentine*, ed. A. E. Qᴜᴀɢʟɪᴏ, Milan, Mondadori, 1964 («*Tutte le opere*», II), XL 4 and XLIV 7.

ladies, seven swans, seven flames — all are the Virtues. The Seven Virtues also appear in the *Filocolo*. Filocolo initially encounters them in a miraculous vision, «seven ladies filled with marvelous beauty», who come unnamed but identified by their traditional iconographic attributes as four preceding three. At the end of the romance, the dying King Felice exhorts his son, Florio, to flee the vices, of which he names seven; next he preaches on each of the virtues: prudence, justice, fortitude, temperance, charity, faith, and hope.[56] For Boccaccio then, the number 7 is a figure of virtue, tied specifically with Diana in the *Caccia* and *Comedia delle ninfe*. This suggests that in the *Teseida* the number of planets, among whom Diana is the virgin seventh, may allusively encompass the Virtues. Since Diana is Emilia's patron and they participate together in the poem as 7's, its chaste heroine Emilia herself would then become a numeric representative of virtue.

Diana appears to share this number in the epic with her mythological twin, Apollo. We have already seen brother and sister joined through a double 7 («7 + 7») in the Glossator's accounts of the Niobe myth. After returning incognito to Athens and just before entering Teseo's household, Penteo worships in the temple of Apollo, a deity whom love had also once driven into servitude. His prayer is in the seventh chapter of Book IV, which has seven stanzas, and on Apollo the commentary reports, «Fu Febo innamorato d'una figliuola d'Ameto, re di Tesaglia, la quale non potendo altrimenti avere, si transformò in pastore, e posesi col detto re, e stette con lui guardandogli il bestiame suo, in così fatta forma, sette anni» (IV 46, gl.).

As Boccaccio notes in the gloss on IV 77, «Phoebus is god of wisdom». In this capacity Apollo could logically attract the number 7 because it is a well-established symbol of wisdom. In addition to the seven pillars of Biblical wisdom,[57] there existed seven branches of secular knowledge. Thus the lady holding book and scepter who personifies *Scientia* in the first triumph of the *Amorosa visione* is surrounded by seven women, «Ma dal sinistro e dal suo destro lato / sette donne vid'io, dissimiglianti / l'una dall'altra in atto ed in parato». They have been interpreted as the seven Liberal Arts, the Trivium on her left, and the more noble Quadrivium in the place of honor at her right.[58] These disciplines and their figuration as women had been fixed by Martianus

---

[56] *Filocolo, cit.*, IV 74, 2-8; V 92, 17-21.
[57] Proverbs 9:1: «Sapientia aedificavit sibi domum, / excidit columnas septem» [Wisdom hath builded her house, she hath hewn out her seven pillars].
[58] *Amorosa visione, cit.*, B, IV 34-36 and n., p. 571. See also below, ch. 2.

Capella in his enormously influential *Marriage of Philology and Mercury*. Accompanying Philology as she marries Mercury are seven maidens-of-honor, none other than the Seven Sciences, each of whom offers in turn a treatise on the category of learning she represents. Although Boccaccio would have been familiar with this famed group of seven from other sources as well,[59] Martianus provides a precedent for placing it in a marriage allegory.

The seven Liberal Arts, a trio and a quartet like the Virtues, also parallel the planets. Dante, we may remember, had correlated arts and planets. Telling what he means by «third heaven» in the *canzone* to its moving intelligences, he says, «Dico che per cielo io intendo la scienza e per cieli le scienze, per tre similitudini che li cieli hanno con le scienze massimamente; e per l'ordine e numero in che paiono convenire». On the last two similarities, his discussion begins, «Sì come adunque di sopra è narrato, li setti cieli primi a noi sono quelli de li pianeti; poi sono due cieli sopra questi, mobili, e uno sopra tutti, quieto. A li sette primi rispondono le sette scienze del Trivio e del Quadruvio, cioè Gramatica, Dialettica, Rettorica, Arismetrica, Musica, Geometria e Astrologia» (*Convivio* II 13, 2-8).

Although Boccaccio does not systematically correlate arts and planets, he implies the possibility of doing so when he couples them sequentially in the epistle *Sacre famis*. The sender's dear friend joins the Chorus of the Muses to study grammar, dialectic, and rhetoric. After a distraction involving activity as a merchant, he returns to take up the remaining four, starting with arithmetic, as we have seen, and concluding with a ranked list of the seven planets, from Moon upward:

And because you had reached a fuller age, having seen through arithmetic the virtues of even and odd numbers, you took up delightful music [...]. You viewed the figures of geometry, carefully exploring its different measures with outstanding eagerness. Thence you proceed to the stars, and you examine the circling of the wandering lights and the constellations, here the various movements of Cynthia are opened to your intellect, and how, when she has laid down her horns, she takes on a circular form, and you are not ignorant of either her recurring waxings or wanings; here you see the regions of Stilbon, harmonious for whomsoever enters hence; thence you ascend to the dwelling of Cytharea, glowing with golden rays of fervent love; and next you enter the bright kingdom of the great son of Hyperion, and you note the effects of this prince of the stars.

---

[59] Cf. Isidore of Seville, *Etymologiae sive origines*, ed. W. M. Lindsay, Oxford, Clarendon Press, 1911, I 2, «De septem liberalibus disciplinis».

But as this much is not sufficient for you, you will approach the camps of warlike Mars, and you will scrutinize the reasons for his rubicund color; and entering into the palace of the king of the silver age, you praise his moderate judgements as you contemplate them. Thence exploring from the cave of the banished father, whose inertia has sent you away, you reach out for Leda's nest.[60]

Next, in a literary motif that encapsulates the plot in the *Teseida*, the friend will abruptly become a warrior, and just as suddenly give up warfare for marriage. This rhetorical exercise actually ends with the writer's request for a glossed copy of Statius's *Thebaid*. As Billanovich speculates, Boccaccio's aim in composing such a formulaic request, never intended for delivery, was not to borrow Statius complete with the canonical commentary by Lactantius Placidus, but rather to announce proudly his recent discovery of that text. It left discernible signs of influence, according to David Anderson, on the latter part of the *Te-seida*.[61] The *Sacre famis* letter thus gives us insights into Boccaccio's literary frame of mind at the time he was working through the first Italian epic. Playing on the parallelism between the Liberal Arts and planets, it presents the Arts as 3 + 4 listed in traditional order ascending to astronomy, the highest, from which there naturally develops a similarly ordered catalogue of the seven planetary bodies.

The venerable number 7 at the center of the *Teseida* is a richly allusive figure. On one level it is planetary and may have ties with the seventh house in a horoscope, 'Nuptials'. As it calls our attention to the

---

[60] *Epistole, cit.*, IV 7-8: «et quia in fortiorem etatem evaseras, viso iam per arismetricam parium dispariumque numerorum virtutes, voluptuosam musicam sequebaris [...] geometrie figuras aspiciebas, diversas suas mensuras studio celebri perquirendo. Hinc igitur ad astra transfereris, et circulationem vagorum luminum rimaris et sydera, hic Cynthie motus varios tuo intellectui reserantur, et qualiter ipsa depositis cornuis formam capiat circularem, non ipsius defectus nec virtutes multiplices ingnorando; hic vides Stilbonis regiones intrantibus quibus-cumque concordes; hinc ferventis amoris radios rutilantes, Cithereie domus ascendis; et per consequens intras rengnum lucidum mangni Yperionis filii, et ipsius stellarum principis notas effectus. Sed tibi non istud sufficiens, aggrederis castra Mavortis belligeri, et rubicundi coloris causam perscruptaris; et argentee etatis tecta regis subintrans, sua moderata iudicia laudas intuendo. Hinc antra patris expulsi perquirens, inertia sua dimissa, tendis ad nidum Lede».

[61] G. BILLANOVICH, *Restauri boccacceschi, cit.*, pp. 75-76 and note. A. LIMENTANI, *Tendenze della prosa, cit.*, found much similarity between Boccaccio's glosses and those of LACTANTIUS PLACIDUS, for the text of which see *Commentarios in Statii Thebaide et commentarium in Achilleida*, ed. R. JAHNKE, Leipzig, B. G. Teubner Verlagsgesellschaft, 1898. R. HOLLANDER, on the other hand, in *The Validity of Boccaccio's Self-Exegesis, cit.*, perceives the Lactantian glosses substantially different in character from Boccaccio's, arguing that even if he was familiar with them, he chose not to imitate them. D. ANDERSON, *Before the Knight's Tale. Imitation of Classical Epic in Boccaccio's Teseida*, Philadelphia, University of Pennsylvania Press, 1988, clarifies that Boccaccio came into possession of them at a late date in his work on the *Teseida* and used them for one passage in Book XI.

heavens and characterizes a book of prayer, the figure could also be a godly hebdomad, expressing the spiritual concept of conversion. A 'virgin' accompanying Diana and Emilia, it can symbolize both chastity and virtue. A 'perfect' number, it is bound as well to the sun, sevenfold wisdom and the heavenly sign of the moral illumination motivating the deeds of Teseo, duke of Minerva's city. By numerical analogy, the meanings of 7 multiply.

Boccaccio surely meant us to recognize manifold possibilities in the number, as would any thoughtful Florentine who paused to study the decorative sculptural scheme on Giotto's campanile, or *The Triumph of St. Thomas* frescoed in the Spanish Chapel at Santa Maria Novella by Andrea di Buonaiuto between 1366 and 1368 (fig. 1). Above the great Dominican enthroned, who displays a book open to the text of Wisdom 7:7, there circle seven winged women, the Virtues. Below him on the right are the seven Liberal Arts, each above a corresponding, representative historical personage; on the left are seven Theological Sciences similarly paired with seven theologians. Over the Theological Sciences preside the Seven Gifts of the Holy Spirit, over the Liberal Arts, the planets.[62]

We have now, I think, gained grounds for better reconciling the author's themes of «love» and «Mars» and his principal characters, Arcita and Palemone, with Fiammetta's title, «Teseida di nozze d'Emilia». His perspective on the poem is accurate, but hers is more penetrating, guiding us beyond the letter to deeper truth conveyed through «closed speech». Venus (3) and Mars (5), coupled in the Seventh Book (VII 30 and VII 50), are emblematic of Emilia's marriage at age fifteen, celebrated in the story of the poem and its numerological plan (5 x 3 = 15). Book VII, which is the longest in the poem and its center, carries a number pointing upward to the planetary gods (7). The number 7 belongs especially to Luna and Emilia but also appears with Apollo, who always shines for Teseo. If we take the *Teseida* as a love story, Arcita and Palemone are indeed its fictional heroes. Allegorically, however, they manifest wrath and lust, and so stand in a secondary, antagonistic relationship to Teseo

---

[62] In connection with my search for simultaneous sequences of 7's, I thank S.I. CAMPOREALE, O. P., for discussing this fresco with me and citing his interpretation of it, in *Lorenzo Valla tra Medioevo e Rinascimento. 'Encomion s. Thomae' — 1457*, «Memoriae domenicani», n.s., VII, 1976, pp. 11-194:22-24. See also M. MEISS, in *Florence and Siena after the Black Death. The Arts, Religion and Society in the Mid-Fourteenth Century*, New York, Harper Torchbooks, 1964², pp. 99-100.

and Emilia. It is these latter, solar and lunar sources of enlightenment, that conquer the appetites and are the moral protagonists in Boccaccio's book of Teseo and the epic of Emilia's marriage.[63]

[63] Research for this essay as originally published was carried out in Florence during 1977-1978, when I was on academic leave with a Fellowship awarded by the Harvard University Center for Italian Renaissance Studies and funded by the National Endowment for the Humanities, a grant generously supplemented by the University of Pennsylvania. For help with this study, which became the subject of a talk on *Boccaccio's Numerology* given at I Tatti in April, 1978, I am deeply indebted to the Fellows, Research Associates, and the Director of I Tatti, Craig Hugh Smyth, who were generous with suggestions and encouragement. I express thanks as well to Richard Seagraves for assistance with some thorny medieval Latin and express special appreciation to Robert M. Durling for his comments on the manuscript as a whole.

2.

AMOROUS VISION, SCHOLASTIC VISTAS

For most readers in this last century or so, the *Amorosa visione* has been Boccaccio's white elephant. Now and again someone takes it down from the attic of his corpus for one of those periodic clean sweeps through the canon. But then, when all the pieces have been dusted off and rearranged in fresh scholarly order, this one goes back to storage, an oversized curiosity, creaky and faded, that we cannot seem to make fit any more with the rest of the furniture. Whatever might call the critic to scrutinize its pages, chances are we hear his patience snap as he comes to Boccaccio's gigantic acrostic allegory. Here, in 4,403 «labored» verses of *terza rima*, is the «most stifling and discouraging of the minor works», the «most bizarre», the «most mechanically clumsy», «most impoverished, colorless, and prosaic». It wobbles «childish», «incoherent», and «confused» allegorically, an «artificial» thing useful only as a «nursery» for the author's later writing. «The most imposing piece of scrimshaw in the history of literature», it seems strangely «unboccaccian» and still remains, as characterized a hundred years ago, «Boccaccio's sphinx».[1]

---

[1] V. BRANCA's philology and rich commentaries have restored the poem to textual dignity. His essay, *L'editio princeps dell''Amorosa visione' del Boccaccio*, «Bibliofilia», XL, 1938, pp. 460-468, laid groundwork for the first critical edition of the poem, which he prepared for the Accademia della Crusca and published with Sansoni, Florence, 1944. Branca, however, felt that the *Visione* rarely «came alive» as poetry, speaking in his seminal article, *L''Amorosa visione' (tradizione, significati, fortuna)*, «Annali della Reale Scuola Normale Superiore di Pisa», s. II, vol. XI, 1942, pp. 20-47, «non può essere — e non è difatti — quasi mai avvivata di poesia». The Crocean line of that early essay, a piece of literary history still powerful for its analysis and coverage, later moderates, but his assessment of the acrostic scarcely warmed. When he republished the text together with its later authorial variant, the B version, *Amorosa visione*, Milan, Mondadori, 1974 («Tutte le opere», III), Branca wrote again (Intro., p. 13) of the poem's «atmosfera incerta, faticosa, fredda». His European colleagues have all concurred. G. CONTINI, reviewing Branca's first edition of the *Amorosa visione* for La Crusca-Sansoni in «Giornale Storico della Letteratura Italiana», CXXIII, 1946, pp. 69-99, labelled it «la più afosa e scoraggiante delle opere minori». R. RAMAT, *Boccaccio 1340 — 1344 II*, «Belfagor», XIX, 1964, pp. 154-174, branded it «l'opera più grossamente macchinosa e poeticamente povera che

Once upon a time, of course, the sphinx did have a place for public display, and those who consulted her, starting with Petrarch, must have listened to her riddles with pleasurable satisfaction and amusement.[2] Girolamo Claricio, the Lombard who published the first edition (Milan, 1521), complimented Boccaccio for creative poetics:

Il Poema tutto è vario, & ordito con maestrevole arteficio, & tessuto di proprieta-te del dire usitata, suave non aspera, luminosa non scura, facile non penosa. Et è

---

il nostro scrittore abbia composto»; N. SAPEGNO, *Dizionario biografico degli Italiani*, Rome, Istituto della Enciclopedia, 1968, p. 845b, echoed that verdict, when he found this «la scrittura più povera, scolorita e prosaica del Boccaccio». C. MUSCETTA, *Giovanni Boccaccio e i novellieri*, in *Storia della letteratura italiana*, II, ed. E. CECCHI e N. SAPEGNO, *Il Trecento*, Milan, Garzanti, 1965, pp. 350-351, accuses Boccaccio of pedantic backsliding when he wrote this «macchinoso poema» with «mediocri meriti»: «era un arretramento pedantesco alle più viete ingegnosità medievali»; again, in *Boccaccio*, Bari, Laterza, 1974, pp. 116-119, MUSCETTA disapproves of the acrostic and finds the work valuable only as a nursery for *De casibus virorum illustrium*, *De mulieribus claris*, *Genealogia deorum gentilium*. On the American side of the Atlantic, a like-minded chorus answered. Here is an 'incoherent' allegory by an author who was not an allegorist, according to E. H. WILKINS, *A History of Italian Literature*, rev. T. G. BERGIN, Cambridge, Mass., Harvard University Press, 1974, p. 105. R. HOLLANDER labelled this 'unboccaccian' invention «the most imposing piece of scrimshaw in the history of literature» in *Boccaccio's Two Venuses, cit.*, 1977, pp. 73, 78. Yet for all its oddity, the piece fascinated him sufficiently to undertake its first English translation, a welcome effort furnished with Introduc-tion by Branca, who upon rethinking it once again, comes to the verge of enthusiasm: *Amorosa visione*, bilingual edition, trans. R. HOLLANDER, T. HAMPTON, M. FRANKEL, with Intro. by V. BRANCA, Hanover and London, University Press of New England, 1986. The trend then does finally seem to be away from that negativism strongest among the positivists late in the last century, scholars like M. LANDAU, who dismissed it tersely as the Certaldan's «most bizarre» work in his *Giovanni Boccaccio. Sein Leben und sein Werke*, Stuttgart, J. G. Cotta, 1877; and C. ANTONA TRAVERSI, *Notizie storiche sull''Amorosa visione'*, «Studi di Filologia Romanza», I, 1885, pp. 425-444, who left us the memorable formula – my own favorite – «la sfinge boccaccesca». J. D. BOSHART, *Giovanni Boccaccio's 'Amorosa Visione'. A New Appraisal*, Unpublished Doctoral Dissertation, Baltimore, Johns Hopkins University, 1974, p. 21, sums up past critics in a well-researched overview: «It is generally credited with being chaotic, impoverished, faded and prosaic».

[2] Two authorial variants of the poem circulated. Eight manuscripts survive that preserve the first, dated to 1341-1342. V. BRANCA lists them in *Tradizione delle opere di Giovanni Boccaccio. I. Un primo elenco dei codici e tre studi*, Rome, Edizioni di Storia e Letteratura, 1958, pp. 16-17. He further documents there three references to codices now lost, a category with two more entries in his *Tradizione delle opere di Giovanni Boccaccio. II. Un secondo elenco di manoscritti e studi sul testo del 'Decameron' con due appendici*, Rome, Edizioni di Storia e Letteratura, 1991, p. 25. A second authorial variant, ca. 1355-65, survives in the *editio princeps*, published by Girolamo Claricio at Milan in 1521. It was reproduced in subsequent imprints (see below, n. 3). These are presented as the A and B texts respectively in Branca's Mondadori *Tutte le opere* edition, *cit.*, of 1974.

BRANCA sketched major directions of the *Visione's* influence in his essay *L''Amorosa visione' (tradizione, significati, fortuna), cit.* G. BILLANOVICH has focussed on its reception by Petrarch, in *Dalla 'Commedia' e dall''Amorosa visione' ai 'Trionfi'*, «Giornale Storico della Letteratura Italiana», CXXIII, 1946, pp. 1-52. When Boccaccio visited Petrarch in March of 1351, he discussed his *Amorosa visione*. After the visit, he sent his new friend a revised copy of that poem in his *terza rima* anthology, along with a copy of the *Divine Comedy* and its cover poem, «Ytalie iam certus honos».

rifertissimo di sententie varie, di figure pieno, d'historie e di favole dipinto: e quando gli è bisogno, usa facondia mira, & moltiplice stilo, hora copioso & abondevole si difonde, hora ristretto & sobbrio si ritiene, hora con florida & luculenta oratione lascivisce, hora con semplici affetti isprimendo donnesca agevolezza intenerisce, & hora sublime e grave con maschile valore rinvigorisce in cotal guisa, che perfetto meritevolmente appellar si puote.[3]

We, on our far side of the Renaissance, can reconstruct historically where she stood, in the years 1342-1343, just after the *Teseida delle nozze d'Emilia* and *Comedia delle ninfe fiorentine*.[4] But what we have lost is the taste to appreciate such a Gothic period piece, for we no longer comprehend her special language. Acrostics today do not classify as literature, any more than copious catalogues of famous people. Personification allegory seems an antiquated form that leaves most of us cold. Besides, has it not been axiomatic to Boccaccio studies that the master was a storyteller, supreme for his realism in prose narrative? Weaker as a versifier, in allegory was he not out of his element?

I think not. The *Amorosa visione* is not a loner, just one isolated experiment with a genre that was Dante's forte, but alien, allegedly, to Boccaccio's more modern spirit. The fact is, what the Certaldan had written before it was almost all allegorical, and in that same mode he would continue to work both as commentator and author for the rest of his life. From his first fiction, *Caccia di Diana*, he busied himself 'hiding' moral truths for readers to uncover, just as he would 'expose' and

---

[3] *Apologia di Gieronimo Claricio Immol. contro Detrattori della Poesia del Boccaccio*, in *'Amorosa visione' di M. Giovanni Boccaccio, nuovamente ritrovata, nella quale si contengono cinque Triumphi, cioe Triumpho di Sapientia, di Gloria, di Richezza, di Amore, e di Fortuna*, ed. G. CLARICIO, Venezia, Zoppino, 1531. Born ca. 1480, Claricio was a modest humanist of the Milanese school and the *Visione*'s most fervid defender in the sixteenth century. An eclectic with special interest in the vernacular, he also published the *Celestina* in 1514. See V. BRANCA, *L'editio princeps dell''Amorosa visione' del Boccaccio, cit.*, and C. DIONISOTTI, *Girolamo Claricio*, «Studi sul Boccaccio», II, 1964, pp. 291-341. Claricio's Milanese edition of 1521 was reissued by Zoppino at Venice in 1531 and 1549, then by Gabriele Giolito in 1558, who, although judging Boccaccio a better 'orator' than versifier, admired the *Visione* for its morality. He finds it «molto dotta, piacevole, e piena di bellissima moralità». A later apologist and editor, I. MOUTIER, *Opere volgari di Giovanni Boccaccio corretti su i testi a penna*, XIV, Florence, Marghera, 1833, could still regard the *Amorosa visione* as «la miglior produzione poetica del Certaldese» and «un vero gioiello di poesia italiana del secolo decimoquarto». Praise as warm as his, reflecting Romanticism's love for medieval esoterica, has not been heard for the last hundred and sixty years.

[4] V. BRANCA's arguments for dating the poem in its two versions can be found in his Introductions to *Amorosa visione, cit.*, 1974, pp. 4-6, and to the trans. by R. HOLLANDER *et al.*, *cit.*, pp. IX-XII.

expound them in his last encyclopedia, *Genealogia deorum gentilium*. Even at mid-career, when he was supposedly keeping well distant from a mode so medieval, and while he had on his drawing boards the very 'realistic' *Decameron*, beneath surface appearances of history and documentary he drew a network of submerged allegory.[5] And if we focus on the date of the *Visione*? We find the poet close to thirty. Financial reverses have brought him back to Florence from a formative sojourn in Naples. To this turning point in his life, which carries him from one literary culture to another, belong two neighboring works: *Teseida* (1339-1341), a heroic poem written largely before the move and finished after; and the bucolic *Ameto*, or *Comedia delle ninfe fiorentine* (1341), the first work fully Florentine, considered a sibling to the *Amorosa visione* because of proximities in time and theme.[6] Both epic and pastoral are deeply informed by allegory.

So no matter how it makes us squirm, we have to confront this quaint rhyming crossword squarely as allegory. Like its lectern mates, the *Amorosa visione* is a fiction that veils moral truth. By Dante's distinction in the *Convivio*, this is «allegory of the poets» because literally speaking the story is not history, rather the author has invented it. It is a lie. From the start, Messer Giovanni shows off tricks and tools of his trade as a fibber. His artifice is conspicuous, deliberately so, for the more signs there are of invention, the loftier the poet's art.

To collect and contain, to synthesize and taxonomize — these impulses ran strong in the medieval mentality. Boccaccio, whom we best remember for one hundred collected tales, won fame among his early publics with other vast assemblies in Latin encyclopedias — the genealogical trees of ancient gods, a gazetteer of the world's geophysical features, accounts of the fallen mighty in universal history, biographies of famous women. For an editor who would compile poetry by Dante and summarize his *Divine Comedy* in *terza rima*, to anthologize his own works in *terza rima* must have seemed a natural step. So, rather than send the *Amorosa*

---

[5] According to BOCCACCIO in the *Esposizioni*, cit., I 2, 17-18: «Fu adunque il nostro poeta [Dante], sì come gli altri poeti sono, nasconditore». Realism is, of course, a narrative stance. Some of the strategies Boccaccio employs to serve it are elegantly analyzed by P. M. FORNI, *Rettorica del reale nel 'Decameron'*, «Studi sul Boccaccio», XVII, 1988, pp. 183-202; *Come cominciano le novelle del 'Decameron'*, in *La novella italiana. Atti del Convegno di Caprarola. 19-24 settembre 1988*, Rome, Salerno Editrice, 1990, pp. 689-700. On submerged allegory, see also below, ch. 4.

[6] As BRANCA has demonstrated, the two works express «mondi e modi strettamente simili». Sharing the great Tuscan theme of «Amore nobilitante e trasfigurante», they both represent the triumph of virtue. See his *Amorosa visione*, cit., 1974, Intro. p. 4.

visione out into the world on its own, or 'widowed',[7] Boccaccio mounted it in a setting with two other pieces of his in *terza rima*.[8] Part of a larger three-part project holding *Caccia di Diana* and a *ternario-ballata*, the acrostic falls under the dominion of the number 3 because it belongs to a trilogy. It is tripartite in a further sense: preceding the 'rhythms' of the *Visione* are three sonnets, not just ordinary ones of fourteen verses, but more imposing *sonetti caudati* with elaborate trains. The words in this trio of 'long-tailed' poems spell out the first letter for every successive *terzina* through fifty cantos, in all 1,451 triplets.

This mammoth acrostic is the central and unique fact-of-art for the *Amorosa visione*. Armature for the work's structure, it is a vehicle conceptually linked to the author's chosen subject matter. Although modern criticism has mostly dismissed Boccaccio's crosswords for spoiling esthetic effect, and in fact, would prefer to peer inside the poem after pushing them aside like some annoying, unsightly overgrowth, we should instead keep them at the forefront of our reading. They are meant to be admired, not deflected and pruned away from the 'real' body of the text. The crosswords *are* the text, a *tour-de-force*, ongoing for all of 4,403 verses.[9]

To appreciate Boccaccio's achievement, with which he won — and still holds — the world record for acrostic length, we can start by mentally restoring the *Visione* to its early manuscript format. Printed copies, beginning with the first, have downplayed the acrostic in two ways. Sometimes the three prefatory sonnets have not been respected. Thus when Girolamo Claricio arbitrarily switched them to an Appendix

---

[7] The notion that a literary text with nothing to follow it could be a «widow» had been established by Dante and would be exploited by Petrarch. N. VICKERS explores the image and its implications in *Widowed Words, Widowed Rhymes*, in *Discourses of Authority*, ed. K. BROWNLEE and W. STEVENS, Hanover and London, University Press of New England, 1989, pp. 97-108.

[8] Technically, the first two sonnets are *caudati*, or 'tailed'; the third is also extended internally, being both *rinterzato* and *caudato*. The three-part anthology must have been Boccaccio's own idea. V. BRANCA, *Tradizione delle opere. I, cit.*, pp. 124-127 and 148-156, deduces that from the manuscript tradition, which preserves the *Visione* transcribed with *Caccia di Diana* and the *ternario-ballata*. See also G. BILLANOVICH, *Dalla 'Commedia' e dall''Amorosa visione' ai 'Trionfi', cit.*, who identifies the occasion for which Boccaccio created this volume, intended as a gift for Petrarch.

[9] In the introductory sonnets themselves there may even be a sort of acrostic double layering, or meta-acrostic. The initial letters of verses 1,3,5,7,9 of the first sonnet form MARIA; counting back from the end of the last sonnet gives PRETE. These coincidences caught the attention of E. H. Wilkins, who suggested that they refer to the *Visione* addressee and sender respectively. Boccaccio could have been nicknamed 'priest' in Naples because of his study of canon law. See WILKINS's note *Maria...Prete*, «Italica», XXVIII, 1951, pp. 101-103.

at the end of his volume, the poem's very cornerstone was pulled out from under it and demoted to a back yard decoration. Worse, other editors separated the sonnets from the *Visione* entirely, as if, even less than ornamental, they were either optional or superfluous. Second, regardless of whether the sonnets assumed their rightful place, modern typography has always set *terzine* for perusal horizontally across the page. Initials bond and flow with the letters that follow, discouraging the vertical cross-reading. By contrast, in a hand-copied codex such initials stood apart from the rest of their verses. Color was one separator; position on the folio the other. Books of finer quality distinguished initials from the body of the text, which was transcribed in black or brown, by inking or retouching them in alternating red and blue. Less costly manuscripts might use a slightly larger letter in the same dusky tone of its companions, sometimes streaked with yellow or red highlighting. Luxury and economy manuscripts alike regularly would place initials well to the left of the line they introduced. This spacing created columns of capitals that ran the folio from top to bottom and invited the eye to follow the acrostic vertically.

Why insist on the acrostic? As form it is more than a mere container. It suggests meaning in and of itself. The medium is a message. Acrostics, with their privileged history as vatic enunciation, were to the Middle Ages a form that signalled communication on a superior, inspired, and mysterious plane. Said to have originated in antiquity, at no less a place than the Greek isle where poetry was born, the art was first practiced by the Erythraean Sibyl, who according to St. Augustine, prophesied in an acrostic «JESUS CHRIST SON OF GOD THE SAVIOR». From its origins the acrostic form is thus linked to the visionary experience, a tradition venerable in its own right — whether rapture vouchsafed prophets and saints, as in the Bible and in Pope Gregory's *Dialogues*, or heavenly ascent to a proper vantage point on our earthly politics, as Cicero imagined and Macrobius glossed in his *Commentary on the Dream of Scipio*. In any event, visions become all the more authoritative when cast in the arcane acrostic medium.[10] Our poet, proud to join a line so

---

[10] V. BRANCA has discussed visionary and acrostic traditions in *L'"Amorosa visione'* (tradizione, significati, fortuna), cit., and most recently in *Amorosa visione*, trans. R. HOLLANDER *et al.*, cit., Intro., pp. XII-XIII. See also E. MÂLE, *The Gothic Image. Religious Art in France of the Thirteenth Century*, New York, Harper Torchbooks, 1958², pp. 336-337. One of the ten Sibyls, a word that in Greek means «female prophet» (ISIDORE, *Etymologiae*, cit., VIII 8), was said to be from Erythraea, the island where poetry was invented. ST. AUGUSTINE in the *City of God*, XVIII 23, gives a Latin rendering of a poem she composed in Greek on the Last Judgment. The first letters of each line spell «JESUS CHRIST, THE SON OF GOD, THE SAVIOR». As Augustine

hallowed, gallantly offers his «mental fantasy» to his lady, Madama Maria, who should find the vision «amazing» for its «original style». Since this particular vision has come not from God or a magnanimous spirit of republican Rome, but direct from Cupid (a lighter-hearted medium whom we could have been led to expect by love numbers writ large in the three-part anthology), it will serve both her private pleasure and a public of amorous readers everywhere. From it, the Author hopes, they will take «fruit» and «delight».

Doubtless with a humorous twist, then, Boccaccio cites a venerable, high form and re-establishes it in the «middle» realm of secular, vernacular poetics.[11] Because visions and crosswords go together, he too will go along with the tradition, his vehicle consonant with the sibylline tenor he smilingly strikes. But he will also go the tradition one better. He must have been thinking that no one before, in Latin or not, had ever created so daringly when sealing acrostic to vision. Of course, Dante's master-piece had its acrostic moments, as did some Old French romances, but nothing like the perfecting continuity of a long vertical calligraphic line from start to finish. Anyway, the *Comedy* did not properly classify as a dream; its Wayfarer's journey into the Otherworld was very much a waking vision.[12]

In contrast, the poet who narrates here leaves no doubt about his bodily status when Amore graciously revealed his Vision. He was asleep. It came to pass during a vigil, as he was lost («smarrito») in desire and daydreams for his lady. There crept over him a sweet drowsiness, to which he gave his every member and, as he meticulously reports, each eye. Then, past all conscious awareness, he wanders alone and frightened on «wide shores», until a queenly lady appears and leads him on a «new path» to a wall with two doors. Rejecting the small one on the right,

---

further points out, if you make an acrostic on the acrostic, the first letters of these five words spell 'fish' (in Greek ἰχθύς = 'ichthys'), a word whose mystic meaning is Christ. A good review of the tradition in early Italian literature is in J. BOSHART, *Giovanni Boccaccio's 'Amorosa Visione'*, cit., ch. 4.

[11] F. BRUNI reads Boccaccio as a «poet in the middle» in his *Boccaccio. L'invenzione della letteratura mezzana*, Bologna, Il Mulino, 1991.

[12] Dante, for example, makes an acrostic on «UOM», repeating each letter for four *terzine*, in *Purgatorio* XII. *Le Parfait du paon*, one of the continuations of the old French *Voeux du paon*, weaves its author's name «JEAN DE LA MOTE» into an acrostic at the close, along with the date 1340. One of the most insistent lines in Branca's Boccaccio studies has been the poet's awareness of himself as an innovator in Italian literature. Recall, e.g., his proud claim at the end of the *Teseida* (XII 84), the first martial epic in the new vernacular, filling the gap noted by Dante in *De vulgari eloquentia*: «tu, o libro, primo a lor [alle Muse] cantare / di Marte fai gli affanni sostenuti, / nel volgar lazio più mai non veduti».

carved above with letters that proclaim it the steep «way of life» and «eternal rest», he accepts an invitation spoken by two young men to follow them back inside the larger, left-hand portal, whose inscription lavishly promises wealth, power, every treasure, fame, and love. Within are two chambers splendidly frescoed. In the first quadrangular space, each of four walls depicts a presiding personage around whom throng dozens of figures. Dreamer recognizes and names them: Knowledge and her seven handmaidens, Worldly Glory in her chariot, Lady Riches enthroned in gold on a mountain of gemstones, Amore seated all-powerful on a pair of eagles with his feet propped on little lions. The narrator and his two young companions then follow the Guide, albeit reluctantly, into a second room where Lady Fortune, painted ghastly of feature beside her wheel, tyrannizes a universal mob. Against Guide's advice, Dreamer escapes this grim spectacle by stepping out into a garden. From a fountain, cunning in the artistry of its marble figures, there flow three streams, and the one Dreamer chooses to follow, a rivulet flowing southward, points his steps to shores along which ladies gather at leisure. One of them is his own. She takes his heart, gives him a ring, and sends him off to find her friend, the Guide whom he had left behind. Guide gladly approves his love match, and he strolls privately with the Lady into some nearby bushes. On the verge of consummating his desire, he awakens with a start. His disappointment, however, soon gives way to amazement and new hope, as the Guide reappears at his side and offers again to lead him through the strait gate and up a hill to happiness. This time he welcomes the climb for the Lady he loves will join in the ascent.

What are we to make of this Dreamer who keeps stubbornly wanting his own way, the castle on a hillock truncated to just a pair of rooms, its watery landscape, and all the ladies who dwell thereabouts? For a dream vision of the Gothic era, Boccaccio's acrostic seems to violate some of the most basic rules. Why, for instance, does he furnish it with a Guide, only to undercut her capacity for guidance? To all appearances a regal lady with super credentials for her mission, she does not last long after dropping in from heaven before we see how problematic are her leadership qualities. What an undignified moment when she tries to stop Dreamer from marching after those two young men into the wide portal, siding against them in a tug-of-war! Here is a «Virgil in skirts»[13] whom,

---

[13] V. CRESCINI called the Guide «un Virgilio in gonne» in *Due studi riguardanti opere minori del Boccaccio. Il 'Cantare di Fiorio e Biancifiore' ed il 'Filocolo'. La Lucia dell'Amorosa visione'*, Padua, Crescini, 1882.

often as not, Dreamer dissuades from the direction she indicates. When that happens, she ends up not leading, but trailing after her charge. Worse, he manages for a time to elude her altogether and wander off through a landscape dotted with ladies. Even after his own Lady has sent Dreamer back to fetch Guide, he still manages to slip away once more and take advantage of her absence, pressing hidden kisses upon Maria in a bower secluded by a rose privet. Undaunted, Guide makes yet another appearance, not to rush upon their recess, separate the lovers, and save decency — there is no need, since sleep's abrupt end takes care of all that — rather to reassert herself outside the dream! But how can she succeed in the everyday order of things while she failed repeatedly in Dreamer's amazing «fantasia»?

Other figures, too, make us wonder. Why do two male youths come out of the wide gate? Why not, say, a happily paired man and a woman, the more predictable Boccaccesque combination? Or a single authoritative spokesman? Or even a whole little company, a *brigata* like the group Filocolo found along the shores of Naples?[14] For that matter, why should Boccaccio have planted any characters at all at this particular textual location? Music alone and sounds of merriment within could surely have been enough to allure Dreamer, always ready for a good time. And what significance, if any, should we attach to the fact that the men are «red» and «white»? Is their clothing or their complexion intended? Is this technicolor detail in the dream a real clue or just a teaser? Can we make symbolic identification on such slim evidence?

The frustrating thing is that Boccaccio seems to have broken his part of the allegorical contract. Has he played fair, told as much as we need to decode the conundrum? The minimal evidence that he does dangle before us dances and flashes, intriguing fragments. Dreamer's ladylove is Maria Aquinas, not a combination of names to pass over lackadaisically. And there are the time references, intermittent but insistent. Whoever remembers his Dante and the well-clocked journey that began on Good Friday must pounce on them as details patly symbolic: the dream starts at dawn; Dreamer and Guide enter the second room in the second hour; the fifth hour is approaching as he nears his lady in the garden; by zodiacal reckoning it is midway through the Ram; he loves Maria for 6 x 4 suns

---

[14] Cf. *Filocolo, cit.,* IV 14: «Filocolo col duca e con Parmenione e con gli altri compagni [...] pervenuti allato ad un giardiano, udirono in esso graziosa festa di giovani e di donne. E l'aere di varii strumenti e di quasi angeliche voci ripercossa risonava tutta, entrando con dolce diletto a' cuori di coloro a' cui orecchi così riverberata venia [...] e mentre che la fortuna così lui e i compagni fuori del giardino tenea ad ascoltare sospesi, un giovane uscì di quello».

plus 5 x 3 x 9 days. Yet no larger calendar connects those specifics. They bob up unanchored, unoriented. So we are left with a time frame tantalizing, incomplete, just short of meaning. And what about the Dreamer's progress? According to the rules of good and proper allegory, the lost soul who is hero of this all ought to be ascending gradually, by degrees. But Boccaccio's visionary is more like a comic anti-hero. He just seems to vacillate and meander without really getting anywhere. We watch him in a perpetual back-and-forth, caught between what he wants to do (abetted by the red and white fellows), and the sounder but more boring itinerary that Guide has in mind. Finally, is not his experience on waking strangely surrealistic? How can the Guide, she who like a queen descended to rescue him within the vision, return to the banal order of reality at his bedside after slumber breaks? Boundaries dissolve between night and day, dreaming and waking, illusion and reason, evanescent fantasy and enduring truth.

How then are we to take this amorous vision? Is it a serious allegory? But seriously flawed? Or is it parody, a mock vision — even, perhaps, a hugely vulgar joke, as Franca Nardelli captiously proposes?[15] Its possibilities, seemingly wide open, push us into confrontation with the classic hermeneutic problem in Boccaccio studies. The protean poet of Certaldo, what was he? Medieval or modern? An orthodox Catholic respectful of social institutions or an amoral iconoclast? A strightforward writer sincere in his optimism or a cynical, wry ironist? According to Giuseppe Mazzotta, the reason critics cannot make up their minds is because of radical, and very deliberate, instabilities in Boccaccio's textual worlds.[16] I take another view. Although Boccaccio did keep moving to new ground in formalist terms, as he experimented ambitiously with literary genres, his work remained remarkably constant in its substance — habits and tactics of style, themes, and value systems.[17] Shifting narrative perspectives need not imply vanishing intellectual points of view. Ambiguities in a text do not have to mean that the author himself is ambivalent. As for

---

[15] F. PETRUCCI NARDELLI, L'"Amorosa visione' rivisitata, «Quaderni medievali», XXIV, 1987, pp. 57-75. Nardelli, in an indiosyncratic and unconvincing reading, constructs a case for taking the poem as an allegory of heterosexual sodomy. Although Boccaccio's Renaissance imitators like Berni certainly practiced this sort of coarse humor, such vulgarity is entirely uncharacteristic of Boccaccio.

[16] G. MAZZOTTA, The World at Play in Boccaccio's 'Decameron', Princeton, Princeton University Press, 1986.

[17] Approaching the subject on philological ground, G. BILLANOVICH, in Dalla 'Commedia' e dall''Amorosa visione' ai 'Trionfi', cit., has also argued the importance of viewing Boccaccio's career as a logical continuum.

an acrostic, is that not by requirements of form sibylline? It relies on riddling language — sleight-of-plot, semantic duplicities, paradoxical possibilities, odd juxtapositions, and binary directions. Without them, where lies the reader's challenge and pleasure?

Like any allegory, the *Amorosa visione* naturally has its ambivalencies. But they are on a literary, not an ethical register. Characters, setting, and plot have perforce double meaning. Our task as readers is to translate those visible symbols into figural signifiers. Once we have cracked the poetic code, the moral of the story comes clearly into focus. It will show something about how a rational human being ought to behave, and will do so fairly unambiguously. Now the fact that allegory is there and that it is there in order to teach a lesson does not mean we are not supposed to enjoy ourselves along the way to understanding. On the contrary, the poet's job is to make sure we do. How does Boccaccio bring us «pleasure» as well as «fruit»? Our delight comes in several ways. We admire how deftly he can play with titles and samples from his stockhouse of literature as over and again we notice citations, twists, reversals; here a bit of the Bible, there a snatch of Dante. We appreciate how adroitly he can handle familiar symbols as he translates philosophy to poetry, so that we see the Pythagorean path of life personified in a myth of Hercules, 'Aquinas' captured in *terza rima*. Then, while the acrostic scrolls longer, we have the delight of a further recognition. It is ourselves, discovered in Boccaccio's humorous, tolerant portrayal. Our foibles and backslidings are funny, not ridiculous or grotesque, because slapstick and farce are not really his style. We are only human, true, but that is not a bad thing. If Dreamer keeps making mistake after mistake, we can sympathize with him as we identify with him. Dreamer is Us. So of course, he wants what is pleasurable. His problem is that he wants it as instant gratification, childishly. Like the toddler Dante describes through Marco Lombardo at the center of the *Comedy*, he is fascinated by anything that moves and glitters. He turns toward it, and he would choose it if his threshold of consent did not raise a barrier. At that threshold stand free will and reason. Within all of us there is that child who does not want to grow up, to become a more serious and responsible person, to forego indulgence for mature discipline, which in the larger picture is supposed to be more satisfying. Although its symbolic language is very medieval, involving concepts articulated by Scholasticism, the allegory of Boccaccio's *Visione* does not speak just to 'medieval Man'. It is about a universal dilemma of the human spirit, the tug-of-war between what looks good for the moment and future insightfulness, between sacrificing short-term pleasure for long-term reward.

When presented with the choice, what is a person to do? What is right and what is wrong? Boccaccio wants us to think about it. He is much cleverer than to set up the alternatives in black and white. The triumphs in his «noble castle» are as splendid as any of Giotto's art; his garden of delights is no land of freaks and monsters in the manner of Hieronymus Bosch, but a pleasance whose sirens at the waterside are beautiful Italian ladies. Temptations have to be appealing, after all. Maybe, Boccaccio would say, if we stroll a primrose path and linger on it for a while, as long as it is only temporarily, no great harm done. In this sense, he posits the dilemma in less stern terms than his predecessor Dante, in a more relaxed mode than his friend Petrarch. He manages to claim the best of both their worlds and touch the whole with a magic wand of 'lightness'. The hero will get his lady, and notwithstanding that, his spiritual prognosis looks good. Progress toward those goals in the *Amorosa visione* is both a mini-Dantean journey and a kind of Petrarchan *processus* as the allegory takes its coordinates from a Pauline conflict on which hang the *Rime sparse*: That which I would do, I do not; that which I would not do, I do. What Boccaccio brings new to the old dilemma is a healthy dose of humor.

* * *

To lay out Dreamer's problem, Boccaccio architects a landscape from Dante. Signs of the *Vita nuova* and *stilnovismo* are easily noticeable in his language of praise for Maria d'Aquino; a motif from the *Convivio* comes back when the Guide condemns whoever cares for status conferred by noble blood. But beyond these early works, Boccaccio's obvious master-copy is the *Divine Comedy*. A sequence of cantos in *terza rima*, the *Amorosa visione* is replete with inventions recycled from Dante's epic.[18] The Narrator is lost, his mind «smarrita». A Guide comes from the Beyond to rescue him. She sets him on a «straight path» toward a «noble castle». They enter a wide portal with an inscription overhead (and in canto III). Canto IV puts them inside the castle, where begins a long catalogue of famous human beings. Art freezes them into postures characteristic of their lives. Some seem happy; others placed elsewhere inside the gate groan with suffering on a wheel. Later, the wayfarer enters a

---

[18] V. BRANCA, *Amorosa visione*, cit., 1974, Intro., p. 12, characterizes this as «la più dantesca delle opere giovanili del Boccaccio», and his commentary notes many echoes of Dante in Boccaccio's verses. Boccaccio pays open homage to «Dante Alighier fiorentino» in the Triumph of Learning at IV 70-88 and V 1-24.

garden and 'looses' this Guide but meets his lady. She will accompany him, so the poem promises, on a journey to a high place.

All this Dante is unmistakable. Still, it is as if we had come upon a house whose contents had been dismantled and spread out on the lawn for a sheriff's auction. We recognize the pieces, but without their familiar setting they seem to have lost some meaning. Now in a different light, loosely reassembled, objects can even reverse appearances. Boccaccio has turned things around or set them upside-down, as if he were not quite sure of their original function. So what strikes us most is not the sameness. Instead, we see discrepancies between the way they used to be and how they are here. Dante's journey began at dusk after an awakening, Boccaccio's at dawn after the Narrator falls asleep. A man rescues the first, a woman the second. Virgil is a shade summoned from Hell, Boccaccio's Guide an apparition descended from heaven. He is only dimly visible («fioco»); she is refulgent («lucente»). Dante first visits Hell, obedient to his guide but with real trepidation, then gladly reaches happier kingdoms. Dreamer starts in Room I by seeing happy souls, against his Guide's wish; then she shows him in Room II the unhappy ones, against his wish. Dante journeys to the center of the earth and the ends of the universe; Boccaccio's Dreamer merely strolls to a hilltop castle, passes through two well decorated rooms, and then saunters along a garden stream to a rose thicket. It is a place far from the celestial rose of the Empyrean and Dante's privileged, but distanced, final 'contact' with Beatrice smiling beside Rachel upon her riser. Dante's vision dissolves, ineffably sweet, with the sight of a triune God *facies ad faciem*; Boccaccio's breaks in a moment of comic bathos, as he tries secretly to snatch kisses from Fiammetta in the bushes. Dante fills one hundred cantos; Boccaccio halts at fifty, halfway to numerical plenitude. He leaves his protagonist suspended, short of a full and perfect resolution to his moral dilemma. He is still on earth, still in the temporal realm. The result, in Robert Hollander's felicitous formula, is «half a *Commedia*».[19]

Less than a model, the *Divine Comedy* is Boccaccio's foil. He did not just pull out pieces haphazardly, then. He has gathered them into a new order and used them to construct a counter-ascent. It is Dante topsy-turvy. And the poetic reversals are amusing.

---

[19] R. HOLLANDER notes in *Boccaccio's Two Venuses*, cit., p. 205 and n. 67, the parallel between the length of the *Amorosa visione* and *Comedia delle ninfe fiorentine*, which has fifty chapters. For Hollander this is one way in which both works «reflect a sense of inferiority to the great(er) Dante».

For instance, Boccaccio follows Dante when he sets up portals on the path of his protagonist. The first one Dreamer sees, «in nulla parte *torta*» (II 39), corresponds to the Gate of Purgatory. As Dante pilgrim had stepped across that threshold, he heard rusty hinges howl. A passageway little frequented, it was «la porta che 'l mal amor de l'anime disusa, / perché fa parer dritta la via *torta*» (*Purgatorio* X 1-2). Boccaccio's Dreamer corroborates Dante when he refuses to enter the strait way in the *Amorosa visione*, deflected like many another because he loves wrong objects. He rejects an ascent that would lead him to salvation, as a message carved overhead announces:

> [...] Questa
> picciola porta mena a via di vita;
> posto che paia nel salir molesta,
>   riposo etterno dà cotal salita;
> dunque salite su sanza esser lenti,
> l'animo vinca la carne impigrita. (II 64-69)[20]

The exhortation to climb swiftly («salite su sanza esser lenti») recalls Cato's rebuke, when at the base of Purgatory, Dante had momentarily let sensual pleasure get the better of him as he and Virgil dawdled to hear Casella's song, «Che è ciò, spiriti lenti? / qual negligenza, quale stare è questo? / Correte al monte» (*Purgatorio* II 120-122). A trek upward, progressively easier, is exactly what Dante accomplished. He made his way to heaven, a realm where souls dwell distributed «from threshold to threshold», and did so gradually, as Boccaccio's Guide wants her charge to proceed, «from threshold to threshold».[21] With such comparisons in mind, we realize right away how ill-advised is Dreamer's preference for gate number two:

> Regni ampii, dignitati e gran tesoro,
> gloria mondana copiosamente
> a color do, che passan nel mio coro.

---

[20] Unless otherwise indicated, I cite the B version of the text. Known only from the first printed edition, Branca accepts it as an authorial revision. As C. MUSCETTA notes, in *Boccaccio, cit.*, p. 118, B has «un moralismo più risentito e una religiosità più preoccupata di ortodossia». I concur and find further a sharpened philosophical vocabulary in B.

[21] Of course, Boccaccio's narrow gate also alludes to Matt. 7:13-14. As for ascent by degrees, cf. *Amorosa visione, cit.*, I 82: «Ir si convien[...]di soglia in soglia» and *Paradiso, cit.*, III 82-83: «noi sem di soglia in soglia / per questo regno». Note that within their respective cantos, the words «di soglia in soglia» fall at exactly the same verse, 82.

Lieti li fo nel mondo, e simelmente
quella gioia gli do ch'Amor promette
a quei che senton la sua face ardente. (III 16-21)

This opening, through which hordes of humans pass, serves the same public as Dante's Gate of Hell: «Per me si va nella città dolente [...]. Lasciate ogne speranza, voi ch'entrate». Structure tightens the parallel, since each gate has an inscription and each stands in Canto III of its poem. This is the way to woe, the end of all hope. We want to call out to the Dreamer, «No! Stop! Not there!» But he is a dense case, and we have to smile as we listen to him wheedle the Guide: «Ogni cosa del mondo all'uom sapere / non si disdice». When in their journey did Dante ever contradict Virgil and coax him into moral hooky by insinuating that «it is not denied man to know everything in the world?» Whose language then does Dreamer speak? It sounds like Ulysses's confession of evil curiosity, «l'ardore [...] a divenir del mondo esperto» in *Inferno* XXVI, and it clinches our understanding of his wrong-headed course.

Boccaccio's habit of playing off scenes against Dante, as he does here in a deft pastiche, often has a humorous effect. Nevertheless, he is not just giving us 'Dante lite'. Humor does not preclude seriousness of purpose on his part. No more do his poetic flips of the *Comedy* comport a denial of Dante's morality and allegory. Literary transformations, through which Boccaccio sets himself apart as a poet with his own identity, as «nuovo autore», need not imply value reversals. It has been our mistake, over the centuries since Renaissance and Reformation, to merge Boccaccio's authorial identity with that of his most famous Narrator, the voice behind the *Decameron*.[22] Those collected tales are the book

---

[22] One learned scholar who makes this assumption is A. SCAGLIONE, *Nature and Love in the Middle Ages. An Essay on the Cultural Context of the 'Decameron'*, Westport, Conn., Greenwood Press, 1976², p. 121: the *Amorosa visione* is an «obvious and miserable failure, logical and aesthetic». Scaglione's reading of Boccaccio descends from a DeSanctisian archetype that conditioned Boccaccio studies well into the twentieth century. Cf. S. SEGALLA DI ARCO, *I sentimenti religiosi nel Boccaccio*. Doctoral Dissertation, Faculty of Letters and Philosophy, Berne, 1909, pp. 19-25, who assumes that the 'real' Boccaccio is a naturalist inclined away from religion, from old medieval forms like allegory. Love is the 'ragione' of all the poet's early works; the religious intent that colors *Filocolo*, like the allegory of *Ameto* and the *Amorosa visione* are old forms that the author cannot quite fully cast off. He struggles between new and old religion and morality, but his true sympathies are with «pagan fantasies». According to this distorted image, moralism supposedly only arose in the old Boccaccio. C. GRABHER, for example, refers to an «ombroso moralismo sorto in lui solo nei tardi suoi anni» in *Il culto del Boccaccio per Dante e alcuni aspetti delle sue opere dantesche*, «Studi Danteschi», XXX, 1951, pp. 129-156.

that has come to characterize him, transforming the philosopher-poet into a legendary Author-construct who caressed racy prose, hence by popular repute must himself have been a priapist.[23] So when Nardelli reads the *Amorosa visione* as an 'allegory' of heterosexual sodomy and a great scatological send up, her enterprise must rest on the premise that Boccaccio was most truly a burlesque spirit. Her revisionist approach tries to save the work that otherwise has seemed so short on merit — bizarre, «unboccaccian», «scrimshaw», the perennial white elephant. As long as we keep supposing that the 'real' Boccaccio was a realist, by nature a sensualist, his *Amorosa visione* will of course look like a miserable failure. Earthy sexuality in the content jars against an allegorical super-structure. Guide is a carping nuisance, much too preachy. Dreamer is frustrated in his sexual fantasy. And realism? Of that there is precious little. In fact, quite the opposite, the poem approaches pure symbolism.

We must distinguish between Giovanni Boccaccio and his fictional narrators. Above all, we must set aside his towering image as an author at one with the *Decameron*. He was not the great truant of the Italian Trecento. Trained as a canonist, he passionately read not only poets ancient and modern, but also the philosophers, encyclopedists, and theologians. In his library Aristotle and Aquinas kept company with Augustine and Andreas Capellanus; Virgil and Ovid with Bernard Silvestris and Alan of Lille; Boethius and Macrobius lay on the shelves beside Isidore, Brunetto Latini, and Dante.

These older authors shed their lights on the new one; they are his *auctoritates*. With reference to them we can unravel the poem. All parts of the *Amorosa visione* are symbolic, from the formal acrostic to the fact of the dream itself. Properly combined, they make a cogent allegory, one whose message Boccaccio often repeated. Dreamer's fantasy dramatizes a psychomachia. A struggle ongoing in Everyman's soul, its victories and defeats decide our choices and actions in life. Scholastic theologians, following Aristotle, defined the psychological faculties that engage in this conflict. Reason is the greater power, and it should by rights control what is below, our sensual appetites of irascibility and concupiscence. In them lie our emotions, such as fear and joy; through them we experience all the pleasures of the senses. But their pull can be irresistibly seductive. When they win, reason suffers a setback. Yet because nature has made us

---

[23] The myth is debunked by V. KIRKHAM, *John Badmouth. Fortunes of the Poet's Image*, in *Boccaccio 1990: The Poet and his Renaissance Reception*, «Studi sul Boccaccio», XX, 1991-92, pp. 355-376.

rational animals, our reason cannot easily surrender and keeps returning to counterattack. In most mortals, folk less perfect than saints, the battle swells and ebbs in continuing tensions, sometimes with an advantage to one side, sometimes to the other. Ideally, as we grow older, reason is supposed to strengthen her sway. Allied with the virtue of wisdom, she brings contemplative detachment from the physical world and increased serenity of spirit.

* * *

Canto I opens as Giovanni di Boccaccio di Certaldo begins to transcribe the vision Amore revealed. While thinking fervently of love, his «fantasy» started to roam with «unaccustomed errancy». He day-dreamed into the night, grew heavy-lidded, and fell deeply asleep:

> In cui vegghiando, allor mi sopravenne
> ne' membri un sonno sì dolce e soave,
> ch'alcun di lor in sé non si sostenne.
>   Lì mi posai, e ciascun occhio grave
> al dormir diedi. (I 16-20)

Thus the first event of the *Visione* is its vehicle, sleep.

As a medium for fictional narrative, the medieval dream-vision had its archetype in *The Dream of Scipio*. Originally a portion of Cicero's *De republica*, it survived past late antiquity thanks to the *Commentarium in somnium Scipionis* of ca. 400 by Macrobius, whose compilation established him as a curriculum author for the European Middle Ages. A copy of his *Commentarium* probably belonged to Boccaccio personally, for he knew Macrobius well. In his preliminary remarks, Macrobius defines five types of dreams. Two are empty nightmares, either nothing more than disturbed sleep from overindulgence in food and drink, or nocturnal phantasms conjured by workaday tensions (what we would call the anxiety dream). But the other three have meaning and value; all overlap with Scipio's privileged sleep. They are the «enigmatic dream», in Latin *somnium*; the «prophetic vision», or *visio*; and the «oracular dream», or *oraculum*. The enigmatic dream is «one that conceals with strange shapes and veils with ambiguity the true meaning of the information being offered». The *visio* will actually come true: a man dreams of a friend long away in a foreign country, then wakes up and goes out and encounters that man. The oracular dream reveals through the agency of some beloved or revered person «what will or will not transpire, and what action to take or to avoid».[24] Like Scipio's dream, Giovanni's partakes of all three varieties with serious import. As an *oraculum* it funnels advice through respected authority, here a queenly Guide. As *visio*, a term that enters Boccaccio's title, its contents spill over from slumber to daytime when Dreamer awakens to find that spokeswoman there right at his bedside. As *somnium*, it speaks enigmatically beneath a veil of ambiguity. It is, then, allegory cast in symbolic language. It needs to be interpreted.

Once Macrobius has alerted us to the conditions for meaningful content, Dante can help orient us in our interpretation. Reading against that Dante, who 'comes to' at the start of his *Comedy*, we could deduce that Giovanni's loss of conscious awareness signals a slip into spiritual darkness. How Dante had wandered into the forest where he reawoke, he cannot say, for he had been «so full of sleep»: «Io non so ben ridir com' i' v'entrai, / tant' era pien di sonno a quel punto». When Boccaccio glosses those lines in his *Esposizioni sopra la Comedìa*, he distinguishes «corporal sleep» from «mental sleep». The former may signify that daily renewal we require for physical survival, or alternatively, the final bodily rest of death. But what caused Dante to «lose the straight way» was a problem in his mind:

Il sonno mentale, allegoricamente parlando, è quello quando l'anima, sottoposta la ragione a' carnali appetiti, vinta dalle concupiscenze temporali, s'adormenta in esse e oziosa e negligente diventa e del tutto dalle nostre colpe legata diviene [...]. E talvolta avviene per sola benignità di Dio che noi ci risvegliamo e, riconosciuti i nostri errori e le nostre colpe, per la penitenzia levandoci, ci riconciliamo a Dio, il quale non vuole la morte de' peccatori; e, a lui riconciliati, ripognamo, mediante la sua grazia, la ragione, sì come donna e maestra della nostra vita, nella suprema sedia dell'anima.

(I 2, 33-34 on *Inferno* I 10-11)

Salubrious in the natural sense, sleep on a 'mental' or moral level is the dead opposite, a most destructive habit. Asleep we are, as it were, blind; we dwell in spiritual torpor. Such metaphors color Biblical language from the prophets to St. Paul. So Isaiah darkly warns, «for the Lord hath

---

[24] MACROBIUS, *Comm. in somnium*, cit., I 3, 2-10: «omnium quae videre sibi dormientes videntur quinque sunt principales et diversitates et nomina [...] est oraculum quidem cum in somnis parens vel alia sancta gravisve persona seu sacerdos vel etiam deus aperte eventurum quid aut non eventurum, faciendum vitandumve denuntiat. visio est autem cum id quis videt quod eodem modo quo apparuerat eveniet [...] somnium proprie vocatur quod tegit figuris et velat ambagibus non nisi interpretatione intellegendam significationem rei quae demonstratur». Boccaccio must have owned the *Commentary* in his library. See G. MAZZA, *L'inventario della 'parva libraria'*, cit., and above, ch. 1, n. 18.

mingled for you the spirit of a deep sleep; he will shut up your eyes, he will cover your prophets and princes» (Is. 29:10); and Jeremiah lowers: «In their heat I will set them drink, and I will make them drunk, that they may slumber, and sleep an everlasting sleep, and awake no more, saith the Lord» (Jer. 51:39). For the Apostle, sleeping is the same as life without Christ, which is to say no life at all: «Awake, O sleeper, and arise from the dead, / and Christ shall give you light» (Eph. 5:14). In the very scriptural passage that St. Augustine credits for his salvation, one of the most dramatic conversions in the history of Christianity (*Confessions* VIII 12), that man whose own sudden enlightenment had come on a road to Damascus urges us all to awake:

you know what hour it is, how it is full time now for you to wake from sleep. For salvation is nearer to us now than when we first believed; the night is far gone, the day is at hand. Let us then cast off the works of darkness and put on the armor of light; let us conduct ourselves becomingly as in the day, not in reveling and drunkenness, not in debauchery and licentiousness, not in quarrelling and jealousy. But put on the Lord Jesus Christ, and make no provision for the flesh, to gratify its desires. (Rom. 13:11-14)

Dante's reawakening, as much as Boccaccio's understanding of it, adduce a commonplace. Sleep figuratively is sin.[25]

Not then in the service of realism does Boccaccio insist on how total was his surrender. To sleep he gave his whole body, every limb and «each eye». Silly as it may sound for him to say that *both eyes* participated in the experience, the poet is not being plodding or pleonastic. He makes a point allegorically. In the sleeper reason has lost her proper seat of power; lower sensual appetites have taken over. As Boccaccio sums up Dante, it is in this «sonno mentale» that «ciascuno, che si diletta più di seguir l'appetito che la ragione, è veramente legato» (*Esposizioni* I 2, 36).

---

[25] BRANCA, *Amorosa visione, cit.*, 1974, Comm. p. 559, notes these scriptural passages, which Boccaccio certainly knew, as well as the connection with Dante's *Inferno* I 11. Is. 19:10: «Quoniam miscuit vobis Dominus spiritum soporis, claudet oculos vestros, prophetas et principes vestros, qui vident visiones, operiet»; Ir. 51:39: «in calore eorum ponam potus eorum et inebriabo eos, ut sopiantur et dormiant somnum sempiternum et non consurgant, dicit Dominus»; Eph. 5:14: «Surge, qui dormis, et exsurge a mortuis et illuminabit te Christus»; Rm. 13:11-14: «Et hoc scientes tempus, quia hora est iam nos de somno surgere; nunc enim propior est nostra salus quam cum credidimus. Nox praecessit, dies autem appropinquavit. Abiciamus ergo opera tenebrarum et induamur arma lucis. Sicut in die honeste ambulemus, non in comessationibus et ebrietatibus, non in cubilibus et impudicitiis, non in contentione et aemulatione; sed induimini Dominum Iesum Christum et carnis curam ne feceritis in desideriis».

Like the acrostic, the *visio-somnium-oraculum* is both container and content. Sleep seals off the world of reality from a realm of art. Closed eyelids enable and encase the oneiric narrative. At the same time, they symbolize Giovanni's confused state, his clouded intellect. As long as he will not 'open his eyes', he sees things wrong. Guide's vocabulary keeps referring semantically to vision blocks. These sight failures cause him to mistake false well-being for true happiness: «Voi che nel mondo state [...] gli occhi alla fulgente aurora / alzare non potete» (II 76-79); «tu ti abbagli / nel falso imaginar» (III 76-77); «Tu t'abbagli te stesso in tanta erranza / con falso immaginar» (XXX 40-42); «seguendo que' beni imperfetti / con cieca mente, morendo perdete / il poter acquistar poi li perfetti» (XXX 58-60).

The sleep of sin belongs to a night of ignorance. So Giovanni's rude wake-up in daylight hours, leaving deflated his sexual hopes, should hold fair promise in a moral sense. Now reason has got the better of concupiscence. Eyes opened again intimate a return to proper order in the faculties of the soul and an attendant possibility of salvation. Why else did Dante return to his senses as he saw the sun rising? Boccaccio's commentary elucidates: «Puossi intorno a questa parte dire, quanto gli uomini involuti ne' peccati dimorano, tanto dimorare nelle tenebre della notte, cioè della ignoranza; la quale, come la notte toglie il poter conoscere o vedere le cose, quantunque nel cospetto ci sieno, così toglie il cognoscere il vero dal falso e le cose utili dalle dannose» (*Esposizioni* I 2, 78). A fiction of sleep, the *Amorosa visione* veils an allegory of life. 'Vision' is at stake in more ways than one.

What does Giovanni see in the first scene of his dream? «Così dormendo, sovra i lidi lati / errar mi vidi». «Sleeping» and «wandering over wide shores», he is errant, in error. Why on «wide shores?» Could not this errancy occur just as well, say, in a forest? Although the Italian 'lito', from Latin *litus, litoris*, can refer to river bank as well as seaside, Boccaccio's qualifier 'wide' implies at first an ocean shore. That is where Dante had been, metaphorically breathless, looking back from a beach to the dangerous waters that had nearly swallowed him down, in the first epic simile of the *Comedy*: «come quei che con lena affannata, / uscito fuor del *pelago* a la riva, / si volge a l'acqua perigliosa e guata». We find Boccaccio's original intention confirmed if we turn back to his earlier version of the *Amorosa visione*, where he left no doubt that Dreamer was rushing along a 'salty' oceanside: «Così dormendo, in su liti *salati* / mi vidi correr». Boccaccio, then, keeps Dante in mind down to the details of his own prologue scene. Giovanni also is «frightened and alone», for those shores on which he stumbles are «uninhabitated places». But literary background for this seascape goes much deeper than Dante. Both poets capitalize on a long familiar image that relates ocean waters to the *fluctus concupiscentiae*, or 'fluxions' and 'commotions' of human passions. Our Dreamer beside the briny deep ambles on the brink of engulfment by sensual attachment.[26]

Later Boccaccio modified his verse, changing «liti salati» to «liti lati». Why? He must have wanted it susceptible to broader meaning, more than just the ocean. 'Wide shores' might be anywhere, inland as well as coastal. The double possibility relates to watery imagery that swirls into one of the most influential portraits of Fortuna from the Middle Ages, a description by the twelfth-century encyclopedist Alan of Lille. In his *Anticlaudianus* Alan imagines that the goddess Nature has decided to fashion a perfect man, but since she can only form the body, she sends Prudence (Phronesis), accompanied by Reason, on a journey through the heavens to obtain from God a soul. Other personified powers, all women, contribute virtue and learning to the new human being, among them Fortuna's daughter, Nobility, whose mission takes her back to her mother's dwelling. The land on which that crazy, bisected house precariously perches lies mid-ocean on a rock, forever pounded by surging waves. Two rivers flow through the craggy island, one with sweet, intoxicating water that leaves those who manage to drink of it even thirstier than before. The other is black and sulphurous, with gigantic crashing waves that have sunk many a victim. Eventually, the foul

---

[26] «Liti salati» may allude to Venus, born of the salty sea foam, whence her name Aphrodite, which Boccaccio says comes from the Greek 'aphrodos', that is, 'foam' (*Genealogia, cit.*, III 23, p. 149). See E. G. SCHREIBER, *Venus in the Medieval Mythographic Tradition*, «Journal of English and Germanic Philology», LXXIV, 1975, pp. 519-535. As for concupiscent fluxions, C. S. SINGLETON, *Su la fiumana ove 'l mar non ha vanto ('Inf'. II 108)*, «The Romanic Review», XXXIX, 1948, pp. 269-277, quotes Augustine's use of the image: «Pronus sum ad omne flagitium, ita me obruunt concupiscentiae fluctus, ut quotidie mergar, et in profundum peccatorum ruam» (Sermo CCCLXV, *Patrologia Latina* 39:1645). Cfr. J. FRECCERO, *The River of Death: Inferno II,108*, in *Dante: The Poetics of Conversion*, ed. R. JACOFF, Cambridge, Mass., Harvard University Press, 1986, pp. 55-69; a volume now in Italian, *Dante. La poetica della conversione*, intro. C. CALENDA Bologna, Il Mulino, 1989. In his *Esposizioni sopra la Comedìa, cit.*, IV 2, 50-53, Boccaccio specifically associates flowing water with worldly riches, which come and go so easily, as well as with the flux of our passions for them. The passage occurs as he describes the 'fiumicello' flowing around the noble castle of the Limbans: «egli intende questo castello il real trono della maestà della filosofia morale e naturale»; the stream one must cross to enter it signifies «le sustanzie temporali, cioè le riccheze, i mondani onori e le mondane preeminenze, le quali sono nella prima aparenza splendide e belle, quantunque in essistenza oscure e tenebrose si truovino [...]. E come l'acqua spesse volte è a' nostri sensi dilettevole, così queste sono agl'ingegni e agl'intelletti nocevoli; e così sono flusse e labili come è l'acqua, la quale è in corso continuo: niuno fermo stato hanno, oggi sono e domane non sono».

turbulence streams into the clear one and corrupts it; «the fetid ruins the fragrant».

When Boccaccio placed his Dreamer in a shaky state upon a shore, he surely meant us to associate that setting not only with the *fluctus concupiscentiae*, but also Fortuna in her flux. What he probably had in mind was the stormy island crossed by two confluent rivers that Alan conceived to allegorize her instability. Even though the Certaldan never cites *Anticlaudianus*, he must have had it in his personal library, and he clearly consulted it again for his dialogue with Fortuna in *De casibus virorum illustrium*.[27]

While retaining Dantean resonance and hinting at Alan, the revised form, «liti lati», is ambiguous enough to have a further advantage. It swings Giovanni into line with the most venerable of visionaries. Just ahead of him had stood the younger Dante, whom Amore once visited beside a river: «ne la mia imaginazione apparve come peregrino leggeramente vestito e di vili drappi. Elli mi parea disbigottito, e guardava la terra, salvo che talora li suoi occhi mi parea che si volgessero ad uno fiume bello e corrente e chiarissimo, lo quale sen gia lungo questo cammino là ov'io era» (*Vita nuova* IX). Love's appearance to Dante recalls in turn experiences reported by Prophets of ancient days. Daniel had a vision on the banks of the Tigris: «On the twenty-fourth day of the first month, as I was standing on the bank of the great river, that is, the Tigris, I lifted up my eyes and looked, and behold, a man clothed in linen, whose loins were girded with gold of Uphaz» (Dan. 10:2-7). So, too, had revelation come to Ezekiel on river banks: «In the thirtieth year, in the fourth month, on the fifth day of the month, as I was among the exiles by the river Chebar, the heavens were opened, and I saw visions of God» (Ez. 1:1). Now, on nameless shores somewhere between the Tyrrhenean Sea and river Arno, it is Boccaccio's turn. *Mutatis mutandis*, the Italian poet's 'celestial' oracle is a classic female: «Così dormendo, sovra i lidi lati /

---

[27] See the description of Fortuna in ALAN OF LILLE, *Anticlaudianus, Patrologia Latina* 210:483-576 (col. 558 for the two rivers that mingle); trans. and comm. J. J. SHERIDAN, *Anticlaudianus, or The Good and Perfect Man*, Toronto, Pontifical Institute of Medieval Studies, 1973, VII-VIII. Two manuscripts in the inventory that includes books Boccaccio bequeathed to the Florentine convent of Santo Spirito contained the *Anticlaudianus*. See A. MAZZA, *L'inventario della 'Parva libraria', cit.*, VII 3: «Item in eodem banco settimo liber tertius, summa magistri anticlaudiani de antirufino, conpletus, copertus corio albo». The same work was part of another manuscript in the library with shelf number III 9. Cf. Boccaccio's portrait of Fortuna, half alive and half dead, in *De casibus virorum illustrium*, VI 1, which surely was inspired by the divided goddess in the Latin epic by Alan. Still standard as an overview of imagery attached to *Fortuna* is the classic study by H. R. PATCH, *The Goddess Fortune in Medieval Literature*, 1927; New York, Octagon Books, 1974.

errar mi vidi [...] / or qua or là, null'ordine tenendo; / quando donna lucente in vista e bella / m'apparve [...] / tal qual nel sidereo coro / Giunon, moveva i passi».

Fluvial settings in which Old Testament prophets had received the divine word forecast Christian baptism.[28] But baptism seems not à propos to the *Amorosa visione*, even though it is a motif recurrent in Boccaccio's early fiction (and one that had furnished the theme for his recently finished *Comedia delle ninfe*).[29] A more socialized fellow than the rustic befriended by seven Virtue-nymphs, this Dreamer shows no need of cleansing waters. He behaves not brutishly, but childishly. Impulse, not firm resolve, rules his decisions. That explains why he first sees himself in aimless errancy, hither and thither along a shoreline. His whimsical fluctuations persist throughout the poem as he flip-flops between Guide's pointers and his own caprice.

The shoreline on which he ambles is actually a moral borderline. Until Guide came along, we can suppose that he might have slipped off the deep end, back into a vortex of passions churned by Fortune. But Guide's arrival, like Virgil's in the *Comedy*, signals a turning point. She takes Dreamer in tow to teach him, and bit by bit he will listen to some of her lessons. One text that medieval readers knew as a *locus classicus* for moralized ocean waters and shores can help us work through this last step in Boccaccio's littoral logic. It is Virgil's *Aeneid*, whose first six books were supposed to convey an allegory of mankind. Aeneas was the human soul; his journey from Troy to Latium our path of life from birth to maturity. The disastrous storm at sea unleashed against him by Aeolus at Juno's instigation, action drama of Book I, naturally attracted commentators' full attention. A twelfth-century scholar traditionally identified as Bernard Silvestris, whose writings had reached Boccaccio's library, can here see resemblance between the sea and the body: «Sometimes the sea is understood as the human body because drunkenness and lustings, which we take to be waters, flow down from it, and in it are the commotions of vices, and through it foods and drink meander [...]. And thus these commotions of the sea, that is, influxions and effluxions of the

---

[28] St. Jerome explained in his commentary on Ezekiel, «To both Daniel and Ezekiel who were in Babylon next to rivers, the sacraments of the future are spread over the waters, in fact, the purest waters so that the power of baptism might be shown forth». Cited by B. NOLAN, *The Gothic Visionary Perspective*, Princeton, Princeton University Press, 1977, pp. 104-105. Nolan assembles examples from *Vita nuova* and the Old Testament of visions beside rivers.

[29] The theme is discussed by A. K. CASSELL and V. KIRKHAM in their introduction to *Diana's Hunt, cit.*, pp. 43 ff.

body, vex Aeneas and his companions, that is, the soul and its powers». Later, in Book VI, as Aeneas comes to harbor in Latium, Bernard equates the ocean now behind him (*pelagum*) with «lust of the flesh and commotions of temporal things». It is another formula for the topos of *fluctus concupiscentiae*. The hero's arrival upon preordained shores (*litora*) signifies allegorically progress in the human soul. After the stormy period of youth, a man settles down to greater stability and maturity: «leaving the sea and entering the port is leaving lust of the flesh and commotion of temporal things and the start of learning».[30] Bernard's gloss on Aeneas could well apply to Boccaccio's Dreamer. He is about to begin an education.

* * *

Enter his Guide. Even though her appearance on the scene parallels Virgil's arrival in *Inferno*, most scholars have supposed that she must symbolize something different than he does. How could such an «awkwardly disguised Virgil», this «Virgil in skirts», be a figure of Reason? But alternatives proposed have been less than persuasive. Is she Faith? the celestial Venus? the terrestrial Venus? Fortitude? the Madonna? Branca settles for a safe, if vaguer, formula: «the aspiration toward virtue in every upright soul».[31]

True enough, Boccaccio does not give us a lot of detail to go on, at least in her physical description. Both versions of the *Visione* present her as beautiful and blond, wearing a crown brighter than the sun and a gown of purple. Dignified in her gait, she holds a royal sceptre and mace. She smiles. The B form of the poem sharpens this generic image to emphasize her refulgence, replacing what had been in the earlier version «donna gentil, piacente» with «donna lucente in vista». After the change — allowance made for a gender shift — she resembles another «shining» apparition of angelic provenance on deserted shores («liti»). He was the

---

[30] *The Commentary on the First Six Books of the 'Aeneid' of Virgil Commonly Attributed to Bernardus Silvestris*, ed. J. W. JONES and E. F. JONES, Lincoln, Neb., and London, University of Nebraska Press, 1977, *Aeneid* I, pp. 10-11: «Mare corpus humanum intelligitur quia ebrietates et libidines que per aquas intelliguntur ab eo defluunt et in eo sunt commotiones vitiorum et per ipsum ciborum et potus meatus fit [...]. Itaque his commotionibus maris, id est influxionibus et effluxionibus corporis, Eneas et Socii eius, id est spiritus et eius potentie, vexantur»; VI, pp. 32-33: «PELAGO: libidini carnis et commotioni temporalium»; «LITORA: exitus a mari et ingressus in portum est exitus a libidine carnis et commotione temporalium et inchoatio studii». On the «pelago» and «flux of concupiscence» see also J. FRECCERO, *The Firm Foot on a Journey without a Guide*, in *Dante: The Poetics of Conversion, cit.*, pp. 29-54:32.

[31] V. BRANCA, *Amorosa visione, cit.*, 1974, Intro., p. 16.

Angel of God who ferried souls in a skiff to Purgatory. Dante had to avert his glance from such overwhelming brightness. So, conversely, Boccaccio stares straight at his heavenly messenger, «fiso pareami di rimirar questa». In spite of reversals, though, there lingers enough likeness to reinforce the idea of escape from dangerous waters, safe arrival on shore, and morally uplifting things to come. A further and more striking modification in B merges the hints of Guide's angelic origins with a simile from the mythographer's stock that likens her to «Juno stepping» among the stars.[32] Boccaccio's comparison, which in contrast to Dante paganizes the letter of the text, stresses her queenliness. Not just any female monarch, she is the highest one, a ruler who presides from heaven over the very peak of Olympus.

Beyond immediate visual impressions, we can deduce more about what she is from her interaction with Dreamer and the other characters. Like Juno, this queen must contend with rival forces and does not always succeed in getting her way. Dreamer himself resists her. Two young men, red and white, pull him away from her. On the other hand, Maria Aquinas is her ally and her «sister». Moreover, she is of stronger stuff than the rest of the vision, evanescent sights that vanish with the dawn. After the enticing castle has been left behind among phantasms of darkness, after its garden with fountain and fair damsels have all dissolved in morning light, after Dreamer breaks out of his 'sleep', the Guide alone remains, close by him in broad day. This woman, whose purpose is to set him on the right path, must after all symbolize Reason. The female noun, whether *Ratio* or *Ragione*, invites a female personification, and in this Boccaccio follows a long line of Neoplatonists from Martianus Capella to Alan of Lille, making a more conventional choice than Dante had.[33] Compared by him to a heavenly queen, she is the authority who should rule «as mistress and *maestra* of our life» from the «supreme seat of our soul». She mimics Virgil as guide and has in

---

[32] Cf. *Amorosa visione, cit.*, A, I 26-44: «donna gentil, piacente e bella, / m'apparve [...] bionda testa, / ornata di corona più che 'l sole / fulgida [...] e mi parea / il suo vestire in color di viole. / Ridente era in aspetto e 'n man tenea / reale scettro, ed un bel pomo d'oro / la sua sinistra vidi sostenea. / Sopra 'l piè grave, non sanza dimoro, moveva i passi»; B: «donna lucente in vista e bella [...] bionda testa / ornata di corona e più che 'l sole / splendida e vaga, ed oltre mi parea / il bel vestir suo tinto di viole. / Ridente in vista, nella destra avea / un real scettro ed un bel pomo d'oro / chiuso nella sinestra sostenea. / Sovra il piè, tal qual nel sidereo coro / Giunon, moveva i passi».
[33] J. FERRANTE discusses the influence of grammatical gender on personification gender in *Woman as Image in Medieval Literature*, New York, Columbia University Press, 1975.

Giovanni a charge like Dante, who will not turn up the direct, steep path. Giovanni, too, will require another, longer route.[34]

It takes him through a wide gate, leftward. Left, the 'sinister side', leads to evil. Everyone knows as much — everyone except Dreamer, that is, and a naive ancestor of his named Amant, who had turned left searching for a shortcut to his red rose in Jean de Meun's romance.[35] In the same direction, but for educational purposes, Virgil and Dante had spiralled down to the Ninth Circle; then much ahead in his journey and far above the yawning Pit, Dante will again exploit such directional language. It comes into play unexpectedly, in the heaven of the Sun, when the pilgrim hears St. Bonaventure refer to his work on earth as General of the Franciscan Order. How did he divide his time between worldly and spiritual activity? He «always postponed the left»: «Io son la vita di Bonaventura / da Bagnoregio, che ne' grandi offici / sempre pospuosi la sinistra cura» (*Paradiso* XII 127-129). Administrative responsibility did not prevent Bonaventure from keeping his priorities 'right', that is, from giving precedence to the contemplative side.

«Postponing the left» was certainly the wiser course, as Bonaventure's heaven-mate Thomas Aquinas could corroborate in an allegoresis of Hebrew religious practice. According to Thomas, the part of the Israelite Tabernacle furnished with an altar, table, and candlestick, denotes «this present world». Its candlestick was fittingly placed on the southern side «because the south is the right-hand side of the world, while the north is the left-hand side, as stated in *De coelo et Mundo* ii.; and wisdom, like other spiritual goods, belongs to the right hand, while temporal nourishment belongs to the left, according to Prov. iii. 16: *In her left hand (are) riches and glory*».[36] Boccaccio's Dreamer does exactly the opposite of the

---

[34] Boccaccio's rationale for introducing the comparison between Guide and Juno in the second version of the *Visione*, which I suggest functions in consonance with the idea of Reason as a personified female who should rule our soul, may have been prompted by another association. The Commentary attributed to Bernard Silvestris explains Juno's part in the storm at sea of *Aeneid* I as an allegorical function of her power over childbirth. In other words, she is part of the textual cluster in the *Aeneid* associated with *fluctus concupiscentiae*, since it was she who set Aeolus against the Trojan fleet.

[35] *The Romance of the Rose*, trans. C. DAHLBERG, Princeton, Princeton University Press, 1972, v. 10029: «After my departure then, I made my way to the left, avoiding the right hand, to seek the shortest road». Further examples of the ancient left-right dichotomy, from the Bible and its exegetes, are cited by V. F. HOPPER, *Medieval Number Symbolism, cit.*, p. 169.

[36] C. S. SINGLETON cites Thomas in his commentary on *Paradiso* XII, *The Divine Comedy*, VI, pt. II, Princeton, Princeton University Press, 1975 («Bollingen Series», LXXX). Cf. T. AQUINAS, *Summa theologica, cit.*, I-II, Qu. 102, Art. 4 ad 6: «Convenienter autem candelabrum ponebatur ex parte australi, mensa autem ex parte aquilonari, quia australis pars est dextera pars mundi, aquilonaris autem sinistra, ut dicitur in II *De Caelo*; sapientia autem pertinet ad dextram, sicut et cetera spiritualia bona; temporale autem nutrimentum ad sinistram».

great Franciscan theologian: he postpones the right. He reminds us of Augustine, who prayed to the Lord for chastity and continence — «but not yet».[37] Time enough for virtue later, Giovanni keeps saying. From the beginning, he wants the wide gate. As if to second his wishes, a pair of young men step forward: «ecco fuore / della gran porta duo giovani uscire, / l'un rosso e l'altro bianco in suo colore» (III 49-51). These red and white characters coax him. Why not have some fun now? You can always make the harder choice just before you die:

> Vien dietro a noi, se vuoli il tuo disire.
>   Solazzo e festa, come molti fanno,
> qua non ti falla, e poscia salir suso
> ancor potrai nell'ultimo tuo anno. (III 54-57)

Guide, who wants to hurry him away from these hustlers, tries to pull him in the right direction. They yank from the other side — the left, of course. In spite of her warning, it is two against one:

> [...] "Lascia costor, andiam su noi".
>   E per la destra man preso m'aveva,
> seco tirando me suso; ma l'uno
> la mia sinestra e l'altro ancor teneva,
>   ridendosene insieme, e ciascheduno
> tirandomi diceva, "Vienne, vienne". (III 63-68)

Later, inside the garden, he refuses to go with Reason along a rivulet that cuts eastward, the direction of Eden. Desire impels him to follow the southerly garden stream that symbolizes sensual love:

> [...] Donna mia, da mia salute
> non pensar più mi stoglia, a tempo e a loco
> cercarò d'operar la tua virtute;
>   ch'ora di nuovo m'è nel cor un foco. (XL 7-10)

If Guide is Reason, then the red and white juveniles must symbolize some kind of Unreason. Jon Boshart was the first to suggest that they

---

[37] St. Augustine, *Confessions*, trans. W. Watts, Cambridge, Mass., Harvard University Press, 1968-1970 («Loeb Classical Library»), VIII 7: «da mihi castitatem et continentiam, sed noli modo». The conflict that Boccaccio dramatizes in the *Amorosa visione* between worldly desires and concern for salvation also recalls Petrarch's *Secretum*. Franciscus and Dreamer have much in common, as do Augustinus and Guide.

signify in allegory the sensitive appetites, an identification also proposed by Janet Smarr. His insight, which dovetails well with what we know more broadly about Boccaccio's debt to Aristotle and the Scholastics,[38] accommodates letter and spirit in the *Amorosa visione*. Red must designate the irascible appetite, for as Boccaccio had explained in the *Teseida*, the passion of anger causes men to wax crimson. White fits the concupiscible appetite, especially as it exerts itself in lovers, who according to Andreas Capellanus lose their appetites, suffer insomnia, and regularly turn pale. The fellows are young because it is in youth that our passions are most turbulent, as Boccaccio explains, commenting on Dante's mental sleep: «dalla nostra puerizia, noi il più diriziamo i piedi, cioè le nostre affezioni, in questi lacci [carne, mondo, demonio], e, quasi non accorgendocene, per ciò che più i sensi che la ragione abbiamo allora per guida, sì c'inveschiamo».[39]

Colored by emotion and still playfully boyish, Red Fellow and White Fellow define themselves most distinctively in their duality. Like twins,

---

[38] J. D. Boshart, *Giovanni Boccaccio's 'Amorosa Visione'*, *cit.*, pp. 184-185. For Boshart, p. 186, the guide was the celestial Venus. J. L. Smarr (who seems not to have been familiar with Boshart's dissertation), found a more persuasive identification of her as Reason, who works to correct the appetites symbolized by the two youths. See her *Boccaccio and Fiammetta. The Narrator as Lover*, Urbana, University of Illinois, 1986, pp. 103-109. Crescini also identified her as Reason: *Due studi riguardanti opere minori del Boccaccio*, *cit.*, p. 59. A systematic study of Aristotle's presence in Boccaccio is still awaited. A. Hortis, *Studij sulle opere latine del Boccaccio*, Trieste, Libreria Julius Dase, 1879, pp. 379-380, sketched some of the poet's Aristotelian connections. For example, as he identifies the shades in Dante's Limbo, Boccaccio's biography of «the master of those who know» appropriately includes a list of the philosopher's writings: on dialectic, on rhetoric, on moral philosophy in three volumes (*Etica, Politica, Iconomica*), on natural science, and on metaphysics (*Esposizioni* IV 1, 250-251). Later in the commentary, Aristotle's *Ethics* serves Boccaccio, as it had Dante, for defining various vices and virtues — magnanimity, avarice, temerity, accidia, docility, ire, and disdain. Although explicit references to Aristotle are few and appear only in the late works, paleographic as well as literary evidence makes it clear that Boccaccio had to know the *Ethics* with the commentary by Thomas Aquinas at least as early as the 1340's. G. Padoan, *Esposizioni*, *cit.*, IV 1 and n. 322, p. 839, says that of Aristotle Boccaccio knew above all the *Ethics* with the commentary by Aquinas, which he personally transcribed into an older manuscript (Biblioteca Ambrosiana, Cod. Ambr. A 204 inf.); also the treatises on meteors, politics, and the soul.

[39] *Esposizioni*, *cit.*, I 2, 37. Boshart paired the irascible appetite with white and the concupiscent appetite with red, but without explaining why. While accepting his identification of the two men and the sensitive appetites, I prefer to reverse the color symbolism. Among the allegorical personifications in the House of Mars are 'Ires', which the Glossator explains, «dice [l'autore] l'Ire, in numero plurale, a dimostrare che due maniere d'ira sono, e ciascuna fa arrossare l'adirato» (*Teseida*, *cit.*, VII 30, gloss, p. 455). See the fifteenth Rule of Love in the treatise by Andreas Capellanus, *Andreas Capellanus on Love*, ed. and trans. P.G. Walsh, London, Duckworth, 1982: «Omnis consuevit amans in coamantis aspectu pallescere»; *The Art of Courtly Love*, trans. J. J. Parry, 1941; New York, Frederick Ungar, 1970, p. 185: «Every lover regularly turns pale in the presence of his beloved». Cf. Filocolo's vision of the theological virtues personified, among whom Charity appears to him red both of dress and face (!), *Filocolo*, *cit.*, IV 74, 1: «vedea l'una tanto vermiglia e nel viso e ne' vestimenti quanto se tutta ardesse».

they form an inseparable couple, always pitted against the Guide. Boccaccio early establishes her antagonism toward them, that turning point before the two gates when Reason and Appetites tug Dreamer right and left. What happens next choreographs the confused state of his soul:

> Seguendo me la donna com'io lei
> pria seguitava, co' duo giovinetti
> a man sinestra volsi i passi miei.
> Intra lor duo avean noi due ristretti. (IV 1-4)

For a little while he had followed Reason, from shoreline to fortress wall. But now that order is reversed. The rightful ruler of his mind has been demoted to second place. Following, not leading, she has lost her power. Appetites propel in their grip both the Dreamer and his guiding light. All four head straight into a four-cornered chamber bright with worldly things. She will briefly make a comeback to show him Fortune's workings, but Dreamer, unphased, once again sides with the seductive red and white boys. Exiting the castle, he makes another left turn at their instigation and leaves Reason altogether behind. Why not? they urge. «Che, non passi / dentro, poiché ardi di vedere?» (XXXVII 74-75).

Dreamer, whose intellect sleeps, 'burns' with desire spurred by his concupiscible appetite. Over and again, as he persists in wrong choices, Queen Reason accuses and admonishes him: «tu se' di coloro / ch'alle mondane cose hanno 'l *disire*?» (XXXI 65-66); «troppo ti volge ogni cosa al *disire* [...] vi è dentro mondana vania» (XXXVII 81-84); «ed io ti lascerò col tuo *disire*» (XXXVIII 12); «ben conosco qual *disio* ti tene» (XLVII 51). Dreamer himself readily admits to being driven by desire: «parve che 'l *disire* mi tirasse» (XXXIX 22); «io mirando / con l'occhio andava pur ove 'l *disio* / mi tenea fitto» (XL 2-3; italics mine). Boccaccio's iterative vocabulary is not an impoverished poetry. The repetitions are deliberate and the lexicon is precise, referring to Dreamer's will. His volitional faculty follows appetite, not reason.

When our will follows the appetites, not reason, those lower faculties in the human soul draw us to worldly things. That is, we desire satisfaction from transient, illusory well-being as opposed to happiness in supernal values. Thus Boccaccio explains Dante's somnambulism in the shadowy forest as a sleep of «temporal concupiscences» (*Esposizioni* I 2, 33). Giovanni sleepwalks, we might say, through a leftside gate, 'sinister' being the 'temporal side', as we know from Aquinas and Bonaventure. The 'world' and the 'flesh' couple by association for Virgil's twelfth-century commentator, who had called the high seas (*pelagum*) «carnal libido and worldly stirrings», landing on shores (*litora*) «leaving those things and the beginning of learning».

Connections between runaway appetites in the soul and desire for temporal goods, which had early been discussed by the Fathers, crystallize in the Scholastic thinkers of the high Middle Ages. One authority who had inherited the terminology was the twelfth-century mythographer known to Boccaccio as Albericus. Following Augustine, he compares Adam and Eve with the higher and lower parts of the human soul.

There are two powers of the soul, one higher, the other lower. The higher power of the soul adheres to celestial and incorruptible things, and desires them, and it is called rational, spirit, mistress [*domina*]), mind, *animus*. The lower is the one that consents to the cravings of the body, and it is called sensuality, animality, servant, *mens*. And it is the nature of the higher to rule the lower. But sometimes, due to negligence of the higher, the lower prevails and seduces the higher. These also figure Adam and Eve. For if Adam the higher had ruled himself with reason, Eve the lower would not have seduced him.[40]

The same psychological terms enter Augustine's scrutiny of our first parents' sin in his treatise *On the Trinity*. For Augustine, the serpent's approach to Eve, her listening, then feeding the fruit to Adam are a chain of events in which we can discern allegorically movements inside the soul that lead to a choice of false over true good. This is so because the «visible marriage» of Adam and Eve in the Garden of Eden corresponds to a «hidden and secret marriage» of the parts of our soul, itself «an excellent paradise». Champions of the Catholic faith before him, Augustine recalls, spoke of «man as the mind, but the woman as the sense of the body». This pairing describes ideally a certain «rational marriage» between contemplation and action in our lives. Action is ruled by reason of the body, which is called 'science' (*scientia*) and perceives whatever is worldly and corporal. Contemplation is ruled by the reason of wisdom (*sapientia*), which has as its object eternal, unchangeable, spiritual things. We could not survive, either as individuals or as a race, without attending

---

[40] *Scriptores rerum mythicarum*, ed. G. H. Bode, *cit.*, III 6, 16: «Animae autem duae sunt vires, una superior, altera inferior. Animae superior vis caelestibus adhaeret et incorruptibilis, et illa concupiscit, vocaturque rationalitas, spiritus, domina, mens, animus. Inferior est, quae voluptatibus corporis consentit, vocaturque sensualitas, animalitas, famula, mens. Estque superioris, ut inferiorem regat. Sed aliquando ex neglegentia superioris praevalet inferior, et seducit superiorem. Est etiam in hac figura Adam et Eva. Si enim Adam superior se ratione rexisset, non illum Eva inferior seduxisset». Boccaccio cites 'Albericus' repeatedly in the *Genealogia*.

in some measure to corporal, temporal things. Thus to 'science' belongs «the reasonable cognition of temporal and changeable things that is necessary for managing the affairs of this life». But 'science' should apply its knowledge to the end of our highest good, meaning that it should quickly lead us beyond temporal to eternal things. Ultimately, we should prefer the reason of the mind, 'wisdom', to which belongs the intellectual cognition of eternal things. 'Science' badly used leads to rejoicing in temporal goods. If the senses induce the mind to rest in false happiness, it upsets the male-female order of our soul. We sin. In the allegory of the Fall, when that happens it means that the serpent addresses the woman in us. If the sin is complete, she has given to her husband of the fruit.[41]

Boccaccio's Dreamer reflects a soul in such disorder. Sensual appetites have persuaded him to rest in false happiness, to linger rejoicing in temporal goods and not speed on to contemplation of things divine. This the Guide tries to tell him, but without persuading him. No sooner does he see that wide gate than he wants in, and she counters: «il corto termine alla vita posto / non è da consumare 'n quelle cose / che 'l bene etterno vi fanno nascosto» (II 55-57); Dreamer insists, «andiamo e vediam questi ben fallaci» (III 38), and she rebuts that what he wants bars the right way: «tu ti abbagli / nel falso imaginar e credi a questi / ch'a ritta via son pessimi serragli» (III 76-78). She loses this round, for within moments Red Fellow and White Fellow are escorting Dreamer and Reason through the gate that gives power, rank, riches, fame, and love. Why is it that sometimes Dreamer listens to her, sometimes not?

We better appreciate his recalcitrance if we recall a bit of Thomism. For Aristotle and Aquinas, our intellectual soul is our substantial form as human beings. Happiness resides in the operation of the faculty that defines us as a species and distinguishes us from the beasts. The intellective soul has primacy over the sensitive powers of irascibility and concupiscence, since those we have in common with the animals. It is the proper role of the sensitive faculties to obey the intellective.[42] Yet rational thought is not absolute in its power. A metaphor borrowed from the language of government explains the limitations of reason's authority. As Aristotle had said, the soul rules the body with a despotic rule, but

---

[41] ST. AUGUSTINE, *On the Trinity*, trans. S. MCKENNA, C.S.S.R., Washington, D.C., Catholic University Press, 1963, XII, pp. 355-367. Boccaccio may not have known this seminal treatise in its entirety, but he certainly was familiar with the concepts it spawned in their theological tradition, especially as discussed by Scholastics like Peter Lombard and Thomas Aquinas.

[42] *Summa theologica, cit.*, I, Qu. 76, Art 1.

reason rules the appetites with a political rule. That is, as hierarchies go, body is perforce subject to soul. Between reason and appetites, however, the relationship is looser. The appetites have some autonomy; they can resist and rebel against reason. Or put another way, in terms Thomas quotes from Augustine, «sometimes the intellect marks the way, while desire lags or follows not at all». Dante was experiencing just that problem in the prologue scene of the *Comedy* as he tried to ascend the hill, his «left foot always lower». His right, intellectual foot led off in the correct direction, but the left leg dragged behind, a handicap indicative of disparity between strength in his intellect and will. He was allegorically *homo claudus*, 'limping man'.[43] Again, as Thomas writes in his *Commentary on the Nicomachean Ethics*, the sensitive appetite «desires what is pleasant to the sense and at times opposes what reason judges absolutely good [...]. This appetite in the continent man is restrained by reason, for he certainly has evil desires, but his reason does not follow them. On the other hand, the appetite of the incontinent man overcomes reason, which is seduced by evil desires».[44]

Aquinas sharpens his argument by antithesis when, in his *Summa contra Gentiles*, he devotes a series of chapters to those worldly goods in which human felicity does *not* consist. It consists not in pleasures of the flesh, which obstruct man's approach to God since sensual pleasure interferes with contemplation. It lies not in honors because they depend on external approval rather than our own operation. It coincides not with glory, that is, «a widely recognized reputation», because glory is sought for the sake of honor, something other than the final end, and it is less noble to be known than to have knowledge. It resides not in riches, which we desire for the sake of something else, whereas the highest good is desired for its own sake. It consists not in worldly power, since that is unstable and often depends on fortune. Thomas concludes that these all — carnal delight, high rank, fame, wealth, power are «exterior goods»

---

[43] *Summa theologica, cit.*, I-II, Qu. 58, Art 2: «interdum praecedit intellectus, et sequitur tardus aut nullus affectus». J. FRECCERO, *The Firm Foot on a Journey without a Guide, cit.*, reconstructs the tradition from antiquity through the Middle Ages that linked the right side of the body with the intellect, the left with the will.

[44] T. AQUINAS, *Commentary on the Nicomachean Ethics*, trans. C. I. LITZINGER, O.P., Chicago, Regnery, 1964, I 20 (237); S. Thomae Aquinatis, *In X. libros ethicorum ad Nicomachum*, Parma, Typis Petri Fiaccadori, 1866, p. 43: «Et hoc est appetitus sensitivus, qui appetit id quod est delectabile sensui, quod interdum contrariatur ei, quod ratio judicat esse simpliciter bonum. Hoc autem in eo qui est continens vincitur a ratione, nam continens habet quidem concupiscentias pravas, sed ratio eas non sequitur. In incontinente autem vincit rationem, quae deducitur a concupiscentiis pravis».

under the sway of fortune: «Man's felicity, then, consists in no exterior good, since all exterior goods [...] are called "goods of fortune"».[45]

Reason knows whereof she speaks when she calls the things inside the wide gate «pessimi serragli», or «the worst obstacles», to true well-being. Those temporal goods block progress toward the steep and narrow way. Fortuna's chamber of horrors will furnish another vivid setting for Dreamer and Guide to converse in language tinged by Scholastic philosophy. Reason reasserts herself, leads her charge into the second room, and she points to the grim spectacle: «Già veder puoi che i mortai poco sanno, / se per aver delle cose mondane / consumansi con non fruttuoso affanno» (XXXIII 58-60). A little later Dreamer acknowledges that she speaks true, for now he has surveyed Fortuna's workings not with «desire», the faculty that had ruled his perceptions in the first painted room, but with his «intellect»: «già pieno / di tal materia aveva *l'intelletto*» (XXXVII 19-20). He assures his Guide that he is ready for the narrow gate since his will is now amenable to her lessons: «Il mio *voler*, che fu ritroso, / ora è tornato fermo, e già non dotto / che questi ben terren son veramente / quei ch'a' vizi ciascun mettono sotto» (XXXVII 30-33; italics mine). The faculty of will for the moment heeds Reason, she who has shown him how volatile and empty are worldly things.

Fortuna's sway over the sensual, worldly realm will again be a central theme in the *Decameron*, where as Branca has noted, Panfilo speaks with language close to that of the Guide in the *Amorosa visione*. Like her, I believe, he is a spokesman in allegory for the rational faculty.[46] Blind Luck, whom Boccaccio depicts in traditional imagery from Boethius, Alan of Lille, and Arrigo da Settimello, forms a leitmotif throughout his writings from as early as the *Filostrato* to his late *De casibus virorum illustrium*. The *Amorosa visione*, an experiment in philosophical poetry, assigns Fortuna a place in the Scholastic scheme of things. Installed between the first castle chamber and the garden of delights, she holds a central ground in the vision that describes a Dreamer strongly and stubbornly inclined toward his appetites. She is the goddess of worldly delights and ambitions, those appetitive desires from which Reason

---

[45] T. AQUINAS, *Summa contra Gentiles*, ed. Fratres Predicatores, Romae, Typis Riccardi Garroni, 1926 («*Opera omnia*», XIV), trans. A. C. PEGIS, F.R.S.C., Notre Dame, University of Notre Dame Press, 1975, III, ch. 27-31, and esp. the end of ch. 31: «Concludit ex supra dictis Sanctus Thomas universaliter quod *in nullo bono exteriori consistit felicitas hominis*: com omnia talia bona sub praedictis [potentiis mundanis] contineantur».
[46] Cf. *Decameron, cit.*, II 7, 3-6 and Comm., p. 1097. Branca notes points of contact between Panfilo's words and *Amorosa visione* XXXIII, XXXVII.

dissuades us with her cautionary voice. If many of the same famous persons who populate the four Triumphs in Room I return in Room II, it is not because Boccaccio ran out of exemplary characters. Rather he shows them to us from two points of view. Dreamer's guides for Room I had been the Red and White Fellows — his lower appetites — so naturally he was impressed by the great followings of Glory, Wisdom, Riches, Love. In Room II, he views the same human spectacle, but this time from Reason's perspective, more penetrating.

Boccaccio's visionary castle demonstrates a Scholastic commonplace. Dante touches on it in *Convivio* IV with succinct formulations that shed light on Boccaccio's intentions. Whoever judges according to sensual appearances rather than rational truth, he asserts, sees only those things that Fortune gives and takes: «costoro che così giudicano, non giudicano se non per quello che sentono di queste cose che la fortuna può dare e torre». Conversely, the more a person is subject to intellect, the less he is subject to Fortune: «quanto l'uomo più subiace a lo 'ntelletto, tanto meno subiace a la fortuna» (IV 11, 9)

We whom modern times have distanced from a mentality with 'contempt for the world' may find it difficult to reject goals like knowledge, fame, wealth, and romance. Knowledge especially is something we have trouble understanding as a 'false good'. First among the Triumphs that Dreamer studies, it is personified as a woman holding a book with seven ladies-in-waiting, symbols of the seven Liberal Arts. How can learning be bad? It can be relatively a *lesser* thing if, according to Augustine's distinction, it is *scientia* instead of *sapientia*. Peter Lombard, one of the great twelfth-century masters at the University of Paris, refers to this dichotomy in his *Book of Sentences*. Under the heading *On Sensuality* he declares:

Now sensuality is a certain lower power of the soul, whose movement is directed toward the senses of the body and appetites of things pertaining to the body. Reason on the other hand is the higher power of the soul, which so to speak has two different parts, one higher and one lower. Through the higher, it directs itself to those higher things that we should desire or reflect upon; through the lower, it regards the disposition toward temporal things [...]. And that application of reason through which we contemplate eternal things is called wisdom [*sapientia*], but that through which we use well temporal things is called science [*scientia*].[47]

---

[47] Peter Lombard, *Liber sententie*, II, Dist. 24.6, *Patrologia Latina* 192:687: «Est enim sensualitas quaedam vis animae inferior, ex qua est motus qui intenditur in corporis sensus,

The lady who appears in Canto IV ruling the first wall in the quadrangular room, must then be 'Science'. Her most prominent follower, the man foremost in Boccaccio's census of thinkers, is Aristotle. Not far behind him sit Socrates and Plato, members of a philosophical family that descend in poetry from souls on the greensward in Dante's Limbo at *Inferno* IV. One of Boccaccio's many retouches to the second version of the *Amorosa visione* bears on this passage. Thomas Aquinas, whom the poet had praised in version A as «ampio fiume di *scienza*», graduates to a more elevated Christian rank and outstrips the ancient philosophers in B, where he merits the epithet, «ampio fiume di *sapienzia*» (XLIII 50).

So far we have seen Dreamer progress from a dangerous oceanside to safer *terra firma*. Still, the tug-of-war between his reason and appetites goes on even after Guide's graphic display of Fortuna's deceptions. Just afterward, Red Fellow and White Fellow entice him into a garden, where for a time he abandons his Reason altogether. Will he ever get straight? Boccaccio leaves room for a hopeful outlook. For one thing, Dreamer does awaken, a positive sign in allegories of sleep. Since this wakeup comes an instant before he reaches sexual climax, some readers have criticized Boccaccio for cutting short the dream at the best part.[48] But the episode is not simply erotic realism. From the letter of the text, which «always must come before», as Dante had dictated, we have to think beyond to allegory. Respecting the poet's moral intention, we realize that Giovanni's *coitus interruptus* signals recovery on a spiritual level.

* * *

Crucial to the turnabout is Madama Maria, Reason's close relative. What Reason alone cannot accomplish, the two ladies together will. The poem ends as Giovanni anticipates returning to his dreamland, but this time, in place of the red and white men, his guides will be two others, Reason and her allegorical «sister». With them he will enter the strait

---

atque appetitus rerum ad corpus pertinentium. Ratio vero vis animae est superior, quae, ut ita dicamus, duas habet partes vel differentias, superiorem et inferiorem. Secundum superiorem supernis concupiscendis vel consulendis intendit; secundum inferiorem, ad temporalium dispositionem conspicit [...]. Et illa rationis intentio qua contemplamur aeterna, sapientiae deputatur; illa vero qua bene utimur rebus temporalibus scientiae deputatur». Cf. D. W. ROBERTSON, Jr., *A Preface to Chaucer. Studies in Medieval Perspectives*, Princeton, Princeton University Press, 1962, pp. 74-75, for an analysis of these parallel passages in Augustine's *Trinity* and Peter's *Sentences*.

[48] C. MUSCETTA, *Giovanni Boccaccio e i novellieri*, cit., p. 351, criticizes the *Amorosa visione* because it ends just where the fun part should begin.

gate. Since traditional readings of the *Amorosa visione* treated Maria in an autobiographical key, she did not seem to 'mean' as an emblematic icon except vaguely, being a stilnovistic lady perfecting in her perfection. Yet she, as much as the Guide, enjoys a precise symbolic status, revealed in three stages as the poem progresses.

Three times Dreamer will see his Maria, first at a distance and only in a painted picture, side by side with the god of Love. His «donna gentile», crowned with roses, resembles an angel from heaven and Cyprian Venus. A ray emanates from her face, shining across the meadow. Young in years, she displays mature wisdom: «Oh quanto nell'aspetto, in detti e fatti, / mostrava in saggio ed alto intendimento / vecchi pensier da giovinil cuor tratti!» (XV 76-78). Love strikes his heart, yet he cannot learn her name, which he promises to tell us later.

The second time, he sees her closer and in person, at leisure in a garden among nineteen high born ladies, each 'named' in a heraldic riddle. Her name, too, he discloses obliquely:

> E come seppi, ella era della gente
> del Campagner che lo Spagnuol seguio
> con la cappa, col dire e con la mente,
>   a sé facccendo sì benigno Iddio,
> che d'ampio fiume di sappienzia degno
> si fece, come chiar poi si sentio,
>   faccendo aperte col suo chiaro ingegno
> le scritture nascoste, e quinci appresso
> da Carlo pinto gì nel divin regno;
>   faccendo sé da quella, in cui già empresso
> stette Colui che la nostra natura
> nobilitò, nomar, che poi l'eccesso
>   absterse della prima creatura
> con la sua pena. (XLIII 46-59)

An intense wish to enter his lady's circle of radiance finds sudden fulfilment, and Dreamer basks in her light «4 x 6 days»: «quattro via sei volte il sole / con l'orizzonte il ciel congiunto avea» (XLIV 62-63). She carves her name in golden letters on his heart, places a ring on his little finger, and chains it into her breast, leading him captive wherever she pleases: «Moveami questa ove pareva a lei» (XLV 28). Amore favors their relationship, «sol che 'l disio non fosse oltre misura» (XLV 47). He continues long following her, for a time enigmatically calculated as «5 x 3 x 9 days»: «Cinque fiate tre via nove giorni / sotto la dolce signoria di questa / trovato m'era» (XLVI 16-18). He begs her to end his pain, and with her consent — or so it seems — he sheds his robe deep in the orchard. They kiss and kiss. Then all at once, as if she had suddenly become aware of their vulnerability in that bosky nook, she sends him off to fetch and follow his Guide, whose job description is the same as Virgil's in Dante: «e lei seguisci però ch'ella è quella / che 'n dritta via ripone chi va errando» (XLVI 71-72). Guide welcomes Dreamer with a motherly embrace and remonstrance:

> [...] "Non cre' tu che io ti guidi
>   in qual parte vorrai? perché perverte
> tua volontate il mio consiglio vero,
> per vanità lasciando cose certe"?
>   Allor risposi: "Madonna, sincero
> m'è il tuo mostrar tornato di colei
> grazia che m'ha disposto a tal sentiero".[49] (XLVII 33-39)

Dubious when he tells her about his lady, Guide supposes that he, as usual, still pursues only desire, but he protests to a «rational» love:

> La qual s'io per terrestre e furiosa
> voglia fruire amassi, in veritate
> con dover ne saresti crucciosa;
>   anzi con quella vera integritate
> ch'ogni razionale amar si dee,
> amo ed onoro la sua gran biltate;
>   la qual, sì come manifesto v'ee,
> non trova par né 'n senno né 'n bellezza,
> per cui ergo la mente all'alte idee. (XLVII 68-70)

At the close of this little colloquium, Dreamer comes to his Lady for a third time, now accompanied by his Guide. To our surprise, when Guide sees for herself whom he loves, she affectionately owns Maria as a dear sister: «Dolce, cara, e benigna mia sorella» (XLVIII 7-8). Restored to authority, Guide puts Dreamer's right hand into his beloved's and pledges them to one another, as if in marriage.

---

[49] At this point, the translation of R. HOLLANDER et al., cit., misses the point, when it gives: «My lady, I sincerely / show myself returned to you / thanks to the favor of her [...]». It implies that Dreamer is now sincerely penitent, and although that is certainly the gist, the Italian indicates more specifically that he now recognizes the truth of her message. The subject is 'mostrar', the indirect object is 'me'.

What is all of this supposed to mean? Boccaccio plants clues in the onomastic riddle that 'labels' his Lady in her second, and central epiphany. First comes her family name, shared with «the man from Campania who followed the Spaniard in wearing the cape», that is, Thomas Aquinas. Born in the region of Campania, he became a brother in the Preaching Order founded by the Spaniard Dominic, earned fame as a learned exegete («ampio fiume di sappienzia»), and was murdered according to legend by King Charles of Anjou. Her given name comes from «the woman in whom He who ennobled our nature was compressed», that is, from Maria, who carried in her womb the world's Redeemer. Since Boccaccio respects the medieval axiom that makes names the consequence of things, Maria Aquinas must symbolize a composite power. As Maria, she is pure and wise, a woman redemptive. This Christian name of hers we already know, since Boccaccio carries it over from his *Filocolo*, the romance where she had originally stepped into her character as his poetic mistress, alias Fiammetta. New to the *Amorosa visione* is her cognomen, Aquinas. As an Aquinas, she must have something to do with philosophy, the intellectual love of wisdom.

Wisdom, in fact, is an attribute of Maria Aquinas that Boccaccio stresses in both versions of the *Visione*. The simple «savia parea» of the A text unfolds to a more elaborate rhetorical formula in B, which contrasts her young beauty with her «old thoughts». That paradox, physical youth infused with mental maturity, is a topos Boccaccio knew from classics both pagan and Christian. One more proximate, high medieval source would have been Alan of Lille, whose *Anticlaudianus* endows Nature's new being as an idealized *puer-senex*. When Youth's turn comes to bestow her gifts on Noys, she does not behave youthfully but as if she were an «aged man», to show how wise she is. Naturally, the freshly minted soul Noys must also receive the character of a man advanced in years, and such maturity is a gift of Reason.[50] As *puella-senex*, Maria Aquinas makes a wise mistress and brooks no disobedience. In her relationship with Giovanni, it is she who gives the orders, ascendency stamped verbatim on his heart and symbolized by the leash on which she walks him. Gothic, courtly conceits at surface, these signs of his subjection wholly to her have a source in Solomon's Proverbs, as Janet Smarr has shown. There Wisdom exhorts: «keep my commandments and live [...]. Bind them

---

[50] *Anticlaudianus*, trans. Sheridan *cit.*, VII and Intro., pp. 30-31, has examples of the topos of the *puer-senex* in Virgil, Ovid, Statius, Apuleius, Claudian, and Gregory the Great. E. R. CURTIUS covers the *puer-senex* in more detail in *European Literature and the Latin Middle Ages, cit.*, pp. 98-101.

upon thy fingers; write them upon the tablet of thy heart. Say unto wisdom, Thou art my sister».[51]

The recognition scene between Guide and her «sister», Maria Aquinas, carries out King Solomon's advice, staged as if in a mystery play: «Say unto wisdom, Thou art my sister». Knowing that Solomon had established Wisdom in her sisterly role, a medieval philosopher-poet could suggest to Boccaccio her kinship with Reason and the two women's potential as personifications for chatting in a dialogue. He was Alan of Lille, in whose *Anticlaudianus* Boccaccio found a whole stockroom of Neoplatonic ideas and images, among them a marvelous picture of Fortuna and the 'young-old' rhetoric that he transfers to his Maria. In Book I of the Latin epic, when Reason takes the floor before the gods assembled in council to discuss how Nature can best achieve a perfect human, Alan stresses Reason's family resemblance to Prudence, who has just argued the need for a soul from God. Their faces, so alike that they seem to mirror each other, have similarities like those between two sisters. Soon after, as the debate continues, Reason defers to Prudence as her «blood sister» and recommends that this «sister» of hers be charged with the journey to God.[52] Alan's epic sisters are models for Guide and Maria in Boccaccio's *Amorosa visione*; both Alan and Boccaccio hark back to God's oldest daughter, Wisdom, portrayed in Solomonic scripture. By nomenclature medieval style, Maria Aquinas has as her consequence 'redeeming prudence'. Paradoxically, Giovanni becomes her vassal because he has freed himself. No longer enthralled by his lower appetites, he gives his allegiance to wisdom, a habit of the higher, rational intellect.

Giovanni, then, does not present as hopeless a case as it may once have seemed, for his vision traces a course that brings him in the end 'to Prudence'. He reaches her by stages, a Neoplatonic three-step ascent from sensory perception to intellectual understanding.[53] First, his view clouded by appetitive interference, Dreamer beholds her in the four-cornered room of the physical world, only a colored image, her god an

---

[51] J. L. SMARR, *Boccaccio and Fiammetta*, cit., p. 124, identifies the source in Proverbs 7:3-4: «liga eam [legem meam] in digitis tuis, / scribe illam in tabulis cordis tui. / Dic sapientiae: Soror mea es, / et prudentiam voca amicam tuam». Smarr argues further for Maria's identification as Wisdom with reference to bestiary lore on the panther and eagle, pp. 112 ff.

[52] ALAN of LILLE, *Anticlaudianus*, cit., I,10; Patrologia Latina 210:497: «[Ratio] Prudentia plurima vultu / Paret [...]».

[53] J. L. SMARR, *Boccaccio and Fiammetta*, cit., p. 127, suggests that Fiammetta's «triple appearance» may parallel the Neoplatonic triplicity formulated by St. Ambrose as «Umbra in lege, imago in evangelio, veritas in caelestibus» [foreshadowing under the Law, the image under the Gospel, the truth in heavenly Afterlife].

omnipotent Cupid. The fact that he is unable to name her reflects his flawed cognition of her. Then, in the garden, he comes upon her person to person.

Now gardens can be places tremendously ambivalent — innocent or corrupt, dangerous or divine. Boccaccio's garden, intermediate between the castle and Dreamer's union with Prudence, merges both possibilities. With its fountain the site is like Eden, but here are only three streams, not four, and they flow from sculpted beasts in the kind of animal trio that could have lurked in Dante's *selva oscura*. Boccaccio reinforces the connection when his Dreamer, happily bedazzled, bursts out with exclamatory rhetoric that counters Dante's shiver of terror at the memory of so dreadful a place: «Ahi quanto 'gli era bello, al parer mio, / quel loco, per cui quanto era contento / dentro da me l'ardente mio disio!» (XXXVIII 19-21). Its occupants are living women who dance, sing, and debate issues of love, not a chorus of blessèd chanting hosannas in white stoles. Plantlife, however, recalls the Terrestrial Paradise: jasmine, rose, cedars, and oranges.[54] In *Caccia di Diana* Boccaccio had imagined a forest, at once infernal and edenic, where wise female virtue hunted, caught, and destroyed appetites disguised as beasts wandering wild. The *Amorosa visione* garden must be a place of sensuality, as long as Dreamer strolls beside his Appetites and without Reason. Instead of taking Guide's advice and the eastern fountain stream, he had brazenly abandoned her and headed south, the cardinal point with amorous thrust. As he hikes this route strewn with female beauty (XLI-XLII), those Red and White Fellows who had pulled him into the wide gate with Reason a poor fourth (III) are still close beside him, but they have disappeared by the time of his third coming to Maria.[55] She tethers him to herself, and he feels «inretito» (XLV 33), as if he were a wild animal just «netted» by a huntress. When Guide ritualistically joins Giovanni to Maria, the captive bond yields to a voluntary vow, and it is as if he has been finally reunited

---

[54] These are all details typical of medieval representations of the Earthly Paradise. See A. GRAF, *Miti leggende e superstizioni del Medio Evo*, I, New York, Burt Franklin, 1971², pp. 16-23. Cf. also CASSELL and KIRKHAM, *Diana's Hunt, cit.*, Intro., pp. 61-67; and below, ch. 6.

[55] The Appetites appear in Canto III 49-51 at the wide gate; they are still with Dreamer at the end of Canto XXX, when all three follow the Guide «with difficulty» into Room II; in XXXVII 74-75 they wheedle him into the garden; in XXXVIII 16 «all four» enter the garden; in XL 16-17 he goes deeper into the garden with «those two, who were pulling me»; at the end of XL they urge him to hasten; at the end of XLI and beginning of XLII he rhapsodizes with «those two» about the female beauties along the river; but in XLVI 65 he only makes reference to them — they are no longer present — as he tells Maria how he came to be in the garden. Red Fellow and White Fellow must drop by the wayside just before or at Canto XLIII, as Dreamer perceives Maria Aquinas on the riverbank.

with his other half. Reason's role here as a kind of high priestess at one of those spiritual marriages so favored by medievals – Christ with his Church, St. Francis with Poverty – nicely fulfils her initial descent from heaven in the guise of Juno, goddess of matrimony. Venus had played the corresponding part in *Caccia di Diana*, whose dénouement anticipates the *Visione* nuptials and a subsequent scene of 'wedded' bliss. In the *Caccia*, Venus had metamorphosed beasts into rational men, given them to Diana's nymphs as if in matrimony, and told them to keep faith with their new mistresses. Then, enacting a Boccaccian idyll, all stroll content upon the meadow, as will Dreamer and Maria. Compare *Amorosa visione* XLVIII 73-75:

> Ridendo e festeggiando insiememente
> sovra l'erbette lieti n'andavamo
> e d'amor ragionando dolcemente.

And *Caccia di Diana* XVII 55-58:

> Nel verde prato diversi diletti
> alcun prendeano, e sospirando alcuni
> givan cogliendo diversi fioretti,
>   tutti aspettando li promessi doni.

At last Giovanni loves wisdom. So, at the letter of the text, he takes Maria into the bushes, intending to consummate his desire while she is napping! At this point modern readers judge the allegory decidedly strained.[56] We must remember, though, that for Boccaccio, the more daring the distance between letter and spirit, the more creative the writer.[57] Here that stretch is no tauter than in the near-contemporary

---

[56] V. Crescini, *Due studi riguardanti opere minori del Boccaccio*, *cit.*, pp. 61-62, touches on the problem in tactful, colorful language: «Dunque a seguire la Ragione ed a procedere sull'ardua via del cielo non lo muove che una speranza affatto sensuale? Non il desio di gloriare con la sua donna nell'eterno bene, ma quello assai poco mistico di aversela realmente tra le braccia? Sta qui l'abisso, che separa il Boccaccio da Dante e da' poeti ontologi». For Crescini, Giovanni's love-making to Fiammetta just before awakening announces the *Decameron* and the rebirth of humanism: «Così nemmeno la vecchia forma asceta della letteratura medievale, la visione, è rimasta salva dalle nuove audacie dell'eterno ribelle». Cf. L. G. Clubb, *Boccaccio and the Boundaries of Love*, «Italica», XXXVII, 1960, pp. 188-196: «Even his excursions into allegory reveal Boccaccio's inveterately, though not exclusively, carnal regard of women [...] the reward promised to the poet at the end of his spiritual journey in the *Amorosa visione* is ultimate pleasure with the enticing lady of his dream».

[57] See Cassell and Kirkham, *Diana's Hunt*, *cit.*, Intro., pp. 63-66, and the quote from Boccaccio's *Genealogia*, *cit.*, XIV 13: «uti mendacium est, fictiones poetice, ut plurimum, non

Comedia delle ninfe fiorentine: seven nymphs boast of adulteries to establish their credentials as the Seven Virtues. Like Ameto, Giovanni progresses toward understanding, but being already a man of the world, he takes longer than the Etrurian shepherd. He procrastinates as he parries with Reason and rationalizes his resistance. Ameto naively longed for Lia as a carnal object, with the eyes of his flesh; afterwards, once the eyes of his intellect had learned to see her as Faith, the rustic could yearn for a union purely spiritual. By contrast, Giovanni seems to desire Maria's body not just at first, but always. Still at canto XLIX, amorous as ever, there he is bent over her sleeping form behind screening roses of Venus. It is dangerously late in his visionary lesson. Is he, then, incorrigible? Maybe not. This time he fails to do the *wrong* thing.

A prudent bride saves the day, when she wakes up and stops him with a warning, «deh, non fare! / Se quella donna vien, come farai?». Her return to active duty, which immediately summons renewed thoughts of Reason to the scene, anticipates Dreamer's own reveille, also 'in time' to prevent a violation of the bounds. Once awake, that is, armed with the protection of his rational powers, he bows before Reason: «Humile e pian, quanto io posso, m'assegno / a te: fa sì ch'al piacer di colei, / di cui son tutto, i' non trapassi 'l segno» (L 34-36).

* * *

Boccaccio's phrase «trapassare il segno» resonates as a double-layered quote. It echoes *Paradiso* XXVI 117 where Dante heard Adam define original sin as «trapassar del segno», literally, a «trespass of the mark» or violation in pride of the boundary set by God. Dante's source for such language was Thomas Aquinas, to whose technical vocabulary Boccaccio likewise alludes with philosophical precision. St. Thomas had written:

Since, in man, the concupiscible power is naturally governed by reason, the act of concupiscence is so far natural to man, as it is in accord with the order of reason; while, in so far as it trespasses beyond the bounds of reason, it is, for a man, contrary to reason. Such is the concupiscence of original sin.[58]

---

sunt nedum simillime, sed nec similes veritati, imo valde dissone et adverse» [Poetic fiction differs from a lie in that in most instances it bears not only no close resemblance to the truth, but no semblance at all; on the contrary, it is quite out of harmony and agreement with the truth].

[58] *Summa theologica, cit.*, I-II, Qu. 82, Art. 3: «Dicendum quod quia in homine concupiscibilis naturaliter regitur ratione, intantum concupiscere est homini naturale, inquantum est secundum rationis ordinem; concupiscentia autem quae transcendit limites rationis, inest homini contra naturam. Et talis est concupiscentia originalis peccati».

Not by accident, Pampinea will martial the very same words as Boccaccio's awakened Dreamer when she, as Prudence, argues the need for the *brigata* to leave Florence in order to preserve their existence — provided they do it «senza trapassar in alcuno atto il segno della ragione».[59]

Moral virtue, Thomas affirms, consists in reason's control of the appetite. The rectitude of reason, in turn, pertains to prudence, the virtue that 'commands' because it perfects our rational faculty.[60] Chief of all the seven virtues, Prudence takes her place at the forefront in Boccaccio's fiction, attuned to Scholastic frequencies. A virtue to which he was partial from his Neapolitan period, it seems to be the driving power behind his Mystery Lady in *Caccia di Diana*, that huntress who «went much like a guardian to the head of the group to guide them safely» (I 49-51). Prudence returns openly as the nymph Mopsa to lead off among the Seven Virtues who tell their stories in *Comedia delle ninfe*. Later, speaking as Pampinea, she is the mature lady who assumes responsibility for protecting the *Decameron brigata* from anarchy and death.[61] In the *Amorosa visione*, as goal and reward of the journey, Prudence retains her favored status. She is Reason's «sister», a sorority as ancient as the Old Testament, as medieval as the *Anticlaudianus*, and as contemporary for Boccaccio as Scholastic philosophy. It is at the confluence of these intellectual currents — the Bible, Alan's Neoplatonism, Thomistic ethics — that we can decipher Dreamer's final moves in the *Visione*. Giovanni, lover then 'husband' of Prudence, thanks to whom he willingly accepts Reason, passes fastforward morally from one phase to another in Life. He learns to overcome youthful impulsiveness and to love disciplined order in the soul. He grows up.

Thus the *Visione*, which began as he drifted off during a night of ignorance into a sleep of sin, comes full circle when it closes with a double

---

[59] The same formula spoken by the Narrator in the *Visione* and Pampinea in the *Decameron* had already found a place in Boccaccio's *Filocolo*, but there King Felice recites it most unreasonably, with iniquitous intent to murder Biancifiore. Before having her executed, he will go through the motions of providing a fair trial «acciò che alcuno non potesse dire che io i termini della ragione in ciò trapassassi». See above, Intro., on the Aristotelian-Thomistic background of this formula, and cf. also *Summa theologica, cit.,* II-II, Qu. 163, Art. 1; St. Augustine, *City of God, cit.,* XIV 12-14.

[60] *Comm. Ethic., cit.,* II 4 (286); II,8 (337); *Summa theologica, cit.,* I-II, Qu. 60, Art. 1; I-II, Qu. 66, Art. 1.

[61] *Caccia di Diana*, ed. V. Branca, Milan, Mondadori, 1967 («Tutte le opere», I), and for the symbolic identity of the Mystery Lady, see Cassell and Kirkham, *Diana's Hunt, cit.,* XVIII 54 and Comm., p. 194. Cf. also below, ch. 4. It would be worthwhile to develop the parallel between the conversation of the seven ladies in Santa Maria Novella and Alan's council of Gods in Book I of the *Anticlaudianus*. In each case life must be reaffirmed, Prudence is the strong lady, and a mission is accomplished with 'superior' masculine help.

awakening. Boccaccio's surprise ending puts a humorous twist on the tale, both as romance and dream-vision. Unlike Filocolo, who bent over his sleeping Biancifiore, awakened her, and made love the night long in a harem chamber, Giovanni is left frustrated in his physical desire. Then, plunged into the bathos of daylight, he finds Reason still lingering beside him. By the rules of dreams what business has she intruding on the morning? Boccaccio could well smile and cite in her defense what Macrobius had said about the prophetic *visio*: one may dream of a friend and then actually happen upon that person in life. Allegorically, since Reason persists in standing by in this *visione*, Giovanni's rightly ordered will can be relied upon to do the reasonable and 'right' thing. As if to stress his new uprightness, Giovanni at the end gets out of bed and takes an upright position; only then, and literally «in piè drizzato» (L 4), does he notice Reason at his bedside. Of course, she also stands. Keeping Reason in the plot to the end, Boccaccio puts a final spin on Dante, whose Virgil had dismissed the pilgrim to his own devices and quietly slipped away. In Boccaccio's poem, it is not Reason, but the Appetites — Red Fellow and White Fellow — who drop by the wayside in silence. Nevertheless, reversal holds the *Comedy* in view, as if we were seeing it stage rear behind a filmy painted curtain. At the last scene in the *Amorosa visione*, we must hear whispered in our mind Virgil's farewell to his pupil at the top of Purgatory: «libero, sano e diritto è 'l tuo arbitrio». Dreamer has reached the same moral summit as Dante — whether or not he has secured it.

For the moment, at least, he is back on track. His will «free, healthy, and straight», Dreamer, once again open-eyed, can make responsible choices. Choosing — between now and later, wrong and 'right', sense and reason, Fortune and God — these are the moral alternatives that Boccaccio's *terza rima* translates into visual images. Now from the last canto, a retrospective view of the whole *Amorosa visione* lays open those choices in patterns of binary poetics.

* * *

At the very center of the poem, in Canto XXVI, Boccaccio embeds a bivium and a figure emblematic of Dreamer's recurrent ethical dilemma. Set apart by its irregular length (it has a supernumerary *terzina*), this swing canto into the second half of the *Visione* is given entirely to the loves and labors of Hercules. By housing the Greek hero here in his poem, as Janet Smarr has shown, Boccaccio alludes to the myth of Hercules at the Crossroads. He symbolizes Everyman, who comes to a point in life when he must decide which way to go, either up a steep path on the right toward virtue, or down the wider road branching left with sensual and temporal enticement. From ancient times, the Greek letter Y represented these paths, and its symbolism was universally understood. Not by coincidence, Virgil put that letter into the central episode of the *Aeneid*, a sign that sparkled with meaning for Servius on the golden bough at Lake Avernus: «We know that Pythagoras of Samos divided human life like the letter Y, and this because the first period is undefined and not yet given either to vice or to virtue, but the bivium of the letter Y begins at youth [*iuventus*], a period in which men either pursue vices, that is, the left side, or virtues, that is, the right side». Isidore transmits the explanation from Servius, with insistence on the moral opposition implicit in the crossroad: «The bivium, above the stem, begins at adolescence. Its right side is steep but leads to a virtuous life; the left is easier but leads to disgrace and destruction». Arrigo of Settimello, whose treatise on the consolation of philosophy against fortune (ca. 1190) Boccaccio undoubtedly knew, also refers to this Y-shaped dilemma: «go by the horns of Pythagoras. No one can reach virtue, unless by the right-hand path; by the other way it is easy to descend to hell».[62] Boccaccio himself, glossing the guard dog Cerberus in his commentary on Dante's *Inferno*, presents Hercules as an example of the «virtuous man» who fights worldliness. Even though he does not name the bivium, he re-hearses temptations typical of the leftward — and wayward — path:

E l'uficio di questo cane non è di vietare la entrata ad alcuno, ma di guardare che alcuno dello 'nferno non esca: volendo per questo che, là dove entra la cupidità

---

[62] J. L. SMARR, *Boccaccio and the Choice of Hercules*, «Modern Language Notes», XCII, 1977, pp. 146-152. Servius, *Commentarii in Aeneidos*, ed. G. THILO and H. HAGEN, 1881; Hildesheim, Georg Olms, 1961, VI 136: «novimus Pythagoram Samium vitam humanam divisisse in modum Y litterae, scilicet quod prima aetas incerta sit, quippe quae adhuc se nec vitiis nec virtutibus dedit; bivium autem Y litterae a iuventate incipere, quo tempore homines aut vitia, ed est partem sinistram, aut virtutes, id est dexteram partem sequuntur». Cf. ISIDORE, *Etymologiae, cit.*, I iii, 7-9: «Bivium autem, quod superest, ab adolescentia incipit: cuius dextra pars ardua est, sed ad beatam vitam tendens; sinistra facilior, sed ad labem interitumque deducens». Cf. Ps.-BERNARD SILVESTRIS, *The Commentary on the First Six Books of the Aeneid, cit.*, p. 58, *s.v.* «ARBORE»: «Arborem Pitagoras appellavit humanitatem que in duos ramos, id est in virtutem et vitium se dividit. Cum enim in initio continuat, deinceps quidam in dextrum, quidam in sinistrum, id est quidam in vitium, quidam in virtutem se dividunt» [Pythagoras called the tree humanity which is divided into two branches, that is, into virtue and in vice. For in the beginning it is continuous, then some people divide to the right, some to the left, that is, some to vice, some to virtue]. ARRIGO DA SETTIMELLO, *Arrighetto ovvero Trattato contro all'avversità della fortuna*, ed. D. M. MANNI, Milan, Giovanni Silvestri, 1815, p. 116: «segui i corni di Pittagora. Niuno può pervenire alla virtude, se non per lo destro sentiero; per l'altra via è leggiero discendimento al ninferno». Cf. CICERO, *De finibus* I 32; ST. JEROME, *Ad Laetam de institutione filiae*; LACTANTIUS, *Divinae institutiones* VI 3.

delle riccheze, degli stati, de' diletti e dell'altre cose terrene, ella non esce mai o con difficultà se ne trae; sì come essi mostrano, fingendo questo cane essere stato tratto da Ercule dello 'nferno, cioè questa insaziabilità de' disideri terreni essere dal virtuoso uomo tratta e tirata fuori del cuore di quel cotale virtuoso. (*Esposizioni, Acc.* 48)

Life's crossroads, inscribed in the letter Y, in the myth of Hercules, and in the magic bough that Aeneas plucks, has meaning similar to that of another great universal, the labyrinth. Boccaccio must have had it in mind when he composed the amusing dialogues between Dreamer and his Guide, forever sparring over which path to follow, whether this way or that, her way or his. The labyrinth through which these characters wend their way in the *Amorosa visione* exemplifies the type of maze Penelope Doob has termed «multicursal», with «many points of choice between two or more paths».[63] In order to advance, over and over again Dreamer must decide at the forking Y which gate, which room, which outdoors — whether low-lying garden or steep path. The binary pattern, imprinted from Canto I, pairs opposites: sleeping and waking, wide and narrow, left and right, downward and upward, crooked and straight, outer and inner, false and true, folly and wisdom, pleasance and austerity, appetites and reason, misery and happiness, multiplicity and unity, vice and virtue, Fortune and God, earthly and eternal. Choices proliferate at the fountain with streams spilling forth in three directions, symbols of three loves. Rejecting utilitarian and virtuous love, Giovanni chooses earthly affection, passion for the sake of pleasure, symbolized by a carved spouting bull and southward watercourse through a landscape subject to seasonal variation.[64] As he pauses before this ornate, enchanting basin to marvel at its artistry, Dreamer stands most deeply inside the walled castle complex. Here, at the trivium, lies the heart of the labyrinth and the point from which he begins to exit, following the rivulet that leads to Maria.

---

[63] P. R. Doob, *The Idea of the Labyrinth from Classical Antiquity through the Middle Ages*, Ithaca, Cornell University Press, 1990, p. 3. Doob calls the other type 'unicursal', just one path that leads to the center and back out again. Doob's broad study includes Boccaccio's *Corbaccio*, or *Labirinto d'amore*, but not the *Amorosa visione*.

[64] Crescini first suggested that the three statuettes at the top of the fountain symbolize the three kinds of love, and Branca accepts his identification. Dante alludes to the bull as a sign of sensuality suited to the sin of lust in *Inferno* V and *Purgatory* XXVI. In *Caccia di Diana*, the huntresses also capture a bull, doubtless with the same implications. See Cassell and Kirkham, *Diana's Hunt, cit.*, Intro. p. 34 and Comm. on XIII 56, p. 184.

We could visualize his path as a tree. Starting at the bottom, his general direction is obvious. It drifts heavily to the left until he wakes up, when his acceptance of Reason announces a switch in direction.

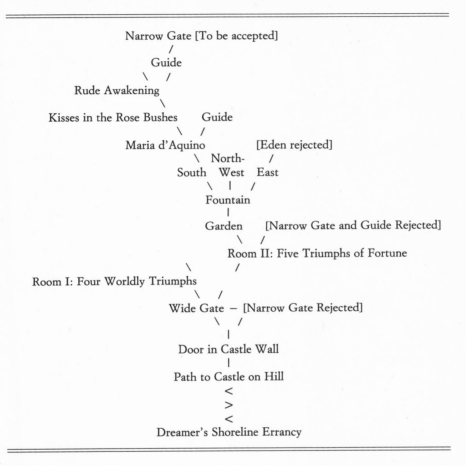

Narrow Gate [To be accepted]
/
Guide
\   /
Rude Awakening
\
Kisses in the Rose Bushes   Guide
\   /
Maria d'Aquino   [Eden rejected]
\ North-   /
South   West   East
\ | /
Fountain
|
Garden   [Narrow Gate and Guide Rejected]
\   /
Room II: Five Triumphs of Fortune
/
Room I: Four Worldly Triumphs
\   /
Wide Gate — [Narrow Gate Rejected]
\   /
|
Door in Castle Wall
|
Path to Castle on Hill
<
>
<
Dreamer's Shoreline Errancy

The dualities, both thematic and semantic, that express Dreamer's alternatives in the labyrinth extend to other doublings in the poem. Dreamer and his Guide are a contending couple. They move through territory divided, part castle and part garden. Its inner wall has two gates. Two young men pull Dreamer into the second. Within the castle are two chambers. The first room doubles the dyad to depict four Triumphs. Twice the poet marks passing time, in lapses of solar units: when the «great topaz» is in the second hour (XXX), and again, in the fortieth canto, when the sun is in the fourth hour. Twice he tells how long he has

~ 101 ~

loved, measured cryptically in diurnal multiples, first in the forty-fourth canto. Such quantities stress not only the dyad, but restate 2 as its square ($2^2 = 4$): for example, Canto XL brings us to the fourth hour; in Canto XLIV Giovanni says he has loved Maria for 24 days (6 x 4 «suns»). Ultimately, Boccaccio will raise the number to its third power ($2^3 = 8$) in the *Visione*'s metrics, which allot as a rule 88 verses to a canto. These 4's and 8's, generated by root 2 as the bivalent sign of the labyrinth and the Pythagorean Y, figure in a well wrought system of numerology.

* * *

Although never confessed, Boccaccio's fondness for numerical composition was keen, especially so in his earlier Italian fiction. From the very start, in *Caccia di Diana*, it was a mode with which he had been experimenting.[65] His interest appears most intense in *Comedia delle ninfe fiorentine* and *Teseida*, those works closest chronologically to the *Visione*. The *Visione* itself forms the centerpiece for the trilogy he made in *terza rima*. As a narrative in verse, the *Amorosa visione* abounds with possibilities for symbolic number play: in canto placement of subject matter, in the quantities that measure thematic categories, in the pacing of the episodes, in time references, in the cast of characters and their appearances, and in canto length.

At Canto IV, Dreamer and his Guide step into a room four-walled (*quadra*) with four painted Triumphs. It reminds us of the Limbo that Dante and Virgil traversed in *Inferno* IV. There Aristotle held central position as the twentieth of forty souls; here he presides as the first on a list nearly twice as long that enumerates sages, heroes, and poets in a Triumph of Knowledge.[66] This fresco program in Boccaccio's first castle chamber, art as magisterial as Giotto's, falls into four parts not just by decorative necessity, in order to cover a quadrangular area. The space and its murals are an architecture also conditioned by symbolism. They correspond to the four-cornered world, made of four elements, moving

---

[65] See CASSELL and KIRKHAM, *Diana's Hunt.*, cit., Intro. pp. 23-27, and cf. above, ch. 1.

[66] In the *Comedy*, the sums of souls named in sequential tallies often have symbolic meaning. For examples concerning the female population, see V. KIRKHAM, *Quanto in femmina foco d'amor dura!*, «Letture Classensi», XVIII, 1988, pp. 235-252; trans. and rev. *A Canon of Women in Dante's 'Commedia'*, «Annali d'Italianistica», VII, 1989, pp. 16-41. In the *Amorosa visione*, by my calculation there are 76 characters in the Triumph of Learning. The number of people listed here and in the other Triumphs does not seem significant. There is no question, however, but that Boccaccio was counting how many he put in certain subgroups. In the first group, sages are pictured in the family of the Seven Liberal Arts by sevens, beginning with 1) Aristotle, 2) Socrates, 3) Plato, 4) Melissus, 5) Alexander, 6) Thales, and 7) Crisippus.

cyclically through four seasons, and inhabited by man, in whose four-elemented body mingle four humors. Learning, Fame, Wealth, and Love assemble as a quartet in the poem because medieval Christian number lore equated the *quaternarius* with man in his physical existence in the temporal realm. By opposition to 3, which as a symbol of our tripartite soul implied man in his spiritual aspect, 4 was understood as a worldly number.[67]

In the second hour of the day, Dreamer and his Guide enter a second chamber (XXX). This room, Fortune's realm, offers a variant list of worldly pursuits with five categories, not four. But we should not be surprised because they correspond exactly to the goods of fortune itemized by Thomas Aquinas (carnal delight, high rank, fame, wealth, power) and advertised on the wide gate: «regni ampii», «dignitati», «tesoro», «gloria mondana», «Amor». If 4 defines the world, 5 stands for Fortune, which is in a sense the fifth Triumph of the *Visione*. Early subtitled by its publishers *Cinque trionfi*, Boccaccio's composition repeats the pentad in overall structure, since it has a total of fifty cantos.[68] His allusion to Hercules at the Crossroads in XXVI splits them evenly into two halves of 25 + 25 cantos, and 25 expresses 5 squared.

---

[67] In his painted microcosm on four walls Boccaccio replicates the four empires of the world as defined by the historian Paulus Orosius (II 1, 5): to the east Babilonia, to the south Carthage, to the north Macedonia, to the west Rome. The meanings associated with 4 − world, elements, humors, man (in his corporeal part) − are commonplaces. See, e.g., MACRO-BIUS, *Saturnalia*, trans. P. V. DAVIES, New York and London, Columbia University Press, 1969 («Records of Civilization», LXXIX), I 19, 15, p. 135: 4 can symbolize the the four corners of the world, or the four seasons of the year, or the arrangement of the zodiac into two equinoxes and two solstices. Martianus Capella's discussion of Arithmetic cites 4 in connection with the first solid body, four seasons, four regions of the sky, four elements, four virtues. Cf. DANTE, *Convivio*, *cit.*, IV 23, 4-5, on the four humors and ages of man. Alan of Lille in *Anticlaudianus* has his team of goddesses put four elements in the perfect new human body. The four elements and the four seasons enjoyed a specific correspondence, explained by the Third Vatican Mythographer, ed. BODE, *cit.*, VIII 6, 1-2, p. 203: «Aestas enim igni, autumnus terrae; hiems aquae, ver aëri assimilatur» [summer is likened to fire, autumn to earth, winter to water, spring to air]. The human body is a 4 because in Platonic geometry 4 forms the first solid body (four points joined make a pyramid). Often 4 was added to 3, the number of the soul, to give 7, a number that passes from Neoplatonism into Christianity with the meaning of 'man'. M.-S. RØSTVIG, *Structure as Prophecy: The Influence of Biblical Exegesis upon Theories of Literary Structure*, in *Silent Poetry. Essays in Numerological Analysis*, ed. A. FOWLER, London, Routledge and Kegan Paul, 1970, pp. 32-72, cites examples of 'man' as the sum of 4/body + 3/soul from Plato, Augustine, and St. Thomas. Cf. also V. KIRKHAM, *Eleven is for Evil. Measured Trespass in Dante's 'Commedia'*, *cit.*, and below, n. 76, for 3 as a soul number.

[68] The fifty cantos of *Comedia delle ninfe fiorentine* also carry the 5, similarly with implications of 'sensuality'. Boccaccio's best literary precedent for the equation of 5 with senses would have been Dante's *Inferno* V. See V. KIRKHAM, *A Canon of Women in Dante's 'Commedia'*, *cit.* R. A. PECK recognizes an association between 5 and Fortune's wheel, perhaps suggested by Boethius, in *Numerology and Chaucer's 'Troilus and Criseyde'*, *cit.*

Why such insistence on 5? The meaning most frequently associated with it was the five senses, certainly appropriate to Boccaccio's Dreamer as he strays about under the sensory sway of his appetites. Like 4, then, 5 has a strong association with our physical nature, our corporeality. And just as five senses find their place in the four-part human body, so from a Neoplatonist perspective 5 defines the cosmic body encasing our four-cornered world. The pentad is rightly «the number assigned to the universe» according to Martianus Capella: «This identification is reasonable, for after the four elements, the universe is a fifth body of a different nature [...]. Then, too, there are five zones of the earth. In man there are five senses; the same number of classes of creatures inhabit the earth: humans, quadrupeds, reptiles, fish, and birds». The five «zones» to which Martianus refers are those great climatic bands marked by the equator, the tropics of cancer and capricorn, the north and south poles. By «fifth body of a different nature» he means the earth's envelope of ethereal matter, which constitutes a fifth «quintessential» element.[69]

Beyond the 'body' integers 4 and 5, Boccaccio's poem turns on a third and more potent symbol, the triad. Anchoring a trilogy in *terza rima*, the *Amorosa visione* unfolds as an acrostic from three prefatory sonnets. At Canto XXXVIII its protagonist happens upon a marvelous fountain, source of three rivers channelled from three female statuettes and through three spouting animals. They seem to symbolize the three kinds of love that Fiammetta had already defined in the *Filocolo* love debate (IV 44). In Boccaccio's numerology, the primary meaning of 3, as well as its variants 9 and 13, is always love.[70] So here he fully describes the fountain in Canto XXXIX, which expresses both the triad and its square (39). The ladies Boccaccio identifies along the river are nineteen (another form of 9), and thirteenth is Maria Aquinas.

---

[69] M. CAPELLA, *De nuptiis, cit.*, pp. 369-370: «Pentas, qui numerus mundo est attributus; nam si ex quattuor elementis ipse sub alia forma est quintus, pentade est rationabiliter insignitus»; «in homine sensus quinque, totidemque habitatores mundi generibus, ut homines quadrupedesque reptantes, natantes, uolantes». Cf. MACROBIUS, *Comm. in somnium, cit.*, I 6, 18. The primary meaning of 5 is the five senses. For example, in Alan's *Anticlaudianus*, the seven Liberal Arts build a chariot for Prudence to ascend the heavens, and then the completed wagon is hitched to five steeds, symbolic of the five senses that must be harnessed by wisdom in the reasonable man. Cf. ISIDORE, *Etymologiae, cit.*, XI 1, 18; V. F. HOPPER, *Medieval Number Symbolism, cit.*, p. 86.

[70] Venus, goddess of the third heaven, determines the connection between 3 and love, naturally reinforced by the Christian Trinity. As for the variants, recall thirteen «questioni d'amore» in the *Filocolo*; nine triumphs of Venus in the gloss on her dwelling at *Teseida* V 50. See further, ch. 1 above.

From a single number several others can be generated, each variant maintaining the same meaning as the base figure. So one may square a number or raise it to the third power, add 10 or multiply by 10, but the arithmetic changes do not alter the symbolic value: 13 expresses 3, so does 30, so do 9, 19, 39. Again, as was true for the *Teseida*, the meaning of a number may be understood as the product of its multiplicands. A cipher with this reductive capacity in the *Amorosa visione* is 15. Going by first appearances and the decimal system, 15 is a variant of 5 (5 + 10 = 15). But one can also articulate 15 as five 3's (5 x 3 = 15). Giovanni's «cara Fiamma» enters the *Amorosa visione* in the first acrostic sonnet, verse 15. She returns within the vision in Canto XV, after the first fifteen *terzine*, to 'couple' on the page with «Giovanni». She will reappear at fifteen-canto intervals in XXIX, in XLIII. All together, Giovanni sees her three times. The Triumph of Love begins at Canto XV, occupies fifteen cantos, and culminates just shy of XXX. Such intersections suggest that Boccaccio meant us to read 15 as the product of 5 and 3, the same formula he himself used in his glosses to the *Teseida* on Emilia's marriage age of 15. Here the equation 15 = 5 x 3 intimates sensual love, which through a process of correction and purification is transformed into 'conjugal' love, the bond that unites in 'matrimony' Giovanni with Lady Wisdom.

Even if Giovanni short-sightedly perceives «Fiammetta» as an object of physical desire, Boccaccio knows she is more than that as he programs her appearances in the poem. Significantly, he reveals the name Maria Aquinas in her central appearance, at Canto XLIII (43). Summing the digits of the canto number, we arrive at a wisdom number: 43 = 4 + 3 = 7. As early as the *Caccia di Diana*, 7 alludes to both virtue and wisdom, meanings that it continues to suggest in *Teseida*. In the *Visione* Triumph of Learning, '*Scientia*' has seven handmaidens, a retinue whose number Boccaccio underlines by repeating the information three times.[71] The number 7 as sum of 4 and 3 acquires fuller meaning when we remember that the virtues are also seven, four cardinal and three theological. Maria thus seems to personify not only wisdom but the totality of virtue.

The nineteen ladies along the river fall into four groups after «the fair Lombard», who relaxes isolated from the others and who occupies a canto on her own.

---

[71] *Amorosa visione, cit.*, 1974, IV 35: «sette donne vid'io»; V 11: «le sette donne»; V 68: «le sette davanti e dintorno».

		1. «la bella lombarda»	(XL 40-)
I)	2.	Agnese di Périgord	(XLI)
	3.	«la ninfa fiorentina»	
	4.	«la bella Lia»	
	5.	Margherita daughter of Filippo di Taranto	
II)	6.	Giovanna di Napoli	(XLII)
	7.	«unica intendanza del Melanense»	
	8.	«donna di quel cui seguita Ungheria»	
	9.	Andrea Acciaiuoli	
	10.	«novella Dido»	
	11.	Dalfina di Barasso	
III)	12.	Eleonora d'Aragona	(XLIII)
	13.	*Maria d'Aquino*	
	14.	Margherita or Gemma dell'Asino	
	15.	Lottiera di Neron Nigi	
IV)	16.	Isabella di Ibelin	(XLIV)
	17.	Alionora Gianfigliazzi	
	18.	Giovanna daughter of Giovanni di Catanzaro	
	19.	Emilia	

Ladies had also come in quadrants in Boccaccio's *Caccia*, where they hunt the forest four by four. Again, as in that earlier poem, Boccaccio may here be thinking of them as embodiments of the four Cardinal Virtues. In any event, stilnovistic numerology multiplies their possibilities. As 19, singing a song of nine *terzine*,[72] they are amorous and remind us of Beatrice, Dante's 9. Grouped by 4's, they are 'virtuous bodies' and have potential for infusing their lovers with virtue. Boccaccio's words of praise for the first lady, «la bella Lombarda», open at XL 40. All told, the four sets of ladies (preponderantly four per group) extend in the territory of the poem from Cantos XL to XLIV. Moments before this lovely vista of women opens unto Dreamer's eyes, he had beheld the fountain, quadrangular at its base with four ladies sitting upon the pedestal. One at each corner, to support the bowl, they must symbolize four virtues.[73]

---

[72] This nine-*terzina* song falls half way through Boccaccio's enumeration of them, at the center of the catalogue (XLII 61-88). He seems to have also been counting 9's when he situated nine women at the beginning of Canto IX in the Triumph of Love.

[73] Their iconography has not yet been fully understood. The three-headed lady (on the right) must surely be Prudence; the lady armed as if with iron should be Fortitude. The other

As in *Caccia di Diana*, Boccaccio establishes a regular number of verses per canto for the *Visione*, but then breaks his own rule. He invokes, as it were, Dioneo's privilege, and well before the *Decameron* these deviations from the norm respect a logic in the economy of the work. The A version has three irregular cantos, and B has four. Two of the odd-length cantos are deficient; two are superabundant.

Canto	Version A Verses	Version B	Canto	Version A Verses	Version B
I	88	88	XXVI	91*Hercules	91*
II	88	88	XXVII	88	88
III	88 Wide Gate	88	XXVIII	88	88
IV	88 Learning	88	XXIX	88 Maria	88
V	88	88	XXX	88	88
VI	88 Fame	88	XXXI	88	88
VII	88	88	XXXII	88	88
VIII	88	88	XXXIII	88	88
IX	88	88	XXXIV	88	88
X	88	88	XXXV	88	88
XI	88	88	XXXVI	88	88
XII	88 Riches	88	XXXVII	88	88
XIII	88	88	XXXVIII	88	88
XIV	88	88	XXXIX	88	88
XV	88 Cupid-Maria	88	XL	88	88
XVI	88	88	XLI	88	88
XVII	88	88	XLII	88	88
XVIII	88	88	XLIII	88 Maria	88
XIX	88	85*	XLIV	85*	85*
XX	88	88	XLV	88	88
XXI	88	88	XLVI	88	88
XXII	88	88	XLVII	88	88
XXIII	88	88	XLVIII	88	88
XXIV	88	88	XLIX	88	88
XXV	88	88	L	94*	94*

The change has occurred at Canto XIX. Why? It is a refinement attributable only to Boccaccio, number-conscious and intimate with

---

two, however, do not as readily match with the remaining cardinal virtues. Perhaps the lady first mentioned with two spirits at her feet is Temperance (or Charity?); perhaps the 'tame' last one is Justice. Why, if there are four ladies at the base of the fountain, does this number not carry through to the streams that flow from it? That ought to be their number *a fortiori* since the fountain sits in a garden that resembles the Earthly Paradise. Given the allegory of the his acrostic.[74] The B version brings the exceptional cantos to four, an integer whose meanings multiply as our familiarity with the *Visione* grows: the four-cornered world, the four-elemented body, the four cardinal virtues.

The two abundant cantos mark the beginning and end of the second half of the poem. One extra *terzina* for ninety-one (91) verses in Canto XXVI, the location where Hercules stands at the Crossroads, reverses the number of the first irregular canto, XIX (19), and the nineteen ladies catalogued. Two extra *terzine* for ninety-four (94) verses in the last canto reverse the total cantos in the *Visione* (49), if we count them from the poet's invocation of Venus at the beginning of II. That is, like Dante's allegory, the *Amorosa visione* has a prologue canto, and only at the start of the second canto does the author signal his 'real' beginning by summoning inspiration. Just as we can count the *Comedy* 1 + 99 = 100 cantos, so we can construe the *Visione* as 1 + 49 = 50 cantos.

The two diminished cantos are short by one *terzina* for 85 verses. They punctuate an internal symmetry since each comes seven cantos from the end of its half of the poem. Canto XIX, whose number replicates the total of ladies praised in Boccaccio's 'sirventese', falls seven cantos before the mid-point of the poem. Its counterpart, seven cantos before the end, coincides with Canto XLIV, which in Arabic numerals (44) doubles the 4.

Visione, I am inclined to see the wondrous marble artifact made of a fourfold base and threefold upper tier as a representation of Man in his dual nature: body (4) + spirit (3). The absence of a fourth river could reflect an exegetic tradition on Genesis going back to Philo Judaeus, cited by A. KATZENELLENBOGEN, in *Allegories of the Virtues and Vices in Medieval Art from Early Christian Times to the Thirteenth Century*, trans. J. CRICK, London, Warburg Institute, 1939; New York, Norton, 1964, p. 49. It is likely that Boccaccio knew it indirectly through a Patristic authority such as Ambrose, who in the *Liber de Paradiso* had linked the four rivers of Paradise to the four cardinal virtues. The idea became a commonplace: Phison-Prudence, Geon-Temperance, Tigris-Fortitude, Euphrates-Justice. Ambrose drew on an allegorical interpretation of Genesis by Philo, whose hermeneutic acrobatics succeeded in superimposing those four rivers on the three parts of the Platonic soul: Pheison-Prudence, Geon-Courage (or Fortitude), Tigris-Self-Mastery (or Temperance). Prudence, the first part of our threefold soul, must rule the other two, namely lustful desire in the abdomen and high-spirited passion in the breast. The fourth river, Euphrates-Justice, only appears when the three parts of the soul are in harmony. See PHILO, *De opificio mundi*, II, *cit.*, pp. 191-195. The fact that the fourth river is absent from Boccaccio's garden would indicate that his soul is not yet dominated by Reason-Prudence.

[74] Although V. Branca has always vigorously argued the Boccaccian paternity of version B, some skeptics have attributed the variants to Girolamo Claricio. But I do not see how any editor could have entered into such subtleties of numerical composition, especially at a distance of two hundred years. Only the author could know his poem so well. Boccaccio's revisions reveal other numerical retouching. For example, in the Triumph of Learning the A text catalogues twenty-nine people; the B text brings the sum to a round thirty.

Each with eighty-five (85) verses, the two diminished cantos in the *Visione* reverse the line sum of its acrostic sonnets, 58:

$$\text{sonnet 1} = 17 \text{ verses}$$
$$\text{sonnet 2} = 16 \text{ verses}$$
$$\text{sonnet 3} = 25 \text{ verses}$$
$$\overline{}$$
$$58 \text{ verses}$$

The integers 5 and 8 in the number 58 anticipate and 'contain' the poem in its larger metrical structures, since by amplification they generate the total number of cantos (50) and the standard length of verses per canto (88). Moreover, 58 exactly repeats the sum of verses per canto in *Caccia di Diana*, the poem that must have stood first in Boccaccio's *terza rima* trilogy. (There, too, he made an exception that reinforced the rule, Canto III with one supernumerary *terzina*). In the *Caccia*, 58 contributes to a significant pattern of 3's, provided we reckon by summing the digits: 5 + 8 = 13. For the *Visione*, it seems not coincidental that summing the digits of 58, 85, 49, and 94 always produces the same number, 13. Thirteen is a variant on 3, as 9 is on 19. Beatrice had appeared «on the number 9» in Dante's epistolary *sirventese*; another of his ladies had fallen «on 30». In the *Caccia di Diana*, Boccaccio had saved number 33 for his Mystery Lady on the tally of huntresses. Now that the scene has shifted from Naples to Florence, 13 takes its turn as the place reserved in the poet's inventory of women for Maria Aquinas.[75]

Love, Boccaccio's theme in the amorous vision, is the primary meaning of its numbers 3, 13, 9, and 19. But the triad has a second connotation, relevant to the poem as a philosophical allegory. All the while Giovanni's dream is unfolding in castle and garden, action is simultaneously taking place in Dreamer's soul, the seat of a psychomachya that pits reason against the irascible and the concupiscible appetites. To personify these three faculties, Boccaccio invented three characters who vie for Dreamer's attention in his mental itinerary: one Guiding Lady, one Red Fellow, one White Fellow. Together they incarnate the tripartite soul.

As 4 corresponded to body and 5 to the senses, so 3 alluded to man's soul. The number 3 designated *anima* by analogy, since our spiritual side was held to have three parts. From Plato and Aristotle, no matter how

---

[75] Examples of ladies listed in symbolic slots are presented by V. KIRKHAM, *Numerology and Allegory in Boccaccio's 'Caccia di Diana'*, cit; cf. also V. KIRKHAM, *A Canon of Women in Dante's 'Commedia'*, cit.

the different schools of perception and behavior chose to name the 'chambers' of the soul, its cameral number was a constant. The Neoplatonists Martianus and Macrobius spoke of a threefold division into «reason», «emotion», and «appetite».[76] Boccaccio preferred a variant vocabulary, more Aristotelian in tone, when he glossed the three male protagonists of the *Teseida* (VII 30 and VII 50) as «reason» (Teseo, duke of Athens), «irascible faculty» (Arcita of Thebes), and «concupiscible faculty» (Palemone of Thebes). In the *Amorosa visione*, the same trio returns to roam and dispute an oneiric landscape, powers of Dreamer's soul externalized. Guide now steps into Duke Teseo's shoes; Red Fellow and White Fellow substitute respectively for the knights Arcita and Palemone. We shall encounter the threesome again when they come back to the *Decameron*, recostumed as Panfilo, Filostrato, and Dioneo. Among all the figures that lend ciphered meaning to the *Amorosa visione* — 2 (4, 14, 40, 44, 88), 3 (13, 9, 19), 5 (15, 25, 50) — the number 3 enjoys the role of numeric 'protagonist'. It functions in a double capacity, both as a love number and as a symbol of the soul, the moral *locus* of the poem.

* * *

The *Amorosa visione* refines to new scientific accuracy a message at the core of all Boccaccio's fiction. From *Caccia di Diana* to the *Corbaccio*, he enunciates a basic Scholastic concept. Virtue is a state of spiritual

---

[76] ARISTOTLE discusses the ways of understanding the soul and its three parts in *De anima*, trans. J. A. SMITH, in *Introduction to Aristotle*, ed. R. McKEON, New York, The Modern Library, 1947, III 3 (428a). See further, e.g., MACROBIUS, *Comm. in somnium* I 6, 42: «ternarius vero adsignat animam tribus suis partibus absolutam, quarum prima est ratio quam λογιστιχόν appellant, secunda animositas quam θυμιχόν vocant, tertia cupiditas quae ἐπιθυμητιχόν nuncupatur» [The number three, indeed, marks the three divisions of the soul, the first being reason, *logistikon*, the second emotion, *thymikon*, and the third appetite, *epithymetikon*].

Vocabulary in Boccaccio's acrostic sonnets and first canto reflects medieval scientific notions of the soul, both its psychology and physiology: I 4: «la *fantasia* ch'è nella mente»; II 1: «Il dolce *inmaginar* che 'l mio chor face»; II 10: «nello '*nmaginar* vostra biltate»; I 11-12: «uscita fuor di sé la *fantasia* / subito corse 'n non usato errore». This terminology describes specifically operations of the 'lower' mind, or sensitive soul, which in its three parts (*imaginativa, logica, memorativa*) receives sensory information. The encyclopedia by Bartholomew the Englishman, *De proprietatibus rerum* (before 1250), explains how our imagination can call things to mind after we have seen them, or allow us to 'imag(in)e' things not yet seen. *Phantasia*, which had quite different connotations for Boccaccio than it does for us, is a technical term for the highest power of imagination. This system also assigns three parts to the 'higher' mind, or intellective soul: reason, intellect (or understanding), will. Memory can store images and render them accessible to the higher powers, reason and will. Images, in short, always present in the mind, are both «likeness and intention» because they can move the soul. From the beginning of his poem Boccaccio describes a mental activity dominated by the sensitive soul because his reason is confused ('smarrita'). Such mechanisms of visual imagination are central to V. A.

order; disorder born in the soul of sin derives from the failure of reason to suppress chaotic movements of the appetites.[77] This credo and the allegorical machinery that Boccaccio devised to propel it as poetry express a medieval cultural tradition that lived on in the masterpieces of Renaissance chivalric narrative. Ariosto exploits it to comic effect, as Boccaccio had with his tug-of-war at the two gates, when he composed the most symbolic episode of his *Orlando furioso* (VI-VIII). Monsters sent by the witch Alcina swarm down over Ruggiero and block his passage on a steep right-hand way, which leads to Logistilla, the good lady whose name means 'Right Reason'. Two damsels, figures cast in the same role as Boccaccio's Red Fellow and White Fellow, then emerge from a gate in a golden wall around a dazzling city and escort Ruggiero into what seems «paradise» but is really a prison where his own sensuality entraps him. Eventually, the good fairy Melissa will liberate him, and he reaches Logistilla with the help of the four cardinal virtues, Andronica, Fronesia, Dicilla, and Sofrosina (Fortitude, Wisdom, Justice, and Temperance). Logistilla's final act is to give Ruggiero a bit to keep in check the Hippogryph, an instrument that symbolizes temperance and rational control of our lower, animal appetites. True to form, Tasso's *Gerusalemme liberata* also has a resident siren, enchantress of many chosen by Fortune and Love. None other than the witch Armida, she seduces Rinaldo hypnotically with a song of sensual pleasure: «Solo chi segue ciò che piace è saggio»; «Goda il corpo securo, e in lieti oggetti / l'alma tranquilla appaghi i sensi frali [...] / Questo è saver, questa è felice vita»; «sì canta l'empia e 'l giovenetto al sonno / con note invoglia sì soave e scorte. / Quel serpe a poco a poco, e si fa donno / sovra i sensi di lui possente e forte». As Tasso himself declared, his three protagonists perform in an allegorical psychomachy hidden beneath the literal plot of the *Liberata*: Goffredo signifies Reason, Orlando is the concupiscible faculty, and Rinaldo is the irascible.[78]

KOLVE's study, *Chaucer and the Imagery of Narrative. The First Five Canterbury Tales*, Stanford, Stanford University Press, 1984, esp. pp. 22, 43-45. They need to be better understood in Boccaccio.

[77] O. LOTTIN, *La doctrine morale des mouvements premiers de l'appétit sensitif aux XIIe et XIIIe siècles*, «Archives d'histoire doctrinale et littérature du Moyen Age», VI, 1931, pp. 49-173, esp. p. 76. Cf. T. AQUINAS, *Summa theologica*, cit., I, Qu. 76, Art. 1-4; I-II, Qu. 56, Art. 4.

[78] An excellent overview with helpful orientation for Ariosto and Tasso is M. MURRIN, *The Allegorical Epic*, Chicago, University of Chicago Press, 1982. On the *Furioso* allegory see A. ASCOLI, *Ariosto's Bitter Harmony*, Princeton, Princeton University Press, 1987, esp. ch. 3.1, *Ariosto between Alcina and Logistilla*, pp. 122-140. I cite Tasso from *Gerusalemme liberata*, ed. F. CHIAPPELLI, Milan, Rusconi, 1982, XIV 62-65. There is debate about whether Tasso

In poetics, psychology and ethics, Boccaccio's *Amorosa visione* is a typical artifact of Trecento Italy. It puts Scholastic thought into Gothic art. Outside his century it connects with a prestigious occidental family vigorous for five-hundred years, one whose most powerful members were the epics, from the *Aeneid* moralized to *Gerusalemme liberata*. Heroes have to make their way from tempestuous youth, when passions run rampant, to the age of reason and wiser serenity.

To edify, Boccaccio constructs an edifice. His pedagogical architecture has a two-room plan, and each space contains numerous personages from various categories of human activity. Such long lists of names are a rhetorical device inherited from the classical epic, but housed as they are here, they exemplify a medieval motif, the «encyclopedic castle». In that form Geoffrey Chaucer plied his art with *The House of Fame* (ca. 1380), Christine de Pisan with the *Livre de la mutacion de Fortune* (1400-1403), Dante Alighieri with the Noble Castle in Limbus.[79]

Authorized by Dante to construct such a building, Boccaccio pillaged its refinements from a more esoteric Latin poem, the *Anticlaudianus*. Although he never mentions Alan of Lille among the learned and famous in his *Amorosa visione*, resemblances between the Chartrian's House of Nature and Dreamer's Tuscan castle are too many to be coincidental. Both edifices enjoy high perches, Alan's on a mountain, Boccaccio's more modestly on a hillock. Pride of each are their wonderfully lifelike frescoes. To introduce Nature and her talent as craftsman at the beginning of his epic, Alan invents a mural. It «depicts men's character» and «apes reality» with incredible verisimilitude: «What can have no real existence comes into being, and painting [...] turns the shadows of things into things and changes every lie to truth». First to be portrayed is Aristotle, followed by Plato, Seneca, Ptolemy, Tullius, Virgil, Hercules, Ulysses, Turnus, and Hippolytus with Venus. But if these men set good examples, a second room in the dwelling of the goddess carries a sadder message. In dark tones are the imperfect and excessive manifestations of Nature's power, represented by evil characters like Ennius, Priam, Maevius, Nero,

---

imposed the allegory *ex post facto* when he wrote his *Allegoria del poema*. M. Murrin, pp. 87-127, accepts the allegory as genuine; for a more recent discussion that argues the allegoresis to be a «red herring for ecclesiastical censors» see W. STEPHENS, *Metaphor, Sacrament, and the Problem of Allegory in 'Gerusalemme Liberata'*, «I Tatti Studies», IV, 1991, pp. 217-24.

[79] See S. CIGADA, *Il tema arturiano del 'chateau tournant'*, «Studi medievali», s. III, vol. II, pt. II, 1961, pp. 576-606. Other examples are the *Pèlerinage de Charlemagne* (12th c.), which describes the palace of Hugo of Constantinople with its speaking statues; *Artus de Bretagne* (14th c.), in which Sophrosyne leads the poet past seven obstacles to her dwelling, painted with images of many famous men.

Midas, and Davus.[80] The French master's precedent can explain the presence in Boccaccio of details absent from Dante: the twin-chambered design, an ekphrasis on didactic wall decoration, Aristotle heading the list of famous men, Fortune's cursèd wailing in the second room. Notwithstanding their natural quality, as Neoplatonic images Alan's frescoes are mere «figures and phantoms of truth». Similarly, while Boccaccio's bemused Dreamer marvels at the realism of the art he beholds, Reason scolds him for confusing empty illusion with truth. From his point of view, «Humana man non credo che sospinta / mai fosse a tanto ingegno quanto in quella / [...] eccetto se da Giotto, al qual la bella / Natura parte di sé somigliante / non occultò nell'arte» (IV 13-18); from hers, «qui dipinto / [...] son cose fallaci e fuor di vere» (XXX 14-15). Alan, we have seen, can also account for other inventions of the Italian work — Fortune monumental beside her wheel, the heroine Maria d'Aquino as a mask of Prudence who recalls Phronesis, sisterhood between Reason and Prudence, the psychomachy.

Of course, Boccaccio took inspiration eclectically, from other sources as recent as Brunetto Latini, as distant as Boethius. In Brunetto's *Tesoretto*, after the Guelph defeat at Montaperti, the disoriented narrator loses his way in a forest, where he encounters a noble lady, Nature. She instructs him and leads him to a plain populated by wise men under the power of Virtue, whose daughters are the Four Cardinal Virtues. Then he enters the palace of Justice, meets Courtesy and her allies, and completes his education in civilized living. Brunetto's treasure-land lessons are a medieval version of the etiquette book and a quaint, but recognizable, ancestor of the modern *Bildungsroman*.[81]

Boethius too, familiar to Boccaccio from his Neapolitan period, had described a journey of sorts. Lady Philosophy raises the suffering exile on wings of wisdom, liberates him from the physical sphere of sense perception, and introduces him to progressively higher forms of knowing, which culminate at the peak of pure Insight. Under her guidance, the narrator in the *Consolation of Philosophy* will learn to despise Fortune's evils, depicted in terms on which Boccaccio clearly drew. But when in the *Amorosa visione* Guide presses upward her slumbrous charge, he denies

---

[80] *Anticlaudianus* I. G. VELLI, *Petrarca e Boccaccio*, Padua, Antenore, 1979, pp. 106-111, documents traces of the *Anticlaudianus* in Boccaccio's first composition, *Elegia di Costanza*.

[81] D. WALLACE outlines parallels between the *Amorosa visione* and il *Tesoretto* in a study that also situates Boccaccio's acrostic vis-à-vis Dante's *Comedy* and Chaucer, in *Chaucer and the Early Writings of Boccaccio*, Woodbridge, Suffolk, and Dover, N.H., D. S. Brewer, 1985, pp. 10-15.

both her and Boethian ascent, «Ben sapete», he replies, «che io non ho penne / a posser su volar, come credete, / né potrei sostener questi travagli / a' quai dispormi subito volete» (III 71-75). Locked into a «tenebrous place», neither can he raise his «fog-mantled» eyes to that «sweet dawn» (II 78-82) his guide talks about, morning that had broken for the Roman prisoner once Philosophy cleared «his eyes of the mist of mortal affairs that clouds them». Forever earthbound, he remains visually impaired and fails to 'see the light'.[82]

Parallels between Boccaccio and Boethius seem to operate inversely, as they had in the *imitatio* of Dante. By taking the wide gate on a little guided outing that leans to the Pythagorean left, Dreamer moves along a descending moral axis. So in Room I of the castle he first sees Learning, then Glory, next the very tangible mountain of Wealth with its greedy grubbers, and last, Cupid amid a throng of carnal servants. In the garden, he disregards the eastern stream of virtuous love, and instead, he selects a southerly course, aimed at cupidinous union with his lady in a retreat whose umbrous red roses designate territory of the lascivious Venus. Both within the castle and without, his route falls from higher to lower things as the weight of his body and senses drags him downward. Inside, he moves away from intellectual knowledge and 'down' to Cupid; outside, he heads away from the direction of spiritual virtue and 'down' toward the shadows of purely sensual gratification. His trip reverses not only Boethius, but also the normal order of events in otherworldly visions.[83] In these declining patterns, directed toward appeasement of the senses, the journey is actually retrograde — as long as Giovanni is dreaming. His turnabout comes with his reawakening. Daytime enlightenment puts him 'back on his feet' for a second chance, this time the 'right' way.

* * *

If the *Amorosa visione* suffers defects, they are not problems of allegorical incoherence. On the contrary, the allegory is almost elementary. Dreamer's route recapitulates a medieval commonplace, that most

---

[82] An illuminating analysis of the Neoplatonic ascent pattern in the *Consolatio* is E. SCARRY, *The Well-Rounded Sphere: The Metaphysical Structure of the 'Consolation of Philosophy'*, in *Essays in the Numerical Criticism of Medieval Literature*, ed. C. D. ECKHARDT, Lewisburg, Pa., Bucknell University Press, 1980, pp. 91-140.

[83] P. PIEHLER, *The Visionary Landscape*, Montreal, McGill-Queen's University Press, 1971, is useful as an introduction to otherworld journeys and their types, both eastern and western.

simple and concise emblem of life known as the Y of Pythagoras. It is so obvious, in fact, that it is funny. Boccaccio, at play with the formal conventions of the Christian dream vision, draws them broadly with comic strokes, and into the scenario he plunks a protagonist who does not understand the script. From the moment Giovanni falls asleep, he is off on the wrong foot, so to speak. Even before they have entered the castle (and still in Canto I), he is already asking Guide, «Siam noi ancora là dove cotanto / ben mi prometti, donna graziosa, / di dovermi mostrar?» Psychologically, he is like a young child who has not yet developed a clear spatial and temporal sense, and so when travelling, impatiently keeps asking his parents, «Is it time yet? Are we there yet?» Morally, within the allegory, he is still in that pre-adolescent stage along the stem of the Y, before the forking when we enter our age of discernment. If things do not happen the way they should in a spiritual journey, the awkwardness is not Boccaccio's as poet, it is his Dreamer's as protagonist. Dreamer is meant to amuse us as a parodic refraction of Boethius, Brunetto, and Dante. What Boccaccio accomplishes is a mock vision, the kind of self-conscious genre parody that Millicent Marcus has ascribed to the *Decameron* as «allegory of form».[84]

Nevertheless, even if we can appreciate the poet's intentions, these verses of his do not touch us as poetry. Had they been unconstrained by the acrostic, they could have moved more freely and gracefully. As it is, machinery gets the better of creativity. In another sense, too, the *Amorosa visione* represents an experiment that could not be repeated. Boccaccio daringly pulled together philosophical systems and literary modes too disparate for a fully successful fusion. Our raconteur's earthy tongue-in-cheek humor is not readily compatible with an intellectual Christian vocabulary that turns on erudite notions from Boethius and Aquinas. Neither can Neoplatonism and Thomism be rolled easily into a single allegorical mechanism. The latter is best couched as a battle, a back-and-forth, the psychomachy between right and wrong. The former translates well into travel, a journey that as linear progression symbolizes gradual moral ascent.[85] In artistic terms, Boccaccio's *Teseida* seems more successful to me than the *Visione* because it is more focussed philosophically.

---

[84] M. MARCUS, *An Allegory of Form. Literary Self-consciousness in the 'Decameron'*, Saratoga, Cal., Anma Libri, 1979.

[85] A. FLETCHER defines the two fundamental patterns of allegory as 'battle' and 'progress', the former being represented by Prudentius's *Psychomachia*, the latter by the allegorized *Odyssey* and *Aeneid*. See his *Allegory. The Theory of a Symbolic Mode*, Ithaca, Cornell University Press, 1964, ch. 3.

The clash between reason and appetites finds a good fictional outlet in the great courtly tournament, the central episode of the epic and its allegorical key. But the *Amorosa visione*, a structure based on dualities, has no such center of gravity. It is both a back-and-forth and a journey, both Aristotle and Plato, both Aquinas and Boethius. Dreamer's tergiversations and Guide's push toward *askesis* result in tension that remains unresolved. The comic and the philosophic do not comfortably mate. Too wide a gap separates the high form of the visionary acrostic and the silly things that Dreamer says. Reversing Dante and Boethius, Boccaccio destabilizes the visionary terrain, where a proper protagonist ought to be goal-directed and upward bound. Dreamer, by contrast, goes now here, now there; he insists on the left; he descends spiritually. In spite of all the time and effort Guide spends on him and his own reiterated best intentions, he cannot *not* retrogress. But no matter. For all his stumbling and slipping, he wins in the end Prudence and Reason!

Twists on tradition, surprise finales — these are favorite Boccaccian games. Here his intention, surely, was to make us smile. It is, moreover, perfectly in character for this traveller to be so juvenile, so delinquent. Dreamer does it all wrong because he is young. Youth must learn. Should we believe that at the end of his dream he has matured? Has he really succeeded in ordering his soul through what, until literally the last minute, was instinctive, compulsive, and physical attraction for Maria? With such a perverse case, can the Neoplatonic cure work? Boccaccio, I think, teasingly leaves open the destiny of his sleepy *Döppleganger*. By the last scene Dreamer's eyelids, both of them, are open again. But all it would take is a momentary nodding, and in the blink of an eye he could slip out of Reason's sight, duck back behind the rose bushes. We can only hope Giovanni has learned enough to turn right — without postponing it until too late — at whatever future gates, rivers, or crossroads come his way in life.

3.

BOCCACCIO'S DEDICATION TO WOMEN IN LOVE

Boccaccio's dedication of the *Decameron* to idle women in love seems an admirably chivalrous gesture. It is just what we should expect, given his image as an inveterate ladies' man. But this amatory 'Author' is not the same man as the Florentine writer who created him. If we look behind the image at the artist who made it, we see his female audience, too, in a less romantic light. The Proem, carrying clear pointers to Boccaccio's own activity as reader, reveals a poet at play with Ovid and mindful of his Dante. Informed by the sources that were his, we can hear a voice speaking not for the lovelorn, but for the lustful. Those idle ladies topple from their courtly pedestal and fall into place as targets for a humorous dosing of misogyny. An emblematic public, they are warning signs of the trouble that can come, not just to women but to anyone in love, when passion runs unchecked by reason.

Just why and for whom he wrote his *Decameron*, the Author informs us in a Proem. A fire of love, life-long and uncontrolled, would have driven him to death had it not been for comfort from friends. With passing time, his own passion has diminished, and now, to repay the debt of gratitude, he offers consolation to others in need. Most deserving are the most afflicted. His book, therefore, is addressed not to men — who find distractions from love-pangs in sport and business — but to amorous ladies. Shut up in their chambers by sheltering families, idly sitting about, they have nothing to distract them from melancholy thoughts of their secret flames:

Adunque, acciò che in parte per me s'amendi il peccato della fortuna, la quale dove meno era di forza, sì come noi nelle dilicate donne veggiamo, quivi più avara fu di sostegno, in soccorso e rifugio di quelle che amano, per ciò che all'altre è assai l'ago e 'l fuso e l'arcolaio, intendo di raccontare cento novelle, o favole o parabole o istorie che dire le vogliamo. (Pr. 13)

Whether by about 1350 Boccaccio had at last matured from the madness of a stubborn, near-fatal affair into sensible middle age, remains a matter for speculation, if not skepticism.[1] His public life and artistic output up to then do not, in any event, accord well with the picture of a man incapacitated by passion. History, moreover, informs us that the *Decameron*'s most avid early readers belonged to the very group whom he is least concerned about reaching: powerful men of business. Marginal account records in the oldest manuscripts attest to the profession of their owners, who bore such distinguished names as Buondelmonti, Acciaiuoli, Bonaccorsi, Cavalcanti, and Verazzano. Some of these entrepreneurs, eager to possess the scarce book, even became *ad hoc* amanuenses, among them Giovanni d'Agnolo Capponi, Prior in 1378 of the great Florentine guild corporations, the *arti maggiori*.[2]

Their womenfolk would also, of course, have been exposed to the stories. Confirmation that they were comes from Boccaccio himself in a letter of 1373 addressed to his friend and patron, Maghinardo Cavalcanti. If anything, though, that communication only complicates matters:

I cannot praise your having allowed the honorable ladies of your household to read my trifles, rather I beg you to give me your word you will not do so again. You know how much they contain that is less than decent and offensive to propriety, how much sting from the unwelcome Venus, how many incitements to vice even for those of iron will; and even if they do not drive to indecent behavior illustrious women, most especially those with brows marked by holy chastity, nevertheless illicit burnings slip in with silent step and not infrequently

---

[1] Within twenty years of Boccaccio's death, folk had begun to accept his fiction as autobiography. The historian Filippo Villani's *Vita* of Boccaccio, 1380/90, is the earliest in a long line of fanciful biographies that were still being produced well into our own century. Romanticism and its epigones rhapsodized his affair with Fiammetta. To her, obviously, the *Decameron* must have been dedicated, as F. DE SANCTIS saw it in *Storia della letteratura italiana*, 1870; rpt. Florence, Sansoni, 1965, pp. 289-291. E. HUTTON, *Giovanni Boccaccio. A Biographical Study*, London, John Lane The Bodley Head, 1910, p. 175, pieced together movingly the 'periods' of this love in the man for whom woman «was the prize of life; he desired her not as friend, but as the most exquisite instrument of pleasure, beyond the music of flutes or the advent of spring». Although Fiammetta has looked more like a literary invention than a real woman ever since the reassessments of G. BILLANOVICH's *Restauri boccacceschi, cit.*, it is reported that Boccaccio, who never married, had five illegitimate children. See V. BRANCA, *Boccaccio. The Man and his Works*, trans. R. MONGES with D. MCAULIFFE, New York, New York University Press, 1976, pp. 76-77.

[2] Over two-thirds of the manuscripts before 1400 belong to this mercantile milieu, as V. BRANCA notes in *Boccaccio medievale*, Florence, Sansoni, 1986⁶, pp. 3-6. See also Branca's fuller profile of the book's fortunes, *Linee di una storia della critica al 'Decameron'*, Milan, Società Anonima Editrice Dante Alighieri, 1939, pp. 2-6, and now the magisterial catalogue with descriptions of the *Decameron* manuscripts in *Tradizione delle opere di Giovanni Boccaccio II, cit.*, pp. 71-146.

penetrate and irritate unchaste souls with the obscene wasting of concupiscence, a thing to be avoided at all costs [...]. Readers will suppose me a smutty panderer, an incestuous old man, an impure person, a foul-mouthed scandalmonger, avid to bruit about people's wickedness. I will not always find someone to stand up and excuse me by saying, "He wrote this in his youth, compelled by the authority of one more powerful".[3]

Has the sixty-year-old poet now sourly resolved that ladies sitting idly at home under the protection of parents, brothers, and husbands are the last people who should read the 'trifles' he penned perforce at thirty-five? No, he has not, we shall soon see. For the time being, let us simply grant that respectable — and presumably active — burgesses had been reading the *Decameron* with just as much pleasure as the businessmen to whom they were bound by ties of marriage and kinship. How, then, are we to understand Boccaccio's decision to single out languorous, lovesick fe-males as his sole beneficiaries?

Questions of real, historical readership aside, the public to whom our Author appeals had existed at least ever since the days of Ovid. Here is how, in a nocturnal epistle, the lonely maiden Hero begs her Leander to come soon:

We burn with equal fires, but I am not equal to you in strength; men, methinks, must have stronger natures. As the body, so is the soul of tender women frail [...]. You men, now in the chase, and now husbanding the genial acres of the country, consume long hours in the varied tasks that keep you. Either the market-place holds you, or the sports of the supple wrestling-ground, or you turn with bit the neck of the responsive steed; now you take the bird with the snare, now the fish with the hook [...]. For me who am denied these things, even were I less fiercely aflame, there is nothing left to do but love.[4]

---

[3] G. BOCCACCIO, *Epistole, cit.*, XXII 19-24, trans. adapted from A. SCAGLIONE, *Nature and Love, cit.*, pp. 117-118: «Sane, quod inclitas mulieres tuas domesticas nugas meas legere permiseris non laudo, quin imo queso per fidem tuam ne feceris. Nosti quot ibi sint minus decentia et adversantia honestati, quot veneris infauste aculei, quot in scelus impellentia etiam si sint ferrea pectora, a quibus etsi non ad incestuosum actum illustres impellantur femine, et potissime quibus sacer pudor frontibus insidet, subeunt tamen passu tacito estus illecebres et impudicas animas obscena concupiscentie tabe nonnunquam inficiunt irritantque, quod omnino ne contingat agendum est [...]. Existimabunt enim legentes me spurcidum lenonem, incestuo-sum senem, impurum hominem, turpiloquum maledicum et alienorum scelerum avidum rela-torem. Non enim ubique est qui in excusationem meam consurgens dicat: «Iuvenis scripsit et maioris coactus imperio». The «one more powerful», we suppose, would have been Cupid.

[4] OVID, *Heroides*, in *Heroides and Amores*, trans. G. SHOWERMAN, Cambridge, Mass., Harvard University Press, 1963 («Loeb Classical Library»), XIX, 5-16: «urimur igne pari, sed sum tibi viribus inpar: / fortius ingenium suspicor esse viris. / ut corpus, teneris ita mens infirma puellis — / [...] / Vos modo venando, modo rus geniale colendo / ponitis in varia

Male and female options at the Hellespont of yore hardly differ from habits in Trecento Florence:

[Le vaghe donne] dentro a' dilicati petti, temendo e vergognando, tengono l'amorose fiamme nascose [...] il più del tempo nel piccolo circuito delle loro camere racchiuse [... gli innamorati uomini] se alcuna malinconia o gravezza di pensieri gli affligge, hanno molti modi da alleggiare o da passar quello, per ciò che a loro, volendo essi, non manca l'andare a torno, udire e veder molte cose, uccellare, cacciare, pescare, cavalcare, giucare o mercatare. (Pr. 12)[5]

Boccaccio's obvious recollection of Ovid's *Heroides* (*in re* Fortune's short shrift to women) establishes a fictional framework for his Proem. The idea that females chambered with time on their hands will be hotly in love, hence benefit from his service, is just one of several literary conventions that shape the way he has staged himself there.[6]

The Author's public also depends on a commonplace according to which women are the proper audience for men who raise topics of amatory import. Boccaccio had already exploited the idea as a younger man in his *Filocolo* (c.1336-1339) when he interrupted the main plot of

---

tempora longa mora. / aut fora vos retinent aut unctae dona palaestrae, / flectitis aut freno colla sequacis equi; / nunc volucrem laqueo, nunc piscem ducitis hamo; / [...] / his mihi summotae, vel si minus acriter urar, / quod faciam, superest praeter amare nihil».

[5] The parallel has long been recognized. See e.g. V. BRANCA, *Decameron, cit.*, Pr. 15 and p. 979, n. 1; C. MUSCETTA, *Boccaccio, cit.*, p. 158.

[6] C. S. SINGLETON saw Boccaccio acting a part in *On 'Meaning' in the 'Decameron'*, «Italica», XXI, 1944, pp. 117-124. Most today concur that the proemial situation is the stuff of fiction, not history, but there agreement ends. It has yielded up signs of revolutionary feminism to D. RADCLIFFE-UMSTEAD, *Boccaccio's Idle Ladies*, in *The Roles and Images of Women in the Middle Ages and Renaissance*, Pittsburgh, University of Pittsburgh, 1975 («University of Pittsburgh Publications on the Middle Ages and the Renaissance», III); of old-fashioned *stilnovo* culture to G. GETTO, *Vita di forme e forme di vita nel 'Decameron'*, Turin, G. B. Petrini, 1972; of a new Occamistic intellectual élite to R. RAMAT, *L'introduzione alla quarta giornata*, in *Scritti su Giovanni Boccaccio*, Florence, Casa Editrice Leo S. Olschki, 1964, pp. 93-107; of broadly popular culture to G. PADOAN (see below, n. 24); of metaliterature to J. H. POTTER, *Five Frames for the 'Decameron'. Communication and Social Systems in the Cornice*, Princeton, Princeton University Press, 1982. R. Hastings, occupying a camp unto himself, takes the Proem literally. He notes that Francesco da Barberino's *Del reggimento e costumi di donna* (1309-1315) requires women to stay confined as the age of marriage approaches and concludes that Boccaccio's concern for them should be understood as genuine, a step toward female emancipation. See R. HASTINGS, *Nature and Reason in the 'Decameron'*, Manchester, Manchester University Press, 1975, p. 52-53. C. DE MICHELIS offers a sensitive gendered reading that associates the strong feminine side of the *Decameron* (including the ladies to whom it is dedicated) with poetry, imagination, and fantasy, while its masculine aspects pertain rather to work-a-day materialism and the course of real history, in *Contraddizioni nel 'Decameron'*, in *Miscellanea di studi in onore di Vittore Branca*, II, *Boccaccio e dintorni*, Florence, Casa Editrice Leo S. Olschki, 1983, p. 95-109; published as ch. 1-2 of his volume *Contraddizioni nel 'Decameron'*, Milan, Guanda, 1983.

the romance to make room for a society game one summer afternoon in a garden of Naples. This episode, the first kernel for the frame tale structure of the *Decameron*, presents a party of young aristocrats who debate questions concerning love under the judgeship and rule of Queen Fiammetta. When Boccaccio set up Fiammetta in court, he was following the lead of Andreas Capellanus, who around 1185 in the French domain of Champagne, had sanctioned women as arbiters in such amorous cases. The Chaplain's manual, a Latin *Art of Courtly Love*, invokes among its authorities in love casuistry Countess Alice of Champagne and her mother, Eleanor of Aquitaine. Andreas in turn had codified the troubadours, who tirelessly addressed poems to women. So, too, would the Italians in highly intellectual *canzoni*, like Guido Cavalcanti's «Donna me prega» and Dante's «Donne ch'avete intelletto d'amore».[7]

Ladies are Boccaccio's appropriate audience because love is his chief subject. Even before starting the stories, we know as much from the book's incipit, «Comincia il libro chiamato Decameron cognominato Prencipe Galeotto». If the first element of its full title implies a category of Christian writing ('hexameral' commentaries on Genesis), the surname calls forth two famous adulteries. Gallehault, the knight who pandered to Lancelot and Guinevere in tales of King Arthur's Round Table, arranged the rendezvous for the lovers' first kiss. That point in fiction would later spark Francesca da Rimini to a romance immortalized by Dante, when he tells through her voice at *Inferno* V, how one day she and her brother-in-law fell into an embrace while reading about Sir Lancelot in a book that was their 'Gallehault'. So, too, is the *Decameron* a go-between. Surnamed «Prince Gallehault», it carries a message of love from Author to ladies, who will find in his tales, as the Proem promises, «piacevoli e aspri casi d'amore».[8]

Courtly and stilnovistic conventions, which make it *de rigueur* to privilege woman, easily account for the sex of Boccaccio's readers. What they do not explain is why his is an *otiose* public that never lays hand to needle, spindle, or reel. Precedent on this point was suggested, we recall, by Ovid's *Heroides*. There women, inactivity, and love go together as a

---

[7] Commentary widely acknowledges courtly and stilnovistic influences in the Proem. Additional discussion of the medieval fashion and reasons for addressing amorous writing to women appears in A. K. Cassell and V. Kirkham, *Diana's Hunt, cit.*, Intro., pp. 7-11.

[8] As noted by Branca, *Decameron, cit.*, p. 976, *Decameron* recalls *Hexameron*, the title of commentaries by St. Ambrose and others on the Six Days of Creation in Genesis. M. R. Menocal has some deconstructionist thoughts on how Boccaccio's «Prencipe Galeotto» is both «written with and against Dante» in *Writing in Dante's Cult of Truth. From Borges to Boccaccio*, Durham, N.C. and London, Duke University Press, 1991, pp. 178-203.

matter of course. Leisured Hero, barred from manly public life, had «nothing left to do but love».

The same circumstantial combination, involving ladies with time on their hands, returns twice after the *Decameron* Proem as a motif in individual stories. During her husband's absence at war, the Queen of France tries to seduce his kingdom's young caretaker with an argument propped on the logic of leisure. Since labor, she points out, is a serf's lot, love-struck peasants endanger their livelihoods, but the life of ease justifies desire. She comes to an inescapable conclusion:

> Egli è il vero che, per la lontananza di mio marito non potendo io agli stimoli della carne né alla forza d'amor contrastare, le quali sono di tanta potenza, che i fortissimi uomini non che le tenere donne hanno già molte volte vinti e vincono tutto il giorno, essendo io negli agi e negli *ozii* ne' quali voi me vedete, a secondare li piaceri d'amore e a divenire innamorata mi sono lasciata trascorrere. (II 8, 15)

Aristocratic *otium* takes a sensual toll, too, on the young widow Ghismonda, as she defiantly apprises her overprotective father:

> Egli è il vero che io ho amato e amo Guiscardo [...]. Esser ti dové, Tancredi, manifesto, essendo tu di carne, aver generata figliuola di carne e [...] quello che gli *ozii* e le dilicatezze possano ne' vecchi non che ne' giovani [...]. Alle quali forze [di concupiscibile disidero] non potendo io resistere, a seguir quello a che elle mi tiravano, sì come giovane e femina, mi disposi e innamora'mi. (IV 1, 32-35)

Both ladies invoke a truism. Idleness predisposes to love. Andreas Capellanus admits disapprovingly, for example, that is is only natural for the clergy to love because they are so well nourished and live in idle solitude.[9] Convent escapades in the *Decameron* — like nine curious nuns' discoveries with «Little Thomas», their silent gardener — prove how vulnerable indeed are the wimpled to «the great powers of leisure» (III 1). The Old French *Romance of the Rose* posts Dame Oiseuse as a gatekeeper at the garden where Amant allegorically pursues his beloved flower. Later the voice of Reason intervenes with reproach, «Love would never have seen you if Idleness had not led you into the fair garden of Diversion».[10]

---

[9] Andreas Capellanus, *The Art of Courtly Love, cit.*, I 7.

[10] *The Romance of the Rose, cit.*, 510 ff. and 2,996 ff. Idleness will come with the largest banner to Love's Parliament at verse 10,449. H. Limoli notes the role idleness plays for some medieval Romance lovers in *Boccaccio's Masetto*, «Romanische Forschungen», LXXVII, 1965, 281-292.

Since idleness leads to love, business/busyness must distance it. Juvenal's sixth *Satire* confirms that toil keeps women chaste, and Dante implies the same thing in his nostalgic picture of Cacciaguida's Florence. Boccaccio agrees in his epic *Teseida*, written about a dozen years before the *Decameron*. Venus's temple boasts as trophies broken bows from Diana's huntresses, nymphs who roamed the forests «a dimostrare che chi vuole interamente servare la sua castità, dee fuggire in quanto può ogni umano consorzio, e similmente l'*ozio*» (VII 50, gl.). That intelligence comes from Ovid. The *Remedies of Love* advise anyone hoping to recover from lovesickness to shun leisure first of all. *Otium* must yield to *negotium*.

Take away leisure and Cupid's bow is broken, and his torch lies extinguished and despised. As the plane rejoices in wine, or the poplar in water, or the reed of the mere in marshy ground, so does Venus delight in leisure; you who seek an end of love, love yields to business: be busy, and you will be safe.

Ovid's recommended tonics are an activity list by now predictable: go out to the law courts; engage in martial exercise, husbandry, and the hunt. Solitude, correct for nymphs committed to virginity, is not advisable for pupils taking this urbane love cure. Since secrecy adds to passion, Ovid's recovering clientele should always seek the crowd — but never, under any circumstances, company of other lovers.[11]

Ovidian theory, supplemented by some medieval updating — commonplaces of courtly love in lyric, romance, and the dialogues of Andreas Capellanus — underlies the *Decameron* Proem. It is not the only textual passage in which Boccaccio plays on the coupling of love and leisure. *Novelle* within the *Decameron*, as we have seen, also feature characters to whose cases that theory applies, the Queen of France (II 8) and Ghismonda, daughter of Tancredi (IV 1). In other writings, too, Boccaccio's protagonists took cues along these lines from his favorite Latin poet. No less a lady than the heroine of *Elegia di madonna Fiammetta* had confessed to a furious passion nourished by secrecy and leisure. The threshold that Panfilo stumbled upon when he walked out of her life is a line she herself

---

[11] How nymphs should live is illustrated by the stories of Callisto, Actaeon, and Daphne in the *Metamorphoses*, myths Boccaccio was fond of citing. The cures are from OVID's *Remedies of Love*, in *The Art of Love and Other Poems*, trans. J. H. MOZLEY, Cambridge, Mass., Harvard University Press, 1969 («Loeb Classical Library»), 139-144: «Otia si tollas, periere Cupidinis arcus, / Contemtaeque iacent et sine luce faces. / Quam platanus vino gaudet, quam populus unda, / Et quam limosa canna palustris humo, / Tam Venus *otia* amat; qui finem quaeris amoris, / Cedit amor rebus: res age, tutus eris». Cf. *Remedies*, 151-210 and 579 ff.

cannot cross, encased as she is by bedchamber walls: «Niuna parte della mia *camera* era che io con disiderosissimo occhio non riguardassi»; «gli occhi all'uscio della mia *camera* rivolgeva»; «dimorando io nella mia *camera sola*». Idle solitude feeds her apprehensive imagination and paralyzes her, «Io piú volte per cacciare da me i non utili riguardamenti cominciai molte cose a voler fare; ma vinta da nuove imaginazioni, quelle lasciava stare». Obsessed with thoughts of her absent Panfilo, she anticipates her melancholy sisters in the *Decameron* Proem, those ladies «nel piccolo circuito delle loro *camere* racchiuse». Ironically, Fiammetta worries that the fatigue of travel might make *him* forget *her* because she remembers «l'avere già letto ne' versi di Ovidio che le fatiche traevano a' giovani amore delle menti».[12]

Boccaccio's amorous Fiammetta, his Phaedra-like French Queen, and Ghismonda of Salerno, along with Ovid's Hero, beloved of Leander, all come to unhappy endings. Their leisure was destructive. It kindled secret, illicit flames that burned with results ranging from unmitigated misery to death *tout court*. Consequently, in the idle circumstances of his *Decameron*'s proemial audience we ought to suspect some potential danger. That love for the sake of pleasure which Fiammetta had rejected at the heart of the *Filocolo* love debate is nourished, she says, by 'ozio'. Sardanapalus, an archetype of lust for both Dante and Boccaccio, not surprisingly «rotted in leisure». Virtue requires that we flee sloth, as does Lia-Faith in Boccaccio's *Comedia delle ninfe fiorentine*. Civic responsibility rejects it, too, for the well ordered community relies on activity. People work and earn, Boccaccio writes in his commentary on Dante, to avoid idleness: «per non star oziosi». Dante himself certainly did not waste his youth in «lascivie e ozii», so Boccaccio communicates in his *Trattatello*.[13]

---

[12] *Elegia di madonna Fiammetta*, ed. M. P. Mussini Sacchi, Milan, Mursia, 1987, pp. 86-88. Fiammetta owes much to Seneca. Cf. *Hippolytus*, in Seneca, *Tragedies*, I, trans. F. J. Miller, 1917; Cambridge, Mass., Harvard University Press, 1979 («Loeb Classical Library»), 204-207: «Whoever rejoices in overmuch prosperity and abounds in luxury is ever seeking unaccustomed [Venearean] joys». See V. Russo, *Il senso del tragico nel 'Decameron'*, «Filologia e letteratura», XI, 1965, pp. 29-83. R. Hollander has an appealing assessment of Fiammetta in *Boccaccio's Two Venuses, cit.*, pp. 40-49.

[13] *Filocolo, cit.*, IV 46, 3: «questo amore niun'altra cosa è che una inrazionabile volontà, nata da una passione venuta nel cuore per libidinoso piacere che agli occhi è apparito, nutricato per ozio da memoria»; *De casibus, cit.*, II 12, 6 paints the Syrian Sardanapalus as a person who «marceret ocio»; *Comedia delle ninfe, cit.*, IV 40; *Esposizioni, cit.*, VII 2, 64; *Trattatello in laude di Dante*, ed. P. G. Ricci, Milan, Mondadori, 1974 («Tutte le opere», III), I 21. Cf. Biblical injunctions, e.g., Prov. 6:6: «Go to the ant, O sluggard; / consider her ways, and be wise». Boccaccio naturally also recognizes a constructive kind of leisure, the «ocia» necessary to poets, as in *De casibus, cit.*, III 14. Cf. Seneca's *Letters to Lucilius*, 82, 4: «Otium sine litteris mors est,

Perhaps the 'ozio' in which the *Decameron*'s feminine public dwells should be construed, then, not as dignified *'otium'* or 'leisure' — what Dante calls «ozio di speculazione» (*Convivio* I 1, 4) — but in a pejorative sense as 'idleness' or 'sloth'. If so, the ladies' secret flames of desire lose connotations of noble love presumed by the courtly canon, and burn rather on the fuel of carnal concupiscence. Love and leisure, in other words, may conceal a more menacing combination, lust and idleness.

Dante had paired them as «lussuria e ozio» to the detriment of a degenerate prince (*Purgatorio* VII 102). In Boccaccio's writings, though, the characters who feed on these vices are more often than not female, usually by sex, but sometimes instead by temperament. A figure who fits the latter description is the male protagonist of Boccaccio's *Corbaccio*, probably composed soon after the *Decameron* (ca. 1355-1356). Like Madonna Fiammetta, he mopes over «carnal love» for a cruel widow — «solo nella mia *camera*, la quale è veramente sola testimonia delle mie lagrime, de' sospiri e de' rammarichii» — until, in a dream, the shade of her husband guides him to recovery by unmasking the shrew.[14] Although the widow often goes out on the prowl to pounce on all sorts of men, her usual haunts are chambers and hidden spots («camere», «nascosi luoghi»). There even crews of men cannot extinguish «one single sparklet» of her fiery lust; there her «paternosters» are French romances about Lancelot and Guinevere, Tristan and Iseult. The *Corbaccio* widow, a figure of lust personified, reads the same Arthurian romances as had Francesca da Rimini, she who dominates Dante's circle of Lust and to whose story the *Decameron* surname, Prince Gallehault, alludes.[15]

Over the book, their «Prince Gallehault», Francesca and Paolo succumb to damning carnal desire. Since the *Decameron*, too, is a «Prencipe Galeotto», Boccaccio invites us to look in his love stories for a message about temptation to love of the flesh. That this go-between should pander to sedentary ladies secretly afire is eminently right. Idleness invites desire; secrecy fans the flames. In woman, what's more, they can be kindled by spontaneous combustion, for she has no weakness greater

---

et hominis vivi sepultura», cited by G. VELLI, *Seneca nel 'Decameron'*, «Giornale Storico della Letteratura Italiana», CLXVIII, 1991, pp. 321-334.

[14] *Corbaccio*, ed. P. G. RICCI, 1952; Milan, Einaudi, 1977 («Classici Ricciardi»), p. 3.

[15] A review of the arguments on the dating, still debated, and an argument for the temporal as well as poetic proximity of *Corbaccio* to *Decameron* appear in R. HOLLANDER, *Boccaccio's Last Fiction. 'Il Corbaccio'*, Philadelphia, University of Pennsylvania Press, 1988. Excellent analysis of the widow and her emblematic character can be found in the introduction and commentary to the *Corbaccio*, trans. A. K. CASSELL, Binghamton, N.Y., Medieval and Renaissance Texts and Studies, 1993[2].

than lust. It is a female sin by antonomasia. Dante well knew that fact because of the thirty-four faults punished in the thirty-four cantos of the *Inferno*, there is only one for which a woman speaks: it is the lust personified by Francesca.[16]

On the aggressive female libido, Boccaccio's authors universally agree. Love's most savvy Latin preceptor, after giving useful hints to men on the look-out, adds in his manual:

Did it suit us males not to ask any woman first, the woman, already won, would play the asker. In soft meads the heifer lows to the bull, the mare always whinnies to the horn-footed steed. In us desire is weaker and not so frantic: the manly flame knows a lawful bound.[17]

A brief, annotated catalogue of names follows to clinch the point: Byblis, Myrrha, Pasiphae, Clytemnestra, Creusa, and Phaedra. Isidore of Seville's highly influential seventh-century encyclopedia, *The Etymologies*, proposes two possible derivations for the word *femina*:

The word *femina* comes from parts near the *femur*, where the species of the sex is distinguished from a man's. Others, using a Greek etymology, say that *femina* comes from *fiery vigor*, because a female is more ardently concupiscent. The libidinous drive is stronger in the female, both in women and animals. That is why among the ancients excessive love was called feminine.

The word for 'man' (Latin *vir*), by contrast, comes from 'strength' (*vis*), cognate with 'virtue', because men are stronger than women, both physically and morally.[18]

Boccaccio's Proem does not privilege ladies to praise them. Women idle, solitary, chambered, and kindled with «hidden flames» are an

---

[16] To my knowledge, it has not been demonstrated that the categories of sins in *Inferno* seem to correlate numerically with the number of cantos. The lustful are in Canto V because 5 is the number of the flesh (cf. five senses) and animal sensuality (God created the animals on the fifth day). Female sensuality and numerology in the *Commedia* are subjects of V. KIRKHAM, *Quanto in femmina foco d'amor dura!*, cit., and *A Canon of Women in Dante's 'Commedia'*, cit.

[17] OVID, *Art of Love*, in *The Art of Love and Other Poems*, I, cit., 277-282: «Conveniat maribus, nequam nos ante rogemus, / Femina iam partes victa rogantis agat. / Mollibus in pratis admugit femina tauro: / Femina cornipedi semper adhinnit equo. / Parcior in nobis nec tam furiosa libido: / Legitimum finem flamma virilis habet».

[18] ISIDORE, *Etymologiae*, cit., XI 2, 24: «Femina vero a partibus femorum dicta, ubi sexus species a viro distinguitur. Alii Graeca etymologia feminam ab ignea vi dictam putant, quia vehementer concupiscit. Libidinosiores enim viris feminas esse tam in mulieribus quam in animalibus. Vnde nimius amor apud antiquos femineus vocabatur». Cf. *Etymologiae* XI 2, 17: «Vir nuncupatus, quia maior in eo vis est quam in feminis: unde et virtus nomen accepit; sive quod vi agat feminam».

audience of readers ripe for a fall like Francesca's. They are a loving public on the brink of lust. Yet their Gallehault-book need not inevitably provoke the same dire consequences as the dame of Rimini's. The gentle readers of Boccaccio's stories may take profit as well as pleasure from their private pastime: «le già dette donne, che queste leggeranno, parimente diletto delle sollazzevoli cose in quelle mostrate e utile consiglio potranno pigliare, in quanto potranno cognoscere quello che sia da fuggire e che sia similmente da seguitare».

Whether the Author's pining shut-ins will take a salutary lesson from his tales depends on which of his characters they choose to emulate. A majority of the *Decameron*'s remarkably high female population are headstrong wives who cuckold a spouse, or women otherwise powerfully sexed. Concupiscent Ghismonda is one. Others are Elena (VIII 7), anticipatory of the *Corbaccio* widow and aptly punished for fiery desire with a day-long roasting in the sun; Alatiel (II 7), who leaves a trail of dead lovers across the Mediterranean and holds the *Decameron* record for sexual coupling — perhaps more than 10,000 times; Madonnna Filippa (VI 7), who evades 'burning' (at the stake) for adultery in Prato on grounds of her unbounded capacity for satisfying men.[19] A significant minority, however, are model wives, the paragon being patient, obedient Griselda (X 10).

Griselda and her lord, Gualtieri, act out a Pauline axiom in the closing tale, which is Boccaccio's last word on a woman's place in the *Decameron*: «the husband is the head of the wife» (Ephesians 5:23). That rule had been pronounced at the beginning of the book by Elissa, who urges the ladies gathered in Santa Maria Novella not to leave Florence without men to guide them: «gli uomini sono delle femine capo e senza l'ordine loro rade volte riesce alcuna nostra opera a laudevole fine» (I Intro. 76). At a moral level, what Emilia appropriates from St. Paul's instruction means that strong, masculine reason and virtue must dominate softer, feminine sensuality and passions in every individual.[20]

---

[19] M. COTTINO-JONES analyzes Elena's lustful fire in *Order from Chaos. Social and Aesthetic Harmonies in Boccaccio's 'Decameron'*, Washington, D.C., University Press of America, 1982, pp. 147-153. Filippa is usually admired for clever eloquence by Italianists, and she has even been cited as a pioneer of feminism («una vera eroina boccacciana», «espressione di cortesia borghese», «una donna moderna») as in *Dieci novelle dal 'Decameron' di Giovanni Boccaccio*, trans. and comm. C. BURA and M. A. MORETTINI, Perugia, Editrice Grafica Perugia, 1980, p. 108. She gets a deserved debunking by a student of canon law: K. PENNINGTON, *A Note to 'Decameron' VI 7: The Wit of Madonna Filippa*, «Speculum», LII, 1977, pp. 902-905.

[20] On reason and the appetites in Boccaccio see above, ch. 2, and below, ch. 4. St. Augustine's treatise *De Trinitate* defined the traditional symbolic relationship linking male-

Florence of the fourteenth century no doubt did mostly confine women to the home.[21] Perhaps some of those women, foreshadowing modern female affinity for the novel, delighted in bedrooms over its ancestral *novelle*.[22] That they lolled about like Hero of Sestos or mournful Madonna Fiammetta, never lifting the time-honored implements of feminine industry, is less than plausible. Conventions of imaginative literature, which determine the parts played by both Author and public in Boccaccio's Proem, also account for his stance in the letter to Maghinardo Cavalcanti. The *peccatum juventatis*, composed by a writer who claims that Cupid gave him no choice in the matter, are a well read poet's professional clichés. Boccaccio never rejected his *Decameron* in old age. On the contrary, he continued patiently to revise it.[23]

The *Decameron*, as Prince Gallehault, brings male guidance for ladies at loose ends. Whoever reads with a healthy mind («sanamente»), answering hope expressed by the Author in his Conclusion, will recognize an

---

female and mind-body. Canon law decreed that women were subject to men *naturaliter*; see R. METZ, *La donna nelle fonti del diritto canonico medievale*, in *Né Eva né Maria. Condizione femminile e immagine della donna nel medioevo*, ed. M. PEREIRA, Bologna, Zanichelli, 1981, pp. 63-71. A good modern survey is J. FERRANTE, *Woman as Image in Medieval Literature, cit.*, pp. 23 ff. and 101-102. See also J. H. POTTER's wry remarks on Boccaccio's implicit misogyny, *Woman in the 'Decameron'*, in *Studies in the Italian Renaissance: Essays in Memory of Arnolfo B. Ferruolo*, ed. G. P. BIASIN, A. M. MANCINI, N. J. PERELLA, Naples, Società Editrice Napoletana, 1985, pp. 87-103.

[21] As historians can confirm, women were more and more confined to domestic spaces from the twelfth century onwards. Division of labor in the cloth guilds, for example, assigned women tasks that were lower paying and carried out at home. Their segregation became so extreme that they were not even permitted to attend funerals of their kinsmen. By 1610 a Frenchman commented, «in Florence women are more enclosed than in any other part of Italy; they see the world only from the small openings in their windows». J. C. BROWN, *A Woman's Place Was in the Home: Women's Work in Renaissance Tuscany*, in *Rewriting the Renaissance. The Discourses of Sexual Difference in Early Modern Europe*, ed. M. W. FERGUSON, M. QUILLIGAN and N. J. VICKERS, Chicago, University of Chicago Press, 1986, pp. 206-224. The 'courtesy' book for women by Francesco da Barberino, *Del reggimento e costume di donna* (1309-1315), requires girls of marriageable age to respect the decorum of domestic confinement. R. HASTINGS, *Nature and Reason, cit.*, pp. 52-53, quite rightly recalls this testimony with respect to the *Decameron* Proem, but at the same time, he is mysteriously able to read Boccaccio's book as «an apologia for women» and «the start, however tentative, of female emancipation».

[22] The suggestion is A. SCAGLIONE's, *Nature and Love, cit.*, pp. 107-108. G. PADOAN calls women Boccaccio's 'natural' readers, in *Mondo aristocratico e mondo communale nell'ideologia e nell'arte di Giovanni Boccaccio*, «Studi sul Boccaccio», II, 1964, pp. 81-216; rpt. with bibliographical update in G. PADOAN, *Il Boccaccio le Muse il Parnaso e l'Arno*, Florence, Casa Editrice Leo S. Olschki, 1978, pp. 1-91.

[23] G. BILLANOVICH, *Restauri boccacceschi, cit.*, p. 162 n.; G. PADOAN, *Mondo aristocratico, cit.*, p. 125. The holograph dates from Boccaccio's last years, as V. BRANCA and P. G. RICCI demonstrated in *Un autografo del 'Decameron' (Codice Hamiltoniano 90)*, Florence, Casa Editrice Leo S. Olschki, 1962 («Opuscoli Accademici, Facoltà di Lettere e Filosofia dell'Università di Padova», VIII).

unspoken warning in the title's allusion to *Inferno* V and the Proem's echoes of Dr. Ovid. Feminine love fed on idleness and secrecy portends a lustful fall. The lovesick — men and women alike — tempted to imitate Francesca's uncritical method of reading[24] and consequent slip into adultery can find in Boccaccio's book a preventive 'remedy' with encouragement toward love of a better kind.

---

[24] Francesca's errors in the enjoyment of her Arthurian book, which she took too literally and failed to finish, are nicely laid out by S. NOAKES, *The Double Misreading of Paolo and Francesca*, in *Timely Reading, cit.*, pp. 38-55.

4.

AN ALLEGORICALLY TEMPERED *DECAMERON*

The *Decameron* frame tale is reticent fiction with hints of underlying allegory. Invented by a poet well practiced in that veiled medieval mode, it repeatedly invites us as readers to collaborate with him in completing his symbolic picture. Ten young Florentines tell ten stories each for ten days, but the Author refuses to reveal their 'real' names. While the book's calendar spans two symmetrical five-day weeks, the storytellers themselves are seven women and three men, a contrastingly lopsided arrangement, and one all the more surprising since it leaves four of the ladies with no lover attendant. Our Author, however, does not say why male and female narrators are not evenly matched, nor will he give away which among the latter is whose beloved. From sanctuary in Santa Maria Novella, the party progresses through three idyllic country settings, places that lie we know not where in spite of their distinctive aspects. Servants accompany them, although not one apiece. Three of the women bring none, no explanations offered. At day's end, the noble brigade takes turns singing curiously allusive ballads, yet what the words mean, no one can tell. Lyrics courtly at surface, they are as much riddles as the amorous pseudonyms given «not without cause» to this chaste mixed company in rational retreat from pestilential mortality.

Backed by a century-long history of failed efforts to crack the frame tale code, most critics today decline Boccaccio's tempting invitation. His clues to the reader, they surmise, may only be red herrings teasingly scattered to sidetrack pedants, earnest souls sniffing out the trail of an allegorical mare's nest. Serious moral symbolism, our contemporaries suppose, would hardly be compatible with a work as modern and playful as the *Decameron*. From their perspective, the *cornice* is primarily an esthetic distancing device, its idealized narrators and the stylized rituals of their daily rhythms reminders that what we are reading is Art. Pseudonyms must serve only to tag the storytellers as purely fictional types, since each name recalls a character in other works by Boccaccio himself, or by poets he especially admired – Virgil, Petrarch, and Dante.[1]

These assumptions, though, are troublesome on several scores. If Neifile is a tribute to Dante, why should she revive the relatively obscure «pargoletta», an anonymous «little girl» of the poet's early period? Would not 'Beatrice' have been a better prospect for new life on later pages? As for Petrarchan Lauretta, what except etymology – or to be exact, a rhetorical figure of *adnominatio* – connects her with Madonna Laura? Does she actually do or say anything in the *Decameron* to justify the namesake? When christening characters, Boccaccio typically went by the maxim of his times, «Nomina sunt consequentia rerum», and here is no exception. In fact, stating his rationale for the seven ladies' pseudonyms, he pointedly invokes that rule: «per nomi alle qualità di ciascuna convenienti o in tutto o in parte intendo di nominarle» (I, Intro. 51). Is it not odd, then, that only Dioneo, Filostrato, and Pampinea possess distinctive

---

[1] Those today who see the *Decameron* as 'antimedieval' descend from the father of Italian literary history, F. De Sanctis. He summed up the spirit of the book with a sweeping dictum: «Qui trovi il medio evo non solo negato, ma canzonato», in *Storia della letteratura italiana, cit.*, p. 254. The Neapolitan professor found a twentieth-century partisan in C. S. Singleton, for whom the stories, purged of any didactic intent, bespeak a new Renaissance esthetic of *ars gratia artis*, as he argued in his article *On 'Meaning' in the 'Decameron', cit.* That point of view, which deracinates the text from its cultural context, still enlists polemical spokesmen. So, for example, J. Markulin with *Emilia and the Case for Openness in the 'Decameron'*, «Stanford Italian Review», III, 1983, pp. 183-189: «Since it departs radically from the norms of fiction as conceived in the fourteenth century, those norms can no longer furnish adequate and reliable guides for its reading».

Others, assuming Boccaccio belonged to his own times, have sleuthed for meaning in the frame tale with various keys – topical, autobiographical, moral, and rhetorical. G. Carducci's *Ai parentali di Giovanni Boccaccio in Certaldo*, Bologna, Zanichelli, 1876, admired the writer's lively characterizations of the narrators, presumably 'real' Florentine people. L. Manicardi and A. F. Massèra, *Le dieci ballate del 'Decameron'*, in «Miscellanea della Valdelsa», IX, 1901, pp. 102-114, constructed parallels between the narrators' songs and phases of Boccaccio's love for Fiammetta: Filostrato, Dioneo, and Panfilo were his amorous frustrations, joys, and 'all-loving' temperament. Rebutting them in a review, H. Hauvette, *Les Ballades du 'Décaméron'*, «Journal des Savants», n.s., vol. III, 1905, pp. 489-500, equated the singers of ballads I-III with Grammar, Rhetoric and Logic; an infelicitous scheme that Boccaccio (alias Dioneo) wisely dropped for IV-X, which simply represent facets of love typical in the popular medieval lyric tradition.

Not until the 1940's did the storytellers begin to assume their identity as symbols of Boccaccio's individual poetic art. Thus Filomena was the 'sweetness' of the *dolce stil novo*, Lauretta his homage to Petrarch, Neifile («lover of the new») pride in his originality, and the three men were symbolic transsexual Muses, according to A. Lipari's ingenious scheme, *The Structure and Real Significance of the 'Decameron'*, in *Essays in Honor of Albert Feuillerat*, ed. H. Peyre, «Yale Romanic Studies», XXII, New Haven, Yale University Press, pp. 43-83. G. Billanovich, *Restauri boccacceschi, cit.*, proposed a similar, but appealingly less Procrustean mold. If Elissa and Lauretta point to Virgil and Petrarch, other narrators have literary names that recur elsewhere in Boccaccio's corpus: Filostrato returns from the early, homonymous 'qualities', while the rest of the group are almost indistinguishably alike?[2] Finally, are there not some puzzling mismatches between source characters and their Decameronian counterparts? Not all reincarnations are as understandable as Filostrato's. Tragic hero of the Trojan romance *Filostrato*, he has every right to resurrect nominally as king for a day in the *Decameron*, when stories end unhappily. But beyond a name, what does

---

romance, as does Filomena, to whom it had been dedicated; Emilia was heroine of the *Teseida*, and Pampinea had appeared both in *Ameto* and Boccaccio's second eclogue. An exception is Neifile, whose name appears for the first time in the *Decameron* and in whom C. Muscetta, *Boccaccio, cit.*, p. 164, later saw an allusion to Dante's «pargoletta».

The first to construct a systematic case for Christian allegory in the frame tale was J. Ferrante, *The Frame Characters of the 'Decameron': A Progression of Virtues*, «Romance Philology», XIX, 1965, pp. 212-226. The female narrators represent the seven Cardinal and Theological Virtues (I Pampinea-Faith, II Filomena-Hope, III Neifile-Perseverance, V Fiammetta-Love, VI Elissa-Justice, VIII Lauretta-Abstinence, IX Emilia-Wisdom); Filostrato and Dioneo, Days IV and VII, are Despair and Sensuality that the mind must overcome in its ascent to All-Virtue, signified by Panfilo, ruler of Day X. A curious psychoanalytical reading by S. Galletti, *Patologia al 'Decameron'*, Palermo, Flaccovio, 1969, labels the women Reason, Temperance, Hope, Justice, Poverty, Faith, and Humility; Panfilo is Charity, Filostrato is Fortitude, and Dioneo is supposed to be «Fear of the Lord» by the far-fetched etymology «m'inchino a Dio». L. Marino, *The 'Decameron' 'Cornice': Allusion, Allegory, and Iconology*, Ravenna, Longo, 1979, pp. 131-179, discovers hints of secular as well as sacred virtues in the narrators, although not in any consistent one-to-one pattern; perhaps the three men are tripartite Prudence. The true purpose of the frame, she asserts, is to proclaim itself art. Similarly, J. H. Potter, *Five Frames, cit.*, pp. 28 and 80 ff., finds in the *brigata*'s stereotyped traits evidence of deliberately and highly coded literature. She is, however, disappointingly noncommittal on its possible message: the group is simply «a varied cross-section of sound qualities for living». Like Marino, Potter provides a good bibliographical retrospective, for which see, too, P. L. Cerisola, *La questione della cornice del 'Decameron'*, «Aevum», XLIX, 1975, pp. 137-156. V. Branca, who surveys major arguments in his commentary on the *Decameron, cit.*, pp. 992-993 and 997, notes that the women are seven to suggest a perfect cycle (cf. days of the week, planets, virtues, liberal arts). «The new inspirational Muses of poetry», they are rhetorical emblems of universal literary themes — fortune, intelligence, love, virtue. The men, in some sense doubles of the Author, likewise have names with etymologies that signal their literary provenance.

[2] Critics have complained about how hard it is, overall, to distinguish narrators one from another. E. Hutton, a Victorian with views very different from his continental contemporary Carducci, could only regret the tedious, terrible sameness of the *brigata* members (except for reprehensible Dioneo), mere «puppets» whom he counsels readers simply to forget in *Giovanni Boccaccio, cit.*, pp. 297-298. More constructive is G. Padoan's idea, which accounts for the «unfocussed» figures as a general «collective character», in the monographic essay *Mondo aristocratico e mondo comunale, cit.* For A. Stauble the narrators are a necessary part of the antiphonal dialogue between tellers and tales; they serve a broad dialectic in the *Decameron* of reality vs. fantasy: *La brigata del 'Decameron' come pubblico teatrale*, «Studi sul Boccaccio», IX, 1975-1976, pp. 103-117. He belongs in a line with G. Getto, who had argued that these vague, deliberately non-realistic portraits contribute to the detached idealism and contemplative atmosphere of the *cornice* in his *Vita di forme, cit.*, pp. 20-23. J. H. Potter, *Five Frames, cit.*, p. 80, perceptively observes: «Unlike the characters and life in the stories, they have the same quality as those figures labeled 'Temperance,' 'Fortitude,' or 'The Prophet So and So' to be found in bas-reliefs or in frescoes, where they were also sometimes used to divide (or frame) the narrative sequence».

Boccaccio's cheerful Elissa have in common with Virgil's despairing Dido?[3] How can fickle, self-serving Panfilo, partner to adultery in *Elegia di madonna Fiammetta*, qualify for comeback in the *Decameron* as a figure who always speaks with the voice of reason? What links Pampinea, merely an early fancy to Caleon in *Comedia delle ninfe fiorentine*,[4] with the mature prime mover of a microcosmic society whose goals are to preserve human life and happiness?

The 'qualities' in the storytellers' names connote more than onomastic moves in a metaliterary game. For a wider perspective on what they may imply, we should admit into evidence Boccaccio's other frame tale clues to the reader, as well as content in his own earlier fictions. This combinatory approach unscreens in the *Decameron cornice* a picture that resonates allegorically, its conceptual space arching from Aristotle's *Ethics* to the virtue system perfected by St. Thomas Aquinas. Boccaccio restages ideas already allegorized in his *Teseida*, *Ameto*, and *Amorosa visione*; once again he assembles a cast of characters — here seven ladies and three young men — to enact a conflict whose locus is the human soul. It pits the rational appetite against the lower irascible and concupiscible appetites, a trio of forces personified by the three male narrators of the *Decameron*. Reason succeeds in dominating, or tempering, the sensitive appetites of anger and lust thanks to assistance from the Virtues, ideal moral qualities adumbrated in the *brigata*'s seven ladies.

* * *

Such Scholastic categories sound quite alien to that jolly, iconoclastic raconteur we still conjure mentally at the drop of the name 'Boccaccio'. But Boccaccio so imagined is a popular legend, filtered through the Romantic imagination, which had formed its notions of the man as an overcompensatory response to the smothering effects of Counterreformation censors. If we backtrack through the centuries to Giovanni Boccaccio's own time, when he held public respect as a canonist and poet, we see this same language of Scholasticism stamped on *Teseida delle nozze d'Emilia*, the epic he created to close a gap in Italy's vernacular letters — a good ten years before the *Decameron*.[5]

---

[3] Dido is sometimes referred to as Elissa in the *Aeneid*.
[4] *Comedia delle ninfe, cit.*, XXXV 78-79.
[5] Striking evidence of the contrast between Boccaccio's popular modern image and his Renaissance dignity surfaces in the history of his portraits, traced by V. KIRKHAM, *Renaissance Portraits of Boccaccio. A Look into the Kaleidoscope*, «Studi sul Boccaccio», XVI, 1987, pp. 284-305. Boccaccio composed his epic, the first in Italian, to satisfy a need signalled by Dante in *De vulgari eloquentia* II 2. Cf. V. KIRKHAM, *John Badmouth. Fortunes of the Poet's Image, cit.*

The *Teseida*, a song of arms and the woman, opens at its very center space for scientific prose on the irrational 'appetites' in the soul, irascibility and concupiscence. The Author's anonymous Commentator (who is Boccaccio himself, writing in another of his vocal disguises) brings those faculties and their potential for self-harm into focus precisely at the twin mid-points of the poem, where we are whisked away from ancient Athens to the exotic castle dwellings of Mars and Venus. Marvellous symbolic structures ghosted with all sorts of personifications, they prompt the Commentator to full-blown allegoresis in mega-glosses that explode over his folios at the central verse of the epic and its central chapter rubric.[6] As part of the preamble to the first, on the House of Mars, we read:

è da sapere che in ciascuno uomo sono due principali appetiti, de' quali l'uno si chiama *appetito concupiscibile*, per lo quale l'uomo disidera e si rallegra d'avere le cose che, secondo il suo giudicio, o ragionevole o corrotto ch'egli sia, sono dilettevoli e piacevoli; l'altro si chiama *appetito irascibile*, per lo quale l'uomo si turba o che gli sieno tolte o impedite le cose dilettevoli, o perché quelle avere non si possano. (VII 30, gl.)

Boccaccio, speaking as his own Commentator, goes on to say that each of these appetites can be good or bad, depending on whether or not it receives the healthy counsel of reason. Although he only alludes to reason's role as guide and curb for wrathful and lustful impetuses, he knew that the rational appetite completes the standard trio of faculties in every man's soul.

The tripartite soul divided between its higher, intellectual power of reason and lower, sensitive powers of irascibility and concupiscence was a piece of spiritual anatomy that the Greeks passed down to the Middle Ages. From Plato's *Timaeus*, the Fathers Augustine and Jerome transmitted it into *Summae* by the medieval Scholastics, men like Peter Lombard and Thomas Aquinas, who could also cite Aristotle even more copiously on the split-level structure of the soul.

For Plato in the *Timaeus* the neck is an isthmus that separates the divine part of the soul, set in our head, from the mortal ones, located in breast and trunk. The heart, manly of spirit, is closer to reason, «which

---

[6] R. HOLLANDER, who speculates that Boccaccio played the part of his own glossator in order to create an «instant classic», first announced in print the central position of the verse with the commentary on the House of Mars in *The Validity of Boccaccio's Self-Exegesis, cit.* Cf. R. HOLLANDER, *Boccaccio's Two Venuses, cit.*, pp. 55 ff. The central rubric announces the dwelling of Venus, as noticed by V. KIRKHAM, '*Chiuso parlare' in Boccaccio's 'Teseida'*, above ch. 1.

commands from its citadel», while below the midriff and about the umbilical lies the belly's appetitive part, tethered there «like a beast untamed but necessary [...] always feeding at its stall and dwelling as far as possible from the seat of counsel». Although not within that part of the dialogue transmitted to the Middle Ages in the Latin version of Chalcidius, the ideas in this passage found other spokesmen to carry them. They were known directly, for example, in the *Commentary on the Gospel of St. Matthew* attributed to St. Jerome, who credits his source:

We read in Plato, and it is widely known in the teachings of the philosophers, that there are three passions in the human soul, τὸ λογικὸν, which we can interpret as "rational"; τὸ θυμικὸν, which we may call "full of ire", or "irascible"; and τὸ πιθυμητικὸν, which we shall call "concupiscible". And that philosopher considers our rational part to dwell in the head, ire in the gallbladder, and desire in the liver. And therefore if we receive the evangelic ferment of holy Scriptures [...] the three passions of the human soul will be resolved into a unity, such that in reason we may possess prudence; in ire, odium against vice; in desire, desire for virtue.[7]

Augustine, meditating on the Fall in the *City of God*, admits the same pagan triad as a useful mechanism for understanding how conflict arose between reason and desire after man's expulsion from Eden:

Here we have the reason why those philosophers too who came closer to the truth admitted that anger and lust are faulty divisions of the soul. They reasoned that these emotions proceed in a confused and disorderly way to engage even in acts that wisdom forbids and that consequently they stand in need of a controlling and rational mind. This third part of the soul, according to them, resides in a sort of citadel to rule the other two parts in order that, as it commands and they serve, justice in man may be preserved among all the parts of the soul.[8]

---

[7] ST. JEROME, *Commentaria in Evangelium S. Matthaei*, Patrologia Latina 26.91: «Legimus in Platone, et philosophorum dogmate vulgatum est, tres esse in humana anima passiones, τὸ λογικὸν guod nos possumus interpretari *rationabile*: τὸ θυμηκὸν quod dicamus, *plenum irae*, vel *irascibile*: τὸ επιθυμητικὸν quod appellamus, *concupiscibile*: et putat ille philosophus rationabile nostrum in cerebero, iram in felle, desiderium in jecore commorari. Et nos ergo si acciperimus fermentum Evangelicum sanctarum Scripturarum, de quo supra dictum est, tres humanae animae passiones in unum redigentur, ut in ratione possideamus prudentiam; in ira, odium contra vitia; in desiderio, cupiditatem virtutum».

[8] ST. AUGUSTINE, *The City of God, cit.*, XIV 19: «Hinc est quod et illi philosophi qui veritati propius accesserunt iram atque libidem vitiosas animi partes esse confessi sunt, eo quod turbide atque inordinate moverentur ad ea etiam quae sapientia perpetrari vetat, ac per hoc opus habere moderatrice mente atque ratione. Quam partem animi tertiam conlocatam ut illa imperante, istis servientibus possit in homine iustitia ex omni animi parte servari».

Among «those philosophers» in Augustine's lump attribution, Plato would have stood accompanied by Aristotle, and it was the Stagirite who was to become much more authoritative for the high Middle Ages. Aristotle speaks about the parts of our soul, higher and lower, in his treatise *De anima* as well as in the *Nicomachean Ethics*, and both are key texts for Thomas Aquinas, who often refers to the three-part *anima*. So in the *Summa contra Gentiles*:

Now, of all the parts of man, the intellect is found to be the superior mover, for the intellect moves the appetite, by presenting it with its object; then the intellectual appetite, that is the will, moves the sensory appetites, irascible and concupiscible, and that is why we do not obey concupiscence unless there be a command from the will, and finally the sense appetite, with the advent of consent from the will, now moves the body.[9] Therefore, the end of the intellect is the end of all human actions.

Aquinas elaborates most fully on intellect and desire when he treats the virtues in his *Summa theologica*. Following Aristotle, he assigns particular virtues to each of the sensitive appetites: fortitude for irascibility and temperance for concupiscence. I shall have more to say about these pairings presently.

Meanwhile, we have now gained a sense of the philosophical tradition on which Boccaccio built an arena of psychological clashes for his «Book of Theseus» and «marriage of Emilia». At surface a tale of love and battle, it meets fourteenth-century requirements for a proper epic by telling another story on the allegorical level. That hidden tale, one we must deduce by reading deeply, takes place not in external events, but within the minds of the protagonists. It is an inner, psychic drama. As Janet Levarie Smarr first argued, the *Teseida*'s three male protagonists symbolize appetites in the soul. Two of them, wrath and lust, lead the Author's 'Commentator' to lecture us for thousands of words in central glosses. Arcita, votary of Mars, personifies irascibility; Palemone, who prays to Venus, doubles for concupiscence. Teseo, Duke of Athens, is Reason, who subdues and governs those sensitive appetites by organizing

---

[9] T. AQUINAS, *Contra Gentiles, cit.*, III 25: "Inter omnes autem hominis partes, intellectus invenitur superior motor: nam intellectus movet appetitum, proponendo ei suum obiectum; appetitus autem intellectivus, qui est voluntas, movet appetitus sensitivos, qui sunt irascibilis et concupiscibilis, unde et concupiscentiae non obedimus nisi voluntatis imperim adsit; appetitus autem sensitivus, adveniente consensu voluntatis, movet iam corpus. Finis igitus intellectus est finis omnium actionum humanarum".

the tournament that will rationally resolve the men's angry amorous rivalry.[10]

* * *

The same trio, I believe, returns allusively to the *Decameron*. Dioneo, who takes his name from Dione, mother of Venus, speaks as a «venerean one» for the concupiscible appetite.[11] Miserable Filostrato, «love's victim», complements Dioneo by personifying the irascible appetite, a force that feeds on violence and despair. Since they team as the two sensitive faculties, it is logical for them to be placed at symmetrical intervals in the *Decameron*. Filostrato, who presides on Day IV over tragic love, is king after the first three Days; Dioneo, who orders as theme for Day VII wiles of adulterous wives, serves as king before the last three Days.

			4 tales						
I	II	III	IV	V	VI	VII	VIII	IX	X
	3 tales		Filostrato			Dioneo		3 tales	

Panfilo, «all loving», points to the soul's higher part, reason. He emerges as ruler at Boccaccio's finale, on the Tenth Day, where powers at work for right in the *Decameron* reach their natural apex. The rational faculty in the soul triumphs over wrath and lust; under its governance tales are told about Magnificence, the crowning virtue in Aristotle's system. They in turn close with a haunting example of Christian perfection, 'Saint' Griselda, whose heroism is humility. It is a ten-story climax set off by a pause from what has preceded, Day IX, which has a free topic, like Day I. Hence we can also understand the progression of Days in the *Decameron* as a structure of 9 + 1, the 'plus one' being the perfecting number, 10.[12]

---

[10] Very different from ours, the medieval conception of an epic called for an allegory complete with glossarial apparatus, not to mention further possible refinements, such as chapter rubrics and framing sonnets. A good reconstruction emerges in D. ANDERSON's archeology of epic in the Middle Ages, *Before the Knight's Tale, cit.* J. L. SMARR reads Boccaccio's epic as an allegory of reason's triumph over sensual and wrathful appetites in *The 'Teseida', Boccaccio's Allegorical Epic, cit.* A fuller discussion of symbolism and allegory appears above, ch. 1.

[11] Commentators cite *Paradiso* VIII 1-8, Dante's entry into the heaven of Venus.

[12] 10 perfects the Pythagorean decad, in which are contained all things; 10 is also the Biblical number of totality, as attested in the Ten Commandments. J. L. SMARR shows how Boccaccio uses a 9 + 1 organizing pattern in the *Decameron*, both for themes in the sequence

I	II	III	IV	V	VI	VII	VIII	IX	X Panfilo
free topic				9				free topic	+ 1 Magnificence

Dioneo, seeking only pleasure, issues the ladies a jocular ultimatum: «o voi a sollazzare e a ridere e a cantare con meco insieme vi disponete (tanto, dico, quanto alla vostra dignità s'appartiene), o voi mi licenziate che io per li miei pensier mi ritorni e steami nella città tribolata» (I, Intro. 93). His are the most salacious tales, starting with I 4, the first in the *Decameron* with an erotic theme. A young Benedictine, flesh unmortified by monastic vigils and fasts, one day espies the fair daughter of a local field worker, and «né prima veduta l'ebbe, che egli fieramente assalito fu dalla concupiscenza carnale». Hidden in his cell after a leisurely interlude, she soon receives a visit from the portly abbot, whose compromising position will lead all three to a discreet, ongoing arrangement.

Dioneo's joyful sensuality, which literally puts «carnal concupiscence» into the *Decameron*, reasserts itself at the end of Day Five, when Queen Fiammetta asks him to sing a song. He counters with risqué titles that announce such activities as skirt-lifting, casking when it is not October, pecking in niches, and rooster shopping. For his own reign, Day Seven, he decrees as theme the practical jokes wives play on their husbands. These 'beffe' are, of course, cuckoldries, ranging from bawdy to cruel. As if to distance and shield itself from such impropriety, the *brigata* removes for the day to a place symbolic of female purity and fertility, the «Valley of the Ladies».[13]

But outside its precincts, both the eve and evening of Dioneo's Thursday reign resound with music of lust. The night before, during entertainment that closes Day Six, good humor prompts him to request tunes for dancing from Tindaro on the bagpipes. (Not coincidentally, Tindaro had been a party in the servants' quarrel over brides' maidenheads at the beginning of Day Six.) Then, when the troupe has departed

---

of Days and for the arrangement on each individual Day, when Dioneo's privilege as last storyteller sets him apart from the preceding nine. See her *Boccaccio and Fiammetta, cit.*, pp. 175-180.

[13] J. H. POTTER, *Five Frames, cit.*, p. 26, refers to the «Valle delle Donne» as a place of ritual female purification. Emblems of fertility (fruit-bearing plants and trees, evergreens, fish) associate it with the 'good' Venus, a goddess of procreation, not lust. See E. KERN, *The Gardens in the 'Decameron' Cornice*, «PMLA», LXVI, 1951, pp. 505-523.

the Valley and as they wind down Day Seven, there is more caroling «to the sound of Tindaro's bagpipe». It is appropriate that only Dioneo's Day evoke the bagpipes. An instrument that Chaucer's earthy miller could also well «blowe and sowne», the evocatively shaped cornemuse was an established Priapic symbol. Among the several illustrators who worked on an early manuscript of the *Decameron*, the codex transcribed by the Florentine burger Ludovico di Silvestro Ceffini, one illuminator conflates the frame music from Day VII with the setting for Day I, when he depicts the *brigata* ruled by Pampinea and beside them, Tindaro playing his bagpipes. The artist, perhaps following Ceffini's instructions, gives us a visual commentary on the book, suggesting its sexual content with the sexual shape of the instrument (fig. 4).[14]

Filostrato is a fitting candidate for the soul's irascible faculty. As Boccaccio defined it in the *Teseida*, ire is activated by deprivation or frustration: «l'uomo si turba o che gli sieno tolte o impedite le cose dilettevoli, o perché quelle avere non si possano». Filostrato suffers because his lady has abandoned him. So he confesses upon taking the crown as Day III draws to a close:

Amorose donne, per la mia disaventura, poscia che io ben da mal conobbi, sempre per la bellezza d'alcuna di voi stato sono a Amor subgetto, né l'essere umile né il seguirlo in ciò che per me s'è conosciuto alla seconda in tutti i suoi costumi m'è valuto, che io prima per altro abandonato e poi non sia sempre di male in peggio andato; e così credo che io andrò di qui alla Morte.

The ballad he then intones as night falls on his narrative territory, Day IV, expresses feelings of despair for love rejected: «Lagrimando dimostro / quanto si dolga con ragione il core / d'esser tradito sotto fede, Amore». Filostrato's song is a lexicon of sorrow: «dolente», «dolore», «doloroso», «'l mio dolore», «dolorosa voce», «doglia». As his dying soul curses crushed hopes, he laments that death will be less painful, «Venga dunque

---

[14] G. CHAUCER, *The Canterbury Tales*, cit., General Prologue, vv. 565-566. Examples of the bagpipe in manuscript decorations, «an instrument with which male lovers make melody», are illustrated by D. W. ROBERTSON, *A Preface to Chaucer*, cit., pp. 128-133. In seventeenth-century Dutch and Flemish paintings of peasant scenes, the pipes retain phallic meaning. See J. HALL, *Dictionary of Subjects and Symbols in Art*, New York, Harper and Row Icon Editions, 1979², s.v., 'bagpipe'. See below, *The Word, the Flesh, and the 'Decameron'*, for more on the language of the servants and their quarrel over brides' maidenheads. The unusual Ceffini manuscript (Paris, Bibliothèque Nationale, Ms. It. 63) has been described by P. F. WATSON, *Gatherings of Artists: The Illustrators of a 'Decameron' of 1427*, «TEXT: Transactions of the Society for Textual Scholarship», I, 1981 (published 1985), pp. 147-156.

[la morte], e la mia / vita crudele e ria / termini col suo colpo, e 'l mio furore».

Not only Filostrato in his language, but other narrators on his Day, gravitate around a medieval vocabulary of wrath. Scholastic terminology that today rings quaint, it recognizes what complex emotions and destructive acts a person's pain of loss can trigger. Boccaccio spelled them out allegorically at the center of his *Teseida*, where a whole architecture of anger styles the House of Mars, that grim allegorical image of man's irascible appetite. Around the palace a sterile forest roars with the noise of «mille furori», eternally dark in drenching rain. The bastion has walls of steel, barred windows, and an adamantine gate to signify stubborn obstinacy and cold-blooded plotting typical of wrathful temperaments. Dwelling within are countless, disastrous guises of rage: Demented Impetuses, Blind Sinning, Woes, Pale Fear, Betrayals, Discord, Threats, Cruel Intention, Glad Furor, and Death.[15]

These personifications return as characters to populate the tragic tales told during Filostrato's reign, a day of wrath on many counts. Not coincidentally, Boccaccio placed on Day IV the only definition of anger in the *Decameron*. Lauretta gives it, her terms precise and technical, in the preface to her story (IV 3). The narrative that follows shows how dire anger can be when it takes control of a woman.

Giovani donne, sì come voi apertamente potete conoscere, ogni vizio può in gravissima noia tornar di colui che l'usa e molte volte d'altrui. E tra gli altri che con più abandonate redine ne' nostri pericoli ne trasporta, mi pare che l'ira sia quello; la quale niuna altra cosa è che un movimento subito e inconsiderato, da sentita tristizia sospinto, il quale, ogni ragion cacciata e gli occhi della mente avendo di tenebre offuscati, in ferventissimo furore accende l'anima nostra. (IV 3, 4)

Ninetta, one of three sisters from Marseilles who all elope, lives out the stages of rage-sickness, ever more intensive and pitched toward death. Trouble begins when she suspects her new husband of infidelity. She sinks into «tristizia», which festers as «ira» and then explodes into «furore». Thus «blinded by wrath», Ninetta ceases loving altogether, and bitter hatred drives her to poison her once beloved Restagnon.

---

[15] *Teseida, cit.*, VII 30, gl.: «In questa parte discrive l'autore la casa di Marte [...] pone qui l'autore il tempio di Marte, cioè questo appetito irascibile, essere in Trazia, la quale è provincia posta sotto la tramontana e molto fredda, nella quale sono li uomini fierissimi e battaglievoli e iracundi per lo molto sangue».

In Filostrato's own story on his Day (IV 9), anger again kills love. Its protagonists are two neighbors, Guiglielmo Rossiglione and Guiglielmo Guardastagno, bound in a fraternal affection symbolized by their shared first name. Up until the final unravelling of their relationship, it recalls in ways that of the two Thebans, Arcita and Palemone, whose rivalry had moved the plot in Boccaccio's *Teseida*. Once Rossiglione hears of his wife's affair with Guardastagno, this friend becomes an object of «mortal hatred». Martially armed, Rossiglione ambushes in the woods his unprotected, unsuspecting rival. Whereas at the corresponding moment in the epic, Duke Teseo came riding onto the scene and separated the duellers (he is in allegory Reason who quells Lust and Anger), the *novella* leaves Rossiglione alone to pounce with felonious wrath («fellone e pieno di mal talento»), run through Guardastagno, and with his very own hands cut out his heart. If wicked Rossiglione exemplifies anger *in malo*, emotion neither rationally controlled nor justified, he has a luckier 'second' about whom Filostrato tells his final tale (X 3). Far away in Cathay, one man vies with another in feats of amazing hospitality. But Mitridanes soon realizes how hopeless it is for him to better Natan's boundless courtesy. Frustration enrages him, and rather than be second-best in generosity, he plots to ambush his defenseless rival in a wood. Then, at the last minute, as Mitridanes is about to murder him, Natan's kind willingness to welcome even death converts to shame his attacker's «furore» and «ira». God opens the eyes of Mitridanes's intellect, which miserable envy had closed.

It is significant that this extreme example of wrath conquered by reason is told under the rule of Panfilo on Day Ten. He is the male narrator who hints at the rational appetite. According to Thomas Aquinas, that appetite is given to man by God so that we may resist the downward pull of the sensitive appetites and rise to contemplative union with our Creator — that is to say, attain happiness.[16] Reason is a kind of median or mediating power in the soul, keeping watch over the 'beast' tethered below while privileged to communicate with the Deity above. In Panfilo we can see philosophical bridges between man and God on the one hand, between intellect and violent sensuality on the other.

On Day Two he had told the story that most strikingly fuses concupiscence and irascibility — Alatiel's Mediterranean odyssey through the hands of multiple impassioned lovers who murder each other in turn. Yet he prefaces all this sex and violence with reasoned words on

---

[16] T. AQUINAS, *Contra Gentiles, cit.*, III 25.

the radical instability of Fortune, ups and downs that Alatiel enacts as she floats her way crazily across the sea in its flux. His counsel is, in a nutshell, much the same as the consolatory wisdom of Boethius's Lady Philosophy: The wise man rejects what Dame Fortune has to give, worldly assets like wealth, power, physical strength, and beauty. Things that Panfilo urges us not to choose, these are what Thomas Aquinas calls «fortuitous goods». Since they are subject to Fortune in her whimsical sway, their appeal is to the sensitive appetites, not reason. Desire for these transient, material things only diminishes our happiness, for it hinders the intellect's approach to God.[17] Panfilo concludes that if we wish to behave rightly, we must entrust ourselves entirely to Him:

E acciò che io partitamente di tutti gli umani disiderii non parli, affermo niuno poterne essere con pieno avvedimento, sì come sicuro da fortunosi casi, che da' viventi si possa eleggere: per che, se dirittamente operar volessimo, a quello prendere e possedere ci dovremmo disporre che Colui ci donasse, il quale solo ciò che ci fa bisogno cognosce e puolci dare. (II 7, 6)

The day before, when privileged to present the tale that Boccaccio places first in the *Decameron*, Panfilo had taken much the same stance. Although it is easy for readers today to dismiss his framing remarks merely as ironic pretense, what he says, at least literally, is something serious. Whether Ser Cepparello, probably the worst man in the whole world, ever made it to 'sainthood' in the only place where it matters, or whether he did not, Panfilo's opening story urges us to fix our hope in God, as in a power unchanging, if we are to survive our temporal climate, where all is transient and mortal:

Manifesta cosa è che, sì come le cose temporali tutte sono transitorie e mortali, così in sé e fuor di sé esser piene di noia, d'angoscia e di fatica e a infiniti pericoli sogiacere; alle quali senza niuno fallo né potremmo noi, che viviamo mescolati in esse e che siamo parte d'esse, durare né ripararci, se spezial grazia di Dio forza e avvedimento non ci prestasse. (I 1, 3)

When Emilia passes the crown to Panfilo at the end of her rule on the Ninth Day, she says it will be his responsibility to «amend» her

---

[17] *Ibid*. III 17-31. Cf. above, ch. 2, *Amorous Vision, Scholastic Vistas*. Fortune is a controlling theme of *Decameron* II, and Alatiel, «Fortune's plaything», its most startling embodiment. See, e.g., M. J. MARCUS, *An Allegory of Form, cit*., pp. 39-42; C. SEGRE, *Comicità strutturale nella novella di Alatiel*, in *Le strutture e il tempo. Narrazione, poesia, modelli*, Turin, Einaudi, 1976, pp. 145-159.

«defects» and those of the narrators who have gone before: «Signor mio, gran carico ti resta, sì come è l'avere il mio difetto e degli altri che il luogo hanno tenuto che tu tieni, essendo tu l'ultimo, a emendare: di che Idio ti presti grazia, come a me l'ha prestato di farti re». Her charge suggests the corrective capacity of reason. On Day Ten stories of magnificence — for Aristotle and Aquinas the virtue that adorns all the others[18] — dramatize reason's conquest of the appetites. We have already seen reason's victory over wrath in Filostrato's tale of Mitridanes and Natan. Analogously, two great kings, Charles of Anjou and Peter of Aragon, wisely repress concupiscent impulses (X 6 and X 7).

Speaking for the soul's rational faculty, Panfilo holds strategic positions in the *Decameron*. Its first queen, Pampinea, selects him to initiate the storytelling. His final turn as narrator coincides with the anthology's penultimate tale, where Franco Fido finds summational resolution of themes from tales throughout the book.[19] More specifically, the tale of Messer Torello and Saladino responds to Panfilo's second-day saga of the Sultan's daughter. Fortune's plaything, Alatiel is a beautiful, all carnal 'femina' mute among men of other lands, who learns from short-lived irascible lovers «con che corno gli uomini cozzano» and joins the sex cult of «san Cresci in Valcava».[20] By contrast, Martian and Venerean actions *in*

---

[18] T. AQUINAS, *Comm. Ethic.*, cit., IV 8 (p. 133): «magnanimitas videtur esse ornatus quidam omnium virtutum. Quia pro magnanimitate omnes virtutes efficiuntur majores, eo quod ad magnanimitatem pertinet operari magnum in omnibus virtutibus. Et ex hoc crescunt virtutes. Et iterum non fit magnanimitas sine aliis virtutibus; et sic videtur superaddi aliis tamquam ornatus earum» [749: Magnanimity seems to be an ornament of all the virtues because they are made more excellent by magnanimity, which seeks to perform a great work in all the virtues. In this way the virtues increase. Likewise, magnanimity accompanies the other virtues and so seems to be added to them as their ornament]. Boccaccio's copy of the *Ethics* with the *Commentary* by Aquinas, the latter in Boccaccio's own hand, is in Milan, Biblioteca Ambrosiana, Cod. A 204 part. inf. It dates from before 1350, hence precedes the *Decameron*. See G. AUZZAS, *I codici autografi. Elenco e bibliografia*, «Studi sul Boccaccio», VII, 1975, pp. 1-20. More on Boccaccio's Aristotelian rationale for making Magnificence his virtue for the closing day appears below, ch. 9.

[19] *Il sorriso di messer Torello ('Decameron' X 9)*, in F. FIDO, *Le metamamorfosi del Centauro. Studi e letture da Boccaccio a Pirandello*, Rome, Bulzoni 1977, pp. 13-41; rpt. *Il regime delle simmetrie imperfette*, cit., pp. 11-35.

[20] The old Italian 'femina', usually pejorative, connoted woman in her physical, sensual nature, as opposed to 'donna' [lady], which implies nobility and dignity. See M. BONFANTE, *'Femmina' and 'donna'*, in *Studia philologica et litteraria in honorem L. Spitzer*, Bern, Francke, 1958, pp. 77-109. G. H. McWILLIAM, translator of the 1972 Penguin *Decameron*, renders as «Saint Stiffen-in-the-Hand» the Italian «San Cresci in Valcava», literally, «Saint Increase in Hollow Valley». Although the euphemism would seem to be purely fanciful, another of Boccaccio's endless puns for sexual parts and play — like mortar and pestle, sausage and mortadella, horseback riding, making the nightingale sing, shaking the coverlet, etc. — there actually is a place called San Cresci in Valcava a few kilometers north of Florence, in the Mugnone, as I have been informed by Alexa Mason of the Villa I Tatti.

bono characterize the ninety-ninth story, Panfilo's last, with its Christian Crusader and love both friendly and familial. The raging bull, which for Dante signified bestiality,[21] here returns as a civilized diminutive, while Torello's saint, an eschatologically promising patron, is San Pietro in Ciel d'Oro. His wife Adalieta, whose name is almost an anagram for Alatiel ('la lieta'), is a model spouse, and both, unlike the Babylonian princess, have Latin to communicate with foreigners. It is linguistic ability indicative of their wisdom and the rational order they maintain in their lives.

Beyond first and penultimate tales, Panfilo's privileged status gives him the role of end rule. His Day Ten subsumes ideally the foregoing nine. Two of those earlier Days are subject to dominion of the lower, sensitive appetites. Under Filostrato's rule, irascibility dominates on the Fourth Day; under Dioneo's, concupiscence dominates the Seventh. It is right for the rational faculty to hold final sway. As Aquinas explains, the intellectual appetite, like the commander-in-chief of all who soldier under him, orders the irascible and concupiscible appetites to its own end. The last end of the intellectual creature is to understand the first truth, that is, God. It is in this understanding that human happiness lies.[22] Reason, adduced in Pampinea's opening speech to justify flight from the city, triumphs as well in the moral order of the narrators' 'giornate'.

* * *

To propose that 'Virtue', figuratively speaking, animates the *Decameron* frame narrators is nothing new. Our Author himself commends them, especially the seven ladies, whose virtues of wisdom and chastity he emphasizes. As we come upon them within the protective Gothic walls of Santa Maria Novella, the temple newly built in Florence by Dominican brothers, we right away hear him single out those qualities by setting them first and last on his list of laudatory epithets. Lovely for their beauty and courtesy alike, these ladies possess moral qualities that run an ideal female gamut, from prudence to temperance: «savia ciascuna e di sangue nobile e bella di forma e ornata di costumi e di leggiadra onestà».

While almost everyone agrees that they are admirable as a group,[23] problems have arisen with schemes devised for pinning a specific virtue,

---

[21] *Purgatorio, cit.*, XXVI 41-42: «Ne la vacca entra Pasife, / Perchè 'l torello a sua lussuria corra!» Cf. the bull as bestiality in *Inferno* XII 22-25.

[22] T. Aquinas, *Contra Gentiles, cit.*, III 25.

[23] Their only detractor, to my knowledge, is Bernardo, who finds them «despicable» because they turn their backs on calls to duty in the city, but his argument does not pay

such as Justice or Charity, to each single person in the *brigata*. So far programs proposed fall short of persuading us. Failing to connect Boccaccio's characters with any obvious medieval canon of moral qualities, scholars have juggled possibilities that complicate rather than simplify. For some frame narrators they could see more than one symbolic meaning, while for others, who seemed too shallow or dimly lit really to 'be' anything, they had to invent labels, arbitrary and suitably noncommittal. Only Joan Ferrante has turned to advantage, and rightly so, the way Boccaccio divided his ten young noblefolk by gender, in groups of three plus seven. Using those numbers for guideposts, when she set Richard of St. Victor's ladder for spiritual progress from the *Benjamin minor* against the *Decameron*, she could correlate the men and sense appetites, matching Dioneo with Lust and Filostrato with Despair (another term for wrath); and she could deduce for the ladies pairings much more commonplace: seven women, Seven Virtues.[24]

Boccaccio's preference for imbalance between male and female narrators, three and seven, is not haphazard. The same numbers operate at other levels in the text. At the beginning of Day IV, for example, the Author's interruption to defend his art drives a wedge between the first three and last seven Days. That is to say, it separates the first thirty from the last seventy *novelle*. Then, too, his pseudonymous Florentines progress through three country settings, moving to the second on the Third Day, and the third is reserved for their Seventh Day. Longest of all the *novelle* in the *Decameron* is the seventy-seventh (VIII 7), the scholar's revenge on a widow; second-longest — nor by coincidence seventh on its day — is the seventeenth (II 7), Alatiel's «four-year vacation from virtue».[25] As rubrics foretell, the third, thirteenth, and thirty-third are all

---

account to Pampinea's defense in her argument for escape — their families are all dead, and now, their greatest responsibility, a rational obligation, is to save themselves. See A. BERNARDO, *The Plague as Key to Meaning in Boccaccio's 'Decameron'*, in *The Black Death: The Impact of the Fourteenth-Century Plague. Papers of the Eleventh Annual Conference of the Center for Medieval and Early Renaissance Studies*, ed. D. WILLIMAN, Binghamton, Medieval and Renaissance Texts and Studies, 1982, pp. 39-64; rpt. «Forum Italicum», XIX, 1983, pp. 18-44.

[24] J. FERRANTE, *The Frame Characters of the 'Decameron'*, cit., does not seem to argue a causal relationship between Richard of St. Victor and Boccaccio; rather we should see the two as inheritors of a common cultural tradition. I depart from Ferrante in her suggestion that there are more than seven virtues, Panfilo being an eighth, who subsumes all the other virtues individually impersonated by the seven women. Nevertheless, her perception that in their ordering as rulers the narrators form a progression toward ever greater virtue, a climb that must overcome obstructing Sensuality and Despair, brought her closer than anyone before to an elegant solution for the frame tale code.

[25] M. MARCUS, *An Allegory of Form*, cit., p. 39.

tales whose plots hinge conspicuously on ternary quantities: three rings (I 3), three spendthrifts (II 3), and three pairs of lovers (IV 3).

We could put it another way and say that as numbers go, Boccaccio privileges 7 and 3 in his «Book of Ten Days». They are the components, technically the addends, of the foundation in arithmetic he laid for that edifice. Its core value is the decad: ten Days of storytelling, each Day with ten stories, told by ten young men and women. But if Boccaccio will symmetrically spread the sum of 100 tales across two calendar weeks, with fifty in each, no such evenness aligns male and female narrators. Quite the contrary. In this particular population women outnumber men by so large a margin, seven to three, that here can be no realistic picture.

Of all possible addends for 10 in combinations of two (1 + 9; 2 + 8; 3 + 7; 4 + 6; 5 + 5; 6 + 4 . . . 9 + 1), the numbers 3 + 7 repeat the coupling that St. Augustine had found most compelling. The perfect 10 of the Decalogue is best understood as a sum of 3 + 7, he believed, because in those integers we recognize the Creator's Trinity plus the hebdomad of the created universe, that is, the week of Creation in Genesis.[26] With the little formula 3 + 7 = 10, then, one can denote comprehensively a Christian world. Boccaccio did not just copy Augustine's symbolic equivalencies, since the three men can hardly stand alone for a perfect Godhead of Power, Wisdom and Love. Nor are the seven ladies simply diurnal entities, one for each day of a week. But he was thinking imaginatively along lines that the Fathers would have liked when he set up an ideal calendar of Ten Days, its title adapted from one of the most widely read commentaries on the week of Creation in Genesis, the *Hexameron* of St. Ambrose. And if 3 is not Trinity strictly speaking for him in the *Decameron* — even though in that sense it cannot ever be totally absent, since for the Christian reader 3 has a primary meaning so potent — the triad does quite nicely as sign of the Soul, another meaning it had borne from antiquity to the Renaissance.[27] So,

---

[26] V.F. HOPPER, *Medieval Number Symbolism*, cit., p. 85, cites Augustine, *Against the Epistle of Manichaeus Called Fundamental*, X 11. Cf. *Confessions*, cit., III 8: «vivitur male adversus tria et septem, psalterium decem chordarum, decalogum tuum, deus altissime et dulcissime» [we live offensively against three and seven, that psaltery of ten strings, thy Ten Commandments, O God, most High and most Sweet]; VI 4: «volebam enim eorum quae non viderem ita me certum fieri, ut certus essem, quod septem et tria decem sint» [my whole desire was to be made so well assured of those things which I saw not, as I was certain that seven and three make ten].

[27] Medieval readings of 3 as the number of the soul are cited above, ch. 2. See also V. KIRKHAM, *Eleven is for Evil*, cit.

too, if 7 is not the Creation, wrought by God in seven days, it can be a series equally close to the life of belief, sevenfold virtue.

Graphic display of number and time in the *Decameron* shows a calendar laid out in 3 + 7 parts, Ten Days with stories from 3 + 7 narrators.

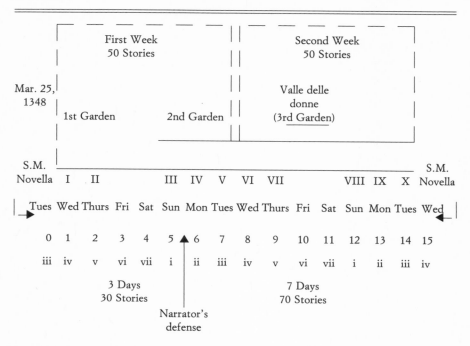

Large Roman numerals: the Ten Days of storytelling
Arabic numerals: the days the *brigata* spends in the countryside
Small Roman numerals: ordinal days of the week counting from Sunday as first

The ennobling power of feminine virtue, a favorite motif in Boccaccio's fiction, had been evident from his first vernacular work, *Caccia di Diana*. There fifty-nine highborn ladies from the Neapolitan court of King Robert of Anjou, led by the goddess Diana, track and kill all sorts of forest beasts, from roebuck to unicorn, from hedgehog to raging bull, from leopard, to lion, to wolf. Then, to everyone's surprise, Venus descends, turning these bestiary denizens into handsome young men. In the end, each woman has 'captured' her man; she has conquered the dark, beastly forces of sin inside him and raised him to a higher form of existence, where reason rather than sensual impulse can dominate his life. Allegorically the *Caccia* is a struggle in the soul, a psychomachy. Virtue defeats vice; rational appetite triumphs over the lower sensitive appetites.[28]

Later the Virtues in person, a familiar sisterhood in the Middle Ages, come forward as an unmistakable set of seven to do storytelling duty in Boccaccio's «Little *Decameron*». That book is the pastoral *Comedia delle ninfe fiorentine*, written like the *Teseida* about ten years before the *Decameron*. One day in prehistoric Tuscany, a coarse rustic called Ameto comes upon a band of nymphs, huntresses who once followed Diana, but now believe in Venus. As one by one, each narrates her life history, we recognize in Mopsa, Emilia, Adiona, and Acrimonia the four Cardinal Virtues (Wisdom, Justice, Temperance, Fortitude); in Agapes, Fiammetta, and Lia the three Theological Virtues (Love, Hope, Faith). These seven ladies join forces with three shepherds to civilize Ameto, a fellow who had lived by animal instinct, teaching him the bond between love and virtue. Just as we took help from the Commentator's glosses in the *Teseida* to characterize the three faculties in the soul loosely personified by Filostrato, Dioneo, and Panfilo, so can we look to the seven Virtue-nymphs in *Ameto* for insights into the nature of the seven ladies in the *Decameron* frame.[29] In order of narration, Day by Day, the female narrators of the *Decameron* are Pampinea, Filomena, Neifile, Fiammetta, Elissa, Lauretta, Emilia.

Pampi-nea	Filo-mena	Neifile	(Filo-strato)	Fiam-metta	Elissa	(Dioneo)	Lauretta	Emilia	(Panfilo)
I	II	III	IV	V	VI	VII	VIII	IX	X

We can start with Pampinea, senior lady and prime mover of the *brigata*. She is the first frame narrator to speak, and what she stresses is reason. We hear it in her first utterance: «Donne mie care, voi potete,

---

[28] A full discussion of the poem's allegory appears in A. K. CASSELL and V. KIRKHAM, *Diana's Hunt, cit.*, Intro., pp. 30-68.

[29] Virtue was that *ninfale*'s true theme, as owners of the early manuscripts understood. See P. F. WATSON and V. KIRKHAM, *Amore e virtù: Two Salvers Depicting Boccaccio's 'Comedia delle ninfe fiorentine' in the Metropolitan Museum*, «Metropolitan Museum Journal», X, 1975, pp. 35-50. More extensive analysis of the *Ameto*, as a later version of *Diana's Hunt*, appears in A. K. CASSELL and V. KIRKHAM, *Diana's Hunt, cit.*, Intro. pp. 30-33.

G. CAVALLINI, *La decima giornata del 'Decameron'*, Rome, Bulzoni, 1980, pp. 8-9, notes the numerical analogy between male and female frame characters in the *Ameto* and *Decameron*. J. FERRANTE, *The Frame Characters, cit.*, properly cites the former to support her interpretation of the latter as the Cardinal and Theological Virtues.

così come io, molte volte avere udito che a niuna persona fa ingiuria chi onestamente usa la sua ragione. Natural ragione è, di ciascuno che ci nasce, la sua vita quanto può aiutare e conservare e difendere» (I Intro. 53). By staying in the city, the ladies are at mortal risk, physically as well as spiritually. The few people left there no longer distinguish between good and evil, behaving as they do only at the urges of bestial, lascivious appetites, doing things «solo che l'appetito le cheggia» (I Intro. 61). Let us then, she argues, flee both death and the dishonest example of others; let us pursue pleasure in the country, «senza trapassare in alcuno atto il segno della ragione» (I Intro. 65). True to this goal, at their destination Pampinea will propose daily rulers to impose order on the group since «le cose che sono senza modo (i.e., 'measure') non possono lungamente durare».

These words suggest that Pampinea, herself chosen by the group to rule the First Day, must signify Prudence.[30] Principal of all the virtues, the purpose of prudence, as described by Aquinas, is to perfect the rational power of the soul. Since it assists the rational faculty by helping reason maintain order, prudence is the intellectual virtue that 'commands'. As «right reason about things to be done», it directs the other moral virtues (Fortitude, Temperance, Justice), which must preserve the good of reason against instinctive movements of the passions, seated in the sensitive appetites. Dante's summary of the virtues from Aristotle's *Ethics* gives us the pith of Prudence in *Convivio* IV 17, 8: «essa [è] conduttrice de le morali virtù e mostr[a] la via per ch'elle si compongono e sanza quella essere non possono». In layman's terms, we could say, wisdom teaches us to order our lives and to make right, not impulsive, choices.[31]

In the *Comedia delle ninfe fiorentine*, Pampinea's counterpart is Mopsa, the lead nymph, whose story comes first and sets the pattern. Mopsa-Wisdom tames Affron, «the unwise one», and sings of Pallas, by whom she was granted the triple gift of memory, understanding, and foresight.[32] Among Boccaccio's pastoral virtues, Mopsa is senior («la più antica»), just as Pampinea in her *brigata* was oldest, («di più età era»). Three times in the *Decameron* Pampinea will tell the seventh story. As it happens, she is so positioned as seventh on the last three Days: VIII 7;

---

[30] Pampinea is prudential to V. Branca, *Boccaccio medievale, cit.*, p. 20; so also for G. Bàrberi-Squarotti, *La cornice del 'Decameron' o il mito di Robinson*, in *Da Dante al Novecento. Studi offerti a Giovanni Getto* Milan, Mursia, 1970, pp. 111-158.
[31] T. Aquinas, *Comm. Ethic., cit.*, I 8 (335 ff.).
[32] *Comedia delle ninfe, cit.*, XVIII-XIX.

IX 7; X 7. In the mini-pattern Boccaccio reasserts his favored 3 + 7 pair. Her seventh placement may signal as well Pampinea's sagacity, since among the many meanings possible for 7, one of the best known in Boccaccio's era was 'wisdom'.[33]

Pampinea's first story rounds off her Day of rule (I 10). Its protagonist is an old doctor of exemplary wisdom, Maestro Alberto da Bologna, a man just seventy years old. Now Bologna, along with Athens and Paris, is a place for scholars to sharpen their wits, as Boccaccio reminds his readers in the *Decameron* Conclusion. Leitmotifs in this tale, whose protagonist has lived to the ripeness of 10 x 7 years, are the words «savio» and «senno». It reveals the embarrassing foolishness in the Maestro's female interlocutor and concludes with an appropriate word to the wise. Pampinea also is the one who tells in VI 2 how Cisti the baker's inborn wit opened Messer Geri Spina's «intellectual eyes». But more important, she has the privilege of the seventy-seventh story. There the scholar Rinieri, after long years of study in Paris, settles a score back in Florence with the widow Elena, vulnerable to his vendetta because she was «più innamorata che savia» — too much in love with someone else to be 'wise' to the spurned student's trap. The lesson of the story is simple: «è poco senno il dilettarsi di schernire altrui». Not only does the tale fall into ordinal position marked by 7's (as 77th in the *Decameron*), it carries those numbers as well 'magically' in its content. The scholar, diabolically clever, will give his victim a tin love-icon that she is to hold while seven times immersing herself nude in a stream; then, again seven times, she must recite with it a spell from some high place. Seven times the credulous woman bathed; seven times from an unshaded tower she spoke the charmed words. The proud female will fall, not to her death, but to a good sound humiliation.

In Pampinea's seventy-seventh tale, a wise fellow downs a fool of a woman. Perfect opposites, Ruggieri and Elena, recall pairs of contraries typical in iconology of the Middle Ages, which often couples Virtues symmetrically with their corresponding Vice. So Boccaccio himself had worked out his pastoral allegory *Ameto*; each nymph is a Virtue who wins a man in whom she conquers an opposing evil. Thomas Aquinas specifies in his *Summa theologica* that for Wisdom or *Sapientia* the opposite is *Stultitia* or Foolishness. Sometimes artists personified it as a jester who plays the fool. In Giotto's program of virtues and vices for the Scrovegni

---

[33] In secular terms it describes universal learning as embraced by the Seven Liberal Arts; in the Bible, too, it is the number of wisdom. See above, ch. 1.

Chapel at Padua (ca. 1305), which pairs seven Virtues personified with contrary Vices, Stultitia is a man crowned with feathers and holding a cudgel who stands opposite Prudentia (Figs. 5a and 5b).[34] The latter figure is kin to the Wild Man, another well known medieval type. That humiliating disguise gets pressed upon the fallen antagonist of Pampinea's fourth tale, Frate Alberto da Imola. Ostensibly to save the friar, his Venetian host costumes and leads him «in forma d'uomo salvatico» to Piazza San Marco, «tutto unto di mele e empiuto di sopra di penna matta, e messagli una catena in gola e una maschera in capo, e datogli dall'una mano un gran bastone e dall'altra due gran cani» (IV 2, 52). Although Pampinea has a preference for smart people like the dignified Dr. Alberto (I 10), she can also remind us of her identity by spinning a tale about someone whose abject foolishness makes him her opposite, the homonymous friar Alberto of Imola.[35]

Allowing Aquinas to continue assisting us in this inquiry, we recall that he assigns two virtues specifically to the sensitive appetites: «Fortitude is assigned to the irascible power, and temperance to the concupiscible power. Whence the Philosopher (*Ethic.* iii) says that these virtues belong to the irrational part of the soul». Just as a craftsman cannot succeed unless both he and his instrument are well disposed, so man's rational faculty, aided by prudence, cannot regulate the lower appetites unless these latter are favorably disposed to accept reason's guidance. The virtues that help bring irascibility and concupiscence into conformity with reason are accordingly fortitude and temperance.[36] Who might they be in the *Decameron*?

We know from what Boccaccio tells us at the outset that each of the three men loves one of the women. Or, as his thoughtful Author wants to put it, *three* of the *seven* ladies are thus favored. Panfilo, Filostrato, and Dioneo «andavan cercando per loro somma consolazione, in tanta turba-

---

[34] T. AQUINAS opposes *stultitia* to *sapientia* in his *Summa theologica, cit.*, II-II, Qu. 46. Further visual examples are in J. HALL, *Dictionary of Subjects and Symbols in Art, cit., s.v.* 'Prudence'. See also R. VAN MARLE, *Iconographie de l'art profane au Moyen Age et à la Renaissance*, The Hague, Nijhoff, 1931-1932, II 66-67. Other kinds of pairings and oppositions in the Scrovegni chapel are discussed by M. ALPATOFF, *The Parallelism of Giotto's Paduan Frescoes*, in J. H. STUBBLEBEIN, ed., *Giotto: The Arena Chapel Frescoes. Illustrations. Introductory Essay. Backgrounds and Sources. Criticism*, New York, Norton, 1969, pp. 156-169.

[35] It seems not coincidental that he suffers the same painful exposure to biting insects («tafani») as Elena, object of Rinieri's vendetta.

[36] T. AQUINAS, *Summa theologica, cit.*, I-II, Qu. 56, Art. 4: «fortitudo ponitur esse in irascibili, temperantia autem in concupiscibili. Unde Philosophus dicit in III *Eth.*, quod «hae virtutes sunt irrationabilium partium». Cf. *Comm. Ethic., cit.*, III 19 (596): «fortitudo est in irascibili, sed temperantia est in concupiscibili».

zione di cose, di vedere le lor donne, le quali per ventura tutte e tre erano tralle predette sette». Although it is difficult to pin down the couples beyond all possible doubt, tradition inclines to see them as Dioneo-Fiammetta, Filostrato-Filomena, and Panfilo-Neifile.[37] Fiammetta, matched with concupiscible Dioneo, would then become not Love his replicate, as she is usually labelled, but his opposite, Temperance.[38]

Temperance counteracts concupiscence and moderates passions.[39] The *Ameto* had paired Adiona (i.e., Temperance, literally, «she who is not Venerean») with 'dissolute' Dioneo. In the *Decameron*, even before storytelling begins, Fiammetta teams to accompany musically a dance with Dioneo, the male narrator whose name and personality identify him with the Venerean appetite. On Day One Fiammetta and Dioneo sit side by side in the circle of narrators, proximity that suggests their symbolic affinity. On Fiammetta's Day, the fifth, Dioneo has the honor of the evening ballad. The two will sing together, paired conspicuously at the Conclusions of Days III and VII. As the Third Day ends, they sing about Messer Guiglielmo and the «Dama del Vergiù», a tragic romance and proleptic taste of the mood to prevail on the morrow. Even more telling, at the Conclusion of Day Seven their song is about Arcita and Palemone, rival knights in the *Teseida* who personified allegorically Wrath and Lust.

Temperance is a virtue suited to the median positions of narrating toward which Fiammetta gravitates, once as queen (Day V) and seven times as story teller. On four Days she has the fifth tale, repeating a slot more often than any narrator except Dioneo, and on three, the sixth. Like fortitude, temperance implies a mean. To achieve a suitable balance of pleasure and sorrow, the temperate person desires the right things, the right way, at the right time, as reason directs. Those pleasures of the flesh to which temperance mainly pertains are food and sex.[40]

Both are conspicuous in Fiammetta's stories on Days I through V. Her first succinctly combines the Thomistic ingredients of palatal and

---

[37] V. BRANCA, *Decameron*, cit., p. 997, gives the traditional names of the couples.

[38] J. FERRANTE, *The Frame Characters of the 'Decameron'*, cit., and L. MARINO, *The 'Decameron' 'Cornice'*, cit., both call Fiammetta 'Love'. S. GALLETTI, *Patologia*, cit., among identifications otherwise idiosyncratic, sees in Fiammetta the «little flame» of Temperance.

[39] T. AQUINAS, *Comm. Ethic.*, cit., II 1 (253); II 8 (337).

[40] T. AQUINAS, *Ibid.*, II 7 (331); II 8 (342); III 19 (595); III 22 (647) on Temperance as a mean in accordance with reason that pertains to food and sex. The artists often represented her as a woman with two vases, tempering water with wine, as on the Loggia dei Lanzi in Florence. Sometimes to indicate her restraint, instead of two vases she holds a bit, as in Orcagna's *Tabernacle* at Orsanmichele, or a sheathed sword as in Giotto's Paduan frescoes and the bas-relief panel by Andrea Pisano for the Florentine Baptistry doors. See R. VAN MARLE, *Iconographie de l'art profane*, cit., II 69.

erotic sensations. With a banquet consisting entirely of dishes made from hens, the marchioness of Monferrato «reprime il folle amore del re di Francia» (I 5, rubric). Although he imagined he could take advantage of that lady whose husband had gone Crusading, he figuratively found instead a locked, armored mountain («Monferrato»). Hers is a bastion of chastity very different from the Venerean «Monte Nero» about which the *brigata*'s servants squabble at the beginning of Day Six, an episode that forecasts Dioneo's accession later the same day. Fortunately, the French king recognizes his error and beats a remedial departure: «così come disavedutamente acceso s'era di lei, saviamente s'era da spegnere per onor di lui il male concetto fuoco [...] e, finito il desinare, acciò che il presto partirsi ricoprisse la sua disonesta venuta, ringraziatala dell'onor ricevuto da lei, accomandandolo ella a Dio, a Genova se n'andò» (I 5, 16-17).

While here a tempering influence represses lust, quite the opposite occurs in Fiammetta's tale on the day of tragic love. As Ghismonda slips Guiscardo a letter hidden in a hollow cane, she jokingly puns about «rekindling the fire».[41] Once discovered, in defense of their secret affair she reminds Tancredi that concupiscence of the flesh is only natural: «Sono adunque, sì come da te generata, di carne, e sì poco vivuta, che ancor son giovane; e per l'una cosa e per l'altra piena di concupiscibile disidero» (IV 1, 34). Guiscardo, in the only line of dialogue Boccaccio allows him, defiantly asserts to his captor Love's omnipotence: «Amor può troppo più che né voi né io possiamo». His statement recalls what Francesca da Rimini, the most memorable of Dante's carnal sinners, had argued to excuse herself in a canto that comments echoically on Ghismonda's emphatic, iterative vocabulary of Love. Her passion is eternal — love past, love present, love future, and love, so we must suppose, even and ever in Hell: «Egli è il vero che io *ho amato* e *amo* Guiscardo, e quanto io viverò, che sarà poco, l'*amerò*, e se appresso la morte *s'ama*, non mi rimarrò d'*amarlo*» (IV 1, 32 - italics mine).[42]

Fiammetta opens the tragic day with this tale of temperance denied to comply with Filostrato's wish for «cruel» stories, a preference she believes he may impose «per temperare alquanto la letizia avuta li giorni

---

[41] *Decameron, cit.*, IV 1, 7: «Essa scrisse una lettera [...] e poi quella messa in un bucciuolo di canna, solazzando la diede a Guiscardo e dicendo: «Far'ne questa sera un soffione alla tua servente, col quale ella raccenda il fuoco».

[42] V. RUSSO, *Il senso del tragico nel 'Decameron', cit.*, notes the 'amore' *adnominatio* at IV 1 in an excellent analysis of lustful and wrathful passions (emphasis on the latter), which Boccaccio understood from Dante, Aquinas, and Seneca.

passati». Reason loses to Ghismonda's lust — and Tancredi's ire — in a tale of two lovers who, in Dante's words, «la ragion sottomettono al talento». On the other hand, Fiammetta's last *novella* (X 6) echoes her first (I 5). The rubric makes clear the connection: «Il re Carlo, vecchio, vittorioso, d'una giovinetta innamoratosi, vergognandosi del suo folle pensiero, lei e una sua sorella onorevolmente marita». In both cases kings guilty of 'folly' in designs of love heed tempering words of advice. Phillip will go on from Monferrato to join the Crusade; old King Charles, his military triumphs all in the past, will now conquer himself.

If Dioneo's lady Fiammetta is Temperance, the virtue that restrains sensuality, the woman loved by irascible Filostrato should be Fortitude. She is Filomena, close to him in name, but not otherwise. Unlike the other two couples in the frame tale, Filostrato and Filomena usually sit apart from each other.[43] Their ballads, too, dovetail negatively. While he asks Love to make his faithless lady delight now in his demise as well as in her new man («Fa costei lieta, morend'io, signore, / come l'hai fatta di nuovo amadore»), she on her part passionately describes a fresh, consummated flame. It sears her as she sings at the end of Day VII: «Io non so ben ridir qual fu 'l piacere / che sì m'ha infiammata, / che io non trovo dì né notte loco. / Per che l'udire e 'l sentire e 'l vedere / con forza non usata / ciascun per sé accese nuovo foco, / nel qual tutta mi coco».

Since she has jilted Filostrato, Filomena would seem at first to epitomize fickleness rather than fortitude. In fact, woman's natural instability is the subject of her initial remarks in the *Decameron*, a cautionary reply to Pampinea's plea for flight from the city.

Donne, quantunque ciò che ragiona Pampinea sia ottimamente detto, non è per così ciò da correre a farlo, come mostra che voi vogliate fare. Ricordivi che noi siamo tutte femine, e non ce n'ha niuna sì fanciulla, che non possa ben conoscere come le femine sien ragionate insieme e senza la provedenza d'alcuno uomo si sappiano regolare. Noi siamo mobili, riottose, sospettose, pusillanime e paurose: per le quali cose io dubito forte, se noi alcuna altra giuda non prendiamo che la nostra, che questa compagnia non si dissolva troppo più tosto e con meno onor di noi che non ci bisognerebbe. (I Intro. 74-75)

Yet Filomena has the name of a bravely resourceful, unwavering Ovidian heroine,[44] and she conforms to the philosophers' definitions of

---

[43] They are together only once, telling in succession on Day VIII tales five and six.

[44] *Metamorphoses, cit.*, VI 424 ff. It may not be an accident that Filomena's Filostrato in the *Decameron* tells the story of the 'nightingale' (V 4).

Fortitude. They knew it in the guise of both perseverance and courage. Cicero, for example, called fortitude the double virtue «by which one undertakes dangerous tasks and endures hardships».[45] Aristotle had affirmed that fortitude treats of fear and aggressiveness, especially in life-threatening situations. It is the mean between rashness and cowardice.[46] In its most general sense, as Aquinas would later explain, fortitude is a condition of every virtue, since virtue must not waiver. But more specifically, it is «bearing and withstanding those things in which it is most difficult to be firm, namely in certain grave dangers», when it curbs fear and moderates daring. Its parts, or facets, on which Aquinas accepts Cicero's authority, are magnificence, confidence, patience, and perseverance.[47]

Fortitude in the *Comedia delle ninfe fiorentine* is Acrimonia, lover of listless, pusillanimous Apaten, «the apathetic one». She makes her entrance in the pastoral allegory together with Mopsa-Prudence and professes loyalty to the mother of Mars. That goddess is Bellona, who 'arms' her followers against the devil, makes them magnanimous, liberal, patient, and accepting of adversity, and always inspirits them with strength («fortezza»).[48] Out of allegory, what this means is that Bellona strengthens by granting fortitude in its various 'facets', or characteristic aspects. Fortitude's attachment to Wisdom in this early allegory will persist in the *Decameron*, where Filomena is Pampinea's satellite.[49] First to answer Pampinea's opening speech in the frame, she crowns her queen of the *brigata* and directly succeeds her as ruler. Five times the two tell consecutive stories: on III, VII, and X Pampinea precedes Filomena; on VI and VIII they reverse the order. In a polemical preface to VI 1, Filomena repeats verbatim what Pampinea had said before (I 10) on the special worth of witty retorts. Not only do the two ladies keep close company; they can even utter exactly the same words.

If Acrimonia took soldierly courage from the mother of Mars, Fortitude in the *Decameron* also speaks with a military turn of mind. Defending the decision to leave for the country, now that three male escorts

---

[45] R. TUVE, *Allegorical Imagery. Some Medieval Books and Their Posterity*, Princeton, Princeton University Press, 1966, p. 59.

[46] ARISTOTLE, *Ethics, cit.*, II 7; III 9.

[47] T. AQUINAS, *Comm. Ethic., cit.*, II 2 (262); II 8 (339-340); III 13 (529 ff.); *Summa theologica, cit.*, II-II, Qu. 123, Art. 2-6; Qu. 128.

[48] Acrimonia and Mopsa join the nymphs at IX 12. See XXIX for Fortitude's story, XXX for her song, and XXIX,43 on her companions.

[49] Branca comments on *Decameron, cit.*, IV 4, p. 1321, n. 4., that she is a «pallida satellite di Pampinea».

have materialized, she objects vigorously to shy Neifile's reservation about the propriety of this venture: «là dove io onestamente viva né mi rimorda d'alcuna cosa la coscienza, parli chi vuole in contrario: Idio e la verità l'arme per me prenderanno» (I Intro. 84-85).

To suggest Fortitude's strength, medieval artists often represented her beside a column, and she is typically armed, either with a club or sword and shield. Thus Andrea Orcagna conceived her for the *Tabernacle of the Madonna*, a project carried out in the decade after the plague of 1348, at Orsanmichele in Florence (fig. 7a). The Bible itself authorized the image in Paul's instructions to the Ephesians: «Put you on the whole armour of God, that ye may be able to stand against the wiles of the devil». This gear includes the shield of faith, the helmet of salvation, and the sword of the Spirit.[50] Boccaccio's Filomena therefore speaks of females as inconstant, pusillanimous, and timorous in her capacity as the virtue that conquers those weaknesses. When she urges caution about rushing out of town without masculine guidance, it is because she has the discretion to recognize the danger of rashness, which fortitude likewise counters.

Filomena's first story presents a situation covertly suited to the virtue she symbolizes. It asks us to recognize Fortitude through her facets, or characterizing parts. In *Decameron* I 3, Melchisedech the Jew escapes «a great danger» devised by Saladino, famous for valor in battle, but now bankrupt from his wars and grand-scale generosity, «avendo in diverse guerre e in grandissime sue magnificenze speso tutto il suo tesoro». How Melchisedech demonstrates Fortitude is fairly obvious: he saves himself by evading sudden entrapment. Saladino's Fortitude, though, is more complicated. We see it first, of course, in his military heroism and defense spending. But surprising to us as readers today, he shows 'strength' by making splendid gifts. His «magnificences», those generous deeds that have contributed to a financial crisis, are the technical term for an Aristotelian virtue, the same Magnificence exemplified by magnanimous spirits like Mitridanes on *Decameron* Day X. It is expressed as expenditures appropriate for a great ruler, huge public works and amazing acts of charity.[51] Now Magnificence, in both the Ciceronian and

---

[50] Eph. 6:10: «Induite vos armaturam Dei, ut possitis stare adversus insidias diaboli». Andrea Pisano's reliefs of Fortitude for the Florentine Campanile and Baptistry door show a woman seated holding club and shield. Giotto vividly represents her as a large, solid female with an enormous shield, opposite Inconstancy, as a woman perilously balanced on a sphere. See R. Van Marle, *Iconographie de l'art profane*, cit., II 67-69; E. Mâle, *The Gothic Image*, cit., pp. 112-113.

[51] Aristotle, *Ethics*, cit.,1124b; T. Aquinas, *Comm. Ethic.*, cit., IV 10 (759-783).

Thomistic scheme of things, is a fixed aspect of Fortitude. So Saladino's need for money, which precipitates the action in the *novella* since he intends to refill his treasury by tricking the Jew, actually comes about because of his virtue, resulting as it does from a nature courageous and strong.

On Pampinea's First Day the stories had followed no assigned theme. For Day Two, however, Queen Filomena asserts her character by restricting the narrators to a single subject. Her choice concerns people who survive adversity: «chi, da diverse cose infestato, sia oltre alla speranza, riuscito a lieto fine». What causes the 'troubles' on Filomena's day is Lady Fortuna, with her wheel and whimsical machinations — the female most fickle of them all. Who could be better qualified to counter Fortune's vagaries than Queen Filomena, resonant with Fortitude? In her own story on her Day of rule (II 9), the Queen returns to the very problem she had raised before the ladies left Florence, woman's inconstancy. Young Ambrogiuolo refuses to believe that Bernabò's wife is any different from the others. Man, being more perfect, must be more stalwart («dee avere più di fermezza»), while a woman, he claims, is just naturally fickle («naturalmente mobile»). Although ironically named after King Arthur's truant wife, Bernabò's steadfast Zinevra turns out to be «stronger than men», as with courage and perseverance she rights the wrongs she has suffered.

So far we have discovered three cardinal virtues among the seven female narrators of the frame tale: Pampinea-Prudence; Fiammetta-Temperance; and Filomena-Fortitude. Who might the fourth be? Since Boccaccio's earlier works clearly designate the Virtues as either cardinal or theological, the ladies here should also comprise a group of 4 + 3.[52] We can sort them by taking our cue from those who travel in the company of a serving maid. As a group the 3 + 7 young Florentines manage with only seven servants. Filostrato brings Tindaro; Dioneo brings Parmeno; Panfilo brings Sirisco. Three of the seven women, then, came without household help. We could say that four are 'tagged', three not. It is just the kind of marker we needed to allocate 4 + 3 cardinal and theological

---

[52] The Seven Virtues present themselves grouped 4 + 3 as early as the *Filocolo* (IV 74), when they appear to Florio in a prophetic fantasy. See below, the analysis of Neifile, for further disussion of this passage. In the *Comedia delle ninfe* the Cardinal Virtues' stories (XVIII, XXI, XXVI, XXIX) precede those of the Theological Virtues (XXXII, XXXV, XXXVIII). Boccaccio had in mind *Purgatorio* XXIX 121-130, where in the procession that comes to meet Dante as he enters Earthly Paradise, the Cardinal Virtues are first introduced dancing on one side of Beatrice's chariot, then the Theological on the other.

Virtues. Since Pampinea, Fiammetta, and Filomena have Misia, Stratilia, and Licisca respectively, the fourth lady with a maid must be the remaining Cardinal Virtue. She is Lauretta, served by Chimera and symbol of Justice.

The Day she rules is the eighth, appropriate to her dominion. Pythagorean number symbolism, transmitted into the Middle Ages by Neoplatonic encyclopedists like Macrobius, equated 8 with Justice because it could be divided into two equal halves of 4, and each of those in turn could be subdivided equally into parts of 2. Not surprisingly, it falls to the queen of Day Eight to narrate tale eighty-eight, and more often than not, she takes her daily turn in the eighth or fourth position (three times each). Matters of law and legalistic terminology rise to prominence during her reign, which has a tale at the center (VIII 5) about a judge seated at the bench meting out justice.[53]

Justice, in the Aristotelian-Thomistic tradition, may be distributive or commutative. Distributive justice deals with apportioning goods and honors among members of the community, while commutative justice pertains to financial transactions. The latter in turn may be voluntary, such as buying, selling, bartering, and loaning; or involuntary and violent, like theft, adultery, and murder. The unjust man, who would rather suffer less deprivation than he ought and enjoy more than his due measure of good, seeks to enrich himself at the expense of others.[54]

Lauretta's first tale, the eighth of Day One, tackles directly matters of the purse strings. At Genoa, a notorious miser of the Grimaldi family holds them unbecomingly tight until a Florentine guest with more sense about largesse in disbursement, Guiglielmo Borsiere, shames him into mending his ways. This William Bursar belonged to a bygone breed of virtuous courtiers who promoted social well-being by arranging peace treaties, marriage contracts, and attacking evil wherever they saw it. Nowadays, expostulates Lauretta, men no longer distinguish between right and wrong or, worse, choose only to reward the dishonest, whence we can see that «le virtù, di qua giù dipartitesi, hanno nella feccia de' vizii i miseri viventi abbandonati». Borsiere, Lauretta's past perfect gentle-

---

[53] Macrobius, *Comm. in somnium, cit.*, I 5, 15: «Pythagorici vero hunc numerum iustitiam vocaverunt, quia primus omnium ita solvitur in numeros pariter pares, hoc est bis quaterna, ut nihil o minus in numeros aeque pariter pares divisio quoque ipsa solvatur, ed est in bis bina» [The Pythagoreans, indeed, called the number eight Justice because it is the first number that may be divided into two equal even numbers and divided again into two more equal even numbers]. To imply equality, a balanced weighting on each side, Justice is depicted in medieval art as on modern court houses holding a scale. On the theme of justice, see below ch. 7.
[54] T. Aquinas, *Comm. Ethic., cit.*, V 1 (885 ff.).

man, might have had as his motto, «Every man his due». What he really disbursed was justice distributive.[55]

Justice commutative accompanies the adventures of Landolfo Rufolo, the Amalfitan trader whose story Lauretta next tells (II 4). He decides to recoup business losses by resorting to piracy, «e diessi a far sua della roba d'ogni uomo». Ironically, Landolfo himself falls victim to robbery at the hands of seafarers from Genoa — no less greedy than their Grimaldi compatriot, since the Genoese — in stereotype the 'Scotch' of medieval Italy — are «men naturally eager and rapacious for money».

These involuntary transactions in commutable goods, simple instances of basic injustice, contrast with Lauretta's last tale (X 4). It is a far more complex case of property ownership, presented by Gentil de' Carisendi of Bologna after serving as visiting judge («podestà») in the next-door city of Modena. By a strange circumstance, he comes into possession of another man's wife, the pregnant Madonna Catalina, whose husband had given her up for dead and laid her in a tomb. Messer Gentile, as noble as his name, generously makes public restitution not only of the wife, whom he loved and has nursed back to health, but also her newborn son, when by rights he could have kept them both. The setting for his grand gesture, Bologna, is a law school town, and Gentile de' Carisendi, scion of one of its most famous families, speaks a language the professors would have appreciated. He turns the question of his property rights into a legal case, argued with precedent, to ask: Who now has claim to wife and child? In favor of his side, he tells about another problem of property rights, where the object of contention was not a woman taken in marriage, but a loyal man-servant.

Egli è alcuna persona la quale ha in casa un suo buono e fedelissimo servidore, il quale inferma gravemente; questo cotale, senza attendere il fine del servo infermo, il fa portare nel mezzo della strada né più ha cura di lui; viene uno strano e mosso a compassione dello 'nfermo e' sel reca a casa e con gran sollicitudine e con ispesa il torna nella prima sanità. Vorrei io ora sapere se, tenendolsi e usando i suoi servigi, il suo signore si può a buona equità dolere o ramaricare del secondo, se egli raddomandandolo rendere nol volesse. (X 4, 26)

Although all the men at the banquet, including Catalina's husband, are quick to assert the logic of finders-keepers, Messer Gentile will give back

---

[55] See V. KIRKHAM, *Lectura Boccaccii* on *Decameron* I 8, Philadelphia, University of Pennsylvania Press, for the American Boccaccio Association, ed. E. WEAVER.

the discarded wife, and what's more, magnify the magnificence of his deed by doubling the gift, Madonna Catalina and her boychild.

Alert to possibilities of tit for tat, Lauretta personally takes a dim view of hasty revenge and will not rush «like a dog» to counterattack King Dioneo (VII Concl. 3). But Pampinea's seventy-seventh tale of the scholar's «rigida vendetta» prompts her to recall for the eighty-eighth a comparably painful vengeance. Its scrappy protagonist is Ciacco, the gourmand and social parasite — «non del tutto uom di corte ma morditore» — who in «less than eight days» evens a score with Biondello. Rich in still largely unexplored intertextual connection with the *Divina Commedia*, this tale's cornerstone is Dante's prophetic encounter in the Circle of Gluttony at *Inferno* VI. When the pilgrim asks Ciacco, wallowing sodden in the rain-pounded River Styx, if any just man is left in their city, «ma dimmi [...] s'alcun v'è giusto», his informant pronounces a grim reply on the state of justice in Florence, «Giusti son due, e non vi sono intesi; / superbia, invidia e avarizia sono / le tre faville c'hanno i cuori accesi». Later, among the usurers (*Inferno* XVI 68-70), Dante names one who epitomized the old «courtesy and valor», gone now that hearts burn with pride, envy, and avarice. He is the ex-pursemaker Guiglielmo Borsiere, the true courtier that Lauretta had praised in her first tale (I 8) for putting his wits to the service of good, promoting justice in times when Virtues still trod the earth.[56]

Three *Decameron* narrators now remain to be identified, those ladies who sojourn in the country without a servant. They are Neifile, Elissa, and Emilia. The Days they rule are the Third, the Sixth, and the Ninth. Such positions — 3, its double 6 and square 9 — are apt for a trio of ladies that resonate symbolically as the Theological Virtues. Moreover, by reserving Days III, VI, and IX for these Christian heroines, Boccaccio repeats a formula he had used in his *Ameto*. Each nymph there, after a spicy report of how she entered the service of Venus, sings a song in *terza rima*. Charity's *ternario* coincides with the thirty-third chapter, Hope's with the thirty-sixth, and Faith's with the thirty-ninth. The virtues return to the *Decameron* triadically placed and in the same order of appearance: Neifile as Charity rules Day Three, Elissa as Hope follows on Day Six, and Emilia as Faith has Day Nine.

The first we meet is Neifile. She bears a name that reminds us of the New Era under Christ, whose Coming brought Charity into the world.

---

[56] F. Fido touches on the intriguing intertextual connections, remarking that *Decameron* IX 8 is «un vero *party* di archetipi danteschi». See his *Dante personaggio mancato del 'Decameron'*, cit.

Its etyma are 'new' and 'love'. Neifile, «Lover of the New» or «New Lover», is entitled to declare the weekend break for religious observances, Friday to commemorate Christ's death on the cross and Saturday for devotion to the Virgin Mary (II Concl. 5-6). She first makes herself heard in the *Decameron* to object that the ladies in Pampinea's church circle ought not leave Florence with the three men who have just so fortuitously stepped inside Santa Maria Novella. Since they are in love with ladies present, might some scandal not ensue? Blushing as she speaks, she gives herself away to our Author-recorder: «Neifile allora, tutta nel viso divenuta per vergogna vermiglia per ciò che l'una era di quelle che dall'un de' giovani era amata, disse [...]». Her lover, we deduce, is Panfilo, whom she succeeds in the ring of narration on Day I. Later, on three other Days (VI, VII, VIII), they will again sit side-by-side. If Fiammetta as Temperance finds her match in Dioneo, the concupiscent part of the soul; and if Filomena stands for the Fortitude that Filostrato misses, he being a figure of irascible appetite; it follows that Neifile's admirer must be the third man, Panfilo. As «All Love» and an emblem of rational appetite, the highest power in man's soul, Panfilo is naturally drawn to Christian love, the Charity radiant in shy, young Neifile.

Neifile's vermilion cheeks betray more than a rush of girlish embarrassment. Beyond realism, they shine with the Christian love that suffuses her being because, by the rules of medieval color coding, red is for Charity. It is a symbolic equivalent of the flaming heart she offers to God in Giovanni del Biondo's Strozzi Chapel ceiling medalion of St. Thomas flanked by Charity and Chastity (Thomas himself holds the heart in his right hand), or on the seated figure by Andrea Pisano (1336), who brought Humility into the company of the seven Virtues beside Charity to fill eight panels that occupy the lower two tiers of the San Giovanni southern doors, below scenes from the life of St. John the Baptist (figs. 2 and 8).

From our point of view, to paint a woman red in the face should not be particularly flattering. But Boccaccio, as we could by now predict, had used before the very same device, and in a context that leaves no mistake about meaning. In the *Filocolo*, Florio one day has a «fantasy» while off musing by himself in a garden enclosed. It is at once an omen of stormy weather ahead in the hero's romance with Biancifiore and a prophesy of his baptism into Christianity (IV 74). Before the eyes of the melancholy youth appear a tranquil sea and little bark, upon its deck «sette donne di maravigliosa bellezza piene, in diversi abiti adornate». They stand four toward the prow, the other three spaced from midships to poop. Separating them rises a mast, high as heaven. First among the four is a lady dressed in black who holds with one hand a book, with the other a mirror. Next is a woman garbed in «ardente colore» beneath a veil of white who grasps a well honed sword. The third seems to wear adamant; with «equal gaze» she looks about, her foot upon a terrestrial globe, in her hand a royal scepter. Fourth stands taciturn a lady in violet, one hand laid across her breast, the other at her lip. Biancifiore rides at the bow as a passenger, cradled in Love's arms. Suddenly, an ugly hag rocks the boat and hurls it into a vortex; when calm waters return, a heavenly lady descends who sprinkles Florio with «most precious water» from her golden ampoule. It washes his eyes, revealing to him in their full glory those three ladies positioned on the far side of the mast: «delle quali tre vedea l'una tanto vermiglia e nel viso e ne' vestimenti quanto se tutta ardesse, e l'altra tanto verde che avanzato avria ogni smeraldo, la terza bianchissima passava la neve nella sua bianchezza».

Florio, still a pagan, has no trouble making out his first four fantasy ladies because they are the four pre-Christian or Cardinal Virtues. Their leader is Prudence, wisely reading a book, she who must precede to 'command'. Boccaccio imagines her as Giotto had in the Scrovegni Chapel, where her attributes are a codex on a lectern, from which she takes instruction, and a mirror, into which she gazes to see 'truth' reflected (fig. 5a). Next, in fiery red reminiscent of Mars, is her satellite, the sword-bearer Fortitude; after her, ruling the world with equality, poises Justice; and finally, Temperance signs restraint with her fingers. Dame Fortune makes waves that threaten the ship of virtue, but in a light-flash, Grace drops personified from the eternal kingdom; with baptismal aspersion she clears Florio's sight so that he can discern each of the Theological Virtues. First is Charity, whose color radiates from her face and dress; then comes Hope in her traditional green, and third, Faith, a vision in shimmering white.

This line-up of women, whose frozen postures and typical attributes have the static quality of Byzantine icons or Gothic bas-reliefs, are ancestors of the seven women who take on flesh, blood, and Florentine pluck to tell seventy stories in the *Decameron*. During the fifteen to twenty years that separate *Filocolo* from *Decameron*, Boccaccio has obviously moved toward greater realism. Yet beneath a surface of plausibility, the later work still carries, submerged, symbolism that had been stark in his earlier period. Florio sees a lady «vermiglia e nel viso e ne' vestimenti»; Neifile only blushes for a moment, the temporary discomfiture of a girl new to love. Whereas we smile at the awkward image of a woman red all over, including her skin, we can accept that picture on symbolic terms, which are its only terms. Neifile's complexion, though, is not naturally crimson. When she turns red, Boccaccio's Author-recorder makes us understand a sign of reciprocal attraction between two young people. But we can see deeper than he does, and in that flush, with hindsight to the *Filocolo*, appreciate Charity infused.

Neifile's Third Day, an optimal numerical dominion for Love, has a garden setting that resembles the Earthly Paradise, and its stories culminate — in humorous metaphor — with a «resurrection of the flesh».[57] Since the salvation promised by Christ's Third Day Resurrection in the Gospels becomes possible through baptism, Neifile will inaugurate her ten tales on a theme of conversion to the Faith, sealed by immersion (I 2). Abraam the merchant loses his Old Testament, patriarchal identity when he rises from the font newly christened Giovanni. Giannotto, who had converted him with prompting from the Holy Ghost, bestows the name, which vouches their Johannine bond in the sacrament.

To put Love before Hope and Faith reverses the sequence usually cited, St. Paul's in I Corinthians 13:13: «So faith, hope, love abide, these three; but the greatest of these is love». Nevertheless, St. Thomas authorizes both ways of naming the virtues. By the order of generation, which proceeds from the imperfect to the perfect, faith comes first and after it, as in the Pauline epistle, hope and love. But according to the order of perfection, in which the perfect precedes the imperfect, charity stands before hope and faith.[58] Boccaccio then, in *Filocolo*, *Ameto* and the *Decameron*, opted for a theological order of perfection, moving from Charity to Hope and Faith.

With Love ruling Day Three in the person of Neifile, Queen Elissa of Day Six must signal Hope. Her congener, Fiammetta in *Ameto* XXXVI, sings of Ariadne's crown, a reward for Greeks and great Romans whose deeds bore witness to hope. In her verses, other ancients of note stand antithetically apart, among them Dido and sad Byblis. They lost sight of that starry promise, sank to despair, and vented their wrath against themselves. Boccaccio's nymph intones a triumphal lyric, for she has delivered her despondent admirer Caleon from a Didoesque death at his own hand. Aspirant to a crown and roborant to despair, Fiammetta in the *Ameto* copies iconographically Hope as imaged by the artists. Giotto's winged *Spes* levitates, stretching her arm toward a crown extended to

---

[57] In Boccaccio's canon 3 is love because it is the planetary sphere of Venus and the number of Christian Trinity. See above, ch. 1 and 2.

[58] T. AQUINAS, *Summa theologica, cit.*, II-II, Qu. 17, Art. 5.

her by an angel, while her contrary *Disperatio* commits suicide by hanging (Figs. 6a and 6b).[59]

Boccaccio's Hope for the *Decameron* takes her name by antiphrasis from Virgil's African queen, a suicide by the sword. To be sure, before flight via Cyprus to Carthage, Dido of Phoenecia had been known as Elissa, a name from happier days. Hence Florentine Elissa begins her first story «tutta festevole» and her second «lietamente». The former (I 9) hovers allusively around Dido's escape: a female protagonist en route from the easternmost Mediterranean puts in at Cyprus; victim of a violent wrong, she despairs of revenge (but finds it with a 'biting' word to the island ruler). Carthage itself, a geographic *hapax* in the century of Tuscan tales, helps locate Elissa's *novella* about Gerbino's long-distance passion for Tunisia's princess, a hopeless affair properly held in store for Hope's turn on the day of tragic love.[60]

If we assume that rule by Temperance on Day Five marks the *Decameron*'s center, Elissa's calendar day (VI) confirms 'Not-Despair' as her nature. Boccaccio schedules her opposite Filostrato, the despairing lover who personifies Irascibility (IV), just as Giotto had set *Spes* against *Disperatio*. Similarly, he opposes Charity in the person of Neifile (III) to Dioneo's concupiscence (VII). Charity, then, acts as a moderating force on lust and in this capacity reminds us of Giovanni del Biondo's pairing of her with Chastity (fig. 2). In the *Decameron*, congruent with the symmetries sketched by Janet Smarr in the Days on either side of the Fifth Day, we see matches between Prudence and Faith, Fortitude and Justice, Charity and Concupiscence, Irascibility (or Despair) and Hope.[61]

At the same time, Pampinea-Prudence as first ruler points structurally to Panfilo-Reason, the last ruler. At opposite extremes of the text, they must be connected in the *Decameron* plan of things as blood relations. From what the Author has told us in his Introduction to Day I, we know that some of the seven women not tied to the three young men in love are otherwise connected to them, as close relatives. Pampinea «a alcun di loro

---

[59] Sword and noose were the death instruments of Dido and Byblis, respectively. Andrea Pisano's Baptistry doors show Hope as a seated, winged woman who reaches for a crown; Orcagna's *Tabernacle of the Madonna* in Orsanmichele has her facing a crown. For these and other examples of hope in the visual arts, see VAN MARLE, *Iconographie*, cit., II 64, and MÂLE, *The Gothic Image*, cit., pp. 113-114.

[60] 'Carthage' is named at IV 4, 13. Boccaccio, of course, knew Dido by both her names from the *Aeneid*. Frequently in his writings he refers to her, and twice he retells her tale: *De mulieribus claris* XLII; *Esposizioni sopra la Comedìa* V 1, 66-83. He etymologizes 'Dido' as 'virago', but he does not hazard an interpretation for Elissa.

[61] J. L. SMARR, *Boccaccio and Fiammetta*, cit., pp. 176-180. Pairings of virtues and their opposites varied. For example, Giotto puts Invidia against Charity.

per consanguinità era congiunta» (I Intro. 87). A good candidate for such kinship is Panfilo, who enjoys sitting just to the right of Pampinea on Day I. Since rational appetite would naturally find a compatible relative in Prudence, they can 'team' again on Day II, when from the complementary third and seventh positions each relegates the things of this world to Fortune's inscrutable power. They are the beginning and the end of the *brigata*, its alpha and omega so to speak, for she initiates and organizes the outing from Florence, while he calls a conclusion to the pastoral retreat and leads the group back into the city.[62] They are a pair of relatives who recall Reason and Prudence, her «sister» in the *Amorosa visione*. Perhaps Panfilo and Pampinea are consanguineous as siblings, then, and he could also say to Prudence, «Thou art my sister».

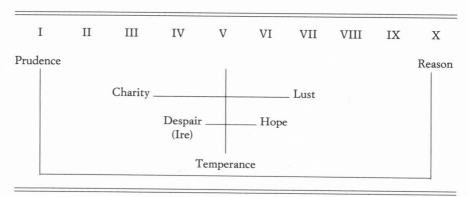

Coming back to Hope, how is it a theme suitable to the topic on Elissa's day? Out of respect for the power of clever speech and witty retorts, which can blunt an adversary's 'bite' and ward off impending danger, she assigns all to prepare, «di chi, con alcun leggiadro motto tentato, si riscotesse, o con pronta risposta o avvedimento fuggì perdita o pericolo o scorno». Boccaccio would have found authorization for Queen Elissa's choice in the Biblical Epistle ascribed to the apostle-martyr James. James had credentials as an exponent of hope, established from the fourth century and still current in the fourteenth. So as Dante stood for his exams on Faith, Hope, and Charity in Paradise, before he could transit to the Most High, the bright soul of St. James interrogated him on

[62] C. De Michelis, *Contraddizioni nel 'Decameron'*, in *Miscellanea di studi in onore di Vittore Branca*, II, *cit.*, pp. 95-109.

hope.[63] Further, it was the Epistle of James that explained the crown toward which Hope reaches in visual representations of the Virtues (fig. 6a). When in his 'Little *Decameron*' Boccaccio has Hope sing to Ameto and her sister nymphs of the constellation known as Ariadne's Crown, he nods to that same tradition, from James 1:12: «Blessed is the man who endures trial, for when he has stood the test he will receive the crown of life which God has promised to those who love him». More important for the 'Big *Decameron*' is James's caveat, couched in a lively series of metaphors, on the tongue's potential for causing trouble:

For we all make many mistakes, and if any one makes no mistakes in what he says he is a perfect man, able to bridle the whole body also. If we put bits into the mouths of horses that they may obey us, we guide their whole bodies. Look at the ships also; though they are so great and are driven by strong winds, they are guided by a very small rudder wherever the will of the pilot directs. So the tongue is a little member and boasts of great things. How great a forest is set ablaze by a small fire! And the tongue is a fire. (James 3:2-6)

The brevity of speech that Elissa's Day advocates, while an ideal of classical rhetoric, is also decorum of a Christian kind. Talk, like the appetites, requires restraint. James thinks in the controlling terms of a rider or helmsman, images that recall the Platonic concept of reason's role in the soul. Not surprisingly, the central spokesman on Hope's day of the well-disciplined tongue is Panfilo-Reason, who praises Giotto for creating a new art with appeal intellectual rather than sensual.

Boccaccio takes his James not just text-to-text, however, but also via the *Divina Commedia*, that is, with benefit of intermediary embellishment on which he in turn capitalizes. Dante admits James — under cover of Ulysses and his 'speechlet' — to *Inferno* XXVI, and later encounters him openly in a corresponding canto, *Paradiso* XXV, for examination on the second theological virtue.[64] Before meeting that test, the pilgrim pauses to express lingering hope for a crown on earth, coronation as poet laureate at his baptismal font in San Giovanni. He remembers with bitterness what cruelty shuts him outside that fair sheepfold where once he slept as a lamb, enemy to hostile wolves: «la crudeltà che fuor mi serra

---

[63] See *Paradiso* XXV, and comm. by C. S. SINGLETON.

[64] *Inferno* XXVI and *Paradiso* XXV correspond numerically in Dante's system of cross-referenced cantos, provided we subtract *Inferno* I as Prologue to the whole *Commedia*. If we count *Inferno* II as the beginning of the first canticle, *Inferno* XXVI drops back one digit to read as the counterpart in Hell of *Paradiso* XXV.

/ del bello ovile ov' io dormi' agnello, / nimico ai lupi che li danno guerra». Elissa, who owes parts of her eclectic character to both Virgil's Dido and St. James's Epistle, takes cues from Dante as well, especially *Paradiso* XXV, when she recites stories with such props as lambs, wolves, and the Florentine baptistry. Treed by voracious wolves, Pietro spends a miserable night separated from his lost lady 'lamb', Agnolella (V 3); contemplating the tabernacle «in the church of San Giovanni», Calandrino hears tell how a body becomes invisible when touched by Bengodi heliotrope — terms laughingly lambent with paradisiacal promise (VIII 3); Messer Betto and his *brigata* corner Guido Cavalcanti outside the door of San Giovanni, «che *serrata* era» in a showdown whose veiled theme — apt for its hopeful narrator on her own Day as queen — is transcendence of the tomb through life after death (VI 9).[65]

The last lady in Pampinea's circle is Emilia. In Thomistic order of perfection, she completes the sequence of theological virtues that starts with Neifile-Charity on Day Three and moves to Elissa-Hope on Day Six. Ninth monarch, she is Faith's embodiment. The name Emilia corresponds by paronomasia to Lia, symbol of Faith in the *Ameto*. As Emilia rules on Day IX, Lia's final hymn is a *credo* in *terza rima* that falls in *Ameto* XXXIX. Lia, privileged as Ameto's chosen nymph, also presents herself in a proemial song, the first *ternario* within the fiction proper (second to Boccaccio-narrator's) and one where we see her seeing herself: «tante fiate, / quant'io veggo onde, tante son costretta / del mio padre [the river God Cefiso] onorar la deitate; / avvegna che ciò far molto diletta / a me perciò che 'n esse riguardando, / mi rendon la mia forma leggiadretta. / La qual come sia bella in me pensando, / di verdi erbette, di rami e di fiori / adorno lei, d'ogni labe purgando» (IV 10-15). Similarly, Emilia sings the first ballad in the *Decameron*, and, like Lia, she mirrors herself with rapture: «Io son sì vaga della mia bellezza, / che d'altro amor già mai / non curerò né credo aver vaghezza. / Io veggio in quella, ognora ch'io mi specchio, / quel ben che fa contento lo 'intelletto» (I Concl. 18-19). Both women are reflective figures, their 'speculation' a metaphor for Faith as it lovingly contemplates.

---

[65] M. CORTI connects the flaming tongue in James with Dante's *Comedy*, *On the Metaphors of Sailing, Flight, and Tongues of Fire in the Episode of Ulysses ('Inferno' 26)*, in «Stanford Italian Review», IX, 1990, pp. 33-47. On the Guido Cavalcanti story, see also R. M. DURLING, *Boccaccio on Interpretation: Guido's Escape ('Decameron' VI 9)*, in *Dante, Petrarch, Boccaccio*, ed. A. BERNARDO and A. PELLEGRINI, *cit.*, pp. 273-304; V. KIRKHAM and M. R. MENOCAL, *Reflections on the 'Arabic' World: Boccaccio's Ninth Stories*, «Stanford Italian Reveiw», VII, 1987, pp. 95-110.

Boccaccio's two Faiths, of whom the second later spins a small tale around truth in a looking glass (VI 8), differ in attribute from that virtue as the artists portrayed her. The mirror they reserved for Prudence (fig. 5a), and so for that matter had Boccaccio in his earlier *Filocolo*, where it accompanies her book as a prop. Boccaccio's Faiths in *Ameto* and *Decameron* have instead a strongly Dantesque cast of character. Indicative is Emilia's opening tale (I 6). Faith is explicitly at stake when a hypocritical Minorite accuses of heresy a man who had spoken lightly of Christ, but only because he happened to have been drinking, «non già per difetto di fede». This inquisitor, greedily devoted to «San Giovanni Barbadoro», was «non meno buono investigatore di chi piena aveva la *borsa* che di chi di scemo nella *fede* sentisse» (I 6, 4). Boccaccio's thumbnail sketch of him raises an image that recalls Dante's examination in faith at *Paradiso* XXIV, where begins the three-part test for which St. James administers the questions on hope. (Dante encounters the theological virtues in order of generation, from Faith to Charity.) After he has recited the proper definition of faith, «fede è sustanza di cose sperate / e argomento de le non parventi», his interrogator on that subject, St. Peter, refers to the virtue of faith as a coin: «Assai bene è trascorsa / d'esta moneta già la lega e 'l peso; / ma dimmi se tu l'hai ne la tua *borsa*» (*Paradiso* XXIV 83-84). Emilia gives a broad hint of her symbolic character with the first story she tells. At issue is keeping the Faith, under scrutiny is a corrupt Inquisitor, who literalizes Saint Peter's metaphor by turning the spiritual coin of that virtue to his personal, material advantage.

* * *

Taken in the order of the days they rule, the three young men and seven ladies now all have a symbolic surname.

I	Pampinea	Prudence
II	Filomena	Fortitude
III	Neifile	Charity
IV	Filostrato	Irascibility
V	Fiammetta	Temperance
VI	Elissa	Hope
VII	Dioneo	Concupiscence
VIII	Lauretta	Justice
IX	Emilia	Faith
X	Panfilo	Reason

Boccaccio has allied the Seven Virtues with Reason to temper Irascibility and Concupiscence, impulses springing from the lower, sensitive appetites. The actions and attributes of his frame narrators, often in monitory contrast to behavior of men and women in the stories they tell, resonate allegorically as the well-ordered soul to which Everyman should aspire.

In this sense, the *Decameron* is a kind of puzzle. Its frame characters are themselves signs to be read. Deciphering them is not so easy as for the Virtues in *Ameto,* each of whom reveals her 'identity' through loops of rhetoric with mythological allusion and punning etymologies. The ladies and gentlemen in the *Decameron* are more elusive, the clues to their nature more scattered. Clearly, Boccaccio does not expect us to click into some drab mechanical This-For-That mode as we track them down. For us to conclude after pouring over the text that Pampinea 'equals' Prudence, Filomena 'equals' Fortitude, Neifile 'equals' Charity, would narrow meaning and run against the poet's grain. Boccaccio invites us to deduce such equivalencies, and in so doing, to unite these young Florentines with fictive names into a literary family. At the same time, his ideal, from his first fiction, was to multiply meanings and slants for reading, to entice us into searching for interpretative panoplies. Once we recognize the patterns of ethical symbolism and psychic allegory in the *Decameron*, the book does not shrink to a single, rigid block. On the contrary, openings into the text proliferate. Those frame narrators whom Edward Hutton found so colorless and unidimensional that he counselled us just to forget about them, are in fact multi-faceted personalities whose parts Boccaccio invites us to discover across the tracks of his prose and pull together into a meaningful whole. Where each person rules, which day on the calendar, in opposition to whom, their frame tale love mates or family kinships, what kinds of stories they tell, the lexicon they use, all contribute to their respective portraits. The more we come to know about them, the better we see how carefully drawn they are, how complex their relationships to each other, how intertwined they are intertextually with Boccaccio's earlier works, with his Dante, with his Aristotle, and with his other authorities, poetic as well as philosophic. Each narrator, if not a symbol strictly speaking, has symbolic resonance. And taken together, they create a situation charged with allegorical resonance.

Seen in this light, the *Decameron* is less radically different in spirit from the works preceding than the traditional dichotomy of a major Boccaccio and a minor Boccaccio presupposes. It retains elements of the allegorical mode in which four of the earlier compositions, starting with the first, were indisputably cast: *Caccia di Diana* (1333-1334); *Teseida delle nozze d'Emilia* (1339-1341); *Comedia delle ninfe fiorentine* (1341-1342); *Amorosa visione* (1342). What all the Italian fictions share, *Decameron* unexcepted, is a point of view that approves of rational behavior and disapproves of irrational behavior.[66] Put in terms of normative, medieval psychology, reason should control the appetites, not the other way around.

---

[66] The chronology is from V. BRANCA's *Profilo biografico, cit.* R. HOLLANDER advanced a hard-hitting argument against the romantic image of a youthful Boccaccio who wrote in praise of carnal love in *Boccaccio's Two Venuses*. He found the *Decameron*, however, 'resistant' to his thesis, a point of vulnerability on which critics capitalized. See, for example, F. FIDO's review, *Speculum* LIV, 1979, pp. 149-152; rpt. *Il regime delle simmetrie imperfette, cit.*, pp. 141-147. A 'rational' *Decameron* has been convincingly reconstructed by T. M. GREENE, *Forms of Accommodation in the 'Decameron'*, «Italica», XLV, 1968, pp. 297-313; J. L. SMARR, *Boccaccio and Fiammetta, cit.*, p. 165-174.

5.

THE WORD, THE FLESH, AND THE *DECAMERON*

The most appealing characters in Boccaccio's *Decameron* are memorable less for what they do than for what they say. A remarkable talent for talking distinguishes two of them in particular. One is Ser Cepparello, arch sinner of the opening tale, who wins the title of sainthood with a blasphemously mendacious confession. His peer in inventive loquacity is Frate Cipolla, that oratorical rival to Tully and Quintilian, whose brilliantly improvised sermon at the end of Day Six metamorphoses an ordinary stroll through Florence into a fabulous Middle Eastern pilgrimage, and enables him to display for the awed peasants of Certaldo not «the angel Gabriel's feather», as he had planned, but «blessed charcoal» from the grate of St. Lawrence's martyrdom. This roguish pair of gifted performers is strategically teamed in the *Decameron*. Its first day of storytelling is a Wednesday, where, after Cepparello's bravura recital, all of the tales revolve in one way or another around well-spoken words. The art of knowing how to speak re-emerges on Day Six, the following Wednesday, which culminates with Cipolla's Ciceronian preaching under a diurnal rubric calling for quick, witty retorts. Calendrically mated, the Wednesdays of Days I and VI are architectural portals leading into both the anthology as a whole and its second half.[1] Their shared theme, implicit the first time around and explicit the second, is symbolically appropriate to the day 'mercoledì', because for medieval mythographers and astrologers alike Mercury was the god of eloquence.[2]

---

[1] P. D. STEWART, *La novella di Madonna Oretta e le due parti del 'Decameron'*, «Yearbook of Italian Studies», III-IV, 1973-1975, pp. 27-40; C. VAN DER VOORT, *Convergenze e divaricazioni tra la Prima e la Sesta Giornata del 'Decameron'*, «Studi sul Boccaccio», XI, 1979, pp. 207-241; T. BAROLINI, *The Wheel of the 'Decameron'*, «Romance Philology», XXXVI, 1983, pp. 521-539.

[2] Boccaccio's own scholarly catalogue of Mercury's attributes in the *Genealogia* (II 7) includes eloquence, good memory, intellectual acumen, sweet delivery in speaking, swiftness,

Mercury's rule at the threshold of each narrative week raises the medium of language itself to high-ranking status in the system of values that informs the Author's message. Although he claims to be writing mainly about love, what Mercury fosters must somehow, on a less superficial register, take priority over those amours prompted in so many tales by his planetary neighbor Venus, since no storytelling at all is permitted on her days, the Fridays. 'Venerdì' is reserved instead for turning away from the flesh to the spirit with penitential meditation on Christ's crucifixion. Readers have long admired the dialogue and direct discourse in the *novelle*, unusual in its frequency, as evidence of Boccaccio's consummate ability to achieve, in alternating rhythms of humor and seriousness, realistic character portrayal.[3] Not until recently has the initial and central structural emphasis on locution been noticed, leading Guido Almansi, Giuseppe Mazzotta, and Millicent Marcus to argue that the *Decameron* is in essence a meta-linguistic text.[4] But these studies, while rightly stressing Boccaccio's mimetic skill and alerting us to the anthology's self-conscious literary nature, have evaded the ethical coordinates of its fourteenth-century rhetorical matrix.

Assuming that communication is indeed a capital topic in Boccaccio's collection of tales, I propose to sound the range of expression it takes there with reference to the philosophical teachings on human locution inherited by the later Middle Ages. This will involve constructing two grids, both necessarily general, given the broad lines of my inquiry. The

---

the tonsure, and writing — all relevant to Frate Cipolla; as well as mendacity and false testimony, two of Cepparello's notarial fortes. Daily astrological determinism of theme in the book's two-week calendar still awaits systematic commentary. Cepparello and Cipolla are an established intratextual couple. See., e.g., R. HOLLANDER, *Boccaccio's Dante: Imitative Distance ('Decameron' I 1 and VI 10)*, «Studi sul Boccaccio», XIII, 1983, pp. 169-198. Each is «an artist of the word» for G. GETTO, *Vita di forme*, *cit.*, p. 163. G. MAZZOTTA sees VI 10 as an amplification vis-à-vis I 1 of «the problems inherent in the duplicity of language», *The 'Decameron' and the Marginality of Literature*, «University of Toronto Quarterly», XLII, 1972, pp. 64-81; rpt. *The World at Play*, *cit.*, ch. 2. His thesis has been provocatively expanded in the analysis of these «companion pieces», portraits of characters similar even in the sounds of their names, by M. MARCUS, *An Allegory of Form*, *cit.*, ch. 1 and 4.

[3] V. BRANCA's seminal monograph, *Boccaccio medievale*, *cit.*, ch. 3, samples dialogue in the *Decameron* for its realistic impact, achieved through the controlled prose cadence of the *cursus* and creative application of rhetorical tropes, the latter sometimes reflected as if «in a fun house mirror»; and surveys «linguistic expressionism» shaded by dialects, colloquialisms, professional jargon, and thieves' slang.

[4] G. ALMANSI, *The Writer as Liar. Narrative Technique in the 'Decameron'*, London, Routledge and Kegan Paul, 1975; G. MAZZOTTA, *The Marginality of Literature*, *cit.*; M. MARCUS, *An Allegory of Form*, *cit.* Building an argument in another direction, C. DELCORNO brilliantly observes, «Nell'intenzione del Boccaccio il *Decameron* si presenta come una vasta e complessa registrazione di voci». See his *Exemplum e letteratura tra Medioevo e Rinascimento*, Bologna, Il Mulino, 1989, p. 266.

first will present an overview of speech patterns in the *Decameron*, which run the gamut from mute gesticulation to perfect linguistic decorum. For the second, a survey of Greek, Latin, and Christian writings on rhetoric, I shall take as primary authorities Aristotle, Cicero, and Augustine. Their reasoning reveals that the words Boccaccio put into the mouths of his characters were not chosen simply for verisimilar, humorous, or esthetic effect. He also knew that speech, the intellectual instrument by which man is distinguished from the beasts, comports a powerful ethical valence. What we say and how we say it is the measure of our humanity. Proper speech mirrors the well-ordered soul and makes possible a harmonious social life; its failure accompanies morally defective behavior and works against the interests of the political community in which all men, like Boccaccio's emblematic frame narrators, must rationally participate to achieve their ontological perfection.

Let us begin by sampling the possibilities of discourse presented in the *Decameron*. It opens with a tale that is the fiction of a fiction, Panfilo's account of Cepparello's confession. That wicked man's tissue of lies transports us into the narrative territory of Day I, where the numbers 3 and 7 join to reiterate Boccaccio's self-conscious narrative line. The third and seventh tales share a structure that sets one story within another. I 3 describes linguistic entrapment eluded, as Melchisedech the Jew answers Saladino's tricky question on true religion by telling his own *novella*; and in I 7 an appositely told anecdote similarly assists the professional raconteur, Bergamino. For the rest of the *novelle* on Day I, pithy replies are the rule, except I 2. But even there words count. A Parisian Jew named Abraam embraces Christianity, in spite of the utter corruption he observes in the Roman clergy, through the proselytizing efforts of his friend Giannotto, an uneducated merchant whose words persuade because the Holy Ghost had put them on his tongue. Formally announced in its governing rubric, the brief tales of Day Six, counterpart to One, generate quintessential models of how people should – and should not – speak: «Si ragiona di chi con alcun leggiadro motto, tentato, si riscotesse, o con pronta risposta o avvedimento fuggì perdita o pericolo o scorno».

Elsewhere in the *Decameron* speech is otherwise conspicuous, sometimes by its absence. This is strikingly the case for the Sultan's daughter Alatiel (II 7), whom Mediterranean language barriers reduce to verbal silence as the vicissitudes of maritime violence send her through the hands and beds of many foreign lovers before final reunion with her long-promised husband, felicitously in the guise of *virgo intacta*. A rich sex life also results from taciturnity for Masetto da Lamporecchio (III 1), the enterprising youth who penetrates a convent as the nun's gardener by pretending to be a deaf mute.

Alatiel and Masetto are, however, exceptions in the *Decameron*'s panoramic range of discursive possibilities, from which, as I have already suggested, readers are most likely to recall the characters more inclined toward loquacity. Their utterances frequently create humorous distortions of speech, which may be dictated on the one hand by naive ignorance, on the other by calculated ingenuity. So the simple-minded Ferondo (III 8) reports, after his presumed resurrection from close to a year «in Purgatory», divinely imparted news of the son that will be born to him, an annunciation he has heard straight from the «Ragnolo Braghiello».[5] Again, Monna Belcolore, partner in the materialistic little country-bumpkinish romance with the priest of Varlungo (VIII 2), has a rustic husband, Bentivegna del Mazzo («May-You-Get-A-Good-Clubbing»), who one day conveniently departs for the city, explaining in nonsensically confused legalese that he is going there «per alcuna mia vicenda [...] per una comparigione del parentorio per lo pericolator suo il giudice del dificio».[6] Conversely, Maso del Saggio, whose name signals his sagacity, can knowingly manipulate language. His double talk on the magical qualities of the heliotrope, aimed at gullible, thick-headed Calandrino (VIII 3), conveys the astonishing fact that whoever possesses on his person the fabulous stone will become invisible, «wherever he isn't».

But Boccaccio's undisputed master of dazzling linguistic legerdemain is the brilliant orator Frate Cipolla. His talent shines in a parodic

---

[5] Ferondo's stumbling tongue, which downgrades the divine messenger into a spiderish thing with trouserlets, tests the mettle of translators. G. H. McWILLIAM's felicitous solution in the 1972 Penguin *Decameron*, «Arse-Angel Bagriel», sacrifices arthropodal allusion for a comparably demeaning emphasis on the *derrière*, and it combines language colloquially as well as classically British, since 'Bagriel' can allude to the slang term 'bags' ('pants'), as in 'Oxford bags' (E. PARTRIDGE, *A Dictionary of Slang and Unconventional English*, New York, Macmillan, 1970, *s.v.* 'bags'). John Payne's Victorian solution was «Rangel Bragiel». See *Decameron*, trans. J. PAYNE, rev. C. S. SINGLETON, Berkeley, University of California Press, 1982. In the first 20th-c. English *Decameron*, London, 1903, the translator J. M. RIGG, who practiced his own form of late Victorian censorship simply by sometimes giving no translation at all − e.g. for most of III 10 − settles for keeping «Ragnolo Braghiello» with an evasive footnote on an elementary orthographic principle. The tale in R. ALDINGTON's pedestrian rendering, New York, Doubleday and Co., 1930, offers only a blandly metathetic «Hangel Gubriel». M. MUSA and P. BONDANELLA's recent American attempt to cope with the spoonerism in their *Decameron*, New York, Mentor, 1982, modernizes spider and breeches by substituting ethnic pastry with a rancid touch («Rankangel Bagel»), but the shift necessitates a footnote, «Ferondo confuses the Rankangel Bagel with the Archangel Gabriel».

[6] One might translate «On an errancy of mine [...] to testimoan on grit of summons from the camisole for the judge of crinimal fences». What he seems to mean is that the judge of the criminal court instructed counsel to subpoena him for an appearance. Even the Italian is here so mangled as to require editorially annotated clarification.

inventory of precious relics: «il dito dello Spirito Santo così intero e saldo come fu mai, e il ciuffetto del serafino che apparve a san Francesco, e una dell'unghie de' gherubini, e una delle coste del Verbum-caro-fatti-alle-finestre e de' vestimenti della santa Fé catolica [...]».[7] Notable on the list is the first item, the finger of the Holy Ghost, true author of sacred writ, celestial power of the Pentecostal gift of tongues, and within the *Decameron*, source of the inspired words that helped simple Giannotto convert his friend Abraam. The relic that was to have been the centerpiece of Cipolla's sermon, «la penna», receives repeated mention in the story, nineteen times by concordance count.[8] Such insistence on the word invites us to associate it with the story's thematic verbal nexus in an alternate application as 'quill' and 'pen'. This exotic feather actually came from a parrot, of course, a non-human creature known for its capacity merely to mimic human pronouncements. Propping the friar's kerystic *tour-de-force*, with its sesquipedalian mockery of the incarnational mystery central to the «santa Fé catolica» are underlying layers of authorial word play, concentrated on communicational media in this climactic tale of the *Decameron*'s second 'mercoledì'.[9]

Other markedly rhetorical moments in the anthology are more seriously cast. This is true, for instance, of the solemn, self-exculpatory declamation delivered by widowed Ghismonda (IV 1) to her jealous father, Prince Tancredi, in defense of her love affair with a page in his household. An even more powerful speech in the high style — and one of the two longest rhetorical displays within the tales — is the diatribe that

---

[7] The problematic rib of the «Verbum-caro-fatti-alle-finestre», confounding John 1:14, «Et Verbum caro factum est», with the joshing image of a swain's fenestral serenade, has given rise to various formulas: Payne had «Verbum Caro Get-you-to-the-windows»; Rigg, «Verbum Caro hie thee to the casement»; Aldington, a nonsensical «Verbum Caro made at the factory»; Musa-Bondanella find «True-Word-Made-Fresh-at-the-Windows»; and McWilliam concocts «Word-made-flash-in-the-pan».

[8] A. BARBINA, *Concordanze del 'Decameron'*, Florence, Giunti-Barbèra, 1969.

[9] R. HOLLANDER, *Boccaccio's Dante*, *cit.*, discusses poetic implications of Cipolla's 'penne'. I am indebted to R. DURLING for pointing out that the feather's last-minute substitute, charcoal, also alludes to writing. Serving Boccaccio's illiterate friar as medium for leaving his signature — Ash Wednesday style — with the credulous Certaldesi at the close of his sermon, it was used from Roman through medieval times in the manufacture of ink, along with gum arabic for emulsification in a solvent medium, the latter often *ad hoc* wine. See W. J. BARROW, *Manuscripts and Documents: Their Deterioration and Restoration*, Charlottesville, University Press of Virginia, 1972. The large black crosses he makes all over their white shirts and veils as protection against «getting burned by fire unless it touches you» also make humorous capital of Ezekiel 9:3-6, where a man in white linen signs those to be spared in the city's destruction. On Ezekiel's signer, see W. NEUSS, *Das Buch Ezechiel in Theologie und Kunst bis zum Ende des XII. Jahrhunderts*, Münster, Aschendorff, 1912, pp. 82, 108, 159-160; and for the tau in Franciscan semiotics, J. FLEMING, *From Bonaventure to Bellini. An Essay on Franciscan Exegesis*, Princeton, Princeton University Press, 1982, p. 112.

bursts from Tedaldo (III 7), who inveighs against hypocrisy in the clergy to justify his own hidden romantic liaison. The longest single speech made by any character in the *Decameron* is that of Tito Quinzio Fulvo (X 8), student of philosophy from ancient Rome and eloquent advocate of perfect human friendship.

Finally, at an opposite pole, the matter at stake is simple abecedarian literacy. Significantly, the alphabet first surfaces at the center of the day whose theme is language itself as distilled in the quick retort. In VI 5 we meet the foremost jurist of the time, that «armory of civil law» Messer Forese da Rabatta, together with Giotto, its leading painter. Both are sights to behold in the ragged, mudspattered peasant garb that a sudden summer thunder-shower has forced them to borrow while returning from their country houses to Florence. Eyeing his companion, Forese asks, «Giotto, a che ora venendo di qua alla 'ncontro di noi un forestiere che mai veduto non t'avesse, credi tu che egli credesse che tu fossi il migliore dipintore del mondo, come tu se'?» With antiphonal word play on the verb 'believe', the artist retorts in the anecdote punchline, «Messere, credo che egli il crederebbe allora che, guardando voi, egli crederebbe che voi sapeste l'abicì». While their sublime wisdom is masked by coarse bedraggled clothing, even the finest fur-lined gowns of another man cannot hide the sheer idiocy of his babbling. He is Maestro Simone, Boccaccio's dim-witted doctor from Bologna, said to have learned his abc's «in sul mellone». The phrase punningly contrasts the physician's brainless, gourd-like head with the 'mela' on which parents were accustomed to carve for their children letters of the alphabet before allowing them to eat the fruit.[10] The message in these two stories is evident: don't believe what you see; people are to be judged by what they say and how they say it, not by the appearance of external trappings.

Sometimes in the *Decameron*, then, the tongue is silenced altogether to be replaced, as in the stories of Alatiel and Masetto, by sign language and mute gesticulation. But facility with speech, starting with one's abc's, is a skill of fundamental value. The ignorant who lack it, unless guided like Abraam's friend by the Holy Ghost, produce amusingly garbled words and can run off at the mouth about miraculous whisperings from the «Arse-Angel Bagriel». They in turn are naturally vulnerable to gulling by those who do possess an enviable gift of gab, even if without benefit of formal education. Frate Cipolla fits this description: «niuna

---

[10] V. BRANCA, *Decameron, cit.*, n. 10, p. 1452. See also below, ch. 7.

scienza avendo, sì ottimo parlatore e pronto era, che chi conosciuto non l'avesse, non solamente un gran rettorico l'avrebbe estimato, ma avrebbe detto esser Tulio medesimo o forse Quintiliano».

Ranging from dumb reticence to polished eloquence, the widely diverse verbal options within the tales of the *Decameron* stand in contrast to the constant propriety and ideal speech of its ten Florentine frame characters. Although Dioneo threatens their rigorously honest code with a bawdy song at the end of Day Five, the *brigata* will not allow him to sing any of the risqué ditties he teasingly proposes. As if to reinforce the dignity of the register on which the group converses, their servants cause a clamorous disruption in the next frame episode, which opens the second Wednesday. Quarreling in broad language, Licisca loudly berates Tindaro for being a «bestia d'uom» if he is foolish enough to believe that women are virgins when they marry, and that on a certain Sicofante's wedding night, «messer Mazza entrasse in Monte Nero per forza e con ispargimento di sangue». Such farcical, erotic double-entendres fall beneath the elevated linguistic norm maintained by their masters and mistresses during conversational interludes between the tales. The high standard will also extend to the world of the stories for precisely the Day on which successful speaking is the enunciated theme, the Sixth, when narrators and *novelle* come into closest expressive proximity.[11]

To be sure, a certain license is permitted in storytelling on other Days, and this becomes an issue under the irrepressible Dioneo's rule, where piquant cases of cuckolding are the order (VII). But as he submits on receiving the crown at the end of Day Six, the exceptional nature of the times can justify some elasticity in subject matter, all the more so because their group seeks only honorable enjoyment. True throughout their sojourn to verbal and behavioral rectitude, the circle will in the end earn praise for it from Panfilo at the close of his concluding reign:

quantunque liete novelle e forse attrattive a concupiscenzia dette ci sieno e del continuo mangiato e bevuto bene e sonato e cantato (cose tutte da incitare le deboli menti a cose meno oneste), niuno atto, niuna parola, niuna cosa né dalla vostra parte né dalla nostra ci ho conosciuta da biasimare: continua onestà, continua concordia, continua fraternal dimestichezza mi ci è paruta vedere e sentire. (X Concl. 4-5)

---

[11] F. FIDO, *Boccaccio's 'Ars narrandi' in the Sixth Day of the 'Decameron'*, in *Italian Literature: Roots and Branches. Essays in Honor of Thomas Goddard Bergin*, ed. G. RIMANELLI and K. J. ATCHITY, New Haven, Yale University Press, 1976; rpt. *Le metamorfosi del centauro*, *cit.*, ch. 2.

Consequently, just as the storytellers' actions remain within the bounds of virtue, so within the confines of the frame does their talk. What they do and what they say are in perfect harmony.[12]

This is an indispensable consonance in the *Decameron*'s ethical system. To see why, we must now turn to the Classical and early Christian rhetorical tradition that had passed into Boccaccio's cultural milieu. It will be appropriate to begin with Aristotle. Although he did author a treatise on rhetoric, Cicero's *De inventione* and the pseudo-Ciceronian *Rhetorica ad Herennium* supplanted it, so the Philosopher's views on language for the Middle Ages are to be sought elsewhere.[13] Linguistic concepts as basic as they were influential receive prominent consideration in both the *Nicomachean Ethics* and the *Politics*.

In the *Ethics*, of which Boccaccio's copy survives together with his own transcription of the *Commentary* by Thomas Aquinas,[14] Aristotle defines moral virtue as a mean between extremes of excess and defi-

---

[12] In spite of what Dioneo and Panfilo say about the *brigata*'s 'onestà', A. BERNARDO, *The Plague as Key to Meaning in Boccaccio's 'Decameron'*, cit., finds motives of hedonistic self-gratification in their flight from the plague, concluding that we should view the group with skepticism, suspicion, and ultimately, contempt. I am in general agreed with his Augustinian reading of the *Decameron*, but cannot accept this idea of the narrators, which departs from the critical consensus on their function vis-à-vis the content of the tales they relate. Indicative of the majority is F. FIDO (*Boccaccio's 'Ars narrandi'*, cit.), who finds that «the *brigata*'s faultless lifestyle constitutes an ideal counterweight to the materiality of the *novelle*». See also F. FIDO, *Silenzi e cavalli nell'Eros del 'Decameron'*, «Belfagor», XXXVIII, 1983, pp. 79-84; rpt. *Il regime delle simmetrie*, cit., pp. 103-110. Bernardo's objections to the group's preference for pleasure-seeking over meditation on death finds an excellent, independent rebuttal in G. OLSON, *Literature as Recreation in the Later Middle Ages*, Ithaca, Cornell University Press, 1982, pp. 87 and *passim*. Olson demonstrates how on medieval medical, psychological, and moral grounds alike, entertainment promotes physical well-being and healing: «Delectare *est* prodesse».

[13] J. MURPHY, *Rhetoric in the Middle Ages: A History of Rhetoric from Augustine to the Renaissance*, Berkeley, University of California Press, 1974, pp. 90-96. See also MURPHY, *The Scholastic Condemnation of Rhetoric in the Commentary of Giles of Rome on the Rhetoric of Aristotle*, in *Arts libéraux et philosophie au moyen âge. Actes du quatrième Congrès international de philosophie médiévale*, Montréal, Institut d'Etudes Médiévales, 1969.

[14] The Ms. is in Milan, Biblioteca Ambrosiana, Cod. A.204 part. inf. The *Commentary* was transcribed into an older copy of the *Ethics* before 1350, hence antedates the *Decameron*. See G. AUZZAS, *I codici autografi*, cit. Flat denials of any Thomistic contamination of Boccaccio's writings were standard in the critical tradition from De Sanctis onward until Branca's vigorous revindication of 'medievalness' restored Aquinas to his cultural heritage. Branca, however, documents no specific textual connections in his various mentionings of Thomas. See, e.g., V. BRANCA, *Boccaccio medievale*, cit., pp. x; 15-16 n.; 168; 193-194 n.; 290. Authoritative among the earlier gainsayers was A. HORTIS, who could firmly avow in his monumental and still helpful *Studj sulle opere latine*, cit., p. 487, that, notwithstanding the codex of Aristotle with Thomas's commentary, «si può affermare che nelle opere del Certaldese non v'ha traccia delle dottrine del grande Aquinate». More tracking is in order of the «Campagner che lo Spagnuol seguio / con la cappa», one responsible to begin with in Boccaccio's gigantic acrostic allegory for Fiammetta's putative family name (*Amorosa visione* XLIII 46-47). See above, ch. 2.

ciency. His three-step scale with its ideal happy medium applies not only to what people do, but just as logically to what they say, that is, to intercourse in words. Such intercourse, he affirms, is of two sorts. One is truth, whose mean is truthfulness; its excessive form is boastfulness, and its defective manifestation is false modesty. The second kind of verbal intercourse relates to 'pleasantness'. It is, in turn, twofold; either friendship, or more to the point for our purposes, the ability to amuse and entertain others: «In the giving of amusement the intermediate person is ready-witted and the disposition ready wit, the excess is buffoonery and the person characterized by it a buffoon, while the man who falls short is a sort of boor and his state is boorishness».[15]

Returning to his assertions about buffoonery and boorishness later in the *Ethics*, Aristotle will offer a variant statement on their mean. Called «tasteful intercourse», it is «saying − and again listening − to what one should and as one should». Representative of such conversational ability is polite joking, through which a person reveals virtuous character with ready wit and sallies tactfully tailored to the audience (1128a). Witty humor does not admit vulgarity or indecent language, but rather conveys its fun in pleasant innuendo.

From the remarks on these passages appended by St. Thomas we learn that in playful conversation the exaggerator is termed a buffoon or *bomolochus* («altar plunderer») after those birds of prey that steal entrails from the sacrificial *bomos*, because he comically misappropriates words and actions to himself. On boorishness Aquinas does not expand. The man who observes the mean, however, «is called witty [*eutrapelus*], as it were "turning well toward everything", and the disposition itself wit».[16] Only a reasonable man who possesses a soul free from slavish passions can enjoy the habit of this virtue, which reveals his internal rational disposition and depends on his education: «The jesting of the cultured man who has been instructed how he should recreate differs from the jesting of the uncultured man who has not been trained by any instruction in jesting. Hence, it is clear that it pertains to the mean habit of virtue to speak and listen to what is becoming in jesting».[17]

---

[15] ARISTOTLE, *Nicomachean Ethics* 1108a, in R. McKEON, ed., *Introduction to Aristotle*, cit.

[16] ARISTOTLE, *Ethics*, cit., 1108a and T. AQUINAS, *Comm. Ethic.*, cit., II 9 (353): «vocatur eutrapelus, quasi bene se vertens ad omnia, et dispositio vocatur eutrapelia».

[17] *Ethics* 1128a and *Comm. Ethic.*, cit., IV 16 (858): «Qui scilicet instructus est qualiter debeat ludere, differt a ludo hominis indisciplinati, qui nulla disciplina in ludo refrenatur. Unde manifestum est quod ad medium habitum virtutis pertinet decentia in ludo dicere et audire».

These Aristotelian-Thomistic ideals of tasteful intercourse may serve as a touchstone for judging some of the talk in the *Decameron*. A *bomolochus* buffoon surfaces, for example, in melon-headed Maestro Simone. He is a boastful fool who yaks cacophonously about student-day conquest by fisticuffs of a puny female in Bologna and his current wenching in 'Cacavincigli'.[18] These risible vaunts are meant to prove his qualifications for admission into a secret orgiastic club that necromantically steals exotic queens for its members' nocturnal gatherings, which always feature first a lavish banquet supplied with fare spirited from others' tables. Boorishness finds its match in niggardly Calandrino's bizarre manners, perfect bait and butt for Maso del Saggio's lapidary joke, or again, in the unpleasant, hypercritical Cesca (VI 8), who doesn't understand that to spare herself disagreeable sights, she should never again face a looking glass. But *eutrapelia*, the desirable mean in playful conversation, initially appears, and probably not by accident, at the center of Day I, when in tale five the Marchioness of Monferrato tactfully cools her royal French houseguest's «folle amore». Adept as well at artfully turning a phrase is the Marchioness's Mercurian and structural 'second' in the *Decameron*, Giotto, who presides at the center of Day Six. But surpassing all in eutrapelian subtlety is the brilliant philosopher-poet Guido Cavalcanti (VI 9), recalled by Elissa, queen for that day, with a story that shows him as deft in deed as he is in word. His vault over a sarcophagus at the San Giovanni door symbolizes the difference between well-mannered, well-spoken «uomini scienziati» like him, and the others, who are «idioti e non litterati».[19]

Boccaccio's *brigata*, too, admirably mirrors the Aristotelian mean, one that underlies Elissa's choice of the witty retort as theme for the Sixth Day. Its initial tale directly recalls the last on Day I. Pampinea, who tells I 10, had prefaced it with words of praise for fair speech and with biting remarks on the sad degeneration of conversational ability among women. Hardly any are left, she complains, who can understand

---

[18] English translators have preferred to let the proper name stand, presumably because of its scatological component. But cf. *Decameron, cit.*, with the commentary by V. BRANCA, who notes, «È un chiasso in Firenze così nominato, cioè calle ovvero ruga sporca e da vil gente abitata [...] Cacavincigli tanto vuol dire quanto *cacavinci* o *vincigli*, cioè di stirpe de' villani». He properly sees in the toponymic an anticipation of the tale's 'malodorous' conclusion.
[19] I cite F. FIDO, *Dante personaggio mancato del 'Decameron', cit.* R. DURLING performs a subtle analysis of Guido in *Boccaccio on Interpretation, cit.* Boccaccio asserts his respect for preserving and transmitting literary culture in Guido's retort, which hinges on a famous dictum from Seneca regarding 'letters' («Otium sine litteris mors est, et hominis vivi sepultura»). See G. VELLI, *Seneca nel 'Decameron', cit.*

or respond to a clever saying. Nowadays they merely chatter with their laundresses and bakeresses instead of engaging in true verbal congress with worthy men. To illustrate the need for pitching one's words to suit time, place, and audience, she then recounts an anecdote about Madonna Malgherida's embarrassing misassessment of her interlocutor, Maestro Alberto, a mature gentleman of youthful spirit who nippingly bests her in banter.

When Filomena presents the first story on Day Six, she repeats Pampinea's lament, echoing almost verbatim her assertions about the special beauty of graceful sallies.[20] These, she says, crown beautiful speech, itself partner to proper moral habits:

Giovani donne, come ne' lucidi sereni sono le stelle ornamento del cielo e nella primavera i fiori de' verdi prati e de' colli i rivestiti albuscelli così de' laudevoli costumi e de' ragionamenti belli sono i leggiadri motti; li quali, per ciò che brievi sono, tanto stanno meglio alle donne che agli uomini quanto più alle donne che agli uomini il molto parlar si disdice.

A reversal of Pampinea's tale, Filomena's significantly situated 'meta-novella' relates the courteous conversational coup of Madonna Oretta, who knew just what to say and when to a knight who did not. Unlike the tale of the scatter-brained cook, Chichibio, whose blurted retort, three stories later, can compensate for the drumstick snatched from a crane, Madonna Oretta's speech-act is not a fluke of one-time luck. Rather it is typical of an aristocratic culture that has taught her the habit of pleasant talk, a conversational mean called *eutrapelia*.[21] Intelligently shaped, pithy remarks and prompt replies, distillations of speech at its most beautiful,

---

[20] The striking repetition forms one of the linkages between I and VI. See, e.g., P. D. STEWART, *La novella di Madonna Oretta, cit.*

[21] G. ALMANSI, *The Writer as Liar, cit.*, pp. 19-20, takes this 'meta-novella', the fifty-first, as center of the *Decameron* and a signpost or «coded invitation» to read the anthology as a book about reading, writing, and telling stories. Its central position and self-conscious content have likewise struck M. BARATTO, *Realtà e stile nel 'Decameron'*, Vicenza, Neri Pozza, 1970, pp. 73-76, for whom the animating power of the *Decameron* is sheer delight in storytelling. F. FIDO, too, in *Boccaccio's 'Ars narrandi', cit.*, perceives there «the poetics in a nutshell» of the whole book, and he recognizes «ben parlare» as an important social virtue alien to the knight's old-fashioned chivalric values. See also G. GETTO, *Vita di forme, cit.*, p. 154. M. COTTINO-JONES has noticed in the 'hiccuping' rhythms of the Chichibio tale «sound effects that suggest correlations with the animal world rather than with a human world of rationalized actions and reactions» in *An Anatomy of Boccaccio's Style*, Naples, Cymba, 1968. The 'Chichibiesco' retort as a rhetorical tactic in vernacular is described by F. CHIAPPELLI, *L'episodio di Travale e il 'dire onestamente villania' nella narrativa toscana dei primi secoli*, «Studi di Filologia Italiana», IX, 1951, pp. 141-153; rpt. *Il legame musaico*, ed. P. M. FORNI with G. CAVALLINI, Rome, Edizioni di Storia e Letteratura, 1984.

have in this venerable Aristotelian context a value that is more than esthetic. They display excellence of character. Tasteful intercourse holds a place in the *Ethics* on a par with such qualities of self-mastery as chastity, truthfulness, friendliness, liberality, courage, and temperance — moral virtues requisite for human happiness.[22]

Why, though, should restraint in speaking be a particularly female virtue? For the unequal measure of speech allotted men and women Aristotle again can offer explanation, provided we turn to his *Politics*. Political order, he asserts, requires the same kind of power hierarchy that should obtain in the soul and individual household. Thus, the head of state, endowed with perfect virtue, must rule his subjects as reason rules our appetites and man his wife. Like their leader, the other members of the state should cultivate virtues suitable to each one's station and sex. So a man displays courage in commanding, but a woman in obeying. Obedience belongs to the human female no less than silence, «a woman's glory». Thus, continues Aristotle, «a man would be thought a coward if he had no more courage than a courageous woman, and a woman would be thought loquacious if she imposed no more restraint on her conversation than a good man» (1260a; 1277b). Given Aristotle's assumption of woman's natural inferiority, her virtues will lie in her submissiveness. It is through wifely obedience and verbal restraint that she fulfills her role in the well-ordered household and, by the same token, in the larger community as well. Boccaccio's vain Venetian blabbermouth Madonna Lisetta, chosen as mistress by the «Angel Gabriel» in his second Decameronian descent (IV 2),[23] foolishly violates this social code. Patient

---

[22] The jocular quipping so prized by Boccaccio's Florentines has a long history passing through Macrobius's *Saturnalia* (ca. 400) and a close vernacular antecedent, the anonymous 13th-c. *Novellino*. Beyond their paradigmatic moral worth, wittiness (*eutrapelia*) and well-told stories further served important therapeutic, restorative purposes, not only in Aristotelian theory, but also in medieval allopathic medical practice, the thesis of G. Olson's *Literature as Recreation*, cit. Dante refers to *eutrapelia* as an Aristotelian moral virtue in *Convivio* IV 17, 6. Boccaccio's debt to the concept of *eutrapelia*, particularly as developed by Roman rhetoricians, is mentioned by C. Muscetta in *Boccaccio*, cit., p. 310. P. D. Stewart, *La novella di Madonna Oretta*, cit., links the «motti di spirito» in the *Decameron* with precepts pertaining to *facetiae* drawn from Cicero and Quintilian. An excellent survey of the history of the «forgotten virtue» of *eutrapelia* from Aristotle to Cervantes can be found in B. Wardropper, *La eutrapelia en las Novelas ejemplares de Cervantes*, in *Actas del Septimo Congreso de la Asociación International de Hispanistas (Venecia 1980)*, ed. G. Bellini, Rome, Bulzoni, 1982.

[23] There are three all told, and they form a curious cross-referential pattern. The first, at III 8 («Ragnolo Braghiello»), is tale 28. The third (VI 10 with Cipolla's feather) is 28 stories after the second (Madonna Lisetta's lecherous Minorite mate in IV 2), which is tale 32, and it is by 32 tales that the last follows the first. All involve corrupt men of the cloth who use the word to serve the flesh with seductions that rise in culpability from the sexual (III 8 and IV 2) to the intellectual (VI 10).

Griselda (X 10) wisely observes it. Disruptive violence results in the first case; reaffirmation and continuity of community in the second, with the reconvergence of Gualtieri's family members.[24]

These ideals of wit and discretion, inherited by the later Middle Ages, depend logically on Aristotle's more famous, primary linguistic enunciation. It stands at the start of the *Politics*:

Nature, as we often say, makes nothing in vain, and man is the only animal whom she has endowed with the gift of speech. And whereas mere voice is but an indication of pleasure or pain, and is therefore in other animals (for their nature attains to the perception of pleasure and pain and the intimation of them to one another, and no further), the power of speech is intended to set forth the expedient and the inexpedient, and therefore likewise the just and the unjust. And it is a characteristic of man that he alone has any sense of good and evil, of just and unjust, and the like, and the association of living beings who have this sense makes a family and a state. (1253a)

Language and its proper use belong to the heart of human behavior, rational and political by definition. Beasts and gods need not speak because they can live in self-reliant isolation, but man achieves perfection only when living communally. Essential to his bonding in the body politic is speech, which, as Thomas Aquinas would later put it, «manifests to another what lies hidden in the mind».[25]

Expanding on the Aristotelian axiom with Thomistic commentary in mind, Dante reiterates in his *De vulgari eloquentia*: «Nam eorumque sunt omnium soli homini datum est loqui» (I 2, 1).[26] Animal behavior, says

---

[24] In this context Biblical injunction on female reticence is certainly also pertinent. See, e.g., I Tim. 2:11-12: «Mulier in silentio discat cum omni subiectione. Docere autem mulieri non permitto neque dominari in virum, sed esse in silentio» [Let a woman learn in silence with all submissiveness. I permit no woman to teach or to have authority over men; she is to keep silent.] Men and women alike, of course, should keep a bridle on their tongues. See, e.g., PETRUS ALFONSI's *Disciplina clericalis*, trans. E. HERMES, London, Routledge and Kegan Paul, 1977, p. 111: «Silence is a token of wisdom: loquacity a sign of foolishness»; and Chaucer's *Canterbury Tales* IX 329: «thy tonge sholdestow restreyne». Cf. Eph. 5:3-4: «Fornicatio autem et omnis immunditio aut avaritia nec nominetur in vobis, sicut decet sanctos; aut turpitudo aut stultiloquium aut scurrilitas, quae ad rem non pertinet» [But fornication and all impurity or covetousness must not even be named among you, as is fitting among saints. Let there be no filthiness, nor silly talk, nor levity, which are not fitting].

[25] *Summa theologica, cit.*, I, Qu. 107, Art. 1, Obj. 1: «Locutio est ad manifestandum alteri quod latet in mente». Boccaccio himself adduces the concept to defend fiction in *Genealogia* XIV 9: «si componere fabulas malum erit, et colloqui malum erit; quod concessisse stultissimum est! Non enim a natura rerum hominibus tantum loqui concessum est, nisi ut invicem conloquamur, et per verba mentium comunicemus conceptus» [if it is a sin to compose stories, it is a sin to converse, which only the veriest fool would admit. For nature has not granted us the power of speech unless for purposes of conversation, and the exchange of ideas].

Dante, is instinctive and consistent, while human behavior is intelligent and unpredictable. Consequently, to communicate our intentions to others, we must enunciate orally the ideas silently formulated in our rational soul. Locution, a divine gift from God for the good of man, he says in the *Convivio*, is an operation proceeding from and proper to the rational soul, man's highest attribute.[27] Indicative of the natural connection between human reason and speech is Isidore of Seville's (early 7th c.) derivation of *oratio* from «*oris ratio*», the «reasoning of the mouth». Boccaccio's Trecento Italian is rooted in the same equation, for 'ragionare' means 'to speak'. The absence of speech, by contrast, is a defining characteristic of brute animals, unreasonable creatures moved by the lower sensitive appetite. Isidore, for example, could say, «*Pecus* dicimus omne quod humana lingua et effigie caret».[28] Creatures of sense only, beasts unlike man need no words to express themselves, as Boccaccio himself will later write in a polemical chapter of his *De casibus virorum illustrium* (c. 1360): «Other living beings show their feelings with nods, hissing, roaring; to man alone has it been granted, and not undeservingly, to express his intention with words. What could Nature have done more prudently than to separate through such an act man, endowed with a divine soul, from the beasts, whose only guide is sensuality?».[29]

In the *Decameron*, failure to communicate articulately often accompanies animal-like behavior. Alatiel remains inhumanly mute through a chain of passive, indiscriminate sexual couplings in dark, silent places; the sensual appetites of nuns and peasants bring to Filostrato's mind Masetto da Lamporecchio, who feigned muteness to lie with the sisters in a convent — nine in all, the same number of lovers through whose 'hands' Fortune passed Alatiel.[30] Silence and beastliness most obviously

---

[26] Boccaccio apparently knew this treatise firsthand since he alludes to it at the close of his epic, *Teseida*.

[27] *Convivio* III 8, 8: «Pruovo questo per la esperienza che aver di lei si può in quelle operazioni che sono proprie de l'anima razionale, dove la divina luce più espeditamente raggia; cioè nel parlare e ne li atti che reggimenti e portamenti sogliono essere chiamati. Onde è da sapere che solamente l'uomo intra li animali parla, e ha reggimenti e atti che si dicono razionali, però che solo elli ha in sè ragione».

[28] *Etymologiae, cit.*, I 5, 3; XII 1, 5. Boccaccio drew frequently on Isidore, beginning with works written well before the *Decameron*.

[29] G. BOCCACCIO, *De casibus virorum illustrium*, ed. P. G. RICCI and V. ZACCARIA, Milan, Mondadori, 1983 («*Tutte le opere*», X), VI 13, 3: «Cum igitur nutu, sibilo vel mugitu animalia cetera suas affectiones ostendant, verbis intentum exprimere homini solo concessum est nec immerito. Quid prudentius potuit fecisse natura quam actu tali hominem, celesti anima preditum, a beluis, quibus sola sensualitas dux est, separasse?».

[30] An excellent analysis of her tale with full biography is offered by C. SEGRE, *Comicità strutturale nella novella di Alatiel, cit.* She remains incommunicate and deprived of a distinct

go together in Cimone (V 1) before Love inspires him to learn the alphabet and join ranks with the philosophers in a suspiciously precipitate turnabout.[31] His pejorative nickname is a consequence of his earlier, primitive nature: «per ciò che mai né per fatica di maestro né per lusinga o battitura del padre o ingegno d'alcuno altro gli s'era potuto metter nel capo né lettera né costume alcuno, anzi con la voce grossa e deforme e con modi più convenienti a bestia che a uomo, quasi per ischerno da tutti era chiamato Cimone, il che nella loro lingua sonava quanto nella nostra "bestione"». Cimone relates in turn by name to Doctor Simone, alias «maestro Scimmione» (IX 3), whose cranial pumpkin scarcely contains even the most elementary letters (VIII 9). Beneath the vair that decorates his academic robes, there lurks a pecorine beast that goes about asking silly, senseless questions and singing «artagoticamente».[32] If he ends up wallowing in a hole full of excrement, it is just where such «pecoraggine» belongs.

Absence of mental acumen also produces garbled speech like Ferondo's annunciation from the «Ragnolo Braghiello» or Bentivegna del Mazzo's «errancies» in the city. Both peasants, they point to a telling line of associations connecting rusticity, illiteracy, and animal sexuality. The «mazzo» in Bentivegna's last name signals his loutishness — and his lustiness. It is an implement related to the «bastone» on which Cimone leans while gazing at Efigenia, the «scure» that the country laborer Masetto bears on his shoulder into the nunnery, and finally, the punning «messer Mazza» in the servants' quarrel over brides' maidenheads. A cluster of coitional symbols, hammers, sticks, axes, and clubs are country tools typifying life at the rudimentary level of the beast and denoting detachment from the sphere of influence of intelligent speech, the linguistic medium that unites men in rational, political community.

---

personality as long as carnal contacts shape her life; her communicability and individuality are restored only when she returns to chastity. Reference to the potentially damning implications of mum Masetto's horticultural work appears below, ch. 6. M. MARCUS elegantly couples the stories, *Seduction by Silence: A Gloss on the Tales of Masetto ('Decameron' III 1) and Alatiel ('Decameron' II 7)*, «Philological Quarterly», LVIII, 1979, pp. 1-15. Arguing the protective function of language, a rational instrument needed for individual and societal survival alike, she concludes that in the very act of «talking about erotica», the frame story youths consign the sexual impulse «to its proper place in the hierarchy of the soul — one rung below right reason».

[31] M. MARCUS, *The Sweet New Style Reconsidered: A Gloss on the Tale of Cimone ('Decameron' V 1)*, «Italian Quarterly», LXXXI, 1980, pp. 5-16.

[32] Another singing animal is the masher priest of Varlungo, «sforzandosi ben di mostrarsi un gran maestro di canto [...] pareva uno asino che ragghiasse» (VIII 2, 10). He has smattered in the dialect family in which Cipolla is so fluent, and he spices his musical courtship with gifts of garlic and scallions. V. BRANCA examines the language of ridicule surrounding doctor and priest in *Boccaccio medievale, cit.*, ch. 13.

To promote social welfare, however, it is not enough that language spring from rational intelligence. Philosophical knowledge is also indispensable to the civilized art of speaking well. This additional qualification finds expression in the Roman tradition on rhetoric. Its primary authority for the Middle Ages was Cicero, whose *De inventione* is posited on the view that «wisdom without eloquence does too little for the good of states, but [...] eloquence without wisdom is generally highly disadvantageous and is never helpful». Whoever wishes to speak well and usefully for the community must complement his study of eloquence with solid grounding in philosophy and ethics. Such a speaker will surpass all other men in excellence: «Furthermore, I think that men, although lower and weaker than animals in many respects, excel them most by having the power of speech. Therefore that man appears to me to have won a splendid possession who excels men themselves in that ability by which men excel beasts».[33]

Among Cicero's many medieval commentators and translators was Dante's teacher Brunetto Latini, who elaborates in his *Rettorica* (c. 1260) on the above passage. Elephants are bigger than men, lions more powerful, he says; the five senses, too, are stronger in animals, as in the boar hearing, the lynx seeing, the monkey tasting, the vulture smelling, and the spider touch. In speech, however, man is always superior to the animals.[34] Even more influential than the *De inventione* was the *Rhetorica ad Herennium*, mistakenly believed to be Cicero's as well, and often distinguished from the master's slightly earlier treatise by the title *Rhetorica nova*. (Boccaccio's library contained both the *Ars nova et vetus Ciceronis*.[35]) A student of philosophy, which he reads with the pupil of oratory addressed in the title of his manual, the wise pseudo-Cicero

---

[33] CICERO, *De inventione*, trans. H. M. HUBBELL, Cambridge, Mass., Harvard University Press, 1949 («Loeb Classical Library»), I 1: «sapientiam sine eloquentia parum prodesse civitatibus, eloquentiam vero sine sapientia nimium obesse plerumque, prodesse numquam»; I 4: «Ac mihi quidem videntur homines, cum multis rebus humiliores et infirmiores sint, hac re maxime bestiis praestare, quod loqui possunt. Quare praeclarum mihi quiddam videtur adeptus is qui qua re homines bestiis praestent ea in re hominibus ipsis antecellat».

[34] B. LATINI, *La rettorica*, ed. F. MAGGINI, Florence, Le Monnier, 1968, p. 38. According to V. BRANCA, *Boccaccio medievale*, cit., p. 48, Boccaccio knew Brunetto's treatise. J. MURPHY surveys Cicero's fortunes, *Rhetoric in the Middle Ages*, cit., pp. 106-115. See also, e.g., E. K. RAND, *Cicero in the Courtroom of St. Thomas Aquinas*, Milwaukee, Marquette University Press, 1946.

[35] See J. MURPHY, *Rhetoric in the Middle Ages*, cit., pp. 18-21; 109 ff. The mid-Quattrocento catalogue that includes books Boccaccio bequeathed to the Augustinians at Santo Spirito in Florence lists two copies of the *De inventione* and three of *Ad Herennium*. A. MAZZA, *L'inventario della 'parva libraria'*, cit. An example of how Classical rhetoric makes its way into the *Decameron* is given by R. KLESCZEWSKI, *Antike und mittelalterliche Traditionen in der Menschendarstellung bei Boccaccio: Das Porträt Ser Cepparellos*, in *Italia viva. Studien zur Sprache*

prefaces his lessons with the injunction that «copiousness and facility in expression bear abundant fruit, if controlled by proper knowledge and a strict discipline of the mind».[36] Such concepts were refined by the second great luminary of rhetorical wisdom in antiquity, Quintilian. As set forth in the Proem of his *Institutio oratoria*, he undertook to describe the perfect orator, «We are to form, then, the perfect orator, who cannot exist unless as a good man; and we require in him, therefore, not only consummate ability in speaking, but every excellence of mind».[37]

Now Boccaccio's convivial Brother Onion, who seemed «Tulio medesimo o forse Quintiliano», becomes a rather less congenial character than commonly thought when weighed against the standards of what his classical archetypes had taught. Although a superlative speaker, Cipolla lacks «scienza» absolutely. This intellectual, ethical defect is externalized and epitomized in his Doppelgänger, the animalistic servant Guccio Balena/Imbratta/Porco, whom the friar proudly credits with traits horrible enough to wreck all the virtue, wisdom, and moral sense in Solomon, Aristotle, and Seneca. The noble, human qualities of his counter-paragons are quite absent in this bloated grease-caked lackey, around whom only filth, stench, and creatures clump. His emphatic, final piggish surname may tag him historically as one Guccio Porcellana, so known from employment at the Trecento hospital of San Filippo in Via del Porcellana.[38] He is about as mean a man, according to his master, as ever was painted by the notorious canvas-spatterer Lippo Topo («Phil the Mouse»). An inveterate womanizer, Guccio appears at his best zeroing in

und Literature Italiens. Festschrift für Hans Ludwig Scheel, ed. W. Hirdt and R. Kleszczewski, Tübingen, Gunter Narr, 1983.

[36] Pseudo-Cicero, *Ad Herennium*, trans. H. Caplan, Cambridge, Mass., Harvard University Press, 1954 («Loeb Classical Library»), I 1: «non enim in se parum fructus habet copia dicendi et commoditas orationis, si recta intelligentia et definita animi moderatione gubernetur».

[37] Quintilian, *Institution oratoire*, ed. and trans. J. Cousin, Paris, Société d'Edition 'les Belles Lettres', 1975, I 1; trans. J. S. Watson, *Institutes of Oratory or, Education of an Orator in Twelve Books*, London, Henry G. Bohn, 1856: «qui esse nisi vir bonus non potest, ideoque non dicendi modo eximiam in eo facultatem, sed omnis animi virtutes exigimus [...] vir talis, qualis uere sapiens appellari possit, nec moribus modo perfectus [...] sed etiam scientia et omni facultate dicendi». Although the complete *Institutio* was not rediscovered until 1416 by Poggio Bracciolini, a fragmentary text had survived into the previous century. Petrarch knew it in that form. Whether Boccaccio had more than hearsay knowledge of Quintilian when he wrote the *Decameron* is unclear, but he could later quote him on the inseparability of oratory and truth when attacking hollow eloquence in *Genealogia* XIV 10. See C. Osgood, *Boccaccio on Poetry, cit.*, pp. 166-167 n. A. Mazza, *L'inventario della 'parva libraria', cit.*, lists a «Quintilianus de institutione oratoria, inconpletus». More about the medieval Quintilian can be found in Cousin's introduction to the text here cited and Murphy, *Rhetoric in the Middle Ages, cit.*, p. 123.

[38] L. Russo, *Letture critiche del 'Decameron'*, Bari, Laterza, 1956, p. 231.

for the pickup on a repulsive scullery lass laden with breasts «che parean due ceston da letame». Perched perspiring by the hearth in August heat, he sets out to con her with scrambled lingo on the high station in life that he has «on credit» and his currently huge fortune, «de' fiorini più di millantanove». Clever in a style copied from the friar, he belongs to that apish clan of the *bomolochi*, who on Thomistic authority get their names from plundering birds. So when Boccaccio envisions him pressing his suit with terms metaphorically avian, he parodies amorous pursuit couched in the courtly mode, and at the same time shows us the big black predator diving for his steal. Happier in kitchens than «sopra i verdi rami l'usignuolo», Guccio swoops down upon fat little Nuta «non altramenti che si gitta l'avoltoio alla carogna».

Figuratively speaking, Cipolla himself has less of the man than the beast, and he literally bears a name that lowers him even further, down into the domain of the plants. It is, for example, his wont to collect alms in Certaldo, because «buona pastura vi trovava» — fields fertile with reference to Isidorian etymology for elemosinary peculation. A member of the mendicant order of St. Anthony, whose iconographic attribute is the pig, he facetiously claims to have embarked on his far-flung pilgrimage in search of «i privilegi del Porcellana». The phrase has porcine odor that replicates Guccio's third moniker and complements Cipolla's sodomistic bent, a tendency announced in the goatish «capitoli del Caprezio» generously given by him to the Patriarch of Jerusalem. This verbal counterfeiter, who descends from the evil family of Antonine 'pigs' excoriated by Dante for distorting Holy Scripture and chattering buffooneries from the pulpit, is named after a lowly vegetative item of agrarian produce and travels the countryside armed with the feather of a bird that just parrots human speech, as the poet's *Convivio* reminds us:

E se alcuno volesse dire [...] che alcuno uccello parli, sì come pare di certi, massimamente de la gazza e del pappagallo, e che alcuna bestia fa atti o vero reggimenti, sì come pare de la scimia e d'alcuno altro, rispondo che non è vero che parlino nè che abbiano reggimenti, però che non hanno ragione, da la quale queste cose convegnono procedere. (III 7, 9)

In view of these associations with subhuman subsistence levels symbolic of his lack of «scienza», it is not surprising that Cipolla's discourse, spun around a prank made into a 'miracle', should turn on twisted words.[39]

---

[39] M. MARCUS analyzes the counterfeiter, *An Allegory of Form, cit.*, ch. 4. M. PASTORE STOCCHI finds pilgrimage «amphibologies» in his sermon, *Dioneo e l'orazione di Frate Cipolla*,

No doubt the real miracle in this tale is Boccaccio's comic prestidigitation of the word on the page, for it is brilliant humor with a sobering latent thrust. Spellbinding, pointless oratory like Brother Cipolla's, while harmlessly amusing for the undeceived, signals serious trouble when those beguiled by it belong to the community of the Lord's faithful, in whatever pastures they may dwell. So we learn from St. Augustine, whose *De doctrina christiana* can grant approval to Ciceronian rhetoric, provided it is for the good in the service of the truth:

But he who is foolish and abounds in eloquence is the more to be avoided the more he delights his auditor with those things to which it is useless to listen so that he thinks that because he hears a thing said eloquently it is true. This lesson, moreover, did not escape those who thought to teach the art of rhetoric. They granted that "wisdom without eloquence is of small benefit to states; but eloquence without wisdom is often extremely injurious and profits no one".[40]

Christian orators, above all, bear a solemn responsibility for addressing their flocks in clearly understandable, truthful terms, for what they say is of the greatest import to the eternal welfare of their listeners.

In the *bon vivant* Cipolla, Boccaccio brings to life a peddler of nonsense utterly nonchalant toward salvation. An incomplete orator by both classical and Christian standards, he specifically answers Dante's description of those degenerate evangelists who fatten on the spoils of 'fables' — hot air, really, which is all they feed their flocks: «Per apparer ciascun s'ingegna e face / sue invenzioni; e quelle son trascorse / da' predicanti e 'l Vangelio si tace». Sermons made of ingenious inventions, but silent on the Gospel, puff up the cowl with self-satisfaction, but for greedy shepherd and gullible lambs alike, the devil lies in wait: «Ora si va con motti e con iscede / a predicare, e pur che ben si rida, / gonfia il cappuccio e più non si richiede. / Ma tale uccel nel becchetto s'annida, / che se 'l vulgo il vedesse, vederebbe / la perdonanza di ch'el si confida» (*Paradiso* XXIX 94-120).[41]

«Studi sul Boccaccio», X, 1977-1978, pp. 201-215; V. BRANCA, *Boccaccio medievale, cit.*, ch. 13, points out its underworld slang.

[40] AUGUSTINE, *De doctrina christiana*; trans. D. W. ROBERTSON, JR., *On Christian Doctrine*, Indianapolis, Bobbs Merril, 1958 («Library of the Liberal Arts»), IV 5: «Qui vero affluit insipienti eloquentia, tanto magis cavendus est, quanto magis ab eo in iis quae audire inutile est, delectatur auditor, et eum quoniam diserte dicere audit, etiam vere dicere existimat. Haec autem sententia nec illos fugit, qui artem rhetoricam docendam putarunt: fassi sunt enim sapientiam sine eloquentia parum prodesse civitatibus; eloquentiam vero sine sapientia nimium obesse plerumque, prodesse nunquam».

[41] R. HOLLANDER stresses the *Decameron*'s ironic detachment from the *Comedy* in Boccaccio's *Dante, Imitative Distance, cit.* I think Boccaccio takes his Dante straighter. Cipolla's appeal

If Cipolla ignores sacred verse in his homily, he has a confrere of sorts who does, so to speak, preach on the Gospel and successfully convert an audience. With Tedaldo Elisei (III 7), castigator of clerical corruption, Boccaccio brings to open, heated attack criticism veiled by humor in his portrayal of the Antonine Onion. Tedaldo has appealed to readers, not only as the author's spokesman against the scourge of the friars, but also as a perfect courtly lover, the intellectual hero of an old-fashioned, bittersweet romance. Appearances in the *Decameron*, though, are often ambiguous. Here we see how eloquence, even from the mouth of a cultured man, can take a dangerously misleading turn.[42]

Grief drove Tedaldo from Florence after sudden rejection by the married lady whose love he had secretly won. During a seven-year absence he makes his fortune in business on Cyprus and then, hopeful of regaining his lady, returns home disguised as a pilgrim from the Holy Sepulcher, only to discover that Ermellina's husband has just been accused of his murder. The error causes him to ponder «la cieca severità delle leggi e de' rettori, li quali assai volte, quasi solleciti investigatori delli errori, incrudelendo fanno il falso provare». Identity still concealed beneath the palmer's cap and cloak, he proves to his lady with sophistry in oratory that she should not have abandoned him just because «un maladetto frate» threatened her with damnation if she persisted in the affair. Those who call themselves friars today, lashes out Tedaldo, en-

---

has long been powerful and validated the critical assumption that Boccaccio was, so to speak, on his side. Thus from F. DE SANCTIS's perspective, those pulpit chatterings that had «turned Dante's stomach» were a source of sophisticated merriment for Boccaccio and his irreverent public. Still writing in that tradition is T. G. BERGIN, who in *Boccaccio*, New York, Viking, 1981, p. 314, continues to see only the tale's comic, *simpatico* Cipolla: «One can admire this outsize specimen of an articulate rascal, without any uneasiness of conscience». More on target are the observations of C. O'CUILLEANAIN, *Man and Beast in the 'Decameron'*, «Modern Language Review», LXXV, 1980, pp. 86-93: Guccio Porco reveals the sordid reality beneath his master's parroted wisdom, which 'falls' from an angelic feather to sizzling coals, dropping the friar into an appropriately infernal iconographic sphere. N. HAVELY offers further intriguing insights into Cipolla's greed and «ciance». Boccaccio may have written him 'against' a treatise on Franciscan poverty composed or commissioned by Robert of Anjou in 1322. Friars in the *Decameron* also seem to be «a distorted image of the story-teller». See *Chaucer, Boccaccio and the Friars*, in *Chaucer and the Italian Trecento*, ed. P. BOITANI, *cit.*, pp. 249-268.

[42] Tedaldo's admirers have included F. FIDO, *Dante personaggio mancato del 'Decameron'*, *cit.*; G. GETTO, *Vita di forme*, *cit.*, p. 98; M. BARATTO, *Realtà e stile*, *cit.*, pp. 141-142. To A. SCAGLIONE, *Nature and Love*, *cit.*, p. 83, Tedaldo shows that there is no sense of sin in the *Decameron*. The story translates courtly love into modern, civic living without any negative value judgment on Boccaccio's part according to A. FRANCESCHETTI, who notes the speciousness in its protagonist's logic, but does not confront the problem: *Dall'amore cortese all'adultero tranquillo: Lettura della novella di Tedaldo degli Elisei*, in *Miscellanea di studi in onore di Vittore Branca*, II, *cit.*, pp. 147-160. N. HAVELY, *Chaucer, Boccaccio and the Friars*, *cit.*, seems more closely attuned to negative undercurrents in the Tedaldo story.

snare the faithful masses with lies to cultivate their own temporal comfort: «E quale col giacchio il pescatore d'occupar ne' fiumi molti pesci a un tratto, così costoro, con le *fimbrie ampissime* avvolgendosi, molte pinzochere, molte vedove, molte altre sciocche femine e uomini d'aviluparvi sotto s'ingegnano» (III 7, 35). To critics these brothers merely reply, «Fate quello che noi diciamo e non quello che noi facciamo». Why, fulminates Tedaldo, do they not follow the holy word of the Gospel, «Incominciò Cristo a fare e a insegnare»?

Tedaldo's diatribe mines Matthew 23, where Christ heaps woe on the scribes and Pharisees. It is the Gospel on hypocrisy:

Then Jesus said to the crowds and to his disciples, "The scribes and the Pharisees sit on Moses's seat; so practice and observe whatever they tell you, but not what they do; for they preach, but do not practice [...] They do all their deeds to be seen by men; for they make their phylacteries broad and their fringes [*fimbrias*] long" (italics mine).

Tedaldo may be right about the clergy, but since all he says is aimed at persuading the lady to resume their affair, he speaks the truth neither for good nor 'in truth'. When he advocates doing what the clergy does, not what it says, he turns Christ's words inside-out, ergotizing all the worse because it evades any reference to the commandment on adultery. Infidelity in marriage, he says, is only a sin of the body, «peccato naturale», trivial compared to her «malvagità di mente» in ending their affair and causing his exile. Ironically, Tedaldo rivals his city's leaders' treacherous ability to contend diabolically for wrong and «prove the false». As Augustine had put it:

There are, moreover, certain precepts for a more copious discourse which make up what are called the rules of eloquence, and these are very true, even though they may be used to make falsehoods persuasive. Since they can be used in connection with true principles as well as with false, they are not themselves culpable, but the perversity of ill using them is culpable.[43]

---

[43] Matt. 23:1-5: «Tunc Iesus locutus est ad turbas et ad discipulos suos dicens: Super cathedram Moysi sederunt scribae et pharisaei: omnia ergo quaecumque dixerint vobis servate et facite, secundum opera vero eorum nolite facere: dicunt enim et non faciunt [...]. Omnia vero opera sua faciunt ut videantur ab hominibus: dilatant enim phylacteria sua et *magnificant fimbrias*». AUGUSTINE, *De doctrina christiana, cit.*, II 36: «Sunt etiam quaedam praecepta uberioris disputationis, quae iam eloquentia nominatur, quae nihilominus vera sunt, quamvis eis possint etiam falsa persuaderi: sed quia et vera possunt, non est facultas ipsa culpabilis, sed ea male utentium perversitas».

Tedaldo is arguing the wrong side of the case. Still, in the story his perversity passes for sanctity because he pretends to be a holy man who has visited the Sepulcher. Then he reassures Ermellina: «Or voi dovete sapere che io son frate, e per ciò li loro costumi io conosco tutti». Were the content of his scathing invective not enough to make us distrust the sincerity of anyone in fraternal garb, this tale's allusion to the hypocrites in Dante's Hell should make it clear that all is not right with 'sepulchral' Tedaldo.

Dante's hypocrites have scriptural ancestors in the scribes and Pharisees of Matthew 23, «whited sepulchers» literalized in the lost souls of *Inferno* XXIII. All friars, they stoop under gilded lead «cappe con cappucci bassi / dinanzi a li occhi».[44] Himself in pious disguise, Tedaldo duplicates the hypocrisy of the clergy he denounces. Friars today, he says, «niuna altra cosa hanno di frate se non la cappa»; yet he himself has nothing of the Christian pilgrim except «la schiavin e 'l cappello». Throughout the story there is always a discrepancy between what Tedaldo seems and is, what he says and does. It parallels the disjunction between Ermellina's behavior and her name, since ermine is a symbol of chastity. Whether as incognito exile or citizen, he is a master of the mask; secrecy and concealment are the hallmarks of his actions. Beneath this onus of duplicity, his romantic glow dims: model lover and enterprising, intelligent citizen, he is also a perfect hypocrite.[45]

If the clerical representatives of Christ should teach like Him by deed and word, so must all right-minded Christians. Boccaccio's deed and word is, of course, the *Decameron*, whose enunciatory registers are a widely ranging, instructive profile of man, the talking animal. When Boccaccio speaks for himself, as in his prefatory evocation of the plague,

---

[44] Dante may have placed the hypocrites in the twenty-third canto of Hell, rather than a canto with some other number, to reinforce the linkage between their *contrapasso* and the twenty-third chapter of Matthew.

[45] Ermine is the small animal carried by Chastity, who accompanies Thomas Aquinas with Charity in Giovanni del Biondo's medalion (fig. 2). The ermine is the ensign of Laura and her handmaidens, victors over Cupid, in Petrarch's *Trionfo della morte*, I 19-20: «Era la lor vittoriosa insegna / in campo verde un candido ermellino». On the ermine as chastity, see also G. de TERVARENT, *Attributs et symboles dans l'art profane. 1450-1600*, Geneva, Droz, 1958, 211-212. Boccaccio's catchword drawing of Tedaldo in his autograph manuscript of the *Decameron* suggests the character's duplicity. He seems first to have given him a beard that fell to a single, sharply triangular point. But in what my colleague P. F. Watson has identified as a *pentimento*, he added a second point that bristles out at the left above the chest. Perhaps he had in mind the kind of forked tongue of false counsel in which Dante hears Ulysses speak at *Inferno* XXVI. See the catchword reproduced in C. S. SINGLETON, *'Decameron'. Edizione diplomatico-interpretativa dell'autografo Hamilton 90*, Baltimore, Johns Hopkins University Press, 1974, *Tavola* III, fig. 5.

he has full rights to the Classical precepts of Ciceronian eloquence. His frame narrators, too, can enjoy the privilege, but not so the majority of characters whose stories they tell. Among the latter, the more 'copious' the discourse, the more socially injurious its potential usually seems to be – at least, until we come to the exemplary protagonists of the Tenth Day.

Before then, though, Tedaldo's specious reasoning does not stand alone. We should also by now see a darker side to Ghismonda's allegedly admirable, feminist declamation (IV 1). Since her father, Tancredi, all too humanly, could not divine her motivations for taking a lover, she must manifest them to him with words, whose necessity Augustine recognizes in Christian parallel to Aristotle:

How did He come except that "the Word was made flesh, and dwelt among us"? It is as when we speak. In order that what we are thinking may reach the mind of the listener through the fleshly ears, that which we have in mind is expressed in words and is called speech.[46]

Although Ghismonda's translation of thought to speech is no doubt perfectly accurate, a problem lies in her thinking itself. It is dictated not by the rational intellect, but «concupiscibile disiderio», as she expressly states, and it claims justification from ideas canonical to the truancy of courtly love. Externalized in stylistically impeccable form, her self-counsel rests on unvoiced premises as morally fallacious as those of Dante's Francesca: The pull of my flesh was an irresistible force.[47]

Tedaldo's and Ghismonda's copious discourse is not a sign of noble character. On the contrary, it argues their preference for cupidinous love over Christian love. As advocates of pleasure, not virtue, they perversely ill-use eloquence. Nevertheless, full-blown rhetoric need not always betoken suspiciously smooth talking. It can express goodness that speaks in the service of good, the ideal both ancient and medieval.

Boccaccio's most accomplished orator, therefore, is the most admirable man he could conceive. He is Tito Quinzio Fulvo (X 8), a Roman

---

[46] AUGUSTINE, *De doctrina christiana, cit.*, I 13: «Quomodo venit, nisi quod Verbum caro factum est, et habitavit in nobis? Sicuti enim loquimur, et id quod animo gerimus, in audientis animum per aures carneas illabatur, fit sonus verbum quod corde gestamus, et locutio vocatur».

[47] Sacred heroine to the Romantics, Francesca has become for most contemporary readers a woman unambiguously in error. Ghismonda's noble reputation, however, persists. T. BERGIN, *Boccaccio, cit.*, pp. 308-309, calls her apologia «rational dialectic» in defense of a refined love that is more than «mere appetite». Poetic echoes of *Inferno* V in *Decameron* IV 1 have been classified by A. BETTINZOLI, *Per una definizione delle presenze dantesche nel 'Decameron', cit.*

student of philosophy in Athens who becomes fast friends with his classmate, Greek Gisippo. Gisippo saves Tito's life (he was dying from lovesickness) by secretly giving him his bride, Sofronia. Later, back home, Tito reciprocates by offering to die in place of Gisippo, who has been wrongly accused of murder. Matters are set straight, and the story ends as Tito gives Gisippo his sister's hand. Tito's splendid speech — longer than any other in the *Decameron* — justifies his *de facto* marriage before the angered parents of Gisippo and Sofronia, and publicly persuades them that he did what was right in every possible respect.

Striking length likens Tedaldo's to Tito's oratory, inviting us to compare the tales. In the former, Fortune is blamed for bizarrely painful events; the logic of divine Providence comfortingly rules the latter. The Florentine is a courtly poet who has sojourned on Cyprus, island of Venus, and who takes his pleasure in physical possession of Monna Ermellina; the Roman is a philosopher who truly falls in love with wisdom (Sofronia is cognate with the Greek *sophrosyne*, 'wisdom'). Tedaldo argues for adultery, Tito for marriage. Tedaldo serves himself above all, while Tito is selflessly magnanimous.

Tito epitomizes Stoic prudence, the highest virtue attainable in his pre-Christian world. His *scientia* in turn makes him a perfect orator, one whose eloquence is coupled with wisdom. First in the book's closing trio of tales, themselves a fictional peroration on virtue, this story spotlights language at an ideal pitch. Rhetoric is the *novella*'s real protagonist, appropriately so, at the *Decameron* finale.[48]

As talk goes within the hundred tales, Tito is a paragon. Touchstones outside the text — Aristotelian, Ciceronian, and Augustinian — help us better understand that talk.[49] Speech suppressed (Alatiel, Masetto, Cimone), misused (Ferondo, Maestro Simone), or abused (Cipolla, Tedaldo, Ghismonda) denotes moral deficiency and sometimes unreasoning behavior akin to the ways of the brute animals. But proper speech (Madonna Oretta, Tito, the frame narrators) reveals man at his highest. In the Classical and Christian traditions alike the better we speak, the better we

---

[48] Rhetoric is protagonist for M. BARATTO, *Realtà e stile, cit.*, p. 65. Tito epitomizes Boccaccio's highest ideals for C. MUSCETTA, *Boccaccio, cit.*, p. 293. Stoic wisdom is his virtue for S. DELIGIORGIS, *Narrative Intellection in the 'Decameron'*, Iowa City, University of Iowa Press, 1975, p. 223. Tito belongs to an older, purer breed than the Romans whom Dante decries for warped, stinking customs that poison their vernacular. It is the ugliest of all in Italy and should really be called *tristiloquium* (*De vulgari eloquentia* I 11, 2).

[49] The Classicism in Boccaccio's rhetoric has been of particular interest to P. D. STEWART, *La novella di Madonna Oretta, cit.*, and A. D'ANDREA, *Le rubriche del 'Decameron'*, *Yearbook of Italian Studies*, III-IV, 1973-1975, pp. 41-67.

are as human beings. Rational, social animals, our perfection requires us to live in groups whose cohesion is made possible by our ability to communicate what we are thinking.[50] Speech at its most urbane thus becomes an art well-fitted to characterize the astrological family of the ancient god of eloquence in the *Decameron*. Finally, the narrators' linguistic decorum is itself politically and morally emblematic. Prompted by reason, they have fled for their lives from a diseased, infernal city of anarchy to reconstitute the community through hierarchically ordered, harmonious daily living, a retreat shaped by virtuous words and deeds in ideal ethical consonance.

---

[50] J. H. POTTER, *Five Frames*, cit., pp. 5-6, posits her theoretically discrete soundings of Boccaccio's «aesthetic idiolect» on the fact that the *Decameron* «is very clearly a book whose focus is on what Aristotle so aptly labelled the *zoon politikon*, whose distinguishing characteristic is sociability, which is in turn based on the ability to communicate effectively». R. RAMAT, *Indicazioni per una lettura del 'Decameron'*, in *Scritti su Giovanni Boccaccio, cit.*, best defines the book's deeply political spirit: «Per non essere anch'essi [i giovani della brigata] travolti dalla bufera bestiale, decidono di ritirarsi per ricostruire nell'intimo del loro animo e in forme simboliche esterne la città dell'uomo armoniosa e razionale». The *Decameron*'s civics thus rest on much the same philosophical assumptions as do those of the *Comedy*, set forth by J. FERRANTE, *The Political Vision of the 'Divine Comedy'*, Princeton, Princeton University Press, 1984, esp. Intro. and ch. 1.

6.

LOVE'S LABORS REWARDED AND PARADISE LOST
(*DECAMERON* III 10)

The Author of the *Decameron* affirms that the stories he has written for women in love will be both entertaining and instructive.[1] Many of the «cento novelle» clearly illustrate this two-fold literary ideal: others do not. Dioneo's tale about patient Griselda (X 10), for instance, brings pleasure to the reader and offers profitable advice for husbands as well as wives, but what useful lesson are we to derive from his delightful account of Alibech's sojourn in the desert with Rustico?

According to Dioneo, its teller, the answer is morally fundamental. He prefaces this story by telling the assembled ladies that it will teach them how to put the devil back into hell, knowledge that may help them save their souls, and concludes, «per ciò voi, giovani donne, alle quali la grazia di Dio bisogna, apparate a rimettere il diavolo in inferno, per ciò che egli è forte a grado a Dio e piacere delle parti, e molto bene ne può nascere e seguire» (III 10, 35). Given its metaphorical implications, however, his opinion would seem no less irreverent than the accompanying fictional exemplum, in which a clever young hermit seduces an ingenuous virgin with analogous words of persuasion: «dicoti che io mi credo che Idio t'abbia qui mandata per la salute dell'anima mia, per ciò che, se questo diavolo pur mi darà questa noia, ove tu vogli aver di me tanta pietà e sofferire che io in inferno il rimetta, tu mi darai grandissima consolazione e a Dio farai grandissimo piacere e servigio» (III 10, 18).

Needless to say, God is not served, nor are souls saved, by humbling the sort of proud devil that happened to be tempting Rustico. Worse still, to sanction lust in the name of the Lord and the vocabulary of Christian piety is blatant sacrilege. Thus it is hardly surprising that Boccaccio's

---

[1] *Decameron*, Pr. 14: «le già dette donne, che queste leggeranno, parimente diletto delle sollazzevoli cose in quelle mostrate e utile consiglio potranno pigliare».

editors and translators should have long considered the tenth tale of the Third Day one of the least edifying in his entire anthology. Their judgments are documented by numerous expurgated versions of the *Decameron*, first published during the early post-Tridentine period, but persisting for nearly four hundred years thereafter, in which this story — when printed at all — was sometimes so radically abridged or altered as to be rendered virtually unrecognizable if not downright nonsensical.[2] Such extreme measures of censorship were necessary, they felt, because devout Catholics and the delicate sensibilities of the fair sex must be spared indecent exposure to the shocking claim that fornication could lead to salvation.

In these pages I am going to argue that the well-intentioned efforts of those textual manipulators were ironically misguided, for although Rusti-

------

[2] In the 1573 Giuntine *Decameron* all that remains is the introduction and conclusion, between which there appears a solitary asterisk to indicate the deletion of nearly 1300 words. Lionardo Salviati's 1572 edition, in some ways more respectful of the original, carries 'revised' passages in a different typeface (e.g., «come il diavolo si rimetta in inferno» becomes «un simile avvenimento» and is adorned with copious asterisks, accounted for in a succint marginal note: «Si lasciano questi fragmenti per salvare più parole, e più modi di favellare che si può». Luigi Groto's Venetian edition of 1588, recalling Dido and Aeneas, resourcefully transforms Rustico into a young moral philosopher who helps Alibech pass the time while they are caught together in a cave during a thunderstorm by teaching her «how to put the dragon into the snake», or, «come il drago (= 'lightning') si rimetta nella biscia (= 'clouds')». The first English version, published in 1620, replaces Boccaccio's thirtieth tale with an account taken from Belleforest's *Histoires tragiques*, thus described in the 1684 edition: The chaste resolved continency of Serictha, Daughter to Siwalde King of Denmark, being sued unto by many worthy persons that loved her, would not look any man in the face, till the time she was married. Another ingenious solution to the problem can be found in the *Contes et Nouvelles de Bocace florentin*, Amsterdam, 1699, where the story of Filippo Balducci, belonging to the Introduction of the Fourth Day, becomes the last of the Third. Balducci also substitutes for Rustico in the 1702 English translation, «accommodated to the Gust of the present Age». The Third Day of the 1751 Bologna *Decameron*, «Per uso principalmente DE' MODESTI GIOVANI», has been reduced to a «Novella unica», and needless to say, it is not the tenth. It does return in 1777 with a London imprint in *Le 'Décaméron' de Jean Boccace*, but since «the chaste French language does not suffer any obscenity», we find, for instance, that Rustico's «resurrection of the flesh» has been demurely rendered as «il a toutes les peines du monde à retenir les mouvements de son impatiente ardeur». Inspired by a modern scientific spirit of obfuscation, the German translation by D. W. Soltan, Berlin, 1860, transforms Rustico's manhood into an «electrometer» that makes an «angle with the horizon»: «Indem nun der Eremit alle Reize des jungen Mädchens vor Augen hatte, [...] wirkte das alles so mächtig auf ihn, dass bei ihm der Elektrometer anfing, einen beträchtlichen Winkel mit dem Horizont zu machen». I thank LEO STEINBERG for this reference, which he cites in *The Sexuality of Christ in Renaissance Art and in Modern Oblivion*, New York, Pantheon/October Books, 1983, p. 185. Even as late as 1903, the entire central portion of the story was deemed a 'detail' unfit for English readers by J. M. Rigg, whose «faithful translation», a standard for many years, leaves it in the Italian. More on the unfortunate fortunes of Alibech and Rustico in the English-speaking world can be found in G. H. McWILLIAM's spirited introduction to the 1974 Penguin *Decameron*. For a general treatment of response to the *Decameron* in Italy, see V. BRANCA, *Linee di una storia della critica al 'Decameron'*, cit., esp. pp. 15-23.

co's rhetoric is a blasphemous lie, Dioneo's advice to the ladies can be taken as the literal truth. Hell, after all, is precisely where the devil belongs, and whosoever has mastered that elementary lesson ought to be a deserving candidate for God's saving grace. The mistake of many readers in the past was to assume that Boccaccio's bawdy tales could not convey any useful message because each novella in the collection was construed as an isolated structural unit, to be praised or condemned, printed or censored, on the merits of its self-contained and singular content. Today, thanks to the efforts of scholars who have discerned unifying patterns linking the individual tales, the Days, and frame passages, we know that the *Decameron* is greater than the sum of its parts.[3] They must be interpreted accordingly in the context to which they rightfully belong.

The moral lesson of Dioneo's most 'immoral' tale can be best understood, I believe, if we recreate that context from a three-dimensional perspective. First, we must discover how his story functions with immediate reference to the others told on the Third Day. Next this narrative decad must be seen within the more extended framework of those that precede and follow it in the *Decameron*. Finally, the *Decameron* itself should be situated in the still broader matrix of Boccaccio's earlier Italian fiction, since the poetic schemes and didactic content of the so-called minor works can provide helpful guidance in our search for patterns and meaning in the major work. I shall proceed by taking these points in reverse order, arguing from the general to the particular.

All of Boccaccio's vernacular fictions written before the *Decameron* are love stories. That is, they are without exception by lovers, for lovers, and about lovers. Although Boccaccio's lover-protagonists create a richly nuanced range of individual personalities and histories, they can be roughly grouped according to three general types: those who are models of virtuous love; their opposites, whose passions are rather to be condemned; and finally those who progress from the latter category to the former through a process of moral enlightenment. Most prominent among the first set would certainly be Florio and Biancifore, «i quali in uno volere per l'amorosa forza sempre furono fermi servandosi debita fede» (*Filocolo* I 1, 25). Here too belongs the fair maiden of the *Teseida*,

---

[3] See, e.g., F. NERI, *Il disegno ideale del 'Decameron'*, in *Mélanges de philologie, d'histoire et de littérature offerts à Henri Hauvette*, Paris, Les Presses Françaises, 1934, pp. 133-138; V. BRANCA, *Boccaccio medievale, cit.*, ch. 2; E. KERN, *The Gardens in the 'Decameron' Cornice, cit.*; H. C. COLE, *Dramatic Interplay in the 'Decameron': Boccaccio, Neifile and Giletta di Nerbona*, «Modern Language Notes», XC, 1975, pp. 38-57.

Emilia, Diana's devout protegée until the day of her nuptials with Palemone. On the other hand, forming a sharp contrast with these exemplary lovers, we have the pastoral protagonists of the *Ninfale fiesolano*. Their violation of Diana's rigidly enforced rule of chastity could hardly have been more flagrant, for Africo rapes Mensola, who subsequently awakens and succumbs to the sweetness of seduction, bearing from their illicit union an illegitimate son. Bringing a courtly variation to this theme, in the *Filostrato* the young prince Troiolo successfully corrupts Criseida, once a proud and honorable Trojan widow. He also pays dearly for this ill-advised affair after her betrayal, when despair drives him to seek death in battle — a miserable end that is mercilessly long in coming. Another victim of abandonment and a would-be suicidal case is Madonna Fiammetta. While this love-blinded lady wants us to believe that her suffering must be blamed on fickle Panfilo's perfidy, we should be inclined to judge otherwise. It is she, an adulterous wife, who surely bears the guilt of a greater betrayal. Her poetic punishment for having violated the sacred trust of the marriage bond, actually a fate worse than death, is to go on living, relentlessly tormented by her superlative, self-imposed bitterness. She will never recover from the disease of her passion because she fails to perceive that it has not been visited upon her by an external agent, but springs instead from inner weakness, as the nurse succinctly reminds her: «tu stessa di ciò se' principalissima cagione».[4]

Between these extremes of 'good' and 'bad' love Boccaccio gives us a third possibility offering the dynamic potential for intellectual and moral correction. Thus the dreamer's heaven-sent guide in the *Amorosa visione* repeatedly warns her recalcitrant charge that he must shun the allurements of secular wisdom and fame, fortune and venereal love, if he is to enter the strait «via di vita», which will require an arduous, uphill journey, but will result in enduring rewards.[5] The *Comedia delle ninfe fiorentine* describes a clearly redeeming transition from wrong to right through the conversion of bestial appetites to desire regulated by the precepts of Christian charity. Thanks to his encounter with the Seven Virtues, Ameto is transformed from a brutish creature motivated solely by instinct to a rational human being, whose amorous yearnings become noble, upright, and pure. A similar argument can be made for *Caccia di*

---

[4] *Elegia Fiammetta*, cit., p. 186. Fiammetta's guilt and self-deception are also stressed by R. HOLLANDER in *Boccaccio's Two Venuses*, cit., pp. 40-48.
[5] The inscription over the gate reads: «Questa / picciola porta mena a via di vita; / posto che paia nel salir molesta, / riposo etterno dà cotal salita; / dunque salite su sanza esser lenti, / l'animo vinca la carne impigrita» (*Amorosa visione*, cit., B, II 64-69).

Diana, which schematically prefigures the *Ameto*, and where the meta-morphosis of the captured animals and a cervine narrator into youthful lovers represents a spiritual reawakening after their release from the dark forest of sensuality.[6]

At this point we may tentatively say that the happy or unhappy endings of Boccaccio's early Italian fiction depend respectively on whether the love described is morally laudable or reprehensible. A decisive factor in the dichotomy seems to be marriage. That is, those whose love will eventually be legitimized through the social institution of matrimony reach an idyllic realm where all is well and will remain so. Sometimes this event is announced explicitly, as in the *Filocolo*, where Florio and Biancifiore are married twice for good measure, and the *Teseida*, which felicitously culminates with «Emilia's nuptials». The sad fates of Africo and Mensola are positively counterbalanced by the long, full life of their son Pruneo, who is given a wife and blessed with ten sons, each of whom in turn also marries. In *Caccia di Diana* marriage is allegorically implicit, signified by the presence of the celestial Venus, whom Boccaccio defines when he describes her dwelling in the *Teseida*: «si può e dee intendere per ciascuno onesto e licito disiderio, sì come è disiderare d'avere moglie per avere figliuoli, e simili a questo».[7] Even in the *Amorosa visione* the last phase of the dreamer's fantasy begins when he and his beloved, Maria d'Aquino, are bound to each other in a ritual resembling a marriage ceremony conducted by the «celestial lady», a figure whose cloak of mystery conceals Boccaccio's personification of Reason.[8] Conversely, lovers like Fiammetta and Troiolo will be brought down from an initially propitious situation to grievous suffering because their passions are motivated by the wanton, worldly Venus, «quella per la quale ogni lascivia è disiderata, e che volgarmente è chiamata dea d'a-more», which by definition does not exist between couples bound in matrimony.[9]

---

[6] See V. KIRKHAM, *Numerology and Allegory in Boccaccio's 'Caccia di Diana'*, cit.; A. K. CASSELL and V. KIRKHAM, *Diana's Hunt*, cit., Intro., pp. 30-63.

[7] *Teseida* VII 50, gl. Cf. Ameto's recognition of the goddess who descends to assist «her sisters», the Virtues, as being «non quella Venere che gli stolti alle loro disordinate conscupi-scenzie chiamano dea, ma quella dalla quale i veri e giusti e santi amori discendono intra' mortali».

[8] She has been given many names — Aspiration to Justice, Virtue, Faith, Reason, Fortitude, the Madonna, the celestial Venus, etc. See above, ch. 2, for a description of her allegorical identity as Reason who contends with the irascible and concupiscible appetites.

[9] *Teseida* VII 30, gl. See the Countess of Champagne's classic judgment on the incompati-bility of love and marriage in ANDREAS CAPELLANUS, *De arte honesti amandi*, ed. P.G. WALSH,

Can comparable patterns be discerned in the *Decameron*? Let us begin our search by returning for a moment to the Third Day. Its theme is to be «di chi alcuna cosa da lui molto disiderata con industria acquistasse o la perduta recuperasse». While the tales told on this day conform to the given topic, they also share a common double denominator not overtly present in the subject established by Queen Neifile. All are love stories, and in every case but one the love is unequivocably 'bad' — either adultery or fornication. (The exception is the ninth, where the Count of Rossiglione lies unwittingly, not with the girl he had hoped to seduce, but rather with Giletta, who is actually his wife.) Now I have argued that in Boccaccio's earlier works bad love can lead to no good, but here each tale has a happy ending. The contradiction can be resolved, however, if these stories are seen as part of a longer narrative unit starting with the Third Day and extending through the Fifth.

The Third Day would seem initially to belong more logically in a structural grouping with the Second, to which it is thematically coupled, than with the tales told on Days IV and V, similarly a narrative dyad, because it is separated from the latter by the Author's defense. But just as the last story of the Fifth Day marks the conclusion of the first half of the *Decameron*, a numerical terminus underlined by the sharp shift in register of the frame situation and tales immediately following, so the beginning of the Third marks an important internal point of departure in the progression of the ten *giornate*. The name of the woman chosen to rule on this Day, Neifile, offers a preliminary clue that starting here we shall be dealing quite literally with something new. Its Greek etyma have been interpreted as meaning 'novice in love', an epithet appropriate to one who sings in her ballad, «Io mi son giovinetta, e volentieri / m'allegro e canto en la stagion novella, / merzé d'amore e de' dolci pensieri» (IX Concl. 8). But the relationship of modifier to modified is ambiguous in her *senhal*. It could also be translated 'lover of the new',[10] and describe not only a maiden discovering love for the first time, but also a young

---

cit., p. 156: «Dicimus enim et stabilito tenore firmamus amorem non posse suas inter duos iugales extendere vires»; *The Art of Courtly Love*, trans. J. J. PARRY, *cit.*, p. 106: «We declare and we hold as firmly established that love cannot exert its powers between two people who are married to each other»; and the Chaplain's first rule of love, *On Love*, p. 282: «Causa coniugii ab amore non est excusatio recta»; *The Art of Courtly Love*, p. 184: «Marriage is no real excuse for not loving».

[10] V. BRANCA, *Decameron*, *cit.*, I Intro., 51 and n. 3, pp. 992-993, translates it «la nuova innamorata» or «l'amante d'amor nuovo». A. LIPARI suggested it is «lover of the new» in *The Structure and Real Significance of the 'Decameron'*, *cit.*

woman with an amorous predilection for the new, one symbolizing a new kind of love.

This latter interpretation is supported by the fact that as queen-designate Neifile initiates major changes in the order of events thus far established in the *Decameron*. The tales told on her Day are, in fact, twice removed from those preceding. On one level the distancing is calendrical; on another it is geographical. After receiving the crown early in the evening of the Second Day, a Thursday, Neifile decrees that the storytelling shall be suspended until Sunday. Friday is to be set aside for penitential abstinence and prayer because on that day «Colui che per la nostra vita morì sostenne passione». Dietary restrictions will similarly be observed on Saturday, when the ladies, in accordance with custom, will wash their hair and bathe to remove «ogni polvere, ogni sucidume che per la fatica di tutta la passata settimana sopravenuta fosse» (II Concl. 5-6). Since 'sabato', as the noun's origin and Neifile's reference to weekend bathing reveal, is the seventh day of the week, Sunday is the first. Hence although she nominally becomes queen on Thursday, the day over which she presides does not actually dawn until Sunday and coincides with the beginning of a new week. In this context her allusion to the Passion may be significant. It reminds us of the dawning of another Sunday on an archetypical Third Day, when Christ's resurrection fulfilled God's promise of salvation, new life for man after death. Our 'new' queen, whose rule is inaugurated on the first day of the new week symbolizing for Christians the beginning of 'new' life, then proposes that before resuming their storytelling, on Sunday morning the group shall move to another place of refuge to obviate the danger of discovery by uninvited strangers. The unusual new retreat that she has chosen for her subjects is described at some length in the introduction to Day Three, and its distinctive features are a matter to which I shall return.

Meanwhile, we may take up the matter of Neifile's reign as it relates to those of her successors, Filostrato and Fiammetta. The Third Day is linked to the next two by virtue of the fact that Days IV and V are also devoted to love. This thematic bond is reinforced by the Author's apology in the Introduction to the Fourth Day. His arguments are surely meant to be read in conjunction with the tale of Alibech and Rustico because he, too, tells a *novella*, (or rather part of one) about a healthy young hermit whose natural sexual instincts were stronger than any theoretical religious convictions. It is no accident that Boccaccio's eloquent defense follows the most blasphemous tale in the anthology, one that marks in turn the culmination of a poetic sequence focusing on examples of illicit love that lead to morally indefensible, happy endings.[11] His decision to interrupt *here*, and not, say, at the beginning of the Sixth Day, when a break in the progression would have been justifiable for reasons of structural symmetry, suggests two things. First, the intervention functions as a signal to the reader, much like Dante's apostrophes in *Inferno* IX and *Purgatorio* VIII, telling us that we should sharpen our eyes to the truth and pay special attention to what has just been — or will be — said. In other words, it indicates that we have reached a crucial moment in the narrative, as indeed we have, for at the end of the Third Day Boccaccio has left us with the untenable notion that bad love is not only good, but may even lead to salvation. At the same time, the ties between his defense and III 10 imply that from the *artist*'s point of view Dioneo's tale and the others told during Queen Neifile's reign are no less inappropriate to the general plan of the work than those illustrating the kind of virtuous love epitomized by patient Griselda.[12]

To understand why a sequence of such 'indecent' tales may play an edifying role in the *Decameron*, we must recall what our Author had said at the outset concerning the «useful advice» that amorous ladies would find in his book. They will benefit by reading it, «in quanto potranno cognoscere quello che sia da fuggire e che sia similmente da seguitare». That is, they will learn from these collected tales what they *should not* do as well as what they *should* do. From this statement we can conclude that Boccaccio's fictional lessons are going to take the form of precept both by negative and positive example. In the Middle Ages the former was a commonly accepted rhetorical procedure, perhaps best exemplified poetically by the magnificent losers in Dante's *Inferno*, Francesca, Farinata,

---

[11] Lipari, noting that «the most indecent stories are contained in the Third Day, and yet no criticism on the score of immorality is reported in the preface to the Fourth Day» (p. 60), argued that the apology is part of the whole work. C. S. SINGLETON, in an otherwise polemical response to Lipari (*On 'Meaning' in the 'Decameron'*, cit.), agreed that it is not an answer to actual criticism, basing his opinion partly on the absence of evidence in the manuscript tradition that any of the stories in the first three days had begun to circulate independently.

[12] By the end of the fourteenth century, Griselda had become a model for all good women to emulate, as attested in the literary tradition by Petrarch's Latin adaptation of the tale. During the 15th century her story was painted on *cassoni*, bridal chests for which subjects were chosen to remind their owners of a wife's obligation to remain faithful, obedient, and virtuous. Two such panels by Pesellino and Apollonio di Giovanni even represent her in the nude, thereby conveying through a visual convention the Job-like quality of her patience. See P. F. WATSON, *A Preliminary List of Subjects from Boccaccio in Italian Painting*, in V. BRANCA, P. F. WATSON, V. KIRKHAM, *Boccaccio visualizzato*, «Studi sul Boccaccio», XV, 1985-1986, pp. 149-166. Griselda may ultimately be a «figura Christi», as M. COTTINO-JONES suggests in *'Fabula' vs. 'Figura': Another Interpretation of the Griselda Story*, «Italica», L, 1973, pp. 38-52. See further below, ch. 9.

Ulisse, and Ugolino. Another representative instance of its application, unfortunately more pedestrian but conveniently more explicit, is to be found in the *Ovide moralisé*, an annotated compendium of Ovid's *Metamorphoses* dating from the first quarter of the fourteenth century. The anonymous author of this didactic text prefaces his work with the following admonition:

> Se l'escripture ne me ment,
> Tout est pour nostre enseignment.
> Quanqu'il a es livres escript,
> Soient bon ou mal li escript.
> Qui bien i vaudroit prendre esgart,
> Li maulz y est que l'en s'en gart,
> Li biens pour ce que l'en le face.[13]

If the tales in the *Decameron* were meant to carry an instructive dimension, those told on the Third Day must have been designed to teach by negative precept. «Li maulz y est que l'en s'en gart». Dioneo's story is a perfect case in point. Fornication, wrong to begin with, becomes particularly reprehensible when practiced by a monk, and all the more so should that monk be an anchorite, one who has adopted extreme measures of self-denial in his flight from the world, the flesh, and the devil. Other hermits in the «Theban deserts» wisely avoid the possible danger posed by Alibech's arrival. The first, a worthy man, «veggendola giovane e assai bella, temendo non il dimonio, se egli la ritenesse, lo 'nganasse, le commendò la sua buona disposizione; e dandole alquanto da mangiare [...] misela nella via» (III 10, 8). The second north African solitary similarly forestalls temptation, but Rustico wrongly succumbs, «like a dissolute man», and through an ironic inversion» becomes himself the devil's spokesman. His sin is further compounded by the fact that the woman he seduces is a virgin, child-like in her simplicity, and even worse, a potential Christian convert who had embarked on her desert journey prompted by an innocent impulse to serve the Lord.

Proceeding on the assumption that we are not to imitate the examples set by some of the characters in the *Decameron*, least of all Rustico's,

---

[13] C. DE BOER, ed., *Ovide moralisé*, in «Verhandelingen der Koninklijke Akademie van Wetenschapen», Amsterdam, n.s., XV, 1915, 1-7: «If Scripture does not lie to me, everything is for our instruction — whatever there is written in books, whether the things written be good or bad. He who would well like to be on guard, the bad is there so that one can be wary of it, the good so that one can do it».

we must ask how Boccaccio uses his art to demonstrate implicitly why everyone should not freely practice adultery and fornication, since the overt evidence presented by the happy endings on the Third Day indicates that such activities produce only positive results. An answer comes, I think, in the Author's interruption and the tales told on Days IV and V.

First, let us reconsider his fragmentary story about Filippo Balducci's son. Although he says (IV Intro. 11) that he has not finished it «acciò che non paia che io voglia le mie novelle con quelle di così laudevole compagnia, quale fu quella che dimostrata v'ho, mescolare», Boccaccio does 'mix' it with those of his praiseworthy company. Its protagonist, like those in the stories on Days III, IV, and V, is a lover, and his circumstances specifically resemble Rustico's. Why then does the *artist* leave us dangling, and what could the missing conclusion have been? The breaking point comes with Balducci's woeful realization that nature is more powerful than human ingenuity. This being the case, we have every reason to supppose that his son is bound to get a 'gosling'. But how? He could do so in one of two ways: either by yielding to lustful inclinations and defying the values of Christian and civic rectitude, or by aspiring to virtuous love and reaffirming those values. We cannot guess what course he will take because he has arrived at the crossroads, and that is where Boccaccio may have deliberately left him in order to let us know that we, as readers, have similarly reached a crossroads in the *Decameron*.[14]

Two paths lie ahead, Days IV and V. On the one hand, we could follow the lead of Filostrato, «sempre di male in peggio andato» on account of an unrequited love. Selecting the subject most consonant with his own experience, he determines that the Fourth Day will be «di coloro li cui amori ebbero infelice fine» (III Concl. 6). On the other, we may go the way of Fiammetta, who in accepting the crown from her predecessor, promises to teach him a lesson and guide us by a better path: «acciò che meglio t'aveggi di quel che fatto hai, infino a ora voglio e comando che ciascun s'apparecchi di dover doman ragionare di ciò che a alcuno amante, dopo alcuni fieri o sventurati accidenti, felicemente avvenisse» (IV Concl. 5). Illustrating examples of love that comes to bad or good respectively, the Fourth and Fifth Days can be taken as the alternative missing conclusions for the Author's story about Filippo Balducci's son. At the same time, they represent a statement on the part of Boccaccio that should rectify any misapprehensions we may have temporarily suf-

---

[14] J. L. SMARR has discussed the concept of the crossroads in an analysis of the *Amorosa visione*, Boccaccio and the Choice of Hercules, cit.

fered regarding the advisability of illicit 'amore'. For if we now ask where the adultery and fornication of the Third Day lead **in the *Decameron***, we find a pattern that recalls thematic motifs of Boccaccio's earlier works. Carnal desire (III), while humanly natural (Intro. IV), leads to tragedy and death (IV) unless legitimized by the life-affirming institution of matrimony (V).

Whatever sympathy Boccaccio may inspire us to feel for the more memorable heroines belonging to the Fourth Day, the «infelice fine» of its stories always seems to be tied with a breach of this socially required moral bond. Thus a friar commmits adultery with a married woman (2); a wife has an affair with her husband's best friend (9); three couples elope without getting married (3); a young woman of an age for marriage takes a lover (5,7); a young widow takes a lover (1); a young woman marries without her father's consent (6); parental constraints prevent an ena-mored youth from marrying the lady he loves (4, 8). Whether foolishly betrayed, unwisely withheld, or wrongly imposed, the redeeming contract of marriage is consistently negated, and the result is the negation of life itself. On no other day in the *Decameron* does death intrude itself so frequently and violently. Tancredi murders Guiscardo, and Ghismonda commits suicide; after being tarred and feathered to resemble a dehuman-ized monster, Frate Alberto eventually dies imprisoned; of the six lovers in the third story, two are murdered, and two die in miserable poverty; Gerbino viciously avenges his mistress's murder by killing the entire crew of a Saracen ship and is then himself beheaded. When Ellisabetta's brothers murder her lover, she dies of sorrow; Gabriotto suddenly ex-pires in the arms of Andriuola; Simona and Pasquino die accidentally from a poisonous sage bush; the thwarted Girolamo and Salvestra die of their love. With the ninth story we come full circle as Guiglielmo Rossiglione murders the paramour of his wife, who like Ghismonda chooses suicide. Finally, even Dioneo, although taking advantage of his usual privilege, tells a story involving a mistaken case of death.

Yet if disaster is certain when love and marriage are driven apart, quite the opposite happens when they are allowed to become allies, as we discover in the tales of Day Five. All have a happy ending, and excluding Dioneo's exception, that happy ending coincides with a marriage. Here there is no adultery and nothing to compare with the grotesque escapades of the «angel Gabriel». In spite of its more dignified tone, however, the Fifth Day echoes important themes of the Fourth. Families again refuse to let a daughter marry the man of her choice (2, 3, 4). We read of an elopement (2); a double abduction (1); and a father who fails to marry his daughter in time (7). Love may be contravened, but nature inexorably triumphs, and sooner or later the nightingale will be allowed to sing. The significant difference between these tales and those falling under Filostrato's reign is that here scandal is averted, sorrow surmounted, and death defeated through a peaceful reconciliation of love and marriage, lovers and the social order.

So far I have tried to demonstrate that the patterns of Boccaccio's earlier fiction are also present in the *Decameron*, where marriage is structurally central (V 1-9) and final (X 10), and becomes society's way of accommodating the threats posed by our natural sexual instincts.[15] It now remains to be seen whether the tales of the Third Day are ordered in such a way as to justify further this Christian interpretation of Boccaccio's literary attitude toward love. I believe they are so ordered, and once the progression they create has been perceived, we should be able to understand why Dioneo's tale, although obscene, is not unedifying.

To document my claim, I shall again proceed by arguing inversely, this time from the end of the Third Day to the Introduction. Let us begin with the concluding frame passage. There we are told that Dioneo and Fiammetta sing of «Messer Guiglielmo» and the «Dama del Vergiù». Their song about «The Lady of the Garden», which has been identified with an Italian *cantare* entitled *La donna del vergiù*, is appropriate to the amorous atmosphere of the Third Day since it also relates a tale of adulterous love.[16] Retrogressing to Dioneo's story, we find ourselves in a desert «putting the devil back into hell». Moving back from III 10 to III 8, we encounter a story in which an abbot with an eye for the ladies comes to the aid of a beautiful young parishioner, the victim of an unreasonably possessive husband, by pretending to put her spouse in Purgatory, where he is cured of his mad jealousy. The summary title indicates how this imaginative abbot accomplished his designs: «Ferondo, mangiata certa polvere, è sotterrato per morto; e dall'abate, che la moglie di lui si gode, tratto della sepoltura, è messo in prigione e fattogli credere che egli è in Purgatoro; e poi risuscitato, per suo nutrica un figliuol dell'abate nella moglie di lui generato» (III 8, rub.). What counts here is that we have passed − humorously and metaphorically − from Hell to Purgatory. Pursuing our reverse reading of Day Three, in the fourth tale we find another cluster of eschatological imagery that sends us on up to Paradise. There a lecherous monk named Dom Felice teaches the pious

---

[15] I refer to T. M. GREENE's essay, *Forms of Accommodation in the 'Decameron'*, cit.

[16] On the question of the source of this song see V. BRANCA, *Decameron, cit.*, III Concl., 8 and n. 11, p. 1194. The text has been published in *Fiore di leggende. Cantari antiche*, ed. E. LEVI, Bari, Laterza, 1914.

but thick-headed Puccio an infallible method for gaining salvation. It will require Puccio to spend forty consecutive nights on the roof in the position of Christ crucified, gazing heavenward and reciting hundreds of Pater Nosters and Hail Marys so that meanwhile, down in the bedroom, the monk may offer nocturnal succcor to Puccio's neglected wife. During this period she often jokingly remarks to her lusty Franciscan benefactor, «Tu fai fare la penitenzia a frate Puccio, per la quale noi abbiamo guadagnato il Paradiso»; «avvenne che dove frate Puccio faccendo penitenza si credette mettere in Paradiso, egli vi mise il monaco, che da andarvi tosto gli avea mostrata la via, e la moglie, che con lui in gran necessità vivea di ciò che messer lo monaco, come misericordioso, gran divizia le fece» (III 4, 31-33).

It should be clear now that we have been progressing along a line of figuratively rising action starting in Hell and leading via Purgatory to Paradise.[17] Of course, the logically sequential chain of metaphors could be merely coincidental, but additional textual evidence indicates that the fourth, eighth, and tenth tales of the Third Day were meant to be poetically conjoined by the reader. In each the industrious protagonist is a monk, and this is not true of any other story told under Neifile's rule. Furthermore, Rustico, the abbot, and Dom Felice all have the outward appearance of holy men, and indeed they would be thoroughly admirable were it not that they share a fatal weakness for women. Boccaccio's description of the abbot, «il quale in ogni cosa era santissimo fuori che nell'opera delle femine» (III 8, 4), may be taken as indicative of this common concupiscent defect. Finally, in order to appease their lustful appetites each one takes advantage of a naive soul in search of God or salvation. Hence the saintly abbot with his hypocritical discourses on the blessedness of eternal life, and Dom Felice, who claims to have inside knowledge from the Vatican on a short-cut to sanctity, are surely literary cousins of the more humble monk Rustico, whose «resurrection of the flesh» inspires him to persuade Alibech that by serving his body she will be saving his soul.

The pattern of metaphors outlined above is strengthened by the situation presented in the first tale of the Third Day. Like the last, it

---

[17] The pattern has not passed unnoticed. For example, Dante Gabriel Rossetti mentioned it in his 1832 treatise *Sullo spirito antipapale che produsse la riforma, e sulla segreta influenza ch'esercitò nella letteratura d'Europa, e specialmente d'Italia, come risulta da molti suoi classici, massime da Dante, Petrarca, Boccaccio, disquisizioni.* The reference is cited by C. O'CUILLEANAIN, *Religion and the Clergy in Boccaccio's 'Decameron'* Rome, Edizioni di Storia e Letteratura, 1984, p. 26.

relies heavily on an obscene euphemism for the sexual act. Here, however, the protagonist is not in a vast desert dealing with the devil, but rather in a small, secluded convent with a «most beautiful garden» that he has been hired to tend. Specifically, his job will be «lavorare l'orto». As the story develops, however, instead of dressing one real garden, Masetto is actually dressing — or undressing — the nuns themselves and working nine tropological gardens.

I deliberately borrow the archaic term 'to dress' from the King James version of Genesis 2:15 because the verb in Boccaccio's pun «lavorare l'orto» literally translates the Latin *operor*, which appears in the same chapter and verse of the Vulgate. There we read that God took man and put him in the garden of Eden «ut operaretur et custodiret illum» [to dress and keep it]. The fact that Masetto entered a cloister to work a garden, especially when coupled with the imagery built into the fourth, eighth, and tenth tales of the Third Day, is surely calculated to remind us of the Garden by antonomasia, Eden. In the Vulgate it is «paradisus voluptatis», and «a garden of delight» is precisely what Masetto enjoys within the sheltered walls of the nunnery, for *voluptas* can mean in one application 'sensual pleasure'. Moreover, the substantive *paradisus* is a Latin transliteration of the Greek word *paradeisos* meaning 'garden', which corresponds to the Italian noun 'orto', cognate with the English prefix 'horti-' and the noun 'orchard'. Its derivation would have been known to Boccaccio from Isidore's *Etymologies*: «Paradise is a place set in the eastern parts; the word translated from Greek into Latin is 'garden' [*hortus*]; moreover, in Hebrew it is called Eden, which means in our language 'delights'».[18]

Should there be any lingering hesitation that Masetto's labors in the convent garden were meant to recall the Earthly Paradise, we may now take one final step into the Introduction of the Third Day. Once again we are in a garden, the most beautiful any of the storytellers has even seen. A quadrangular area walled off from the surrounding countryside, it is permeated by a floral perfume so sweet that the young Florentines imagine themelves to be «tra tutta la spezieria che mai nacque in Oriente». All manner of plants grow in this timeless, terrestrial garden, «dipinto tutto forse di mille varietà di fiori, chiuso dintorno di verdissimi

---

[18] ISIDORE, *Etymologiae, cit.*, XIV 3, 2: «Paradisus est locus in orientis partibus constitutus, cuius vocabulum ex Graeco in Latinum vertitur *hortus*: porro Hebraice Eden dicitur, quod in nostra lingua deliciae interpretatur». For a modern explanation of the etymology of 'paradise' see A. B. GIAMATTI, *The Earthly Paradise and the Renaissance Epic* Princeton, Princeton University Press, 1969, pp. 11-15.

e vivi aranci e di cedri, li quali, avendo i vecchi frutti e' nuovi e i fiori ancora, non solamente piacevole ombra agli occhi ma ancora all'odorato facevan piacere». In addition to an indeterminate number of singing birds, it shelters harmless wild animals; and at the center of the enclosure there is a beautiful marble fountain, the waters of which are channelled into a cleverly devised system of canals flowing out in every direction. The distinctive aspects of this *hortus amoenus* are suspiciously similar to those of Eden as described in Genesis, and the resemblance is no mere coincidence:

Il veder questo giardino, il suo bello ordine, le piante e la fontana co' ruscelletti procedenti da quella tanto piacque a ciascuna donna e a' tre giovani, che tutti cominciarono a affermare che, se Paradiso si potesse in terra fare, non sapevano conoscere che altra forma che quella di quel giardino gli si potesse dare.[19]

In summation, the thematic patterns and moralistic content of Boccaccio's minor works, which reappear in the general plan of his major work, are also allusively present within the narrower confines of the Third Day of the *Decameron*. Its frame passages lead us from a paradise of innocent delights, described in the Introduction, to a garden of evil recalled at the Conclusion, when Dioneo and Fiammetta sing of Messer Guiglielmo and «la Donna del Vergiù». The story of these lovers, set down in the Italian *cantare* «per dare esemplo a chi intende d'amare» is surely mentioned here to teach us a lesson as well. Boccaccio's allusion to their courtly but star-crossed romance, completing the hell-bent trajectory of the Third Day and anticipating the tragic atmosphere of the Fourth, is particularly apt because the lovers' trysts, which took place in the lady's private «vergiero» ('garden' in the sense of 'orto', or 'orchard'), were ultimately responsible for her suicide, an attempted suicide on the part of her lover, and the murder of his lawful wife. Within this descending narrative framework we find a sequence of tales carrying us metaphorically from a bawdy version of Adam in Eden to a blasphemous re-enactment of the devil's damnation. What the progression implies is elementary. Illicit love leads to perdition.

To the foregoing conclusion I would add a corollary. Since the Third Day contains a metaplot of falling from innocence to corruption, it can be

---

[19] Neifile's garden contains many of the features commonly associated with the Earthly Paradise during the Middle Ages. They are described in A. GRAF's classic study, *Miti e leggende e superstizioni del Medio Evo*, I, *cit.*, pp. 16-23.

read as an ironic commentary on the given theme for Neifile's reign, «di chi alcuna cosa molto disiderata con industria acquistasse o la perduta recuperasse». Taken individually, the protagonists of these stories all get what they desire, which is to say that they are all winners in love. When judged from the broader perspectives of the *Decameron* and the earlier works, however, they all get exactly what they deserve, because 'bad' lovers are inevitably losers, and what they have lost is Paradise.

7.

PAINTERS AT PLAY ON THE JUDGMENT DAY
(*DECAMERON* VIII 9)

The dirtiest joke in the *Decameron* is on Maestro Simone, that dim-witted doctor from Bologna, whom Bruno and Buffalmacco initiate as «cavaliere bagnato» in the *Brigata*-of-the-Privy. Italianists have mostly kept a decorous distance from this malodorous *beffa*, touching on it only tangentially in connection with the Calandrino cycle. Anyway, scatology aside, Lauretta's eighth *novella* has not seemed to warrant much interpretative probing because literary and artistic traditions alike confirm its historical plausibility. But even though the story certainly rests on some anecdotal truth, it belongs less to the mode of chronicle than creative prose fiction. For when he set about relating the painters' prank, Boccaccio was playing his own game as poet. He conceived a text that in language, imagery, and structure programmatically fuses four subjects of reference: first, medieval medicine; second, Dante's *Comedy*; third, popular lore and learned opinion on sorcery; and finally, visual iconography of the Judgment Day. The well-plotted synthesis can explain, to begin with, why *Decameron* VIII 9 should involve these particular protagonists in this particular practical joke. Its parodistic implications, in turn, open new possibilities for exploring a theme implicit throughout the storytelling on Day Eight, namely, the Last Judgment. Identification of that numerologically apt motif then permits Boccaccio's Eighth Day to be read in the overall calendrical plan of his 100 tales as counterpoise for the Third, that is, the Resurrection Day.

Bruno and Buffalmacco's sport with simple Simon starts soon after the latter returns from Bologna to set up practice in Florence. Capitalizing on his credulity, the fun-loving painters tantalize him with tall tales of their privileged secret life as members of a magical *brigata*. Disciples of the great necromancer Michele Scotto founded this club, claims Bruno, and its initiates revel twice monthly in lavish banquets, followed by heavenly chambering with all the queens of the earth. Such fabulous entertainment supposedly materializes through piratic sorcery, fare and ladies borrowed by conjury from those to whom they rightfully belong. In hopeful anticipation, Simone himself becomes the artists' mealticket, while to repay the courtesy, Bruno graciously decorates the doctor's house with an ensign of the urinal, paintings of Lady Lent, an *Agnus Dei*, and the battle of the cats and mice. At last, the physician's dear friends inform him that the date of his initiation has arrived. Shortly before midnight, robed in his finest scarlet academic regalia, he is to wait on one of the newly built tombs in front of Santa Maria Novella, where a beast will come to fetch him. The creature, none other than Bruno's hefty cohort Buffalmacco, charges howling into the piazza on all fours hidden beneath an inside-out haircloth and horned mask. Trotting his terrified passenger past the convent of Santa Maria della Scala, Buffalmacco reaches the city's outskirts near the Prato gate and deftly throws him headfirst into a ditch filled with human excrement. As Simone wallows abandoned in this abominable mess, he has indeed earned his promised knighthood and embraced «la Contessa di Civillari», the royal lady of 'Latrineland' who was to be his occult consort in the *brigata* of those who «course upon the waters». In the end the doctor will conceal his humiliation and content the painters with continuing hospitality. Lauretta closes her narration on an aphoristic note, «Così adunque, come udito avete, senno s'insegna a chi tanto non apparò a Bologna».

Vittore Branca, whose commentary offers the single best discussion, cites archival evidence on the story's proper names and places that make it possible to estimate an ideal date for Dr. Simone's dunking. The gullible physician, Simone da Villa in Boccaccio's texts, might be the same Maestro Simone Medico who was buried in Santa Croce toward the mid-fourteenth century. His program of home decoration from the ensign of the urinal to the battle of the cats and mice would have been executed by one Bruno di Giovanni d'Olivieri, mentioned in a notarial act of 1301 and again as a member of the Guild of Doctors and Druggists (which was also the painters' guild) alongside Buffalmacco and Giotto in the year 1302.[1] Pejoratively tagged a «dipintore di camere», this brush-wielder must have been a rather pedestrian practitioner of the craft. Giorgio Vasari recalls an altarpiece of his deemed so lifeless that at the teasing instigation of Buffalmacco, the uninventive Bruno added explanatory

---

[1] V. BRANCA, *Decameron, cit.*, VIII 9, 5 and n. 11, p. 1445; VIII 3, 4 and n. 10, p. 1411.

phrases emerging in scrolls from the figures' mouths.[2] By contrast, Buonamico Buffalmacco was a naturally gifted and «excellentissimo maestro» in Lorenzo Ghiberti's admiring appraisal, so much so that «when he put his heart into his works, he surpassed all the other painters».[3] Accorded a full chapter in Vasari's *Vite*, Buffalmacco is said to have lived from 1262 to 1340 and carried out a number of important Tuscan commissions, among them some work at the Camposanto in Pisa, to which I shall return. For the time being, we should remember that Boccaccio's Buffalmacco, disguised as a beast, presents himself to Simone in a Florentine sepulchral context, that is, «on one of those raised tombs [avelli rivelati] which have been lately made outside Santa Maria Novella». They were constructed for the most part in 1314. Thence Buffalmacco carries Simone toward Santa Maria della Scala. These topographical details, together with what we otherwise know about the artists and doctor, suggest an ideal date for the events in Lauretta's story of about 1320.[4]

Nevertheless, whether such a broadly humorous *beffa* actually took place or not is another question. If so, Boccaccio was its lone chronicler. And if not? No doubt Bruno and Buffalmacco did live historically, but the same cannot be said with certainty of Simone da Villa, laureate in medicine from the University of Bologna and practitioner on Florence's Via del Cocomero. As for the artists' legendary prankish reputation, our primary sources are *novelle* — first Boccaccio's, and later in the Trecento, those of Franco Sacchetti. Vasari seems to take both writers for reliable authorities,[5] but in light of his own creative bent, he may have been more cognizant of the fictions surrounding their 'facts' than we yet realize. We are, however, definitely coming to see today that when Boccaccio puts real people in one of his stories, it does not follow that their actions

---

[2] Life of Buffalmacco in G. VASARI, *Le vite de' più eccellenti pittori scultori ed architettori scritte da Giorgio Vasari pittore Aretino*, I, ed. G. MILANESI, 1906; Florence, Sansoni, 1981, pp. 503-519.

[3] I cite Ghiberti from L. BELLOSI, *Buffalmacco e il Trionfo della Morte*, Turin, Einaudi, 1974, p. 69: «quando metteva l'animo nelle sue opere passava tutti gl'altri pictori». Franco Sacchetti, writing in the generation after Boccaccio, had ranked him «grandissimo maestro», second only to Giotto (*Novelle* 136, 161).

[4] V. BRANCA, *Decameron, cit.*, VIII 9, 98 and n. 1, p. 1456.

[5] Following Boccaccio and Sacchetti (see also *Novelle* 169, 191, 192), the artist-biographers emphasize Buffalmacco's penchant for play. Ghiberti terms him «huomo molto godente»; Vasari, who begins by referring to him «come uomo burlevole celebrato da messer Giovanni Boccaccio nel suo Decamerone», and retails several of Sacchetti's anecdotes, concludes: «troppo lungo sarei se io volessi raccontare così tutte le burle come le pitture che fece Buonamico Buffalmacco».

duplicate actual events.[6] Even when a story appears to be true, chances are he has worked less from life than literature. The poet's task, after all, is not to record, but to invent. This being the case, the 'realism' of *Decameron* VIII 9 becomes only a point of departure for the tale of Bruno, Buffalmacco, and Simone. What the artists and doctor proceed to say and do comes not from chronicle, but Boccaccio's imagination.

To see why, let us begin by approaching the matter into which Simone takes his nocturnal plunge. To be sure, he is not the only character in the anthology to suffer such undignified exposure to this inevitable natural product, which Thomas Aquinas affirms was even present in the Earthly Paradise, since after all, Adam and Eve did eat.[7] Andreuccio da Perugia, too (II 5), had had a scrape with that matter in the ill-famed Malpertugio when he fell through the floor boards of a second story loo. But that was only one episode in the small town horse-trader's Neapolitan adventures. The story of Simone, on the other hand, is dominated by puns and imagery pertaining to human excrement. For instance, as prelude to the finale, Buffalmacco announces that the noble lady scheduled for Simone in their clandestine club will be «la contessa di Civillari, la quale era la più bella cosa che si trovasse in tutto il culattario dell'umana generazione». Civillari, as one early gloss had it, «è un chiasso così detto in Firenze, sopra il monastero di San Jacopo a Ripoli, nel qual luogo si caca senza rispetto [...] e a tempi debiti poi di quel sterco i lavoratori ingrassano gli orti». Such a great lady is this Countess of Civillari, continues Buffalmacco with dazzling word play, that «poche

---

[6] A. BETTINZOLI, *Sul comico e sulla 'metamorfosi': appunti in margine a una novella del 'Decameron'*, in *Miscellanea di studi in onore di Vittore Branca*, II, cit., pp. 169-180, meditates on the fluid boundaries between fact and fiction in *Decameron* VIII 9, showing how, for example, contaminatory effects of Boccaccio's humor undermine his so-called realism and seem to change actual Florentine settings into objects more like cardboard props; P. F. WATSON, *The Cement of Fiction: Giovanni Boccaccio and the Painters of Florence*, «Modern Language Notes», XCIX, 1984, pp. 43-64, uncovers persuasive literary antecedent for the behavior of Giotto, Buffalmacco, and Calandrino in Pliny the Elder's *Natural History*. R. DURLING has argued that the poet Guido Cavalcanti's leap over a tomb must be explained with intertextual reference to *Inferno* X, in *Boccaccio on Interpretation*, cit.

[7] T. AQUINAS, *Summa theologica*, cit., I, Qu. 97, Art. 3, adduces Genesis 2:16: «De omni ligno quod est in Paradiso, comedetis» [Of every tree in Pardise ye shall eat], and specifies (Rep. Obj. 4): «Dicendum quod quidam dicunt quod homo in statu innocentiae non assumpsisset de cibo nisi quantum fuisset ei necessarium; unde non fuisset ibi superfluitatum emissio. Sed hoc irrationale videtur, quod in cibo assumpto non esset aliqua faeculentia, quae non esset apta ut converteretur in hominis nutrimentum» [Some say that in the state of innocence man would not have taken more than necessary food, so that there would have been nothing superfluous. This, however, is unreasonable to suppose, as implying that there would have been no faecal matter. Therefore there was need for voiding the surplus, yet so disposed by God as not to be unbefitting].

case ha per lo mondo nelle quali ella non abbia alcuna giurisdizione, e non che altri, ma i frati minori a suon di nacchere le rendon tributo» (VIII 9, 74). Naturally, Simone, born and raised in Bologna, fails to penetrate the glib Tuscan language barrier, and so is delighted at the prospect of his forthcoming tryst with such a high-born lady.[8]

As a doctor, Simone is especially deserving of the linguistic and literal treatment practiced on him by the painters. Given medical diagnostic methods, the association between physicians and human waste was taken for granted. In Machiavelli's *Mandragola*, for example, it is Lucrezia's urine that permits Callimaco to discourse on the alternative causes of her childless union with Nicia. Elsewhere in the *Decameron* itself (IX 3) Calandrino's distressing pregnancy is similarly ascertained by the accommodating Dr. «Scimmione» for purposes of another witty scheme devised by Bruno and Buffalmacco. Then as now, urine was analyzed to reach a diagnosis, hence the 'urinal' that Bruno so kindly painted to advertise the Maestro's office.

We learn more about medical practice during the period contemporary with the composition of the *Decameron* from Petrarch's *Invective contra medicum* (1352). Although Petrarch had a heavy ax to grind with the arrogant, ignorant Aristotelian whom he so mordantly attacks, woven into the *Invectives'* satire are realistic reminders of the procedures and tools of that mechanical trade. The Papal physician, addressed by Petrarch as a «great sewer» («cloaca es magna»), is condemned for passing judgment on poetry and liberal arts, and told to mind his own business «inter latrinas, inter urinas». Continually exposed to anal winds and foul chamber pots, he is likened to the hoopoe, a coprophagous bird called 'bochipuzola' in the fourteenth-century Italian translation.[9] If poets bring sublime solace to the soul, this dolt wreaks a merciless mission of

---

[8] The allusion suggests breaking wind explosively. On the unusual word 'naccheri' ('nakers' = drums, trumpets), of Arabic origin, see A. K. CASSELL and V. KIRKHAM, *Diana's Hunt, cit.*, pp. 188-189. V. BRANCA cites the gloss on 'Civillari' in *Decameron, cit.*, VIII 9, 73 and n. 2, p. 1453. See also his *Boccaccio medievale, cit.*, pp. 55, 63, 75, 114 for the mocking word fun with Simone. Boccaccio is much more circumspect and circumlocutious in his scatological language than his glossator, who speaks a straightforward popular language. Such reserve on the poet's part is well documented by F. BRUNI, *Boccaccio, cit.*, pp. 357-363.

[9] ISIDORE of SEVILLE, *Etymologiae, cit.*, II 7, 66, says: «Upupam Graeci appellant eo quod stercora humana consideret, et foetenti pascatur fimo» [The Greeks call it hoopoe because it contemplates human excrement and feeds on foul ordure]. Aristotle had stated that the hoopoe constructs its nest out of human excrement, and for Pliny it was «avis obscenu pastu» [the bird with abominable food]. 'Bochipuzola' ['Stinkmouth'] has European vernacular counterparts in 'coq puant', 'Mistvogel', 'Kothhahn', and 'Stinkvogel'. See ARISTOTLE, *Historia animalium* 616b and note in *The Works of Aristotle*, IV, trans. D. W. THOMPSON, Oxford, Clarendon Press, 1910.

mayhem on the body by distributing purgatives that sicken the healthy and kill the infirm.[10]

Not only did doctors thus encourage the production of excrement with their laxatives, they also prescribed it. No less an authority than Avicenna, whose name Boccaccio's story amusingly distorts to «Vannacena», enthusiastically recommends a canine variety, «stercus canis album» as proper and suitable at all times. Described as white, we can assume it was used in dried, powdered form. It was given for angina in solutions to be gargled and was administered as a topical treatment for maladies of the mouth and throat. A Florentine guild statute dating from 1498 required druggists to stock at least eight separate kinds of excrement, and that salubrious organic matter remained part of the standard pharmacopoeia well into the seventeenth century.[11] This said, we can see that Boccaccio was giving the doctor a dose of his own medicine. Or to use a term of Dante's coinage, Bruno and Buffalmacco arranged the perfect *contrapasso* for an idiotic laureate in medicine — a 'punishment' quite in keeping with the doctor's daily diagnostic and prescriptive crimes.

Simone's *contrapasso* leads now to a second ground of inspiration for Boccaccio's story, namely the *Divine Comedy*.[12] The orgiastic club in which Bruno and Buffalmacco vaunt membership is said to have been founded by disciples of Michele Scotto pursuant to a sojourn of his in Florence. Whether the city ever really did host him or not is uncertain,[13] but we know at any event that he would have lived in Florentine memory thanks to his presence among the soothsayers of *Inferno* XX. There Dante singles him out as the man «che veramente de le magiche frode seppe il

---

[10] F. PETRARCA, *Invective contra medicum. Testo latino e volgarizzamento di ser Domenico Silvestri*, ed. P. G. RICCI, Rome, Edizioni di Storia e Letteratura, 1978, II 55, 105, 645-650. Scatological insults abound, e.g., II 745-781: «tu vai pe' luoghi oschuri e neri, lividi e puzzolenti; i chatini imbrattati degli infermi tu cerchi; tu ragguardi l'orina». At III 612-615, the doctor's trumpets are «i borbotti degli infermi corpi [*ventris crepitus*] e i brutti rochi chatini pieni di fastidio [*raucas pelves*]».

[11] M. PASTORE STOCCHI, *Altre annotazioni. 7. Le galle del cane ('Decameron' VIII 6)*, «Studi sul Boccaccio», VII, 1973, pp. 200-208.

[12] The dynamic relationship between *Decameron* and *Comedy* has become a lively interpretive subject. See, e.g., F. FIDO, *Dante personaggio mancato del 'Decameron'*, cit.; R. HOLLANDER, *Boccaccio's Dante*, cit.; and R. DURLING, *Boccaccio on Interpretation*, cit.

[13] Documents cited by M. CORTI, *Dante a un nuovo crocevia*, Florence, Sansoni, 1981, p. 22, place him in Bologna in 1220 and 1231. He did not live beyond 1235/6 according to L. THORNDIKE, *A History of Magic and Experimental Science During the First Thirteen Centuries of our Era*, II, New York, Macmillan, 1923, p. 308. Bruno and Buffalmacco could hardly therefore have been invited to join a *brigata* established by men who knew Scotto personally. Is the anachronism Bruno's or Boccaccio's? Either way it is a point that further undermines the story's veracity.

gioco». One kind of magic in which this court astrologer to Frederick II was adept is related in the commentary on the *Comedy* by Jacopo della Lana (1322-28). It resembles strikingly Boccaccio's description of the banquets sponsored by his piratic Florentine adherents. Jacopo's gloss on Dante's reference explains, «si rasona che stando a Bologna e uxando cum genti homini e cari, e manzando cum s'usa tra loro im brigada a casa l'uno de l'altro che quando venia la volta a lui d'aparecchiare mai non facea fare alcuna cosa de cusina in soa casa, ma avea spiriti a lo comandamento, che 'l facea tôrre lo lesso della cusina del re de França, el rosto de quella del re d'Ingelterra, le trasmesse de quel de Cecilia, lo pane d'un logo, el vino d'un altro; confeti e frute donde li piaxea, e queste inbandisiuni deva alla soa brigada».[14]

Boccaccio's allusion to Michele Scotto is not the only detail in his story of the doctor and the painters with an infernal Dantesque counterpart. Consider, for example, the repeated references to the unmitigated stupidity of this M.D. trained in Bologna. We first hear how he came to Florence in vainglorious pomp from his Alma Mater, «una pecora [...] tutto coperto di pelli di vai». Squirrel skin, or vair, which was used to line the ceremonial capes of medical graduates in Boccaccio's time, fails to disguise this physician's cerebral, pecorine simplicity. Our Simone will then install himself on the Via del Cocomero, an address eminently suited to one who has learned his abc's «in sul mellone» rather than the conventional 'mela', the apple on which parents used to carve letters of the alphabet for their children to learn to read.[15] Bruno coos at Simone with derisive flattery, calling him «zucca mia da sale», «pinca mia da seme», «maestro mio dolciato», and «Maestro Scipa». These appellatives all revolve around the doctor's head, a brainless, gourd-like receptacle unseasoned by the salt of wit. But the epithets «zucca mia da sale» and «Maestro Scipa» redound with even more biting condemnation when coupled with the passage they echo in the *Comedy*. The word 'scipa', while appearing twice in the *Inferno* at moments when Dante directs our thoughts to God's harsh judgement for sinners, also recalls 'sipa', a Bolognese dialect variant for the affirmative particle 'sì'.[16] Dante uses

---

[14] G. BIAGI, *et al.*, *La 'Divina Commedia' nella figurazione artistica e nel secolare commento*, I, Turin, UTET, 1924; *Inferno, cit.*, XX 116-117.

[15] *Decameron, cit.*, VIII 9, 64 and n. 10, p. 1452. The child could then eat the apple after he had read out its letters correctly.

[16] 'Scipa', in parallel rhyme with 'stipa' and 'ripa', occurs at *Inferno* VII 21 and XXIV 84. It is from the transitive verb 'scipare', a variant of 'sciupare', to spoil or waste. Branca's 1965 Le Monnier edition of the *Decameron* gave «maestro Scipa»; his Mondadori edition of 1976 has instead «maestro sapa» (VIII 9, 60). «Sapa» signifies, he explains, a kind of honey made from

'sipa' in *Inferno* XVIII, where in the first ring of the Malebolge a great population of greedy Bolognese weep for the sin of pandering. Interestingly, the same canto gives us a gourd-head, the 'zucca' shouldered by Alessio Interminei da Lucca. Like his fellow flatterers, Alessio suffers punishment in the second pouch (still *Inferno* XVIII) immersed in «uno sterco / che da li uman privadi parea mosso». So caked is the sinner in this «privy shit» that the pilgrim Dante cannot even distinguish his station in life, «Vidi un col capo sì di merda lordo, / che non parëa s'era laico o cherco». Commentary links the «merda» caked to Alessio with that in which Simone became «impastato» because both recall the common medieval sight of ditches just outside cities where human ordure was deposited and stored for use as manure.[17]

Boccaccio, we see then, seems to have scattered several signals in *Decameron* VIII 9, to cantos XVIII and XX in Dante's poem. These involve 1) the game of magic frauds, in which on a rhetorical level, at least, Bruno and Buffalmacco equal their predecessor Michele Scotto; 2) Bolognese greed, flattery and empty-headedness; and 3) human ordure. These two cantos from the *Comedy* form, I suggest, the outer limits of a sequential group with a significant center for Boccaccio in *Inferno* XIX. Since that is reserved for the simonists, who take their name from Simon Mago, we might suspect that the tale of our doctor from Bologna should have more than a name in common with them.

The simoniac whom Dante meets there is Pope Nicholas III, Giovanni Gaetano Orsini. He identifies himself with the «orsa», the animal on their family cognizance: «sappi ch'i' fui vestito del gran manto; / e veramente fui figliuol de l'orsa, / cupido sì per avanzar li orsatti, / che sù l'avere e qui me misi in borsa» (XIX 69-72). When Buffalmacco comes to whisk Simone away from the tomb, he does so in the guise of a devil-headed-bear: «pareva pure un orso, se non che la maschera aveva viso di diavolo ed era cornuta» (VIII 9, 92). Thus if Dante gives us a Pope-bear in Hell, Boccaccio answers with a bear-like infernal impersonator, that is, Buffalmacco in his fake fur and diabolical headgear.

A more obvious and important parallel between Bocccaccio and Dante here hinges on the fact that both Maestro Simone and Simon Mago were believers in magic, and as a consequence, became the victims of falls that sent them plummeting headfirst to earth. The reason for the

grapes. Although as he points out, the latter form continues the imagery of sweetness (opposed to saltiness) used to describe the doctor's mental dullness, the reading 'Scipa' remains appealing because of its intertextual relationship to Dante's *Inferno*.

[17] *Inferno*, cit., XVIII 113-114; 116-117 and comm., e.g., C. S. SINGLETON.

simonists' upside-down punishment has been explained as an eternal reminder of the magician Simon's presumptuous attempt to fly. It abruptly terminated in a headlong fall when Saint Peter called on Christ to prove that God's power is greater than sorcerers' arts.[18] Although properly speaking, Maestro Simone does not fly and travels instead on the back of a beast who has spirited him away into the night, his precipitous plunge headlong certainly recalls that of the magician from the Gospels and the *Comedy* after whom Boccaccio surely named him. Nearing their destination of the cesspit with Simone on his back, Buffalmacco pushes up one of the doctor's feet with his hand, flips him off, and deftly dumps him headfirst into the ditch: «messa la mano sotto all'un de' piedi del medico e con essa sospintolsi da dosso, di netto col capo innanzi il gittò in essa».

What are we to infer from the artistically calculated resonances of *Inferno* XVIII-XIX-XX in *Decameron* VIII 9? My answer is that Boccaccio, who certainly meant to arouse the reader's appreciation of his poetic virtuosity, may also be inviting us to ponder the moral side of Simone's fall. The *beffa*, that is, may portend Simone's damnation. But before pursuing this possibility, I should like to take up my third point, the matter of belief in witchcraft.

Surviving medieval descriptions report rituals not dissimilar to the practices of the painters' *brigata*. According to one widely held superstition, certain people, usually women, travelled in bands by night transported by animals, or devils disguised as beasts, to witches' sabbats and other secret meetings where they would indulge in gluttonous feasting and lascivious debauchery. Varying mentions of these putative customs occur in a range of sources, religious as well as secular. Universally condemned as satanically inspired, such blasphemous gatherings, over which the devil himself would preside, were imputed to the heretics — Templars, Cathars, and Waldensians. Alan of Lille, for one, even derived the word Cathar from the Latin 'cattus', because it was supposedly in the

---

[18] C. S. SINGLETON, *'Inferno' XIX: O Simon Mago!*, «Modern Language Notes», LXXX, 1965, pp. 92-99. It is perhaps not coincidental for Boccaccio's story that in the apocryphal Acts of Peter, prior to his attempted flight Simon gets credit for dining room magic: «Simon the magician, after a few days were past promised the multitude to convict Peter that he believed not in the true God but was deceived. And when he did many lying wonders, they that were firm in the faith derided him. For in dining-chambers he made certain spirits enter in, which were only an appearance, and not existing truth». *The Apocryphal New Testament: Being the Apocryphal Gospels, Acts, Epistles, and Apocalypses, with other Narratives and Fragments Newly Translated*, trans. M. R. JAMES, Oxford, Clarendon Press, 1966², Vercelli Acts, ch. XXXI, p. 331.

form of a cat that Lucifer appeared to the heretics and received their obscene kisses.[19]

A twelfth-century reference to the phenomenon of surreal night riders appears in Gratian's *Decretum*, the compilation on church law that became a standard teaching text and constituted, together with its glossarial apparatus, the introduction to ecclesiastical law for the next eight centuries. Boccaccio was among those university students who read it, having studied canon law in his youth for five years at Naples. The relevant passage, called *Canon episcopi*, admonishes bishops to uproot vigorously sorcery from their parishes:

some wicked women, perverted by the Devil, seduced by illusions and phantasms of demons, believe and profess themselves in the hours of the night, to ride upon certain beasts with Diana, the goddess of pagans, and an innumerable multitude of women; and in the silence of the dead of night to traverse great spaces [...] whoever believes such things or similar loses the faith, and he who has not the right faith in God is not of God but of him in whom he believes, that is, of the Devil. For of our Lord it is written "All things were made by Him." Whoever therefore believes that anything can be made, or that any creature can be changed to better or to worse or be transformed into another species or similitude, except by the Creator himself who made everything and through whom all things were made, is beyond doubt an infidel.[20]

Simone's night ride on the back of a beast for an evening of necromantic debauchery mocks just such superstitions.[21] The fun in Boccaccio's satire, though, has sobering implications. What Christian exegetes had said about magic should make it clear that «Maestro Scipa»

---

[19] N. COHEN, *Europe's Inner Demons. An Enquiry Inspired by the Great Witch-Hunt*, New York, Basic Books, 1975, pp. 21-22 ff. and 215-219, cites accounts by Jacobus de Voragine and John of Salisbury. Still valuable is the trove in H. C. LEA, *Materials Toward a History of Witchcraft*, I, ed. A. C. HOWLAND, Philadelphia, University of Pennsylvania Press, 1939, which gives Jacopo Passavanti's thoughts on «la tregenda» in *Specchio della vera penitenza*.

[20] E. V. PETERS, *The Magician, the Witch and the Law*, Philadelphia, University of Pennsylvania Press, 1978, pp. 71-74. A general discussion with theological focus is H. A. KELLY's *The Devil, Demonology and Witchcraft. Christian Beliefs in Evil Spirits*, Garden City, N.Y. Doubleday, 1974².

[21] The orgies were inquisitional myths, as Cohen has demonstrated, but many disbelieved them even in the Middle Ages. So the *Romance of the Rose* (18, 411-418, 460) has only derision for the credence. An enlightened eighteenth-century reader, G. G. BOTTARI, *Lezioni sopra il 'Decamerone'*, II, Florence, Gaspero Ricci, 1818, pp. 209-229, finds similar satirical skepticism in *Decameron* VIII 9: «A queste empie sciocchezze pensò di dare addosso il Boccaccio». V. BRANCA, *Decameron, cit.*, VIII 9, 1 and n. 1, p. 1445.

is in some parlous moral trouble. Rabanus Maurus affirms, for example, that divine law revealed through Scripture 'execrates' all who believe in it. Whoever wants 'salvation' without the 'Savior' is headed for eternal perdition: «not saved, but sickly; not wise, but foolish he will labor in unremitting sickness, and a demented fool he shall remain in harmful blindness; and just as when a person's every inquiry and every responsibility is supposed to be answered by diviners and magicians, or by the very demons in the cult of idols, it should rather be called death than life, so those who pursue such things, unless they correct themselves, are heading for eternal perdition».[22]

So far all roads in Boccaccio's story have been leading to Hell. The same is ironically true of the route taken by Buffalmacco as he trots Simone to his scatological destiny. He proceeds westward, the cardinal point reserved in church orientation for scenes of the Last Judgment, when the arc of salvational history that moves temporally from east to west will reach an end with the end of time itself. The devil-beast and his passenger ride toward Santa Maria della Scala. The ladder, of course, figures ascent to Heaven, precisely where Simone imagines he is going. Confiding the marvels of their club, Bruno says that after the banquet, each man retires to a private chamber with his chosen consort (Bruno usually borrows the queen of England, Buffalmacco the queen of France). «E sappiate che quelle camere paiono un paradiso a veder, tanto son belle, e sono non meno odorifere che sieno i bossoli dalle spezie della bottega vostra, quando voi fate pestare il comino» (VIII 9, 25). But the Maestro never gets to Paradise. Rather he is lobbed into a hole and ends up smelling exactly like what we now realize would have been some of the less heavenly items in his stock of drugs, not to mention micturition and gasses induced among patients whose problems called for a cumin cure.[23] Simone's tumble from precincts known as the place of the ladder finds parallel in medieval Christian texts and their illustrations. They have left us many *scalae paradisi*, some with graphic depictions of what happens to

---

[22] RABANUS MAURUS, *De magis*, in *De universo*, *Patrologia Latina* 111:424-425: «non salvus, sed aeger; non prudens, sed stultus in aegritudine assidua laborabit, et in caecitate noxia stultus et demens permanebit: ac proinde omnis inquisitio, et omnis curatio, quae a divinis et magis, vel ab ipsis daemoniis in idolorum cultura expetitur, mors potius dicenda est quam vita; et qui ea sectantur, si se non correxerint, ad aeternam perditionem tendunt».

[23] ISIDORE, *Etymologiae, cit.*, XVII 11, 7, implies that cumin is a diuretic, grouping it with its botanical relative anise, which is «accerrime fervens, mictualis» [stingingly hot, urinary]. *The Oxford English Dictionary*, s.v. 'cumin', reports that the seeds were used medicinally as a carminative.

climbers who belong in Hell rather than Heaven. Targeted, lassoed, and tugged by devils, they fall off.[24]

Bruno and Buffalmacco's *beffa* has other eschatological ramifications. Thus Bruno paints «la Quaresima» for the doctor. Probably an emaciated figure of Lent personified as a lady, it would have been designed to remind the home's owner of the importance of penitential fasting during the Paschal cycle in preparation for Easter's promise of resurrection and salvation. Simone, however, does not abstain. On the contrary, he provides rich repasts for the painters and longs to gorge in their *brigata*. Another of the mural decorations made by Bruno for the doctor is an *Agnus Dei*, the lamb of the Apocalypse that symbolizes Christ's sacrifice for man's redemption and is canonically present in visual representations of the Last Judgment. Boccaccio would have often seen the mystic lamb in his local churches — crowning the baptistry mosaics at Florence, in exterior decorations of Santa Maria Novella — as well as in illuminated manuscripts of the Book of Revelation, where it naturally presides over resurrection of souls. Needless to say, the gluttonous Simone with his credence in magic is too morally myopic to appreciate the lesson of John's vision on Patmos: «I saw a great multitude which no man could number [...] standing before the throne and the Lamb, clothed in white robes and with palms in their hands. And they cried with a loud voice saying, "Salvation belongs to our God who sits upon the throne, and to the Lamb"»; «Blessed are they who are called to the marriage supper of the Lamb» (Rev. 7:9; 19:9). If the lamb's blood will wash the raiment of these elect to purest white, Simone gets bathed in an infernal paste that turns his gown from scarlet to black. Since he would rather feast in Florence than banquet in Heaven, the story's imagery well suits his attitude toward food — merely the stuff of consumption and evacuation as summed up in Matt. 15:17: «Whatsoever entereth into the mouth, goeth into the belly, and is cast out into the privy».

More puzzling, though, is Bruno's pictorial offering of the battle of the cats and mice. It receives Boccaccio's narrative emphasis because

---

[24] The seventh-century Sinai ladder of ascent and judgment by Johannes Climacus is archetypical. Its diffusion has been discussed by J. R. MARTIN, *The Illustration of the Heavenly Ladder of John Climacus*, Princeton, Princeton University Press, 1954. Spurred by demonic attack, headlong plunges from the rungs also befall unmeritorious souls in the late twelfth-century *Ladder of Virtue* in Herrad of Landsberg's *Hortus deliciarum*. Reproductions of illuminations from both texts appear in A. KATZENELLENBOGEN, *Allegories of the Virtues and Vices in Medieval Art*, cit. Other ladder texts are mentioned by M. W. BLOOMFIELD, *The Seven Deadly Sins. An Introduction to the History of a Religious Concept, with Special Reference to Medieval English Literature*, East Lansing, Michigan State College Press, 1952, pp. 76, 359-360.

Simone finally gathers his courage to plead for admission into the club while holding a lantern to help Bruno complete his execution of that *loggia* adornment, and not until the finishing strokes have been applied to the mice's tails does the painter pretend to be reluctantly persuaded. Why should this subject find fitting expression with an *Agnus Dei* and *Quaresima* in a home whose owner cares more for body than soul?

Cats and mice were frequently represented in medieval and Renaissance art. Contexts vary widely, as does intent. Artists usually took inspiration from the animals' natural antagonism. So a nestled embellishment on the Chi Rho page in the *Book of Kells* (c. 800) shows two mice confronted around a piece of cheese, and behind them, two cats confronted.[25] Centuries later Albrecht Dürer would capitalize allegorically on the same inexorable enmity in his engraving *The Fall of Man* (1504), where a sleek fat cat beneath Eve is about to pounce on the tiny mouse at Adam's feet.[26] Church decoration of the High Middle Ages has bequeathed us felines and rodents carved on misericords, as at Astorga,[27] and on capitals, as in the cloister at Tarragona. The Tarragona relief shows a cat feigning death borne to its funeral on a litter propelled by rats. Obscure in meaning, the scene may refer to a struggle between vassals and their suzerain,[28] as would a later conclave of rats and mice who assembled to discuss belling that cat in *Piers Plowman*.[29] Cats and mice often turn up in margins of illuminated manuscripts, favored subject for drolleries. Sometimes a solitary mouser jealously clamps his catch in mouth.[30] But the weaker creature can triumph, too, and he does so in one English codex by hanging his perennial, silent stalker.[31]

---

[25] F. HENRY, *The Book of Kells. Reproductions from the Manuscript in Trinity College, Dublin*, New York, Knopf, 1974.

[26] E. PANOFSKY, *The Life of Albrecht Dürer*, 1945; Princeton, Princeton University Press, 1955, pp. 84-85.

[27] I. MATEO GÓMEZ, *Temas profanas en la escultura gótica española. Las sillerias de coro*, Madrid, Istituto Diego Velásquez, 1979, pp. 78-80.

[28] *Espagne*, 1935, («Guides Bleus»), p. 66; P. TISNÉ and D. JOSÉ MILICUA, *Guide Artistique de l'Espagne*, 1967; trans. *Spanien. Bildatlas der Spanischen Kunst*, Cologne, M. DuMont Schauberg, 1968, p. 468. I thank Georg Nicolaus Knauer and Elfrieda Regina Knauer for these references.

[29] F. KLINGENDER, *Animals in Art and Thought to the End of the Middle Ages*, Cambridge, Mass., Massachusetts Institute of Technology Press, 1971, pp. 368-370.

[30] *A Cloisters Bestiary*, ed. R. H. RANDALL, JR., New York, Metropolitan Museum of Art, 1960, p. 27.

[31] L. M. RANDALL, *Images in the Margins of Gothic Manuscripts*, Berkeley, University of California Press, 1966. *Three Rats Hanging an Untroubled-looking Cat* from a pew carving in Great Malvern Abbey are reproduced, undated, in a drawing by M. O. HOWEY in that author's popularizing volume, *The Cat in the Mysteries of Religion and Magic*, New York, Castle Books,

If none of these examples constitutes a battle of cats and mice proper, another manuscript from fourteenth-century England does depict it in sketchy, yet clear miniature. Mice, one operating a catapult, besiege a castle defended at its crenellated summit by a stocky rock-dumping cat.[32] A far better monument of the motif, though, is the full-scale military encounter frescoed during the latter half of the twelfth century in Austria for a chapel dedicated to Saints John the Baptist and Evangelist at Pürgg. Reversing the positions of the battling creatures, it shows cats — even rigged with armored shields — attempting to scale a fortified structure busily garrisoned by a troop of martial mice. The subject evidently continued to be painted into the fifteenth century. A letter written by the merchant Benedetto Dei from Paris to his brother at home in Florence, June 15, 1468, reports that he had bought «a great storied painted paper, about twelve feet or so, which had the battle of the mice and cats, a pleasant thing to see, and a bargain». Although Benedetto's Parisian souvenir has not survived, it confirms, along with the English drolleries and the Austrian fresco at Pürgg, the battle of the cats and mice as a real subject dealt with by artists. Bruno's foray into the field was not just the work of Boccaccio's fantasy.[33]

What might the subject mean? On the cat there is consensus. Associated with supernatural evil from antiquity, it became a typical Christian sign of the Devil.[34] So in the *Divine Comedy* when Malebranche descend on a sinner from the kingdom of Navarre (*Inferno* XXII 58), Dante can liken the swindler to a mouse trapped among demon-cats, «Tra male gatte era venuto il sorco». Hence, too, Cathars and other social undesirables were accused of helluous cannibalism at orgies presided over by Satan appearing as a cat. Artists likewise knew the symbolism. In an

---

1956, p. 226. Howie also cites, p. 231, inimical cats and rats in heraldic devices. Their instinctive antagonism brings a feline and rodent into natural coupling in the whimsical Gothic alphabet drawn around 1390 by Giovanni dei Grassi, a sculptor and architect who worked on the Milan cathedral. He forms the letter 'C' out of a woman who stands on a cat and protectively holds a mouse while a hovering dwarf wraps her in a mantle. The letter is reproduced by J. BALTRUŠAITIS, *Réveils et prodiges. Le gothique fantastique*, Paris, A. Colin, 1960, fig. 25.

[32] See L. M. RANDALL, *cit.*, above n. 31.

[33] O. DEMUS, *Romanische Wandmalerei*, Munich, Hirmer Verlag, 1968, pl. 236, reproduces the Pürgg scene. C. GILBERT cites Benedetto's letter in *Italian Art 1400-1500. Sources and Documents*, Englewood Cliffs, N. J., Prentice Hall, 1980, p. 182.

[34] B. ROWLAND, *Animals with Human Faces. A Guide to Animal Symbolism*, Knoxville, University of Tennesee, 1973, pp. 52-53, adduces Ovid's Hecate, who transformed herself into a cat, and the cat-witches in *The Golden Ass*.

Annunciation by Lorenzo Lotto, for example, Gabriel puts to flight a cat, image of Satan incarnate,[35] and the motif recurs in Annunciations by Veronese, Alessandro Vitale, and Lelio Orsi. More specifically, the cat, to whom Aristotle had imputed a libidinous nature, could also be an emblem of sexual promiscuity. Friezes of menacing, erotic cats' heads appear prominently in combination with Luxuria personified on the Aquitainian Romanesque church façades at Parthenay-le-Vieux and Vouvant. Even the resting and seemingly innocuous domestic cat that accompanies *St. Jerome in his Study* by Antonello da Messina presumably connotes the same carnal temptation. Alternatively, when in combination with Madonna, Child, and goldfinch, the animal may suggest man in his bestial as opposed to spiritual nature, the latter being signified by the bird. In whatever context it appears, that cat betokens evil, often none other than the Evil One himself, who has been ensnaring unsuspecting victims ever since the time of Adam. Dürer's depiction of the Fall, like others by Bosch and Breughel, makes that point with perfect clarity.[36]

Mice, on the other hand, could have either positive or negative implications. Carriers of the latter occur in early legends surrounding the life of St. Francis. Two of these report, among the holy man's tribulations, fifty days of painful blindness, during which he was plagued in his cell, day and night, by a diabolical infestation of mice that severely interfered with sleep, meals, and meditation.[37] Such popular lore has a learned counterpart in the exegetical wisdom of St. Augustine, on whose thinking the Flemish Master of the Flémalle capitalized for the Mérode Altarpiece. There the artist envisioned Joseph in the act of carpentering mousetraps, instruments symbolically capable of capturing the Devil. They are *muscipula diaboli*, little wooden boxes allusive to the cross of

[35] L. Réau, *Iconographie de l'art chrétien*, I, Paris, Presses Universitaires de la France, 1955, pp. 108-112. The rats gnawing at the Tree of Life in the *Legend of Barlaam and Jehosophat* also make their way as diabolical symbols into the visual arts. See Réau, *cit.*, p. 212; Mateo Gómez, *cit.*, pp. 107-108; G. De Terverant, *cit.*; G. Ferguson, *Signs and Symbols in Christian Art*, Oxford, Oxford University Press, 1954, p. 24.

[36] The cats at Parthenay are illustrated and briefly discussed by L. Seidel, *Songs of Glory. The Romanesque Façades of Aquitaine*, Chicago, University of Chicago Press, 1981, p. 66 and figs. 8, 68. Reference to the Aristotelian tradition (*Historia animalium, cit.*, 540a) and symbolic cats in Renaissance painting, northern as well as southern, appears in P. H. Jolly, *Antonello da Messina's 'Saint Jerome in his Study': An Iconographic Analysis*, «The Art Bulletin», LXV, 1983, pp. 238-253. Jolly's survey, although supported with useful bibliography, points to a need for fuller, systematic inquiry.

[37] The texts, from the *Legenda antiqua perusina* and *Speculum perfectionis*, are printed in appendices to V. Branca's critical edition of *Il Cantico di Frate Sole*, Florence, Leo S. Olschki, 1950, pp. 106 and 113.

Christ's sacrifice, by which the Devil was entrapped.[38] But by contrast, a quite different tradition, more relevant for our purposes, is the entry 'mus' in the encyclopedia *De universo* by Rabanus Maurus. The mouse is a «pusillanimous animal», says Rabanus. «Mistice autem mures significant homines cupiditate terrena inhiantes et praedam de aliena substantia surripientes».[39] A variation on the idea passed into medieval sermons that used fables of cats and mice to preach a spiritual reminder. There the mouse stands for the human soul that must vigilantly shun worldly wealth to avoid being pounced on and swallowed up by the ever menacing cat-Devil.[40]

Consequently, if Boccaccio's Bruno finishes the mice's tails exactly when Simone greedily takes the bait for the painters' ambush, we may read the situation as a game of cat and mouse with moralistic overtones. Just as Lady Lent and the Lamb of God should summon Simone to Christian meditation, so might the battle of the cats and mice. The fact that the theme is present in the sacred context of the Johannine chapel at Pürgg yields visual evidence of its seriousness. Aside from the two St. Johns, its frescoes include the Cardinal Virtues, Christ Pantocrator, the Offerings of Cain and Abel, the Annunciation to the Shepherds, the Feeding of the 5,000, the Wise and Foolish Virgins, and a Devil. The Foolish Virgins and Devil are on the same side of the chapel as Cain; on the side with Abel are the Wise Virgins and the cats and mice, whose battle faces symmetrically the Devil painted just opposite. Holding their castle against what may then well be demonic feline aggression, the mice are on the wall with the saved. A recent interpreter of this unusual cycle speculates that the battle and its opposing Devil, which both appear at the far west end of the chapel's lateral surfaces, are iconographically associated with the Last Judgment that must have originally occupied its west wall, where now only traces of color remain.[41]

Shifting to another motif of judgment, we may remember that Bruno initially refused to reveal the secret of his happiness as a poor painter

[38] M. Shapiro, *'Muscipula diaboli', The Symbolism of the Mérode Altarpiece*, «The Art Bulletin», XXVII, 1945, pp. 182-187; C. I. Minott, *The Theme of the Mérode Altarpiece*, «The Art Bulletin», LI, 1969, pp. 267-271.

[39] Rabanus Maurus, *De universo, Patrologia Latina* 111:226: «In the mystical sense, mice signify men open-mouthed with cupidity for earthly things and secretly stealing away booty from other people's property».

[40] B. Rowland, *cit.*, p. 53; I. Mateo Gómez, *cit.*, pp. 78-80.

[41] O. Demus, *cit.*, pp. 208-209, thus rejects the possibility that Pürgg's cats and mice had literary antecedent in the Byzantine *Katomyochia* by Theodoros Prodomos.

because it would be his undoing and send him straight into the mouth of the San Gallo Lucifer. The Florentine hospital of San Gallo, destroyed in the sixteenth century, had painted on its façade, «il Diavolo grandissimo con più bocche, laonde i fanciulli avevan grandissima paura a vederlo».[42] But if San Gallo's frightening, multimouthed Lucifer is lost, others are not. To the Byzantine blue angel at Torcello's Last Judgment are attached devouring orifices in the form of serpents. Subsequent chomping Devils, with which Dante's Dis has much in common, become more ferocious and efficient.[43] Such is the infernal king in the Florentine baptistry mosaics of the Last Judgment, or Giotto's Lucifer in the Scrovegni Chapel (fig. 10).[44] Details of the damnation side in San Giovanni are reminiscent of Maestro Simone's appointment at a tomb with a demon. As the souls on the Last Day rise out of their sepulchres beneath the cosmic emperor, those at his left hand are met by devils who deliver them to Hell. Some carry their victims bodily; some push them into the abyss. The damned fall helter-skelter, and often, in headlong dives (figs. 9 and 11).[45]

One more Last Judgment invites consideration, that at the Camposanto in Pisa. Although damaged, its presiding Devil still devours the damned in magnificently grotesque splendor (fig. 12). He is a beast with features resembling a bear, perhaps not unlike the horned ursine monster of Buffalmacco's disguise (fig. 13). Authorship and dating of the Pisan Last Judgment with its contiguous Triumph of Death have long been controversial. Roberto Longhi and Millard Meiss assigned these burial-ground frescoes to the years after the plague of 1348, but a 1974 monograph by Luciano Bellosi shifts their time of composition back to the mid-1330's and attributes them to none other than Buffalmacco himself. Bellosi's argument, now winning acceptance among art histor-

---

[42] V. BRANCA, Decameron, cit., VIII 9, 15.

[43] The apocryphal Vision of Saint Paul, of which manuscripts survive from the eighth century on, has in Hell a tricephalous dragon agape to absorb souls, with a body spouting snakes, frogs, and worms. Dante probably knew the text, and this Behemoth must have inspired as well the Lucifers in mosaic. T. SILVERSTEIN, Visio Sancti Pauli. The History of the Apocalypse in Latin together with Nine Texts, London, Christophers, 1953, pp. 1-13; 154-156.

[44] A. DE WITT, Le storie del giudizio universale in I Mosaici del Battistero di Firenze, III, Florence, Cassa di Risparmio, 1958; C. SEMENZATO, Giotto: La Cappella degli Scrovegni, Florence, Sadea/Sansoni, 1967.

[45] Upside-down sinners are normal in Hell's chaos. Giotto has some, and for others see F. VAN DER MEER, Apocalypse Visions from the Book of Revelation in Western Art, London, Thames and Hudson, 1978.

ians, is appealing.[46] If the talented Buffalmacco was indeed responsible for those powerful images of death at Pisa, it would make him a particularly well-chosen actor for the role in which Boccaccio cast him: as the painter who stages a Last Judgment drama for a soul on the way to perdition.

Although Buffalmacco's career remains largely in shadow because little of his known work survives, he came from Florence, and that is the city where he matriculated into the artist's guild. His part in the demonic Decameronian *beffa* could then take cues not only from the Camposanto, but also from projects undertaken at home. Two traditions come to mind in this context, one from Vasari. According to the *Vite*, Buffalmacco and Maso del Saggio helped organize a Florentine May Day celebration that featured a memorable representation of *Inferno* in a boat on the Arno. Unfortunately, neither Vasari nor his sources are always reliable, so the float can only be counted speculatively among Buffalmacco's credentials as an expert on Hell. There is a stronger possibility, however, that his professional experience brought him into contact with magic. He has sometimes been attributed a fresco cycle at the Badia a Settimo, near Florence, extant in spite of serious deterioration. Based on stylistic evidence, Bellosi now inclines to see in it Buffalmacco's hand. The narrative subject of the paintings is the life of St. James, and they include a great miracle related in the *Golden Legend*. As Simon Magus had challenged St. Peter, so James must deal with a magician called Hermogenes. After James has compelled the wizard to appear before him, bound and transported by his own demons, Hermogenes quickly surrenders all his books on magic, which are destroyed at the apostle's command by being thrown into the sea.[47]

My suggestion then is this. Just as Doctor Simone, at the ensign of the urinal, has professionally earned his midnight bath, so the painterly scene that starts with Simone at the tomb is one that Boccaccio's pair of artist-friends would have been well qualified to orchestrate. What unites Simone, physician, with Bruno and Buffalmacco, painters, is their socio-

---

[46] *Buffalmacco e il Trionfo della Morte* did not quite convince C. BRANDI, who reviewed it for «Studi sul Boccaccio», VIII, 1974, pp. 336-338. However, E. BORSOOK's *The Mural Painters of Tuscany from Cimabue to Andrea del Sarto*, Oxford, Clarendon Press, 1980², follows Bellosi in giving the Pisan *Triumph of Death* and *Thebaid* to Buffalmacco. See pp. XXXIII-XXXV; 39, 44, 51. L. BATTAGLIA RICCI also cautiously accepts the attribution for working purposes in *Ragionare nel giardino*, cit., pp. 12-13 and *passim*.

[47] JACOBUS DE VORAGINE, *The Golden Legend*, trans. G. RYAN and H. RIPPINGER, 1941; New York, Arno Press, 1969, pp. 368-377.

logical bond as fraternal members of the same Florentine guild – doctors, druggists, and painters.

Like its protagonists, the position of this *novella* in the overall scheme of the *Decameron* was chosen for poetically plotted reasons. Boccaccio placed it on the «ottava giornata». In medieval tradition 8 is a number that signifies Baptism, whence octagonal bapistries, and maybe, too, Simone's sardonic title of «cavaliere bagnato». But by association with rebirth, 8 also figures the Judgment Day. An ancient Pythagorean number of Justice, it became conflated in Patristic thought with the adjudication of souls foreseen at the Eschaton. Augustine explains in his exposition on Psalm 6 that the 'octave' aptly signifies the Day of Judgment because its arrival will mark the end of the worldly time, which always revolves through periods of seven days. The eighth day will also come at the end of two sweeping, temporal generations, one pertaining to man in the quaternary body and the Old Testament, the second to man in his ternary soul and the New Testament. The Bishop concludes: «When therefore the numbers of the body pertaining to the Old Man and the Old Testament are fulfilled, and when also the numbers of the soul related to the New Man and the New Testament are fulfilled, as when the septenary number is fulfilled, because it refers to all temporal things – divided between the quaternary number in the body, the ternary in the soul – the eighth day will come, which paying due reward to merits, now will transport the saints not to temporal goods, but to eternal life, while the impious shall be damned eternally».[48]

Consecration of 8 as a cipher shadowing the Lord's final Judgment gained widespread acceptance that persisted for well over a thousand years. So in the Sistine Chapel, beneath the cloud-borne Christ in Judgment, Michelangelo frescoed a total of eight trumpeting angels.[49]

Simone's devil-prodded dive into a pit is not the only tale on the Eighth Day in the *Decameron* that calls to mind such justice. Thus VIII 8 describes an exchange of wives in a neighborly vendetta dependent for

---

[48] St. AUGUSTINE, *Enarrationes in Psalmos*, *Patrologia Latina* 36:91: «Peractis igitur numeris corporis ad veterum hominem et ad Vetus Testamentum pertinentibus, peractis etiam numeris animi ad novum hominem et ad Novum Testamentum relatis, sicut septenario numero transacto, quia unumquodque temporaliter aitur, quaternario in corpus, ternario in animum distributo, veniet octavus dies, qui meritis tribuens quod debetur, jam non ad opera temporalia, sed ad vitam aeternam sanctos transferet, impios vero damnabit in aeternum».

[49] On 8 as baptism: R. KRAUTHEIMER, *Introduction to an 'Iconography of Medieval Architecture'*, «Journal of the Warburg and Courtauld Institutes», V, 1942, pp. 1-33; as Justice: MACROBIUS, *Comm. in Somnium, cit.*, I 5, 15; in Michelangelo's fresco: L. STEINBERG, *A Corner of the 'Last Judgment'*, «Daedalus», CIX, 1980, pp. 207-273.

effect on a household chest to which illustrators of the *Decameron* gave distinctly tomb-like features.[50] Robert Durling has uncovered signs of the Last Judgment in VIII 7, where the scholar Rinieri renders unto the vain widow Elena «just retribution». In VIII 3 Bruno and Buffalmacco make their initial Decameronian appearance to convince Calandrino that he has been rendered invisible by a heliotrope stone collected from the bed of the Mugnone. The stream was a millrace, and the millstones that are an important part of the tale's imagery, as Ronald Martinez has shown, carry weight as well in the Apocalypse, when as tokens of worldliness, they shall be cast into the sea (Rev. 18:21-22).[51] Significantly, the fifth — and central — story of the Eighth Day has for protagonist a judge, whom two notorious jokesters successfully untrouser while he sits at the bench meting out justice.

If the Eighth Day of the *Decameron*, a Sunday, is Boccaccio's parodistic version of the Last Judgment, its counterpart in his sequence of one hundred tales is the Third, also a Sunday. We have already seen how salvation is a key matter, metaphorically anyway, in the tales of Day III.[52] Narrated in a garden resembling the Earthly Paradise, they tell us of Fra Puccio's hopes of gaining Heaven by copying on his roof the position of Christ crucified, and of Ferondo's time in Purgatory before the «Ragnolo Braghiello» announced his miraculous fatherhood. The day climaxes in III 10, when Rustico's «resurrection of the flesh» inspires him to instruct Alibech on putting the devil in Hell. Now it was, of course, the Third Day that Christ arose. That Resurrection of the Flesh on an archetypical Biblical Sunday foreshadows the Sunday noon judgmental resurrection of all souls at the octave of universal history. Linked numerologically as resurrectional numbers by the Christian exegetes,[53] 3 and 8 are similarly coupled in the calendrical plan of the *Decameron*. Getting to Heaven is certainly at stake on its first Sunday, Day III, with the blasphemous *imitationes Christi* of such protagonists as Rustico. But were Christian justice to pass ruling on his «resurrezion della carne», it would send him when the world ends on the Eighth Day to the same place where he lustfully teaches Alibech to put his devilish appendage. The fate

---

[50] *Decameron*, 3 vols. illus., ed. V. BRANCA, Naples, Marotta, 1966.

[51] R. DURLING, *A Long Day in the Sun ('Decameron' VIII 9)*; R. MARTINEZ, *Calendrino and the Numbers of the Sun*, both presented at the International Medieval Institute, Kalamazoo, Mich., 1981.

[52] V. KIRKHAM, *Love's Labors Rewarded and Paradise Lost ('Decameron' III 10)*, above, ch. 6.

[53] ST. AUGUSTINE, *Contra Faustum manichaeum, Patrologia Latina* 42:335.

that may be awaiting him finds at the same time facetious, but seriously monitory fulfillment in the destiny of another forgetful Christian, one who puts demonically orgiastic pleasure on earth ahead of God the Creator's long-term rewards in Heaven. He is Maestro Simone, delivered to Lucifer by two painters at play on the Judgment Day in the *Decameron*.[54]

[54] This study would not have been possible without generous offerings from friends and colleagues. Some are acknowledged above, but special thanks go to Paul F. Watson and Charles I. Minott, fellow sleuths on cats and mice at Pennsylvania, who so willingly shared what they know of the subject in the visual arts. My discussion of the battle scene in Simone's house relies heavily on their information. I am grateful as well to Anna Arnaud of Novara for the thought-provoking gift of *Buffalmacco e il Trionfo della Morte* when it was still in print.

8.

THE CLASSIC BOND OF FRIENDSHIP
IN BOCCACCIO'S TITO AND GISIPPO
(*DECAMERON* X 8)

The long tale of Tito and Gisippo, Boccaccio's account of a 'classical' friendship, strikes modern readers as one of his least successful *novelle*. But this story had a powerful appeal in the Renaissance, and Boccaccio himself considered it a privileged component of the *Decameron* since he put it antepenultimate in the anthology. Tito and Gisippo join company with Torello and Saladino, Gualtieri and Griselda, creating the trio of heroic couples whose virtues cap the day that crowns the book. The last characters to appear in the *Decameron* from ancient times, theirs is a story that unfolds during the Golden Age of Latin culture, a historical milieu and ethical climate that heralds the Christian era.

Set between Athens and Rome under the triumvirate of Octavian, the eighth story of Day Ten has as its theme the holy bond of friendship. A young Roman patrician, Tito Quinzio Fulvo, sent to Athens to study, stays with his father's best friend, Cremete, and becomes bosom friends with Cremete's son, Gisippo. Together the youths learn philosophy with Aristippo. After Cremete dies, Gisippo is affianced, but Tito falls passionately in love with the lady, Sofronia. Tito agonizes over the dilemma: if love is all-powerful, can friendship be stronger? To save Tito from his mortal lovesickness, Gisippo decides to give him his bride. The two devise a plan whereby on the wedding night, in the darkness of the chamber, Tito will consummate the marriage in place of the groom, Gisippo. This *ménage-à-trois* continues for some time, unbeknownst to anyone else — including Sofronia, until the death of Tito's father recalls him to Rome. Now the truth must be revealed. Sofronia and her family are furious, but Tito delivers an eloquent oration, successfully defending the ruse. He returns with Sofronia to Rome, where Gisippo, reduced to impoverished exile by the scandal, arrives for help. But when Tito, living in high estate, appears to snub Gisippo, the latter, in despair, allows himself to be arrested for a murder he did not commit. As he is sentenced to death by crucifixion, Tito happens on the scene, this time recognizing miserable Gisippo, and to save him, claims that he, Tito, committed the crime. Meanwhile, the real murderer, moved by compassion for the two innocent friends, comes forward and confesses. Octavian summons and pardons all three, Tito marries his sister to Gisippo, and everyone lives happily ever after.

This tale enjoys a status unique in the *Decameron* on several scores. Second-longest of the stories (outdistanced only by the seventy-seventh, Rinieri's vengeance on the widow), its leading men are given leave for speaking to the most extraordinary lengths. Although Tedaldo (III 7) and Ghismonda (IV 1) are almost as multiloquent in their apologies, Tito's defense of his secret marriage to Sofronia sets the record for the book's single longest speech. It is no mean distinction in a narrative territory populated by nearly 350 characters rarely reluctant to talk.[1]

Chronological setting further gives an unusual identity to the ninety-eighth *novella*. Among a handful of tales not set historically within one, or at most two, generations before the Black Death of 1348, it alone is entirely classical in period, location, and cast. As he launches Filomena into her narration of the events proper, Boccaccio is emphatically precise about where we are and when:

Nel tempo adunque che Ottavian Cesare, non ancora chiamato Augusto ma nello uficio chiamato triumvirato, lo 'mperio di Roma reggeva, fu in Roma un gentile uomo chiamato Publio Quinzio Fulvo; il quale avendo un suo figliuolo, Tito Quinzio Fulvo nominato, di maraviglioso ingegno, a imprender filosofia il mandò a Atene. (X 8, 5)

Since Octavian became a triumvir in 43 B.C. and sole ruler in 30 B.C., our story takes place during the years between 43 B.C. and 30 B.C.

Finally, Tito and Gisippo's case is singular because they have suffered such a painful fall from grace with the reading public. Their story was among the top three from the *Decameron* in Renaissance Europe.[2]

---

[1] The census estimate is T. G. BERGIN's, from *An Introduction to Boccaccio*, in G. BOCCACCIO, *The Decameron*, sel. and trans. M. MUSA and P. E. BONDANELLA, *cit.*, p. 162. S. BATTAGLIA, *La coscienza letteraria del Medioevo*, Naples, Liguori, 1965, p. 517, notes that Tito's speech is the longest in the *Decameron*. For a study of that speech in context with the talk of other *Decameron* characters, see above, ch. 5.

[2] L. SORIERI, *Boccaccio's Story of 'Tito and Gisippo' in European Literature*, New York, Institute of French Studies, 1937 («Comparative Literature Series»), p. 99. Beroaldo's Latin

The others, Ghismonda and Tancredi, and Griselda and Gualtieri, are still subjects of lively interest. But ideal friendship seems not to have the enduring appeal of fornication with hints of incest or sado-masochistical marriage.

Of the modern commentators, some say the story is disadvantaged to begin with since it belongs to the Tenth Day, where the *Decameron*'s atmosphere becomes cold and artificial[3] and the actors' behavior verges on the monstrous.[4] Others object that an overdose of analysis, intellectual and psychological, spoils this tale,[5] or they regret that Boccaccio was not able to create a realistic situation here, the ultimate failure for a 'realistic' writer of fiction. Rather, being best at describing his own times, he could only make these remote, ancient characters come out «draped with philosophy like antique statuary»[6] in a story stale, forced, and «bogged down» in oratory.[7] Referring to the «frigid solemnity» of its structure, Salvatore Battaglia gives the *novella* a particularly thorough roasting. He finds it the least approachable in the entire *Decameron*, one whose protagonists operate more like con-men («patenti bricconi») than gentlemen, their behavior verging on idiotic criminality.[8]

Boccaccio, though, not to speak of his Renaissance readers, must have thought otherwise. For him, Tito and Gisippo are models of magnanimity and generosity, motif of the *Decameron*'s final day. Their well-planned response to an unlucky circumstance resolves a life-threatening conflict, reconfirming what Cicero had called that «natural fraternity» where men are united by reason and speech.[9] Tito and Gisippo should be

---

translation of 1492 was an important medium for the European diffusion of X 8. The tally by F. N. JONES, *Boccaccio and his Imitators in German, English, French, Spanish, and Italian Literature. 'The Decameron'*, Chicago, University of Chicago Press, 1910, lists only two tales with more imitators, IV 1 and X 10. To the thirty-five titles she cites in the posterity of X 8, others can be added, e.g., a Latin translation (Vatican Ms. 3336, inc. fol. 45r: *Urbanitas Boccatii*) noted by A. HORTIS, *Studij sulle opere latine, cit.*, pp. 940-941; Françoys Habert d'Yssouldun en Berry, *L'Histoire de Titus et Gisippus et autres petiz oeuvres de Beeroalde latin interpretés en ryme françoyse*, Paris, 1551, mentioned in the exhibit catalogue by F. AVRIL and F. CALLU, *Boccace en France. De l'humanisme à l'erotisme*, Paris, Bibliothèque Nationale, 1975.

[3] G. PADOAN, *Mondo aristocratico e mondo comunale, cit.*, pp. 81-216, esp. pp. 167-168; V. RUSSO, *Il senso del tragico nel 'Decameron', cit.*, pp. 29-83.

[4] S. BATTAGLIA, *La coscienza letteraria, cit.*, p. 510.

[5] G. GETTO, *Vita di forme, cit.*, p. 225; A. SCAGLIONE, *Nature and Love, cit.*, p. 74.

[6] C. MUSCETTA, *Boccaccio, cit.*, p. 293.

[7] G. CAVALLINI, *La decima giornata, cit.*, p. 138.

[8] S. BATTAGLIA, *La coscienza letteraria, cit.*, pp. 487-522. In spite of his disapproval, Battaglia presents an excellent close study of this tale's relationship to its source in the *Disciplina clericalis*.

[9] CICERO, *De officiis*, trans. W. MILLER, Cambridge, Mass., Harvard University Press («Loeb Classical Library»), I 16.

read, not as miscreants in a morally repugnant situation, but as exemplars of the most noble classical virtue, friendship. Filomena eulogizes its powers in her rhetorically elevated summation, powers comparable in secular terms to those of Christian *caritas*:

Santissima cosa adunque è l'amistà, e non solamente di singular reverenzia degna ma d'essere con perpetua laude commendata, sì come discretissima madre di magnificenzia e d'onestà, sorella di gratitudine e di carità, e d'odio e d'avarizia nemica, sempre, senza priego aspettar, pronta a quello in altrui virtuosamente operare che in sé vorrebbe che fosse operato.

Friends, she finally asserts, are more precious and more loyal than whomever we know in any other personal relationships, even immediate family. On this note the story ends:

Disiderino adunque gli uomini la moltitudine de' consorti, le turbe de' fratelli e la gran quantità de' figliuoli e con gli lor denari il numero de' servidori s'acrescano; e non guardino, qualunque s'è l'un di questi, ogni menomo suo pericolo più temere che sollecitudine aver di tor via i grandi del padre o del fratello o del signore, dove tutto il contrario far si vede all'amico.

Bizarre peripeties in Filomena's tale dramatize classical definitions of friendship to which her closing remarks allude. A first-century Roman exponent of the tradition on which Boccaccio capitalizes, author of a factual cache that was a medieval favorite, is Valerius Maximus. Discussing this virtue in typically axiomatic form, Valerius affirms that true friends prove themselves in adversity, not prosperity. The bond of friendship is stronger than consanguinity because we have the latter by destiny, but the former is voluntary. Various examples illustrate his dicta. First among the foreigners are the Pythagoreans Damon and Phintias. When Dionysius of Syracuse condemned one to death, the other came as surety until his friend had set his affairs in order and returned to be executed at the appointed time. The tyrant was so impressed that he asked to become a third member in their friendship.[10]

Tito and Gisippo, literary descendants of Damon and Phinthias, stalwartly withstand trials imposed by Fortune. For the dying Tito's sake Gisippo sacrifices his betrothed, his reputation, his inheritance, and his fatherland. For Gisippo, Tito offers himself to the pretorian crucifier, then gives the homeless, destitute Athenian his own sister as wife, and

---

[10] VALERIUS MAXIMUS, *Fatti e detti memorabili*, trans. L. RUSCA, Milan, Rizzoli, 1972, IV 7, 1.

makes him partner in all his property. To Roman and Greek, who defied the marriage contracted by Gisippo's family, friendship is the ultimate allegiance. It must take precedence over more ordinary 'relationships' among kith and kin, as Filomena had pointed out in her finale. So Gisippo would rather surrender his wife than his friend: «forse così liberal non sarei, se così rade o con quella difficultà le mogli si trovasser che si trouvan gli amici: e per ciò, potend'io legerissimamente altra moglie trovare ma non altro amico, io voglio innanzi [...] transmutarla che perder te» (X 8, 38).

Who else belongs to Tito and Gisippo's spiritual ancestry? We can pursue the genealogy, turning first to other works by Boccaccio himself. His *Filocolo*, a learned romance written fifteen to twenty years before the *Decameron*, has a set piece on the subject of friendship. Florio mourns the death of his dear companion, the knight Ascalion:

Alcuni vogliono lodare per amicizia grandissima quella di Filade e d'Oreste, altri quella di Teseo e di Peritoo mirabilemente vantano, e molti quella d'Achille e di Patrocolo mostrano maggiore che altra; e Maro, sommo poeta, quella di Niso e di Eurialo cantando sopra l'altre pone, e tali sono che recitano quella di Damone e di Fizia avere tutte l'altre passate: ma niuno di quelli che questo dicono la nostra ha conosciuta. Certo niuna a quella che tu verso di me hai portata si può appareggiare (V 75, 4-5).

The motif returns, but this time to serve vituperation, in one of Boccaccio's early rhetorical Latin epistles, *Nereus amphytritibus* (1339). Its unknown (and perhaps imaginary) recipient is accused of having betrayed that sacred tie of friendship, which «unites various and diverse wills, joins, makes equal, and associates alien souls», as the deeds of Perithous, Nisus, Damon «and others» declare. Closer to the *Decameron* is Boccaccio's letter of 1348 to the poet, Zanobi da Strada. The epistle opens with reverent praise for friendship: «Who could describe with fitting words how pious, how holy, how venerable friendship is? Not I».[11]

---

[11] *Epistole, cit.*, III, *Nereus amphytritibus*; and, to Zanobi, *Epistola* VI 1: «Quam pium quam sanctum quam venerabile sit amicitie numen, quis posset verbis debitis explicare? Non ego». Sanctity of friendship notwithstanding, Boccaccio would later turn against Zanobi. But the topos is frequent in his writing. Friendship will again be a theme in the *Teseida*. Boccaccio has Pirithous come in a vision to pull Theseus away from an overlong honeymoon with Ipolita (II 4); the main plot will turn on another pair of friends created by the poet, Arcita and Palemone. The «metaphsyics of friendship» as a «philanthropical ethic» in Boccaccio's epistles has been magisterially investigated by G. AUZZAS, '*Quid amicitia dulcius*', in *Miscellanea di studi in onore di Vittore Branca*, II, *cit.*, pp. 181-205:187, «con gli antichi è condivisa e accolta l'idea che l'amicizia vada anteposta e preferita a tutte le cose umane».

Words, needless to say, do not entirely fail the writer, though, who goes on to marshal some sterling examples: Damon and Phinthias, Theseus and Pirithous, Nisus and Euryalus. What we have in both cases is a catalogue, names of the male couples most memorable in world history for their unswerving, reciprocal devotion.

To this canon of male bonding, whose members were all Greek by birth, must be added another duo of Roman origin. I refer to Publius Scipio Africanus and Gaius Laelius, celebrated subjects of Cicero's *De amicitia*. Cicero imagines that after Publius Scipio has died, Laelius, for the benefit of his two sons-in-law, recreates the picture of their friendship. Expressing the wish that its memory might always endure, he continues, «this thought is the more pleasing to me because in the whole range of history only three or four pairs of friends are mentioned; and I venture to hope that among such instances the friendship of Scipio and Laelius will be known to posterity».[12]

Although Laelius does not name them, Cicero would have had in mind a list identical to Boccaccio's, minus one couple whose fame rests on Virgil, the Trojans Euryalus and Nisus. When Boccaccio shaped the tale of Tito and Gisippo, his aim was to admit one more rare pair into the cycle he had inherited from antiquity. Going the ancients one better, though, he devised a 'mixed' partnership, half Greek and half Roman, uniting «animo romano e senno ateniese» (X 8, 55).

That his bid to enter them in friendship's hall of fame succeeded we know from the story's remarkable diffusion. Spurred as much by Filippo Beroaldo's Latin translation of the early 1490's as by circulation of the Tuscan *Decameron*, Tito and Gisippo's popularity carried them throughout Europe to destinations ranging from Matteo Bandello to Ludovico Ariosto to British balladry to the plays of Hans Sachs.[13] Boccaccio would have been pleased to discover that his mark had, for example, made its way into *The Faerie Queene*, where, in the temple of Venus, Spenser visualizes an elect company of truest friends. Its members, Biblical as well as classical, number Hercules and Hylas, Jonathan and David, Theseus and Pirithous, Pylades and Orestes, Titus and Gesippus, Damon and

---

[12] CICERO, *De amicitia*, trans. W. A. FALCONER, Cambridge, Mass., Harvard University Press, 1971 («Loeb Classical Library»), IV 15: «eo mihi magis est cordi, quod ex omnibus saeculis vix tria aut quattuor nominantur paria amicorum, quo in genere sperare videor Scipionis et Laeli amicitiam notam posteritati fore». Boccaccio was already thinking about these names in his *Filocolo*, when he christened Biancifiore's father Quinto Lelio Africano, a figure descended from Scipio Africanus.

[13] L. SORIERI, *Boccaccio's Story of 'Tito and Gisippo'*, traced this diffusion.

Phinthias: «All these and all that ever had been tyde / In bands of friendship, there did live for ever».[14]

When read in light of the ancient literature on friendship, Tito and Gisippo reassume an identity that would have been taken for granted by their Renaissance interpretative community — not as hypocrites or con men, but as paragons of a virtue that is the cement of society. At the head of the tradition stands Aristotle, whom Boccaccio cites in several works on the three types of friendship or love (*Ethics* VIII). His earliest treatment of the Aristotelian trinity — friendship for the sake of pleasure, for the sake of utility, and for the sake of virtue — occurs in a key passage of the *Filocolo*, Fiammetta's central ruling in the love debate (IV 44). Speaking in medieval terms of 'amore' and not 'amicizia' literally, she asserts like Aristotle the superiority of virtuous friendship over ties cultivated for pleasure or utility:

amore è di tre maniere, per le quali tre, tutte le cose sono amate [...]. La prima delle quali tre si chiama amore onesto: questo è il buono e il diritto e il leale amore, il quale da tutti abitualmente dee esser preso. Questo il sommo e primo creatore tiene lui alle sue creature congiunto, e loro a lui congiunge. Per questo i cieli, il mondo, i reami, le province e le città permangono in istato. Per questo meritiamo noi di divenire etterni posseditori de' celestiali regni. Sanza questo è perduto ciò che noi abbiamo in potenza di ben fare.

For the Middle Ages it was Aristotle who had first seen in friendship the noble, binding force necessary to life and civic unity. He attributed to it a special kinship with just government, for both serve the common advantage. Perfect friendship, he acknowledged, is rare, since it cannot ripen until friends have eaten the proverbial peck of salt together.

Cicero's Laelius develops this line of reasoning when he holds that «friendship cannot exist except between good men», for «without virtue friendship cannot exist at all». By his etymology (which surely had played in Fiammetta's pronouncement on 'love') 'amicitia' derives from 'amor': «For it is love, from which the word 'friendship' is derived, that leads to the establishing of goodwill».[15] A natural urge, it is best practiced by the wealthy and powerful, since they are the most self-sufficient, hence most

---

[14] E. SPENSER, *The Faerie Queene*, ed. T. P. ROCHE, Jr. with C. P. O'DONNELL, Jr., New Haven, Yale University Press, 1981, IV 10, 27.

[15] *De amicitia, cit.*, V 18: «nisi in bonis amicitiam esse non posse»; VI 21: «sine virtute amicitia esse ullo pacto potest»; VIII 27: «Amor enim, ex quo amicitia nominata est, princeps est ad benevolentiam coniungendam».

given to generosity. Hypocrisy, flattery, or feigning stay far from faithful friends, who mirror each other in a «rivalry of virtue», and are always there when Fortune is fickle. Pure and faultless friendship subdues the passions, self-serving by definition, and promotes justice, creating the human bonds necessary for cohesion of household and state.

Scions of patrician households, closer than blood brothers, Tito and Gisippo, who vie to outdo each other in ascending tests of virtue, answer ideals in Cicero's *De amicitia*. Likewise they conform to specification in the same philosopher's treatise on moral duty, *De officiis*. Boccaccio summons it to our attention with a signal clearly sounded at the beginning of his story:

You must know, then, that at the time when Octavianus Caesar, not yet styled Augustus, ruled the Roman Empire in the office called Triumvirate, there was in Rome a gentleman called Publius Quintius Fulvus, who, having a son of marvelous understanding, by name Titus Quintius Fulvus, sent him to Athens to study philosophy and commended him as most he might to a nobleman there called Chremes, his very old friend.

In this *mise-en-scène* readers who remember their classics hear the echo of another opening, Cicero's exordium for *De officiis*. He addresses his son, «My dear Marcus, you have now been studying a full year under Cratippus, and that too in Athens, and you should be fully equipped with the practical precepts and the principles of philosophy». Just like Marcus junior, who left Rome to learn with Cratippus, Boccaccio's younger Tito is sent by his father to study in Athens under Aristippo.[16]

In this treatise, following the Stoics, Cicero investigates three questions: Is an act morally right or wrong? Is it expedient? When the good and the expedient conflict, how do we chose? Now Boccaccio's *novella* raises precisely such concerns. To a reader like Battaglia, the supposed heroes are really scoundrels because they put the expedient above the good, abetting Tito's lust at the expense of Sofronia's dignity and Gisippo's honor. Still, does Tito's appetite really triumph, as Giuseppe Mazzotta has argued, in a solution to the friends' dilemma that is at best darkly ambivalent, at worst, an act of violence and self-delusion?[17]

---

[16] CICERO, *De officiis, cit.*, I 1: «Quamquam te, Marce fili, annum iam audientem Cratippum, idque Athenis, abundare oportet praeceptis institutisque philosophiae». V. BRANCA points to the parallel, *Decameron, cit.*, X 8, 5 and n. 4, p. 1532: «Secondo il costume della nobiltà romana (cui appartennero i Quinzi) che già Cicerone accenna nell'introduzione al *De officiis*».

[17] G. MAZZOTTA, *The World at Play, cit.*, pp. 254-60.

With Cicero in mind, we can, I think, take a brighter view of the story's ambiguities. Deliberate to be sure, they are meant more to dazzle than to disturb. Reason not passion, community not selfishness, are the powers that win out in Boccaccio's plot. From the first word of this tale's rubric, 'Sofronia', the tale emphasizes rational endeavor.[18] Her name is formed from the Greek adjective that means «soundness of mind», hence 'wisdom'. Tito and Gisippo, who both desire her, pursue wisdom twice over while students of philosophy in Athens, city of Minerva and wisdom.[19]

Steeped in this atmosphere, Tito does not, after all, succumb to the fatal threat of his *coup-de-foudre* for Sofronia. As he mentally struggles with the dilemma, intellect tells him what is right: «dà luogo alla ragione, raffrena il concupiscibile appetito, tempera i disideri non sani». Alone, however, he has not sufficient strength of will, and had not the selfless friend heroically come to his rescue, the outcome of their conflict would have been, if not Tito's suicide, at least adultery. As Cicero puts it, men united by ties of goodwill «will first of all subdue the passions», for «friendship was given to us by nature as the handmaid of virtue, not as a comrade of vice; because virtue cannot attain her highest aims unattended, but only in union and fellowship with another».[20] In Boccaccio's story amity assures probity; the heroic triumphs over the erotic. Tito's love can be accommodated to marriage, which, as the life-affirming tie that binds, is the most basic unit of political cohesion and harmony.[21]

---

[18] The full rubric is unusually long, anticipating complexities of plot: «Sofronia, credendosi esser moglie di Gisippo, è moglie di Tito Quinzio Fulvo e con lui se ne va a Roma, dove Gisippo in povero stato arriva; e credendo da Tito esser disprezzato sé avere uno uomo ucciso, per morire, afferma; Tito, riconosciutolo, per iscamparlo dice sé averlo morto; il che colui che fatto l'avea vedendo se stesso manifesta; per la qual cosa da Ottaviano tutti sono liberati, e Tito dà a Gisippo la sorella per moglie e con lui comunica ogni suo bene».

[19] S. DELIGIORGIS, *Narrative Intellection, cit.*, p. 223, etymologizes the name. See also G. MAZZOTTA, *The World at Play, cit.*, p. 257. Athens is a prominent symbol of wisdom in Boccaccio's epic, *Teseida*, and it returns more than once in later works with the same essential identity. In the *Decameron* itself (Concl. 21), Athens again crops up as a learning center for men. Its culture is also remembered in *De casibus, cit.*, I 10: «Athene civitas, phylosophorum poetarum et oratorum olim egregia altrix» [the city of Athens, she who once nourished philosophers, poets, and orators]. Cf. *De mulieribus claris*, ed. V. ZACCARIA, Milan, Mondadori, 1967 («Tutte le opere», X), VI 7: «Ob tot comperta, prodiga deitatum largitrix, antiquitas eidem [= Athenis] sapientie numen attribuit» [For all her discoveries the ancients, generous bestowers of divinity, attributed to Athens the numen of wisdom].

[20] *De amicitia, cit.*, XXII 83: «Virtutum amicitia adiutrix a natura data est, non vitiorum comes, ut, quoniam solitaria non posset virtus ad ea quae summa sunt pervenire, coniuncta et consociata cum altera perveniret».

[21] V. BRANCA, *Boccaccio medievale, cit.*, pp. 105-106, sees X 8 as an antiphrastically obscene situation. That is, the adultery that could have been exploited for comic or tragic

More than anything else, what makes the dominance of reason evident in this tale is the predominance of logical discourse, particularly Tito's apologia, a tour-de-force of epideictic oratory. Mario Baratto is quite right to pick out rhetoric as the story's real protagonist.[22] Balm and protection for storms of the soul, it is the rational word that rules this tale. Gisippo must persuade Tito to accept Sofronia, then Tito must convert her family from fury to reason («ramarichii, più da furia che da ragione incitati»), persuading them that friendship led to the right decision, one optimally expedient and good. Through painstaking elaboration of his medieval source tales,[23] Boccaccio recreates for the moderns a classical mythos of friendship, a Ciceronian ideal of style, and a Stoical philosophy of life.

* * *

I should like to add a note on nomenclature and dates in *Decameron* X 8. Some of the characters' names, beginning with Sofronia's, have allusive value in accordance with the traditional norm, «Names are the consequence of things». Gisippo's father, Cremete, has a congener in Chremes, one of the two father-friends from Terence's play *Andria*, and men who had in turn inherited the bond from their fathers before them. Aristippo, preceptor to Tito and Gisippo, has a name aristocratic in ring. The mythographer Fulgentius, familiar to Boccaccio, had explained 'ariston' as meaning 'the best' in Greek. A real Greek philosopher of the fifth century B.C. had been called Aristippo, and Boccaccio uses the name once before in the *Decameron* for the Cypriot father of Cimone, whom he characterizes «a most noble man» (V 1, 3).[24] Tito's agnomen Quinzio

---

purposes is transformed by Boccaccio into a heroic example of virtue. G. CAVALLINI, *La decima giornata*, *cit.*, pp. 127-145, agrees that the story expresses «an authentic ideal» for Boccaccio; so does M. COTTINO-JONES, in *Order from Chaos*, *cit.*, p. 175. She speaks of an «apotheosis of friendship». On the relationship of reason to appetites, see above, ch. 4.

[22] M. BARATTO, *Realtà e stile*, *cit.*, pp. 34-42, 73.

[23] See S. BATTAGLIA, *La coscienza letteraria*, *cit.*, p. 519. A complementary discussion of the story's antecedent in Alexander de Bernay can be found in L. SORIERI, *Boccaccio's Story of 'Tito and Gisippo'*, *cit.*, ch. 1.

[24] The positive Greek connotations of the name could have been known to Boccaccio via a source such as Fulgentius, who reports that Eurydice stumbled on a snake as she was fleeing the shepherd Aristaeus and allegorizes the incident. She was desired by 'the best' because *ariston* in Greek means 'the best'. See FULGENTIUS, *The Mythologies* III 10 in *Fulgentius the Mythographer*, *cit.*, p. 97. G. MAZZOTTA, *The World at Play*, *cit.*, pp. 255-257, takes Aristippo as an emblem of ethical hedonism, basing his argument on tradition in the Church Fathers. I prefer to see the story's hedonism as a danger surmounted by reason and ethical Stoicism. Athenian philosophy always seems to be positive in potential for Boccaccio.

attaches him, by a fictitious branch, to an illustrious Roman family, the *gens* Quintia.[25]

These allusions, clearly, enhance the story's classical flavor. Others, terms that conjure the ghost of Dante, function differently. Consider Octavian, whose role in this *novella*, the 'octave' on its day, calls attention both to the number 8 and the future emperor's name. Why did Boccaccio set *Decameron* X 8 specifically during the triumvirate of «Ottavian Cesare»? The period, as Filomena's exordium qualifies it, is significant for what it precedes: «Nel tempo adunque che Ottavian Cesare, *non ancora* chiamato Augusto [...] lo 'mperio di Roma reggeva». Octavian the triumvir became Octavian Augustus, that same emperor under whom our world reached the providentially ordained time for Christ's Incarnation. This is, in other words, not just a Roman setting. To be more precise, it is a pre-Christian setting. Octavian, the crucifixion to which Gisippo is sentenced, and his rescue by a man called Tito all point forward to the Christian era – Christ's Coming, his sacrifice on the Cross, and the avenging of it by Emperor Titus.[26]

So, too, does the number 8 adumbrate his Coming, since it is an emblem of baptism, resurrection, and life eternal.[27] The salvific potential of the ogdoad found expression in the tremendously popular twelfth-century *Speculum humanae salvationis*, where Advent, 8, and Octavian all symbolically converge. The eighth chapter of this historiated encyclopedia is illustrated by the Nativity. Three typologically parallel pictures accompany that scene: Pharoah's cup-bearer dreaming of the vine, Aaron's rod, and the Tiburtine Sibyl foretelling Christ's birth to the Roman Emperor Octavian.[28]

Octavian, who ruled as Caesar Augustus when Christ was born, had in medieval memory a second connection with the Nativity: he had been vouchsafed a vision of the Child's Advent. The story, widely known in versions narrated by writer and painter alike, would have been familiar to Boccaccio from both the *Mirabilia urbis Romae* and *Legenda aurea*. Ac-

---

[25] V. BRANCA, *Decameron*, cit., X 8, 5 and n. 2, p. 1532. In this context, we might also recall the name Cratippus, not unlike Aristippus, Cicero's Athenian professor.

[26] The Dantesque undertexts here include, beyond *De monarchia*, *Purgatorio*, cit., VII 4-6: «Anzi che a questo monte fosser volte / l'anime degne di salire a Dio, / fur l'ossa mie per Ottavian sepolte»; *Ibid.*, XXI 82-84: «Nel tempo che 'l buon Tito, con l'aiuto / dell sommo rege, vendicò le fóra / ond' uscì 'l sangue per Giuda venduto».

[27] Discussion and documentation for the medieval symbolism of 8 appear in V. HOPPER, *Medieval Number Symbolism*, cit., pp. 77, 114; H. MEYER, *Die Zahlenallegorese im Mittelalter. Methode und Gebrauch*, Munich, Wilhelm Fink, 1975, pp. 140-141. See also above, ch. 7.

[28] D. ROBB, *The Art of the Illuminated Manuscript*, Philadelphia, Art Alliance Press, 1973, p. 26.

cording to the latter, when the Roman Senate wanted to deify the emperor for having brought the world to peace, he wisely inquired of the Sibyl whether there would one day be born a man greater than he. In response, there came an amazing apparition of the Virgin, holding her infant Son, on an altar high in the noonday sky:

Now on the day of the Nativity the Sibyl was alone with the emperor, when at high noon, she saw a golden ring appear around the sun. In the middle of the circle stood a Virgin, of wondrous beauty, holding a child upon her bosom. The Sibyl showed this wonder to Caesar; and a voice was heard which said: "This woman is the Altar of Heaven [Ara Coeli]"! And the Sibyl said to him: "This child will be greater than thou". Thus the room where this miracle took place was consecrated to the Holy Virgin; and upon the site the church of Santa Maria in Ara Coeli stands today.

The revelation gave its name to the spot in his palace chamber where Octavian had stood to witness it, commemorated by the church of Saint Mary on the Altar of Heaven, next to the Campidoglio.[29]

Tito and Gisippo, whose era overlaps with the Golden Age of Latin literature, Octavian's privileged rule, and the Pax romana, embody the historical culmination of pagan culture. Friends, orators, and Stoic philosophers, they come as close to being Christian as conceivably possible, by nation, epoch, and ethics. Emblems of Hellenic and Latin civilization at its finest moment, they are a fitting pair for the closing sequence in the Decameron's magnificent finale.

---

[29] A. GRAF devotes an entire chapter to Octavian Augustus and his medieval mystique in Roma nella memoria e nelle immaginazioni del Medio Evo, I, Turin, Ermanno Loescher, 1882, pp. 308-331. The vision of Caesar receives prominent attention in The Marvels of Rome where it introduces the list of the city's monuments (II 1). See The Marvels of Rome. Mirabilia urbis Romae, ed. and trans. F. M. NICHOLS, rev. E. GARDINER, New York, Italica Press, 1986, pp. 17-18. In The Golden Legend, cit., Jacobus de Voragine affirms for December 25 that the Nativity was revealed to «every class of creatures, from the stones, which are at the bottom of the scale of creation, to the angels, who are at its summit». The revelation that came to Octavian was a theme that flourished in the visual arts from the thirteenth through sixteenth centuries. See, e.g., Emperor Augustus and the Tiburtine Sibyl, an engraving by the German Master E.S., active ca. 1450-1467/68, at the Philadelphia Museum of Art. E. KIRSCHBAUM, S.J., ed., Lexikon der Christliche Ikonographie, I, cit., pp. 226-227, cites other examples of the theme. Among those who painted the scene was Rogier van der Weyden, who illustrates the belief that the Church of Aracoeli was built over Caesar's palace chamber, the spot where he had his vision. See the analysis by E. KNAUER, A CVBICVLO AVGVSTORVM. Bemerkungen zu Rogier van der Weydens Bladelin-Altar, «Zeitschrift für Kunstgeschichte», XXXIII, 1970, pp. 332-339.

9.

THE LAST TALE IN THE *DECAMERON*

The tale of patient Griselda, a disturbing puzzle to its modern public, met with phenomenal success among Boccaccio's Renaissance posterity. Griselda's unique international fortune springs from the effort of Petrarch, first to separate her from the rest of the *Decameron*. He implies that what attracted him to this «story so sweet» was its seriousness of subject, but by that criterion alone he could have Latinized instead the moving account of Ghismonda's romance (IV 1), as would Leonardo Bruni a few decades later. When deciding to 'tackle' X 10, Petrarch took up a *novella* significant on a second count: aside from gravity of matter, it is privileged by finality of position. The Aretine man of letters well knew that an author's ending is the point of greatest poetic emphasis.[1]

---

[1] Petrarch's Latin adaptation of Boccaccio's last tale, *De insigni obedientia et fide uxoria, sive historia Griseldis*, fills one of the epistles to Boccaccio that form the last book of his final letter collection, the *Seniles* (XVII 3). He declares it a story so dulcet («tam dulcis ystoria») that he memorized it and then decided, as he puts it, «to attack» a translation: «ystorium ipsam tuam scribere sum aggressus». E. KADISH presented and Englished Petrarch's aggressive enterprise in *The Proem of Petrarch's Griselda*, «Mediaevalia», II, 1976, pp. 189-206 and *Petrarch's Griselda: An English Translation*, «Mediaevalia», III, 1977, pp. 1-24. Petrarch's Griselda vis-à-vis Boccaccio's along with pertinent documents has now been republished in the fine small volume *Griselda*, ed. L. C. ROSSI, Palermo, Sellerio, 1991. It is Rossi's Latin edition of the letter, p. 76, that I cite. V. BRANCA marshals evidence of the tale's remarkable Renaissance reception in *Boccaccio medievale*, *cit.*, pp. 388-393. Branca reports the survival of approximately 100 manuscripts of the *Seniles* with Petrarch's *Historia Griseldis*, and about another 100 manuscripts containing just the translation. J. B. SEVERS recreated her path into the *Canterbury Tales* with his classic study *The Literary Relationships of Chaucer's Clerkes Tale*, New Haven, Yale University Press, 1942, pp. 3-37. For a comprehensive bibliography of Griselda's fortunes, see further the excellent report by R. MORABITO, *La diffusione della storia di Griselda dal XIV al XX secolo*, «Studi sul Boccaccio», XVII, 1988, pp. 237-285. Documentation of the heroine's popularity in the visual arts appears in P. F. WATSON, *A Preliminary List of Subjects from Boccaccio*, *cit.* See also V. BRANCA, *Un 'lusus' del Bruni cancelliere: Il rifacimento di una novella del 'Decameron' (IV 1) e la sua irradiazione europea*, in *Leonardo Bruni. Cancelliere della Repubblica di Firenze. Convegno di Studi (Firenze, 27-29 ottobre 1987)*, Florence, Leo. S. Olschki, 1990, pp. 207-226.

On cue from Petrarch, I should like to probe for meaning in Boccaccio's ending, my premise being that an end conditions its own meaning, and in so doing, comments by privilege of cloture on whatever is prior. Griselda's finest quality, her humility, correlates historically with Humility's new prominence as a virtue in fourteenth-century Italy. Theological definitions of Humility help in turn explain why *Decameron* X 10's last position should be of first importance. 'Cornerstone' in the edifice of virtues as constructed by Christian thinkers, Humility is a fitting theme for the *novella* that perfects Boccaccio's finale.

Humility complements the secular acme to which tales on the closing day ascend, Aristotle's privileged moral virtue called 'magnanimity'. In the *brigata*'s vocabulary it becomes 'magnificenzia'. As Neifile embarks on X 1, she likens this fulfilling quality to the sun: «come il sole è di tutto il cielo bellezza e ornamento, [la magnificenzia] è chiarezza e lume di ciascun'altra virtù». Her simile, which implies uplifting enlightenment, came to Boccaccio from the Philosopher's definition in the *Nicomachean Ethics* (IV 3): «it seems that magnanimity is an embellishment of the virtues, since it makes virtue more excellent and does not exist without them». To reinforce the idea of magnanimity as the perfecting virtue, Boccaccio also had clearly in mind the gloss by Thomas Aquinas, whose commentary on the *Ethics* he personally had transcribed:

Magnanimity seems to be an ornament of all the virtues because they are made more excellent by magnanimity, which seeks to perform a great work in all the virtues. In this way the virtues increase. Likewise, magnanimity accompanies the other virtues and so seems to be added to them as their ornament.[2]

---

[2] T. AQUINAS, *Comm. Ethic., cit.*, IV 8 (749): «magnanimitas videtur esse ornatus quidam omnium virtutum. Quia pro magnanimitate omnes virtutes efficiuntur majores, eo quod ad magnanimitatem pertinet operari magnum in omnibus virtutibus. Et ex hoc crescunt virtutes. Et iterum non fit magnanimitas sine aliis virtutibus; et sic videtur superaddi aliis tamquam ornatus earum». The virtue Boccaccio calls 'magnificenzia' on the last Day of the *Decameron* incorporates some aspects of Aristotle's 'magnificence' (*Ethics* 1122a-b), or generosity on a scale that surpasses 'liberality'. Liberality in this higher form of magnificence is well exemplified in the *novelle* by Saladino (I 3). But what Boccaccio clearly has in mind for Day X is the virtue Aristotle discusses after magnificence, 'magnanimity', or *megalopsychia* (1123a-1124b). Boccaccio's copy of the *Ethics* with Thomas's *Commentary* is in Milan, Biblioteca Ambrosiana, Cod. A 204 part. inf. G. AUZZAS describes it, *I codici autografi, cit.*

Most modern readers suppose some fundamental, repugnant defect in Griselda. A. MOMIGLIANO, *Decameron. 49 novelle commentate*, Milan, Francesco Vallardi, 1936, believed that she was a «poor idiot». T. G. BERGIN, *Boccaccio, cit.*, p. 323, cannot help diagnosing her «pathologically submissive». A. BONADEO, *Marriage and Adultery in the Decameron*, «Philological Quarterly», LX, 1981, pp. 287-303, sees her poor personality «violated and destroyed» in this «sordid tale of sadistic abuse and rejection».

Magnificence (Magnanimity), «light and luster of every other virtue», merges at tale 100 in Griselda with Humility, cornerstone virtue in the Christian scheme of things. At the outer limits, in the *novella* that brings Boccaccio's anthology to numeric perfection, she will call us back across the *Decameron* to its point of departure, for her silent obedience counterpoises saturant pride in Ser Cepperello, that dapper fiend and 'father of lies' who 'falls' to death in tale number one. Her passive wifedom, far from the sheer idiocy or the shocking pathology it has bespoken for our century, dramatizes a medieval existential hierarchy by which order and life are preserved, both in the individual and the *polis*, within man's soul and throughout his social cosmos.

In work first published more than fifty years ago, the art historian Millard Meiss traced development of a major new iconographic type in European painting. It was the Madonna of Humility, whose invention Meiss attributed to Simone Martini of Siena and whose earliest extant Florentine example he placed in a panel by Bernardo Daddi dating from 1348. These devotional images, which quickly became extremely popular, represent the Virgin not enthroned, but sitting on the ground nursing her child, «more like a simple housewife or a poor peasant than the Queen of Heaven». Her lowly position as *Madonna Lactans*, allegorically the mother who breasts and nourishes us all, refers to her preeminent Biblical virtue, Humility (fig. 14). The depiction recalls Isidore of Seville's explanatory derivation: «Humble, as it were bent down toward the earth» [Humilis, quasi humo adclinis].[3]

Other artistic contexts confirm a new importance for the concept of Humility in the first half of the Italian Trecento. One is the traditional cycle of female figures personifying the Virtues. The canonical seven, which Giotto had rendered in grisaille in 1305 at Padua's Arena Chapel (figs. 5 and 6), sometimes now take on an eighth. So Andrea Pisano's

---

[3] Modern lexicographers still accept Isidore's derivation, advanced in *Etymologiae, cit.*, X 115. Cf. Webster, who traces 'humility' to Latin *humilis* ('low', 'small') and compares it to the Latin word *humus* ('soil'). R. FREMANTLE's census of *Florentine Gothic Painters from Giotto to Masaccio, cit.*, lists nearly forty surviving Madonnas of Humility that were made between the mid-14th and 15th centuries in Boccaccio's city alone. As early as the 1350's, this same type of the Virgin, *mater omnium* and *nutrix omnium*, appears in Bologna, Padua, Modena, Pisa, Pistoia, Venice, and the Marche. See M. MEISS, *The Madonna of Humility*, «The Art Bulletin», XVIII, 1936, pp. 435-464, and *Florence and Siena after the Black Death, cit.*, pp. 135-141. By the third quarter of the Trecento, Simone's influential model has spread to such distant areas as Catalonia and Bohemia, fostered in its diffusion by preaching friars, especially the Dominicans. E. SCHIFERL, in a paper presented at the International Medieval Institute in Kalamazoo, Michigan (May, 1986), documented connections between the Madonna of Humility and the Confraternities, whose members commissioned such paintings and also practiced the virtue of humility, more feasible for them as laymen than the monastic virtues of chastity and poverty.

doors of 1336 for the south side of the Baptistry in Florence expand the sequence to keep symmetry by inserting Humility as a bridge between the four Cardinal and three Theological Virtues (fig. 8).[4]

Andrea Pisano may have been following the lead of Giotto's pupil, Taddeo Gaddi, whose *Scenes of the Life of the Virgin* at the Franciscan church of Santa Croce (1328-30) two series of Virtues accompany. One sheds benevolent influence from ceiling sectors; a second frames the windows. Overhead, the outer vault of the Baroncelli Chapel has the four Cardinal Virtues; the inner vault, their theological counterparts plus Humility, who stands holding her symbolic attribute, a lamb. Among Virtues enclosed by roundels in the window splays, Humility fittingly appears in horizontal juxtaposition to the Virgin Annunciate. As Creighton Gilbert has suggested, the Madonna of Humility as a type probably originates in such representations of the Annunciation, where Mary is shown sitting on the ground.[5]

Gaddi's chapel contains eighteen Virtues all told, and they influenced the decoration of the Strozzi Chapel at Santa Maria Novella. About 1356, Giovanni del Biondo frescoed its vault with medalions that depict St. Thomas Aquinas attended by eight Virtues (fig. 2). Twelve further Virtues appear in octagons within the decorative bands that articulate the ceiling divisions, among them Poverty, Chastity, Obedience, Penitence, Purity, and Humility. A choice so Franciscan in flavor, based on Gaddi's Baroncelli program and related to allegorical representations of the Franciscan Vows at the Lower Church in Assisi, makes a sisterhood surprising at first retrospective glance in Florence's great Dominican church.[6]

---

[4] K. CLARK, Intro. to *The Florentine Baptistry Doors*, New York, Viking, 1980, pp. 78-85.

[5] J. HALL, *Dictionary of Subjects and Symbols in Art, cit., s.v.* 'Humility', gives the lamb as that virtue's symbol; contrast, *s.v.* 'Pride', attributes of the opposing sin, the lion and the eagle. A. LADDIS, in *Taddeo Gaddi. Critical Reappraisal and Catalogue Raisonné*, Columbia, University of Missouri Press, 1982, pp. 33-34, describing the Baroncelli Chapel ceiling, erroneously identifies the lady who kneels before an altar with chalice and cross as Humility. She is, rather, Faith. Cf. the Faith of Orcagna's *Tabernacle*, who holds a chalice; and Andrea Pisano's Baptistry doors, where Faith holds both chalice and cross. For additional discussion and reproductions, see J. GARDNER, *The Decoration of the Baroncelli Chapel in Santa Croce*, «Zeitschrift für Kunstgeschichte», XXXIX, 1971, pp. 89-113. I thank C. GILBERT, who made the important point about the Baroncelli Chapel Annunciation after reading this essay as first published, in a letter to me of February 18, 1991.

[6] For the Strozzi Chapel program, see R. OFFNER and C. STEINWEG, *A Critical and Historical Corpus of Italian Painting*, IV 4, *cit.*, pp. 21-23. For other virtue cycles, L. RÉAU, *Iconographie de l'art chrétien*, I, *cit.*, pp. 177-182; E. KIRSCHENBAUM, *Lexikon der Christlichen Ikonografie*, IV, *cit., s.v.* 'Tugenden'. Under the influence of Scholasticism, Humility had by the early thirteenth century already found her place in virtue cycles in the cathedral art of Northern France. She appears with a dove at Notre Dame de Paris (c. 1210) accompanying

Yet the paradox comes down to acceptable eclecticism in cultural currents of those times. If Humility's rising status, chronicled by shifting virtue configurations in the visual arts, occurs favored by a climate of Franciscan piety, it was the Dominican Scholastics who had provided systematic conceptual definitions, promoting that habit of self-effacement to the forefront of right demeanor. Andrea Orcagna, for example, follows St. Thomas's classification from the *Summa theologica* when he designs his *Tabernacle of the Madonna* in Orsanmichele (1359) as a domed aedicule with the Cardinal Virtues at the four corners. Each one is flanked by a pair of its facets, or subordinate virtues. Humility, joined by Virginity, is of the couple that accompany Temperance. Between Patience and Perseverance presides Fortitude (figs. 7a and 7b).[7]

Humility, according to Aquinas, is «praiseworthy self-abasement». It regards «the subjection of man to God, for Whose sake he humbles himself by subjecting himself to others». A virtue that in Greek was called 'measure', or 'moderation', Humility belongs to Temperance, since it restrains impetuous movements of the will. It is in this intellectual context that we should understand the virtue Chastity who joins Charity to keep company with Aquinas in Giovanni del Biondo's medalions for the Strozzi Chapel (fig. 2).

Although *humilitas* should not be deemed the greatest virtue (that is Charity's honor), for Thomas it is absolutely basic: «as the orderly assembly of virtues is, by reason of a certain likeness, compared to a building, so again that which is the first step in the acquisition of virtue is likened to the foundation, which is first laid before the rest of the building». In the sense then that Humility expels Pride and opens man to Grace, Thomas sees it as the foundation of the entire spiritual edifice.[8]

Jacopo Passavanti's *Specchio della vera penitenza*, a devotional treatise based on Lenten sermons delivered in 1354, gives an indication of how these Thomistic ideas were transmitted to the Florentine people by friars of the Dominican Order at mid-Trecento. From 1340 he preached in Santa Maria Novella, the church which became the setting for the *Decameron* and where Boccaccio would have heard his sermons. His *Mirror of True Penance* is a 'medicinal' manual, composed on the assump-

---

Prudence, Chastity, Charity, Hope, Faith, Fortitude, Patience, Mansuetudo, Concordia, Obedience, Perseverance. The same twelve virtues were copied at Amiens (1230) and again Chartres (1240). The Italian Duecento also knows Humility as companion to the cardinal and theological virtues, as attested in Nicola Pisiano's Siena cathedral pulpit (1265/68).

[7] N. RASH FABBRI and N. RUTENBERG, *The Tabernacle of Orsanmichele in Context*, «The Art Bulletin», LXIII, 1981, pp. 385-405.

[8] T. AQUINAS, *Summa theologica* I-II, Qu. 161, Art. 1.

tion that vices, which cause infirmity of soul, can be cured by their corresponding virtues. Brother Jacopo begins with Pride, root of all evil, and then proceeds to treat it with a good instructional dose of Humility. On that virtue an impressive array of authorities, Biblical and exegetical, are assembled to animate his argument, a homeopathic line that proceeds as follows.

Christ says, «Learn from me, for I am meek and humble of heart». His school taught Humility to Mary, handmaiden of the Lord, for as we read in the Book of Job, «He who is humbled will be glorified». So, too, does the Gospel promise that the mighty shall be cast down and the lowly exalted. Solomon's Proverbs remind us that to be humble is to be wise: «Where there is humility, there is wisdom». Or, as Augustine phrased it, Humility opens the mind to truth, while Pride closes it. True Humility, according to the same Father's sermons on John, consists in «counting oneself nothing», for self-reliance is self-defeat. Declaring this virtue synonymous with self-vilification in his Book of Degrees, St. Bernard offers the simplest formula for achieving it: «L'umiliazione si è via all'umiltà».

Without Humility, all other virtues are worthless: «chi raguna tutte l'altre vertù sanza l'umiltà, è come se portasse la polvere contra il vento» – that is what St. Gregory's accommodating image shows us. Why Humility is both a moral prerequisite and cornerstone, San Giovanni Boccadoro (St. John Chrysostom, or the 'Golden Mouth'), whose architectural metaphor for Humility would find its way into the *Summa theologica*, makes clear in the fine summation that Passavanati cites: «Ella è capo d'ogni vertù: ella è madre della sapienza: ella è fondamento di tutto l'edificio spirituale, sanza la quale l'altre vertude periscono, non avendo dove s'appoggiare».[9]

---

[9] J. PASSAVANTI, *Specchio della vera penitenza*, Florence, Accademia della Crusca, 1725, pp. 180-187. Among the biblical loci on humility to which Passavanti refers are Matt. 11:29: «Take my yoke upon you, and learn from me; for I am gentle and lowly in heart, and you will find rest for your souls»; Mary's *magnificat* at Luke 1:48: «for he has regarded the low estate of his handmaiden»; and Luke 1:52: «he has put down the mighty from their thrones, and exalted those of low degree»; Job 5:11: «he sets on high those who are lowly, and those who mourn are lifted to safety»; Job 22:29: «For God abases the proud, but he saves the lowly»; Prov. 15:33: «The fear of the Lord is instruction in wisdom, and humility goes before honor»; Prov. 29:23: «A man's pride will bring him low, but he who is lowly in spirit will obtain honor». Helpful to me in tracing them was an unpublished manual prepared for his seminar at Johns Hopkins University on the *Divine Comedy* by C. S. SINGLETON, *Humility: The First Goal of the Journey*.
The importance of Jacopo Passavanti, a charismatic preacher who became prior of Santa Maria Novella, was considerable. Biographies can be found in *Enciclopedia italiana* and *Storia della letteratura italiana*, II, *cit.*, pp. 652 ff. M. MEISS, *Florence and Siena, cit.*, p. 149, implies that a case of exemplary humility in Passavanti's *Specchio* may have had some impact on the

Humility, primal by definitions of Dominican deontology, is also a virtue fundamental to the Franciscans. The general rule for attaining it had been enunciated by St. Bernard: «Humiliation is the way to humility». How, in practice, can humiliation make us humble? One example was set by Saint Francis himself (d. 1226), at least, as popular legend codified his life story. Anecdotes retailed in *I fioretti di San Francesco*, a late Duecento compilation that achieved wide diffusion with its vernacular rendering in the 1370's, include a simple, but lovely dialogue to dramatize joyful mortification and self-abasement, *Della pazienzia, dove è perfetta letizia, scrive santo Francesco*:

Quando noi giungneremo a Santa Maria degli Angeli, cosí bagnati per la piova e agghiacciati per lo freddo, e infangati di loto e afflitti di fame, e picchieremo la porta del luogo, e 'l portinaio verrà adirato e dirà: "Chi siete voi?", e noi diremo: "Noi siamo due de' vostri frati", e colui dirà: "Voi non dite vero, anzi siete due ribaldi che andate ingannando il mondo e rubando le limosine de' poveri, andate via", e non ci aprirà, e faràcci stare di fuori alla neve e all'acqua, col freddo e colla fame, infino alla notte, allora, se noi tante ingiurie e tanta crudeltà e tanti commiati sosterremo pazientemente sanza turbazioni e sanza mormorazione, e penseremo umilemente e caritativamente che quel portinaio veracemente ci cognosca, e che Iddio il faccia parlare contra noi: o frate Leone, scrivi che ivi è perfetta letizia.

Imagine, continues St. Francis, that we knock again, and the porter drives us away with his fists; yet again, and he beats us back, down into the snow and mud, with a knotted club. If we endure patiently, recalling Christ's suffering — in this is perfect happiness. For the greatest gift we have from Him is to conquer ourselves and share in the tribulation of the cross.[10] The virtue Aquinas called «praiseworthy self-abasement», risen to unprecedented prominence by the middle of the fourteenth century, finds here its Franciscan *exemplum* in an imaginary, rhetorical drama of rejection and brutal outcasting. Humility so understood seems to infuse as well the last story of the *Decameron*.

---

low-seated Madonnas that evolved from Simone Martini's prototype. L. BATTAGLIA RICCI gives good background on Dominican culture in Tuscany during Boccaccio's lifetime, but she comes to conclusions very different from mine: Boccaccio wrote the *Decameron* in open polemic with the Dominicans and their penitential literature. See *Ragionare nel giardino, cit.*, esp. p. 90 and n. 69; p. 178.
    [10] G. D. BONINO, ed., *I fioretti di San Francesco*, Turin, Einaudi, 1964, pp. 25-27. I would like to thank P. M. Forni for suggesting this passage in the *Fioretti* as an example of praiseworthy humiliation.

The subject itself, trials supernaturally visited on a mysteriously chosen mortal, has roots that reach deep into universal narrative. But Boccaccio actualizes the archetype. An impossible plot becomes believable, in the realm of fiction and readers, because its coordinates have taken on realistic qualities.

While keeping expressive formulas typical of a magic-wand-world, Boccaccio gives the story a specific geography in the Piedmontese Marquisate of Saluzzo (Bologna and Rome lie in the wings), and he populates it with a cast of characters positioned from end to end in the social hierarchy of his historical era: the Pope, Gualtieri, the Marquis; his off-stage relatives, the Counts of Panago; Griselda, the peasant herdgirl; her rustic father, Giannucolo. For the matrimonial union that takes place, there is plausible need, an heir to assure political stability. Even in the wedding, crudely unceremonial as it seems today — a bride stripped naked, no benefit of clergy — and Gualtieri's repudiation of his spouse, a woman reified as his possession except for her dowry, there are signs typical of fourteenth-century custom in Florentine marriage rites.[11] Just

---

[11] K. MALONE, *Patient Griselda*, «Romanic Review», XX, 1929, pp. 340-345, put the source of this story «in fairyland», arguing an oriental archetype. Others, such as W. A. CATE, *The Problem of the Origin of the Griselda Tale*, «Studies in Philology», XXIX, 1932, pp. 389-405, have pointed out its resemblance to the Cupid and Psyche tale. G. BÀRBERI-SQUAROTTI, *L'ambigua sociologia di Griselda*, «Annali Facoltà di Magistero Università di Palermo», 1970, pp. 32-75, shows how Boccaccio achieves a double-speak («un parlare doppio») that pairs the language and logic of fable with those of the Christian relationship between God and his creature, but concludes that he deliberately undermines the magical and hagiographic modes by squaring the story with sociological reality: it marks the rise of the lower classes through intermarriage. C. KLAPISCH-ZUBER, *Zacharie, ou le père évincé. Les Rites nuptiaux toscans entre Giotto et le Concile de Trente*, in «Annales. Economies. Sociétés. Civilisations», VI, 1979, pp. 1216-1243, documents mutual consent, usually pronounced in the absence of a priest but often the presence of the bride's father, as the necessary, sufficient condition of legal marriage in Tuscany during the 1300's and 1400's. In *Le Complexe de Griselda. Dot et dons de mariage au Quattrocento*, «Mélanges de l'Ecole française de Rome, Moyen Age-Temps Modernes», XCIV, 1982, pp. 7-43, she has also shown how the bridegroom, who must clothe his new wife in a ritual of 'vestition', often reclaimed his marriage gifts to her, even — and notably — the wedding ring, because wide circulation of such objects through repeated use in a large family symbolically strengthened its unity. Bridal vestiture and the husband's repossession of what he had given, both emphasized in Boccaccio's plot, confirm as well the husband's authority to possess absolutely his wife. Klapisch-Zuber's premise is worth stating: «Boccaccio has rationalized the supernatural elements of the old tale by lending the Marquis of Saluzzo — a plausible avatar of the monster or of the being come from beyond the grave to marry a mortal woman — the gestures, or I am tempted to say, the ritual automation of a husband from his times. By historicizing the supernatuaral gifts of the monstrous groom, he has adapted the tale to contemporary taste while respecting its structure». See now for this material C. KLAPISCH-ZUBER, *Women, Family, and Ritual in Renaissance Italy*, trans. L. C. COCHRANE, Chicago, University of Chicago Press, 1985. A militant feminist rebuttal to the French social historian, provocative but not to my mind persuasive, comes from Cristelle L. Baskins, *Griselda, or the Renaissance Bride Stripped Bare by her Bachelor in Tuscan 'Cassone painting'*, «Stanford Italian Review», X (1991), pp. 153-175.

Fig. 1. Andrea di Buonaiuto da Firenze, Triumph of St. Thomas (fresco), 1366-68. Florence, Santa Maria Novella, Strozzi Chapel.

Fig. 2. GIOVANNI DEL BIONDO, St. Thomas Aquinas flanked by Charity and Chastity (fresco), ca. 1354. Florence, Santa Maria Novella, Strozzi Chapel.

Fig. 11. GIOTTO, The Last Judgment. Detail: Devils dumping souls headfirst into Hell (fresco), ca. 1305. Padua, Scrovegni Chapel.

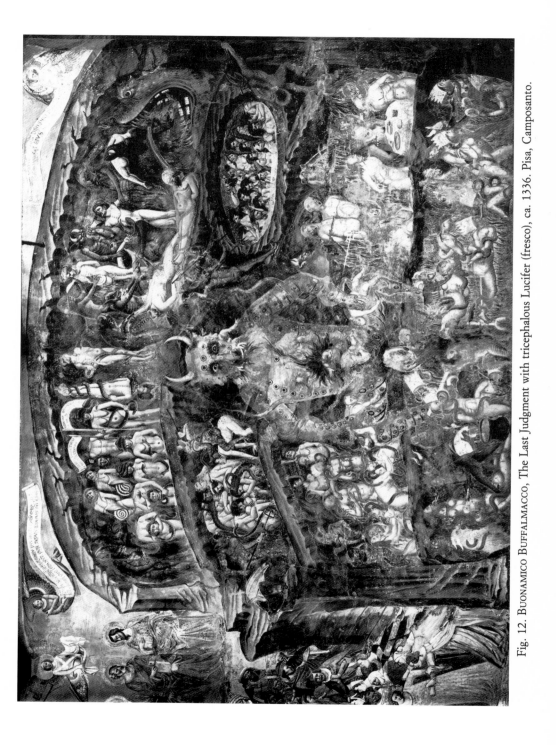

Fig. 12. Buonamico Buffalmacco, The Last Judgment with tricephalous Lucifer (fresco), ca. 1336. Pisa, Camposanto.

Fig. 13. BUONAMICO BUFFALMACCO, The Last Judgment. Detail: Bearlike head of Lucifer (fresco), ca. 1336. Pisa, Camposanto.

Fig. 14. ORCAGNA and JACOPO DI CIONE. Madonna and Child
with Angels (wood panel), ca. 1370. Washington, National
Gallery of Art, Samuel H. Kress Collection.

Fig. 15. Nardo di Cione (d. 1365). Madonna of Humility enthroned with St. Gregory and the Prophet Job (triptych). Florence, Santa Croce.

as Boccaccio anchors this tale, at its literal level, to societal structures of his own times, so he may have had in mind for it a moral sense suggested by those contemporary ideals of virtue that stressed the value of Humility.

Beginning with her earliest published belle-lettristic admirer, Griselda has seen a succession of allegorizers. Petrarch stressed her similarities to Job, concluding that such heroic constancy should give Christian readers the courage to endure trials visited by God. Recent scholars have advanced identifications of Griselda as Christological, or alternatively, Marian. A keeper of sheep, whose father, Giannucolo ('Little John'), is onomastic kin to the Baptist and whose own name can be interpreted as meaning 'annointed image', she is the sacrificial victim «needed to restore her surrounding community to the harmony and happiness emblematic of a Golden Age condition of existence». Griselda's virtue, selectively highlighted, echoes the «Ecce ancilla domini» of Luke 1:38, and recalls the Queen of Heaven whom Dante addresses at the end of his pilgrimage, «umile e alta più che creatura» (*Paradiso* XXXIII 1-2). Dante's vision of Mary face to face fulfills her *figura* as he had earlier enshrined it, in marble relief on the shelf of Pride in Purgatory. The first exemplum of Humility, she appears at the moment of the Annunciation: «iv'era imaginata quella / ch'ad aprir l'alto amor volse la chiave; / e avea in atto impressa esta favella / "*Ecce ancilla Dei*"», (*Purgatorio* X 41-44).

The long-suffering wife's likeness to Job, Christ, and Mary implies a common denominator. It is her Humility, of which all three Biblical persons are types, as Passavanti's guidebook recognizes. Orcagna's brother Nardo di Cione (active 1343-1365), illustrates the kind of religious climate that flourished under Passavanti's spiritual leadership in a painting of the Madonna preserved at Santa Croce. Mary's posture and companions, moreover, put her very close to the spirit of Boccaccio's Griselda. Although enthroned, Mary sits with veiled head humbly bent. Flanking her are St. Gregory, he who saw all the other virtues without Humility as so much dust thrown into the wind, and the prophet Job, an Old Testament model for Humility, patience, and obedience. As an ensemble, the triptych is an allegory of Humility (fig. 15).[12]

---

[12] G. MAZZOTTA, *The World at Play*, pp. 123-124, cites Biblical parallels between the Book of Job and Boccaccio's phrasings in *Decameron* X 10. M. COTTINO-JONES sees Griselda's chrism and prelapsarian purity in '*Fabula*' vs. '*figura*', cit., V. BRANCA, *Boccaccio medievale*, cit., pp. 17-18, mentions her Marian nature. Cf. G. BOCCACCIO, *Esposizioni* II 2, 20: «Gran forze son quelle dell'umiltà nel cospetto di Dio [...] sì come essa medesima Vergine testimonia nel suo cantico, quando dice: "*Respexit humilitatem ancille sue*"; per che da questa parola degnamente essa medesima segue: "*Deposuit potentes de sede et exaltavit humiles*"». On Nardo's panel see R. FREMANTLE, *Florentine Gothic Painters*, cit., pp. 147-148 and fig. 315.

Among that Dominican preacher's expert witnesses, another, not yet mentioned, further corroborates the particular nature of Griselda's allusive character. I refer to St. Benedict, whose Rule, cited at length by Passavanti, articulates twelve steps or degrees in Humility against Pride. Excluding those that apply strictly to the monastic life, they comment aptly on Boccaccian Griselda.

At the first step one must show Humility with heart and body; the second, say few words; the third, not laugh readily; the fourth, keep still until spoken to. Continuing by degrees, one must believe himself baser than everyone else, be patient in harsh things, be obedient, do only the will of others, and fear the Lord.[13]

Boccaccio presents Griselda practicing Humility with heart and body by performing lowly tasks: when first sighted, she is carrying water from a well («con acqua tornava dalla fonte»); upon Gualtieri's repudiation she readily resumes her poor existence as a shepherd («guardiana di pecore»); when summoned back to prepare for his 'second wife', she sets her hands to hard chores of housekeeping, «come se una piccola fanticella della casa fosse».

Never betraying contrary emotion, she speaks only when spoken to, except, significantly, when she greets the new bride. Her statements are also strikingly terse, although again there is an exception, when she asks permission to return to her father clothed at least in a shift. Recurrent in her language is the noun 'onore', and properly so, for Aristotle and Aquinas had taught that «magnanimity has to do with honor» because the magnanimous never deem themselves worthy of honor above their deserts. The first words we hear from her are in response to her lord, and they set the pattern for subsequent dialogue, in which she reiterates her unworthiness for such a high honor as being his wife and her complete subjection to his will: «Signor mio, fa di me quello che tu credi che più tuo *onore* o consolazion sia, ché io sarò di tutto contenta, sì come colei che conosco che io sono da men di loro e che io non era degna di questo *onore*»; «Signor mio, pensa di contentar te e di sodisfare al piacer tuo e di me non avere pensiere alcuno, per ciò che niuna cosa m'è cara se non

---

[13] Benedict's twelve steps to humility against pride, as listed by Passavanti, are: 1) show humility with heart and body, eyes to the ground; 2) say few, reasonable words, and say them not loudly; 3) do not laugh readily; 4) keep silent until spoken to; 5) keep the rule of the monastery; 6) believe and say you are more vile than the others; 7) confess and believe you are worthless and unworthy of everything; 8) confess your sins; 9) have patience in harsh, hard things; 10) be obedient; 11) delight not in having your own way; 12) fear the Lord. For a modern presentation of the text, see E. HEUFELDER, O.S.B, *The Way to God According to the Rule of St. Benedict*, Kalamazoo, Mich., Cistercian Publications, 1983.

quanto io la veggo a te piacere»; «Signor mio, io conobbi sempre la mia bassa condizione alla vostra nobiltà in alcun modo non converirsi»; «Signor mio, io son presta e apparecchiata».[14]

Hand in hand with this Humility comes the wifely virtue so admired by Renaissance husbands: perfect, unswerving Obedience. Like patience, it is integral to Humility by St. Benedict's standards, being enjoined by the tenth rule. Passavanti hints at the reason for an affinity between Humility and Obedience when he asserts that prompt Obedience is just the opposite of Adam and Eve's disobedience through Pride. Perhaps he had in mind Augustine's more extended argument on the theological nexus at which Humility, Obedience, and Pride converge. It belongs to the discussion of the Fall in his *City of God*. Dante would capitalize on it for his dialogue with Adam in *Paradiso* XXVI: «non il gustar del legno / fu per sé la cagion di tanto essilio, / ma solamente il trapassar del segno».

Sin came into the world, setting the flesh against the spirit, not for a trivial offense of eating, but for transgression of our creator's command:

in God's command obedience was enjoined, and this virtue is, in a sense, the mother and guardian of all virtues in a rational creature, inasmuch as man has been naturally so created that it is advantageous for him to be submissive but ruinous to follow his own will and not the will of the creator.

By pleasing themselves, not their creator, Adam and Eve were guilty of perverse self-exaltation, synonymous with Pride, «the start of all sin».

It is a good thing to have an aspiring mind, yet aspiring not to oneself, which belongs to pride, but to God, which belongs to obedience, and obedience can belong only to the humble.[15]

Obedience then, like Humility, opposes the arch sin, Pride. In the dynamics of the *Decameron*, Griselda's polar opposite is Ser Cepparello. Protagonist of the first tale, he is the most evil man who ever lived.

---

[14] For the connection between magnanimity and honor, see *Ethics* 1123a and *Commentary* 743. In the brevity of her speech, as in significant other features (some noted by G. BÀRBERI-SQUAROTTI, *L'ambigua sociologia di Griselda, cit.*), she is the opposite of Ghismonda (*Decameron* IV 1), a figure immortalized in her flowing oratory. Concerning the range of discursive possibilities in the *Decameron*, from silence to sonorous oratory, see ch. 5 above.

[15] ST. AUGUSTINE, *City of God* XIV 12: «oboedientia commendata est in praecepto, quae virtus in creatura rationali mater quodam modo est omnium custosque virtutum, quando quidem modo est omnium custosque virtutum, quando quidem ita facta est ut ei subditam esse sit utile, perniciosum autem suam, non eius a quo creata est facere voluntatem»; XIV 13: «Bonum est enim sursum habere cor, non tamen ad se ipsum, quod est superbiae, sed ad Dominum, quod est oboedientiae, quae nisi humilium non potest esse».

Heroine of the last, she is the world's most saintly woman. Since obedient Humility is her distinguishing virtue, his diabolical vices emerge by theological contrast as those sins of the flesh that Augustine traces to Pride. St. Paul's Epistle to the Galatians (5:19-21) furnishes that Father with a profile in evil for which Boccaccio's mendacious notary is every bit the match. «Now the works of the flesh are plain: fornication, impurity, licentiousness, idolatry, sorcery, enmity, strife, jealousy, anger, dissension, party spirit, envy, drunkenness, carousing, and the like». They are vices that have primacy in the Devil, «the father of lies», and all originate in Pride: «the head and source of all these evils is pride».[16]

The apostate Cepparello, whose name hinges on an Adamic allusion,[17] answers to repeated counts of Pride in its medieval ramifications. By St. Benedict's scale, this 'Old Man' scores high for 'non-humility'. He speaks much and boasts. He confesses his sins insincerely and most elaborately, the opposite of Rule Nine's precept on patience: «nelle cose aspre e dure abbracciare la pazienza; ed è contrario al nono grado della superbia, che è confessare il peccato non sinceramente e semplicemente, ma a malizia, per iscampare della pena debita per lo peccato».[18] Cepparello, rebel to God's law, has lived a lifetime of evil, freely following his own will. Instead of fear of the Lord, he has the habit of sin, which causes disdain for God and his commandments.

Passavanti, adducing Peter Lombard, sharpens our perspective on this worst possible of men.

Non è maggior peccato, che apostatare da Dio, che ciò fa fare il vizio della superbia (apostare è propriamente partirsi dalla religione e non volere esser suggetto ne obbediente alla regola, ch'altri ha promessa) così fa la superbia, che non vuole osservare gli ordinamenti della Cristiana religione, né esser suggetta alla volontà d'Iddio, la quale è la regola, secondo la quale si dee vivere. Anzi spergia Iddio, e' suoi comandamenti.[19]

Griselda, the heroine and *figura humilitatis* of Boccaccio's final tale, responds to Ser Cepparello, the 'father of lies' and *figura superbiae* who falls prostrate unto death in the first. His elaborate, comic, confessional

---

[16] *Ibid.*, XIV 2: «Manifesta autem sunt opera carnis, quae sunt fornicationes, inmunditiae, luxuria, idolorum servitus, veneficia, inimicitiae, contentiones, aemulationes, animositates, dissensiones, haereses, invidiae, ebrietates, comisationes et his similia»; XIV 3: «quorum omnium malorum caput atque origo superbia est, quae sine carne regnat in diabolo».

[17] G. MAZZOTTA, *The 'Decameron' and the Marginality of Literature, cit.*

[18] J. PASSAVANTI, *Specchio della vera penitenza, cit.*, pp. 190-191.

[19] *Ibid.*, p. 161.

histrionics belong to the book's infernal, 'fetid' beginning. Her simple, sober, enduring sense of duty — what Petrarch admired as «matters pious and grave» [quedam pia et gravia] — quietly earn Griselda's triumph, which crowns the idealistic plane of the *Decameron*'s concluding day.[20]

At issue in Griselda's end position is a paradox central to the synoptic Gospels. Illustrated by the parable of the vineyard, it is Christ's word on admission to Heaven, a Kingdom where earthly values are reversed. «Many that are first will be last, and the last first», Matthew records (19:30), and Mark is mindful of the same message (9:35), «If anyone would be first, he must be last of all and servant of all». Griselda, lowliest of all Boccaccio's characters, acts out the axiom. In an exemplary Christian sense — and in narrative placement within the one hundred tales — she is the last who will be first.

Taken together, Cepparello and Griselda attest to a Gospel truth: «whosoever exalteth himself shall be abased; and he that humbleth himself shall be exalted» (Luke 15:11).

Other contrastive analogies between *Decameron* X 10 and I 1 appear if we extend our territory, annexing for purposes of argument Day One's Introduction. Here themes that couple beginning and end are preservation of the race; the threat posed to such vital continuity by 'bestiality'; woman's nature and her need for masculine guidance; necessity for disciplined submission to the hierarchical social order. In this broader context, perhaps Gualtieri's «matta bestialità» is more than an irascible appetite that Griselda's fortitude finally tames.[21] His short-sighted ab-

---

[20] Although Deconstruction denies ascensional dynamics in the *Decameron* (thus, e.g., G. MAZZOTTA, *The World at Play*, cit.), literary historians see it clearly. BRANCA's overarching view best represents the latter, in his vision of a broad movement from vice to virtue, from comically humble to tragically sublime, described in *Boccaccio medievale*, cit. Among scholars in this country, E. KERN persuasively outlined an allusive progression from Hell to Heaven in *The Gardens of the 'Decameron' Cornice*, cit. Comedy as 'stinking' at the outset is from Dante's lexicon in the *Letter to Can Grande*. The Cepparello-Griselda polarity is by now, of course, a commonplace of Decameronian criticism. Cf. V. BRANCA, *Boccaccio medievale*, cit., pp. 95 ff.; J. POWERS SERAFINI-SAULI, *Giovanni Boccaccio*, Boston, Twayne, 1982, p. 84.

[21] Animals inhabit three panels that depict Griselda's story by the Griselda Master in the London National Gallery (c.1500). They include a bear chained to a column beside Gualtieri. Perhaps the artist had in mind lore of the bestiaries, where that animal can imply irascibility. The irascible appetite, clearly under scrutiny in Boccaccio's tale, as G. MAZZOTTA has noticed (*The World at Play*, cit., pp. 127-128), is a force strongly felt all across the *Decameron*, most often in connection with Filostrato. See above, ch. 4. In much of Boccaccio's Italian fiction the irascible and concupiscible appetites operate powerfully. These medieval psychological agents figure significantly, for instance, in his epic. See above, ch. 1. J. L. SMARR richly documents examples of the passions contending with reason in the chronology she traces of *Boccaccio and Fiammetta*, cit., *passim*. Gualtieri's fierceness, astrologically considered, is a Martian trait tamed by his wife's Venusian docility. Approaching I 1 and X 10 via *Inferno* XI 79-84, M.

sorption in hunting and fowling shuts out any thought of marriage and children. Although Dioneo jestingly approves, it is behavior on which Boccaccio seems to frown. Rhetorical repetition casts in negative grammar the consequences of this bachelor's sporting life: «essendo senza *moglie* e senza *figliuoli*, in niuna altra cosa il suo tempo spendeva che in uccellare e in cacciare, né di prender *moglie* né d'aver *figliuoli* alcun pensiero avea». Young Gualtieri is foolishly denying his mortality in a way that recalls Pampinea's plea for flight from the plague: «crediamo la nostra vita con più forti catene esser legata al nostro corpo che quella degli altri sia, e così di niuna cosa curar dobbiamo la quale abbia forza d'offenderla? Noi erriamo, noi siamo ingannate: che *bestialità* è la nostra se così crediamo?» (I Intro., 63-64).

Pampinea's ladies will not, however, leave the city alone, since Filomena points out that women without men are «mobili, riottose, sospettose, pusillanime e paurose», remarks to which Elissa adds that men are «truly the head of women»: «Veramente gli uomini sono delle femine capo». Griselda, whose name is ironically similar to Criseida, ficklest of all Boccaccio's heroines,[22] counters Filomena's every criticism and embodies Elissa's Pauline wisdom. A paragon of constancy, courageous and unquestioning, she is absolutely subject to her husband's absolute power.

Griselda, of course, is not the only one of the two who obeys. Gualtieri also bows to another will — that of his subjects — and bends to the yoke of matrimony. When individual and society come into conflict, the former must yield to protect the latter, whose future rests on perpetuation of the species. Thus is preserved the Aristotelian chain of command on which the politics of the Decameronian microcosm are posited. This hierarchy expects subjects to obey their ruler, members of a household to obey its head, the wife to obey her husband, the appetites to obey the intellect, the body to obey the soul. William Bouwsma, from a political perspective, powerfully states the hypostasis:

the *respublica christiana* was necessarily organized as a hierarchical system in which lower ends were subordinated to higher, and inferior powers to superior; authority in the entire structure descended from above [...]. Self-determination,

SHERBERG reported a significant tie between Ciappelletto's 'malizia' and Gualtieri's «matta bestialità», the latter synonymous with brute violence, in *Boccaccio, Dioneo, and 'matta bestialità'*, paper presented for the American Boccaccio Association at the Modern Language Association Meeting, Chicago, 1985. C. HAINES, proposing another connection between the Introduction to Day I and X 10, suggests an analogy between the plague, «an appalling cavalcade of horrors» visited by God on man, and Gualtieri's tests of his wife, in *Patient Griselda and 'matta bestialitade'*, «Quaderni d'Italianistica», VI, 1985, pp. 233-240.

[22] V. BRANCA, *Decameron, cit.*, X 10, 16 and n. 3, p. 1556.

in this view, could only appear, in the deepest sense, as a violation of the very structure of reality, and political duty appeared to consist only in patient submission and obedience. Man, in this system, was always and necessarily a subject; he could not be a citizen.[23]

Boccaccio dramatizes these relationships in a Tuscan fairy tale about the fiefdom of Saluzzo, its Marquis, and his model wife. It is anachronistic misreading to criticize a *novella* so deliberately stylized — and stylized its structure remains in spite of details consistent with plausibility — by faulting its author on the count of psychological realism. Boccaccio certainly could probe the psyche when he chose, as the romance of Madonna Fiammetta amply attests, but that is not here his concern. Whatever we chose to call his Griselda tale, — *exemplum, mysterium, fabula*, or allegory — perhaps he himself, choosing from the four possible terms in his Proem, would have labelled it a 'parabola'.[24]

In her goodness Griselda is as exaggerated as is in evil Ciappelletto, «il piggiore uomo forse che mai nascesse». Both, by Judith Serafini-Sauli's sensible reading,[25] are a «*reductio ad absurdam*», characters whom Boccaccio pushes «beyond credible limits» for the joy of narrative flourish and places at either end of his work «as emblems of the extreme limits within which human experience on earth is contained». Through Griselda's example at end position on Day X — under Panfilo's rule of Reason, the rubric of Magnificence, and the 'silent' theme of Humility — virtue *in extremis* completes the anthology's structural program.

Beneath the prevailing winds of post-Romanticism, in the gusts of Deconstruction so fashionable today, it is *de rigueur* to doubt that Boccaccio could ever have intended anything very seriously in the *Deca-*

---

[23] W. BOUWSMA, *Venice and the Defense of Republican Liberty*, Berkeley, University of California Press, 1971, p. 6. Dante's *De monarchia* makes a good, representative statement on the Aristotelian political hierarchy. How Boccaccio's *brigata* re-establishes ideal political order R. RAMAT outlines in *Indicazioni per una lettura del 'Decameron', cit.* Cf. also M. COTTINO-JONES, for whom the idea is a thesis in her book *Order from Chaos, cit.* E. KRIEGER, *Re-reading Allegory: The Clerk's Tale*, «Paunch», XL-XLI, 1975, pp. 116-135, finds the hierarchy built into the story as told by Chaucer, who «uses the hierarchic structure of allegory to defend the hierarchic structure of society and to attach an idealized eternality to political institutions from which the feudal ruling class derived its power and attendant benefits».

[24] E. DE' NEGRI referred to the tale as an *exemplum* and a 'mystery' in *The Legendary Style of the 'Decameron'*, «Romanic Review», XLIII, 1952, pp. 166-184; rpt. abr. in *Critical Perspectives on the 'Decameron'*, ed. R DOMBROSKI, London, Hodder and Stoughton, 1976, pp. 82-98; M. COTTINO-JONES used the term fable, in *'Fabula' vs. 'Figura', cit.*; Petrarch was the first literary critic to consider it allegory. Recall *Decameron, cit.*, Proem 13: «intendo di raccontare cento novelle, o favole o parabole o istorie che dire le vogliamo».

[25] J. POWERS SERAFINI-SAULI, *Giovanni Boccaccio, cit.*, pp. 83-84.

meron, excepting, of course, his metapoesis and constant self-irony. So we can be confidently told that the last Day in the *Decameron* does not, in fact, mark a progression to a nobler esthetic and ethical plane. Is not good evidence for this conveniently at hand in Griselda's suffering and the coarsely lascivious remarks with which Dioneo judges her? As a heroine she is so ridiculously exaggerated that her story almost has to undercut sardonically any pretended movement toward perfection on the *Decameron*'s concluding Day.[26]

Yet the *brigata*'s journey has an ascensional direction, as Edith Kern should have persuaded us, and apart from the gardens, there are other symbolically resonant elements in the frame tale to suggest rising moral action.[27] Further, by the precepts of Ciceronian rhetoric, which Boccaccio knew well and practiced, the end is always reserved for what is most important, since that is the part that we best remember. So the treatise *Ad Herennium* can advocate this strategy: «since what has been said last is easily committed to memory, it is useful, when ceasing to speak, to leave some very strong argument fresh in the hearer's mind». Dante had restated the rule in his *Convivio* II 8, 2: «sempre quello che massimamente dire intende lo dicitore sì dee riservare di dietro; però che quello che ultimamente si dice, più rimane ne l'animo de lo uditore».[28]

Petrarch, too, naturally understood this dictum. His rhetorically elevated *canzone* to the Virgin, rounding off the *Rime sparse*, permits the book to close on a higher, sacred note, one doubly tagged as 'final' since

---

[26] Boccaccio 'metaliteratus' is an epithet implicit in the approaches of G. ALMANSI, *The Writer as Liar, cit.*; M. MARCUS, *An Allegory of Form, cit.*; and G. MAZZOTTA, *The World at Play, cit.* Typical of many readers is R. KIRKPATRICK, who argues the open-endedness of Dioneo's presence as a narrator and believes that the *Decameron* ends with debate rather than closure: *The Griselda Story in Boccaccio, Petrarch and Chaucer*, in *Chaucer and the Italian Trecento*, ed. P. BOITANI, *cit.*, pp. 231-248.

[27] E. KERN, *The Gardens in the 'Decameron' Cornice, cit.*, and ch. 4 above.

[28] [CICERO], *Ad Herenniium, cit.*,: III 10, 18: «quoniam nuperrime dictum facile memoriae mandatur, utile est, cum dicere desinamus, recentem aliquam relinquere in animis auditorum bene firmam argumentationem».

The earliest surviving inventory of books in Boccaccio's library (A. MAZZA, *L'inventario della 'parva libraria', cit.*) lists copies of Cicero's treatises and the Pseudo-Ciceronian *Rhetorica ad Herennium*. S. WENZEL, *Chaucer's Parson's Tale 'every tales strength'*, in *Europäische Lehrdichtung. Festschrift für Walter Naumann zum 70 Geburtstag*, ed. H. G. ROETZER and H. WALZ, Darmstad, Wissenschaftliche Buchgesellschaft, 1981, pp. 86-98, recalls *Troilus and Criseyde* II 260 («th'ende is every tales strengthe») and advances the case for «a pattern of cloture» in the *Canterbury Tales*, where the Parson agrees «to knytte up all this feeste», as it were, «wrap up» the merriment. S. S. ALLEN, *The Griselda Tale and the Portrayal of Women in the 'Decameron'*, «Philological Quarterly», LVI, 1977, pp. 1-13, intuits the importance of *Decameron* X 10's end position, but decides for a disappointingly antihistorical interpretation: «The hundredth tale is an ironic argument for women's liberation», six centuries ahead of its time, like madonna Filippa's (VI 7) defense of adultery.

it copies the template fashioned by Dante, who had saved St. Bernard's prayer to the Virgin for the culminating moments of his *Comedy*. His earlier epistolary anthology, the *Familiares*, had ended grandly with a sequence of ten letters to the ancients, and his collection from old age was to have concluded, by symmetrical opposition, with the letter he wrote to Posterity. That self-portrait, which alone would have constituted an eighteenth book and epilogue for the *Seniles*, survives only in partial form, but the semi-final seventeenth book of the later letters has come down to us complete. Dedicated as a unit to Giovanni Boccaccio, its capstone is the Griselda story, adapted into Latin for broad dissemination.

Petrarch singled out that tale, he says, because he had scanned the *Decameron* with special attention to its start and finish, «as readers are wont to do». Boccaccio's correspondent, though, was self-consciously playing an 'end game' when he chose *Seniles* XVII as the setting for his version of the last tale in the *Decameron*. In that effort, we can now see a tacit tribute to his friend's entire anthology.[29]

A final gloss on Boccaccio's Griselda may fittingly close these remarks. It is from the *Praise of Obedience* found in a work conceived in Florence about 1350, at a period contemporary with the *Decameron*:

It is not without reason that I should like to urge people to embrace and exhibit obedience with all their strength; by obedience ferocity of spirit is tamed; humility of mind is revealed; vices are restrained; virtues are exalted; order is maintained in all things; the sword of justice lies idle; by obedience kingdoms flourish, cities grow, and peace of mind is preserved.

The book to which these words belong is the *De casibus virorum illustrium*.[30] Its author is Giovanni Boccaccio, to whom I have given the last word on the last tale in the *Decameron*.

---

[29] E. KADISH, *Petrarch's Griselda: An English Translation, cit.*; A. MIDDLETON, *The Clerk and his Tale*, «Studies in Chaucer», II, 1980, pp. 121-150.

[30] G. BOCCACCIO, *De casibus, cit.*, II 2, 4: *Obedientie commendatio*: «Quam non immerito suaserim amplexandam et maioribus totis exhibendam viribus: ea quippe domatur ferocitas animorum, ostenditur mentis humilitas, comprimuntur vitia, exhilarantur virtutes, ordo servatur in cunctis et redditur ociosus iustitie gladius: hac regna florent, ampliantur urbes, et mentium tranquillitas servatur».

LIST OF ILLUSTRATIONS

Fig. 1. ANDREA DI BUONAIUTO DA FIRENZE, Triumph of St. Thomas (fresco), 1366-68. Florence, Santa Maria Novella, Strozzi Chapel. Photo: Alinari/Art Resource, New York.

Fig. 2. GIOVANNI DEL BIONDO, St. Thomas Aquinas flanked by Charity and Chastity (fresco), ca. 1354. Florence, Santa Maria Novella, Strozzi Chapel. Photo: Alinari/Art Resource, New York.

Fig. 3. ANDREA ORCAGNA, Christ in Glory with the Virgin, Saints Michael, Catherine, Thomas Aquinas, Peter, John the Baptist, Lawrence, Paul. 1357. Florence, Santa Maria Novella, Strozzi Chapel, Altarpice. Photo: Alinari/Art Resource, New York.

Fig. 4. The *Brigata* with Queen Pampinea and Tindaro on the bagpipes. Paris, Bibliothèque Nationale, *Decameron*, Ms. It. 63 (1427), fol. 10 v. Photo: Bibliothèque Nationale.

Fig. 5a. GIOTTO, Prudence (grisaille), ca. 1305. Padua, Scrovegni Chapel. Photo: Alinari/Art Resource, New York.

Fig. 5b. GIOTTO, Foolishness (grisaille), ca. 1305. Padua, Scrovegni Chapel. Photo: Alinari/Art Resource, New York.

Fig. 6a. GIOTTO, Hope (grisaille), ca. 1305. Padua, Scrovegni Chapel. Photo: Alinari/Art Resource, New York.

Fig. 6b. GIOTTO, Despair (grisaille), ca. 1305. Padua, Scrovegni Chapel. Photo: Alinari/Art Resource, New York.

Fig. 7a. ANDREA ORCAGNA, Fortitude (marble bas-relief), 1359. Florence, Orsanmichele, Tabernacle of the Madonna. Photo: Alinari/Art Resource, New York.

Fig. 7b. ANDREA ORCAGNA, Humility (marble bas-relief), 1359. Florence, Orsanmichele, Tabernacle of the Madonna. Photo: Alinari/Art Resource, New York.

Fig. 8. ANDREA PISANO, Charity and Humility below scenes of John the Baptist (bronze panels), 1331. Florence, San Giovanni Baptistry, south doors. Photo: Alinari Anderson/Art Resource, New York.

Fig. 9. The Last Judgment (mosaic), ca. 1290. Florence, San Giovanni Baptistry, cupola. Photo: Alinari/Art Resource, New York.

Fig. 10. GIOTTO, The Last Judgment with Lucifer gobbling souls (fresco), ca. 1305. Padua, Scrovegni Chapel. Photo: Istituto Centrale per il Catalogo e la Documentazione.

Fig. 11. GIOTTO, The Last Judgment. Detail: Devils dumping souls headfirst into Hell (fresco), ca. 1305. Padua, Scrovegni Chapel. Photo: Istituto Centrale per il Catalogo e la Documentazione.

Fig. 12. BUONAMICO BUFFALMACCO, The Last Judgment with tricephalous Lucifer (fresco), ca. 1336. Pisa, Camposanto. Photo: Istituto Centrale per il Catalogo e la Documentazione.

Fig. 13. BUONAMICO BUFFALMACCO, The Last Judgment. Detail: Bearlike head of Lucifer (fresco), ca. 1336. Pisa, Camposanto. Photo: Istituto Centrale per il Catalogo e la Documentazione.

Fig. 14. ORCAGNA and JACOPO DI CIONE. Madonna and Child with Angels (wood panel), ca. 1370. Washington, National Gallery of Art, Samuel H. Kress Collection. Photo: National Gallery of Art.

Fig. 15. NARDO DI CIONE (d. 1365). Madonna of Humility enthroned with St. Gregory and the Prophet Job (triptych). Florence, Santa Croce. Photo: Alinari/Art Resource, New York.

INDEX

Iconography, Numerology, Proper Names

Misia (*Dec.*) 159.
misogyny 84-85, 117-129.
Mitridanes (*Dec.* X 3) 142, 144.
Momigliano, A. 250n.
Monferrato 154, 182.
Monges, R. 118n.
Monte Nero (*Dec.*) 154, 179.
Months
— April 41
— May 28
Mopsa (*Com. ninfe*) 97, 149, 150, 156.
Morabito, R. 249n.
Morettini, M. A. 127n.
mouse 230.
Moutier, I. 57n.
Mozley, J. H. 123.
Murphy, J. 180n, 188n.
Murrin, M. 111n, 112n.
Musa, M. 176n, 177n, 238n.
Muscetta, C. 56n, 68n, 89n, 120n, 133n, 184n, 196n, 239n.
Muses 17, 24, 34, 45, 50.
Mussini Sacchi, M. P. 124n.
Myrrha 126.
mythography 39, 84.

Naples 121.
Nardelli, F. Petrucci 64n, 70.
Nardo di Cione 10, 257, 268, fig. 15.
Natan 142, 144.
Nature (goddess) 75.
Neifile (*Dec.*) 132, 149, 153, 157, 161-164, 165, 168, 204-206, 250.
Neoplatonism 93, 110, 113, 115, 116, 159.
Neri, F. 201n.
Nero 112.
Neuss, W. 177n.
Nicholas III, Pope 222.
Nichols, F. M. 248n.
Ninetta (*Dec.* IV 3) 141.
Niobe 25, 33, 35, 49.
Nisus and Euryalus 241-242.
Noakes, S. 38n, 129n.
Nobility 66, 75.
Nolan, B. 77n.
Number Symbolism: gender of numbers 42-43 and n, 50; numerical composition 18-19, 25ff, 48n, 102, 114n; Pythagorean number theory 29, 33, 42, 48.
— 1 (monad) 42.
— 2 (dyad) 101-102; first even number 42; dualism and dualities 101, 110.
— 3 (triad) 104 and n, 109-110, 146-147; first odd number 42.

Diana-Luna-Proserpina as threefold deity 27.
figures on fountain (*Am. vis.*) 24.
kinds of love/friendship 23-24, 100, 104, 243.
man's threefold nature 23n.
Maria d'Aquino sighted three times (*Am. vis.*) 90.
pairs of lovers (*Dec.* IV 3) 147-148.
Palamon (*Knight's Tale*) 28.
Palemone (*Tes.*) 34.
Resurrection 164, 215, 234.
rings (*Dec.* I 3) 147-148.
rivers from fountain (*Am. vis.*) 100, 104.
soul of man in three parts 103, 108n, 109, 135-136, 147, 233.
spendthrifts (*Dec.* II 3) 147-148.
terza rima 24, 59, 102, 104.
third heaven 22, 23 and n, 28, 50, 104n.
trilogy in *terza rima* by Boccaccio 59.
Trinity 23, 48, 104n, 147.
trivium 100.
Venus 21-25, 28, 35, 46, 48, 104n, 164.
3 and 7 (*Dec.*) 146-148, 151, 158, 166.
— 4 (tetrad) 101-103, 106, 110.
body of man in four parts 104, 108, 233.
cardinal virtues 106, 108 and n, 111.
corners of the world 102, 108.
elements 102, 108.
empires of the world 103n.
humors 103.
Inferno IV with 40 souls 102.
quadrangular fountain (*Am. vis.*) 106.
quadrants of ladies (*Am. vis.*, *Caccia*) 106.
quaternarius 103.
rectangular, four-walled room (*Am. vis.*) 102.
regions of sky 103n.
rivers of Paradise 108n.
seasons 103.
solid body, pyramid 103.
Triumphs (*Am. vis.*) 101, 103.
— 5 (pentad) 33, 42-43, 103 and n, 104n, 110.
against Thebes (as opposed to seven) 32.
Arcita, Penteo, Fively (*Tes.*) 24, 33-34, 49.
body of man 104.
classes of creatures 104.

TABLE OF CONTENTS

FINITO DI STAMPARE
NELLA TIPOGRAFIA GIUNTINA
FIRENZE - DICEMBRE 1993

BIBLIOTECA DI «LETTERE ITALIANE»

STUDI E TESTI

SAGGI DI «LETTERE ITALIANE»